BIOS Option	Quick Review	Detailed Description	BIOS Option		
Memory Subsystem (Continued)					
MD Driving Strength	84	236	SDRAM Cycle Time Tras/Trc	121	288
Memory Hole At 15M-16M	85	236	SDRAM ECC Setting	121	288
OS Select For DRAM > 64MB	94	248	SDRAM Idle Limit	122	289
OS2 Onboard Memory > 64M	94	247	SDRAM Leadoff Command	122	291
Rank Interleave	111	271	SDRAM Page Closing Policy	123	291
Read Around Write	111	271	SDRAM Page Hit Limit	123	292
Read Wait State	111	272	SDRAM PH Limit	124	293
Refresh Interval	112	272	SDRAM Precharge Control	124	293
Refresh Mode Select	112	273	SDRAM Precharge Delay	124	294
SDRAM 1T Command	116	278	SDRAM RAS Precharge Time	125	295
SDRAM 1T Command Control	117	279	SDRAM RAS Pulse Width	125	295
SDRAM Active to Precharge Delay	117	280	SDRAM RAS-to-CAS Delay	126	296
SDRAM Bank Interleave	117	281	SDRAM Row Active Time	126	297
SDRAM Bank-to-Bank Delay	118	282	SDRAM Row Cycle Time	126	297
SDRAM Burst Len	119	283	SDRAM Tras Timing Value	127	298
SDRAM Burst Length	119	284	SDRAM Trc Timing Value	127	298
SDRAM CAS Latency Time	119	285	SDRAM Trcd Timing Value	128	299
SDRAM Command Leadoff Time	120	285	SDRAM Trp Timing Value	128	300
SDRAM Command Rate	120	286	SDRAM Trrd Timing Value	129	300
SDRAM Cycle Length	120	287	SDRAM Write Recovery Time	129	301

(Continued on Inside Back Cover)

"Adrian has done the tech community a great service by making this guide. It has personally saved me time on both repairs and evaluations. With BIOS options as numerous as they are today, it's wonderful to have a one-stop-source to decipher them all."

—**Nathan Warawa**, GamingIn3D.com

"You know, I couldn't count the amount of times I've referred people to your BIOS Guide…it's very informative, and saves me the time of explaining why people should disable Video BIOS Shadowing, why Fast Writes isn't such a big deal for today's games, and much more."

"Just wanted to say thanks for saving me time and also helping me out. (I learned a lot from it, too!) Keep up the most excellent work."

—**Matt Burris**, 3DGPU.com

"…this isn't so much a Knowledge base but a labor of love. Not only has this guide had a place in both Titch's and My Favorites for many years, but I'm really excited to see it still going after many, many years. Well done, Adrian. Keep up the excellent work."

—**JohnL**, The ModFathers.com

"Adrian Wong of Adrian's Rojak Pot has been building up his BIOS guide since late 1999. Today, he hit version 6.0, and the guide is now comprehensive in its scope. It comes highly recommended from me due to the fact that BIOS optimizations can yield positive results in performance and compatibility for everyone. Adrian also goes into far greater detail than even your best motherboard manual and even debunks some "myths" that some manufacturers still propagate."

—**Ryu Connor**, Tech-Report.com

"This is one of the most comprehensive and user-friendly guides I have found to date. I was able to do various tweaks with my mem/cpu that increased my overall system performance by about 15%.

Many of the BIOS tweaks will depend on your mobo and whether certain options are even available in your BIOS menu. However, I do recommend that even ppl that aren't familiar with working with the BIOS give it a go with this guide… Really helps to answer all your questions."

—**James**, TimSoft.com

"Some bookmarks occupy space in my Favorites folder just in case I need such a resource in the future, but others are frequent visits. I can easily see this one being a resource to which I refer often. This site contains very good explanations of the numerous configuration options you see in the BIOS.

…this truly is a link you'll want to keep around. This one is already sync'ed to my iPaq!"

—**LockerGnome.com**

"This is the most comprehensive BIOS Guide available. Just about every option in a modern BIOS is explained. The best performance setting is usually pointed out, and the explanations are easy to follow. A must for any overclocker wanna-be."

—**Tim B.**, OCWorkbench.com

"I'd like to congratulate the author of the BIOS Optimization Guide. This is absolutely marvelous. I was looking specifically for advanced information on the AGP Aperture Size setting, and you guys have got TEN paragraphs on it."

—**Sherman**, Microsoft Support Services

Breaking Through the BIOS Barrier

Breaking Through the BIOS Barrier

The Definitive BIOS Optimization Guide for PCs

Adrian Wong

PRENTICE
HALL
PTR

An Imprint of PEARSON EDUCATION

Upper Saddle River, NJ • New York • San Francisco • Toronto

London • Munich • Paris • Madrid

Capetown • Sydney • Tokyo • Singapore • Mexico City

www.phptr.com

Library of Congress Cataloging-in-Publication Data

A CIP catalog record for this book can be obtained from the Library of Congress

Managing Editor: Gina Kanouse
Production Supervision: Lori Lyons
Composition: Tolman Creek Designs
Cover Design Director: Jerry Votta
Cover Design: Anthony Gemmellaro
Manufacturing Manager: Dan Uhrig
Acquisitions Editor: Bernard Goodwin
Editorial Assistant: Michelle Vincenti
Marketing Manager: Robin O'Brien
Copy Editor: Sarah Cisco

2005 Pearson Education, Inc.

Publishing as Prentice Hall Professional Technical Reference

Upper Saddle River, New Jersey 07458

Printed in the United States of America

First Printing: August 2004

ISBN 0-13-145536-2

LOC 2004106506

Pearson Education Ltd.
Pearson Education Australia Pty., Limited
Pearson Education South Asia Pte. Ltd.
Pearson Education Asia Ltd.
Pearson Education Canada, Ltd.
Pearson Educacion de Mexico, S.A. de C.V.
Pearson Education—Japan
Pearson Malaysia S.D.N. B.H.D.

Contents

Acknowledgments

Like every new author, I started this project with the idea that all I needed to do was write the guide on BIOS options. It would be a cakewalk—or so I thought. Unfortunately, writing a book is really a lot more complex than it seems.

As I worked with my editor on the book, I found myself adding more and more material. Unlike the online version of the BIOS Optimization Guide, this book covers everything about the BIOS. This book is the truly complete BIOS Optimization Guide.

Unfortunately, because of my busy schedule, the development of this book has taken almost a year longer than we planned for. A thousand apologies to everyone, including my exasperated editor!

Now, I would like to thank my parents (*as everyone should!*) and my girlfriend, Jenny, for believing in my abilities and supporting me all the way through. Although they never understood why anyone would want to optimize the BIOS, I couldn't have done all this without them!

I would also like to thank the individuals who made significant contributions to this exhausting project—my editor, Bernard Goodwin; Lance Leventhal and Jim Markham at Prentice Hall; and of course, my pal, Chan Jo Wee!

Bernard, if you did not persist and guide this new writer through the pitfalls of writing a book, it wouldn't have become a reality. Thank you!

A big thank you also goes to both Lance and Jim for commenting on my work. You really helped me raise the standard of this book. Thank you!

I would also like to thank my pal, Jo Wee, for helping me handle the mundane aspects of this project. He was invaluable in allowing me to concentrate on writing the book instead of getting bogged down in clerical work. You are a savior, Jo Wee!

Finally, I would like to thank my buddies and core members of Team ARP—Ken Ng and Chai Ser Loon for helping me with Adrian's Rojak Pot while I finished the book. This book is as much a tribute to Team ARP as it is to everyone else who contributed to the book. Thank you, guys!

Foreword

Breaking Through the BIOS Barrier: The Definitive BIOS Optimization Guide for PCs is absolutely the best guide of its kind.

Recent advances in technology have turned the user-friendly BIOS of the past into an engineer's maze of jargon and techno-babble. Most descriptions of BIOS settings from motherboard manufacturer's manuals give little more than a list of the available settings options. A description of the settings and an indication of how to set timings are virtually nonexistent.

Breaking Through the BIOS Barrier solves all that by providing easy-to-understand, layman's descriptions for all of the latest BIOS settings.

Combining these descriptions with real-world reasons for choosing certain options makes the guide an invaluable resource to any computer "tweaker" or enthusiast. For the advanced user and the curious, the book is full of technical information that delves deeply into the mysterious and uncharted waters of the modern BIOS setup.

Memory timings are an extremely important part of performance and stability in today's high-end computers. At Mushkin, Adrian Wong's online BIOS Optimization Guide (http://www.rojakpot.com/bog.aspx) has helped us give accurate, bleeding-edge suggestions to our customers to increase performance and stability. It has been an indispensable tool for our technical personnel to use in R&D and troubleshooting.

Kudos to Adrian Wong!

Lewis Keller
Technical Services Manager,
Mushkin Enhanced Memory Systems, Inc.
http://www.mushkin.com/

Introduction

What Is the BIOS?

Welcome to the first edition of *Breaking Through the BIOS Barrier: The Definitive BIOS Optimization Guide for PCs.*

Most people never think about what actually goes on when using a computer. To many, a computer simply reacts to a series of keyboard entries and clicks. Whatever the computer is commanded to do, it just does. No questions asked.

In reality, it isn't as simple as that. Behind the facade of the user-friendly graphical user interface, many things have to be done by the system for a command to be carried out.

Enter the BIOS, which is short for **Basic Input/Output System**.

By definition, it is the interface between software and hardware that allows them both to communicate and interact with each other. While you may think that the BIOS only exists in the form of the motherboard BIOS, it is actually the combination of the motherboard BIOS, the BIOS of all add-on cards in the system, as well as their device drivers.

In the early days of personal computing, the BIOS was off-limits to the user. Access was restricted to only a few basic functions, just enough for the system assembler to get the computer running. Knowledge about the BIOS at that time was nothing short of arcane.

Yet today, the situation is not much better. Yes, motherboard manufacturers are allowing a lot more access to the various BIOS options. This gives us more flexibility in setting up and optimizing the computer. However, little has been done about educating the user about what each BIOS option actually does.

Take a look at the BIOS section of any motherboard manual. It would be very surprising if you manage to extract anything useful out of the terse, cryptic explanations. How is anyone expected to optimize the BIOS when no one knows what each BIOS option does?

I started writing this BIOS guide back in 1999 as a simple online guide on how to optimize the BIOS. Today, it not only covers BIOS optimization, it has also become a comprehensive guide on over 250 BIOS options.

This book not only teaches you how to optimize each BIOS option, you also learn what each BIOS option does and the reason behind each recommended setting. In the end, you will be able to optimize the BIOS like a professional!

Book Objectives

Breaking Through the BIOS Barrier was written with several key objectives in mind.

It was primarily written to help the reader optimize the BIOS. Unfortunately, BIOS optimization isn't a clear-cut problem that can be solved by simply following some fixed guidelines.

Although many simple guidelines and recommendations are covered in this book, hardware and software configurations vary from computer to computer. Therefore, it is important that the reader understands what each BIOS option does so that he or she can make the best decision for the computer in question.

To that end, this book not only helps you optimize the BIOS with many guidelines and recommendations, it also helps you understand what each BIOS option does, so you can make the necessary adjustments for your system.

This book aims to dispel the misinformation about many BIOS options that have been propagated by both media and manufacturers alike. For too many years now, motherboard manuals and various computer books have been spreading inaccurate information and recommendations on many BIOS options. It's time to change that for good!

This book also discusses basic topics about the BIOS to provide a solid foundation on the BIOS and how to keep it updated as well as access its setup menu.

When you finish reading this book, you will have all the necessary knowledge you need to fully optimize the BIOS of your computer!

Who Is This Book For?

This book is for those (novice or advanced) who are interested in optimizing the BIOS for performance and stability.

You will learn what the BIOS is, the different types of BIOS, how to access your BIOS, and how to update it. You also will learn what each BIOS option does and what you should set for optimal performance and stability.

This book also teaches you about BIOS emergencies like an unbootable computer or a corrupted BIOS. What should you do? How can you correct the problem? This book covers all that, including a look at the hot flash method.

For the novice, Chapters 1 and 2 are just what you need. If you are familiar with computers and want to understand what each BIOS option really does, turn to Chapters 3 and 4.

Chapter Breakdown

Breaking Through the BIOS Barrier is really two books in one. Chapters 1 and 2 provide a solid foundation of BIOS basics and special topics in a narrative fashion, while Chapters 3 and 4 are presented in a more structured manner for easy reference. Here, you not only learn everything about each BIOS option, you also learn the logic behind each optimization.

Chapter 1: BIOS Basics

Chapter 1 serves as an introduction to the BIOS. It deals with basic topics on the BIOS. In this chapter, you learn what the BIOS really is, how it works, how to keep it updated, and how to access it.

Chapter 2: Special Topics

Chapter 2 deals with special topics like BIOS emergencies and hot flashing. If you ever run into trouble with the BIOS, head straight for this chapter. It can help you restore your BIOS.

Chapter 3: Quick Reviews

Chapter 3 offers a simplified explanation of each BIOS option as well as its recommended settings. Flip to this chapter if you need a quick overview of a BIOS option and its optimal settings. This is targeted at those with little hardware knowledge.

Chapter 4: Detailed Descriptions

Chapter 4 deals with each BIOS option in much greater detail. If you already have a moderate level of hardware knowledge, this section allows you to achieve a greater understanding of the various BIOS options and the logic behind their recommended settings.

Please note that certain BIOS options may appear similar in both the *Quick Reviews* and *Detailed Descriptions* sections.

Acronym List

Following Chapter 4, you will find a complete alphabetical list of acronyms used throughout the book. Refer to this list if you want to quickly see an acronym spelled out.

Category Lookup Table

Printed on the inside front and back covers of this book is the Category Lookup Table. The BIOS features have been arranged according to different sub systems so that you can easily search for the BIOS feature of your choice. If the BIOS feature you are interested is not listed within the book (because it has a different name), you can try checking the Category Lookup Table for a similar BIOS feature.

Chapter 1
What Is the BIOS?

The **BIOS** is short for **Basic Input/Output System**. By definition, it is the interface between software and hardware that allows software and hardware to communicate and interact with each other.

The BIOS is made up of everything that allows software and hardware to interact with each other. While you may think that the BIOS only exists in the form of the motherboard BIOS, it is actually the combination of the motherboard BIOS, the BIOS of all add-on cards in the system, as well as their device drivers.

How Does the BIOS Work?

Most people never think about what actually goes on when they do something on the computer. To most people, whenever they command the computer to do something, it just does it. No questions asked.

It isn't as simple as that. Behind the facade of the user-friendly **GUI (Graphical User Interface)**, many things have to be done by the system for the command to be carried out.

Let's visualize the computer system as three separate layers that communicate with each other through different interfaces. The diagram to the right is of that layered division:

In our layered system, the application is the highest level. It cannot directly interact with the hardware. It can only communicate with the operating system through the **API** or **Application Program Interface**.

The API is a set of common functions that the application calls upon to get the operating system to do what it wants. Because the API is operating system-specific, it differs from operating system to operating system.

However, irrespective of the operating system, the API allows the application to get the job done without knowing how the operating system does it. The application doesn't need to know anything about the computer's hardware.

The operating system then communicates to the BIOS what it needs to carry out the application's request. The operating system never communicates directly with the hardware.

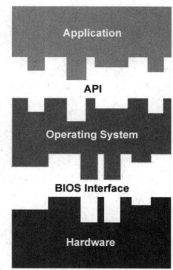

The different layers and interfaces.

The BIOS layer allows the operating system to support all manners of hardware. Each piece of hardware comes with its own BIOS and/or driver, which become part of the system's BIOS.

Therefore, the BIOS layer is dynamic and changes to match the computer's hardware configuration. It serves to mask the differences between different hardware by presenting a common interface to the operating system.

The operating system only needs to know how to communicate with the BIOS layer. It is up to the BIOS layer to translate the operating system commands into action by the hardware.

Without the BIOS layer, there's no way the operating system can access the hardware layer. The BIOS layer is the operating system's key to the hardware layer. That's how important the BIOS layer is in the computer system.

The Motherboard BIOS

Although, by definition, the BIOS consists of the motherboard BIOS, the BIOS of all add-on cards in the system, as well as their drivers, we will be concentrating on the motherboard BIOS in this book.

The motherboard BIOS is the most important component of the BIOS layer. This is because it contains all the software needed to get the computer started. It also comes with basic diagnostics and configuration utilities.

The BIOS Chip

The motherboard BIOS is stored in a chip on the motherboard. The BIOS chip normally comes in the form of a rectangular **DIP (Dual In-line Package)** or a square **PLCC (Plastic Leaded Chip Carrier)** package.

The capacity of BIOS chips is measured in Megabits (Mb). Most BIOS chips these days are 2Mb (256KB) in size. These higher capacity chips allow the manufacturer to offer more features than is possible with the smaller 1Mb chips.

However, please note that the size of the BIOS chip has nothing to do with its performance. The choice of type and size of the BIOS chip is a matter of economics and requirements, rather than performance.

PLCC-type BIOS chips.
(Photo by author.)

What Does It Do?

Here is a breakdown of what the motherboard BIOS actually consists of:

- Power-on diagnostic tests
- System configuration utility
- Bootstrap loader
- BIOS interface

When you boot up the computer, it initiates the **POST (Power-On Diagnostic Test)**. The POST serves as a quick-and-dirty way to make sure that all the critical components are functioning.

After the POST sequence completes, you are given the opportunity to access the system configuration utility. This utility allows you to configure and modify a range of features. These BIOS features show you just how important the BIOS is.

These BIOS features control every aspect of the computer, from the speed at which the processor runs to the transfer mode of the hard disk. It goes without saying that these BIOS features are the reason why I'm writing this book. We go into details later in Chapter 4.

After the short delay, the BIOS starts the bootstrap loader routine, which scans for a valid master boot sector on all available drives. This can be anything from a hard disk to a CD-ROM drive. The master boot sector is just a predetermined area containing code that initiates the loading of the operating system.

When executed, the master boot sector turns over the booting process to the operating system by loading the operating system's boot sector. The operating system then starts loading up its core files.

In most cases, this is where the BIOS' role ends because current operating systems employ their own 32-bit or 64-bit drivers, which offer far superior functionality and performance to the BIOS' basic drivers. However, the BIOS' core drivers still have some importance.

Even modern operating systems like Microsoft Windows still need to use the BIOS' basic drivers, albeit only in their troubleshooting or "safe" modes. This is because the core BIOS drivers have been standardized a long time ago, and every piece of hardware made since then is backward-compatible with them.

While these core BIOS drivers may be slow and primitive, they are guaranteed to work with any hardware designed for the PC. That's why they are still an integral part of every PC.

Why Optimize the BIOS?

Although the BIOS only functions from the time you press the Power On button until the operating system takes over, its effects last as long as the computer is operational. Whatever you set in the BIOS greatly determines your computing experience.

If the BIOS is not configured properly, you may be able to boot up the operating system and run it for a while. However, the system will become unstable and eventually crash. This will go on and on, ad nauseum.

You may send it back to your computer dealer and, more likely than not, the technician will simply reset the BIOS to its fail-safe settings and send it back to you. However, is that the best solution?

Most definitely not! An unoptimized BIOS means an unoptimized system. Not only will it take longer to boot up or initialize devices, it will also slow down the entire computer. It's like knee-capping someone before sending him out to do the long jump!

BIOS optimization is critical not only to the optimal performance of the computer, but also to the proper functioning of the system's components. Computers these days are made up of a hodge-podge of different components from different manufacturers. This presents a real problem when it comes to getting them all to work together.

Because of the variety of components that make up any one computer, it is impossible for man-ufacturers to optimize their motherboards for any particular configuration. That's why all moth-erboards come with configurable BIOS.

The BIOS allows the OEM (Original Equipment Manufacturer), as well as the end-user, to modify settings and timings to support different configurations. Without them, manufact-urers would be forced to use the most conservative settings, which would greatly degrade performance.

How Do I Optimize the BIOS?

The key to optimizing the BIOS lies in its built-in system configuration utility. As mentioned earlier, this is where you can configure or modify a variety of BIOS features and options.

These BIOS features show you just how important the BIOS is. They control every aspect of the computer, from the speed at which the processor runs to the transfer mode of the hard disk.

This book teaches you how to optimize your BIOS for proper operation and maximum per-formance. Let's turn that snail into a road hog!

BIOS Updates

First of all, you should know that the BIOS that ships with your motherboard is not necessarily the latest version or the most stable version. Reputable motherboard manufacturers constantly improve on their motherboard BIOS and regularly release BIOS updates.

These BIOS updates are important because they correct bugs and sometimes provide additional capabilities. You can think of them as driver updates or software patches. You should always keep the motherboard BIOS up to date.

In the following figure, you can see the list of changes in two BIOS updates for the ABIT NF7-S motherboard.

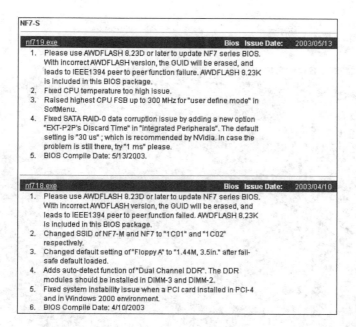

Details of BIOS updates for the ABIT NF7-S motherboard.
(Courtesy of ABIT Computer Corporation. Used with permission.)

As you can see, the bug fixes and feature enhancements are both numerous and important. It really pays to keep your BIOS updated!

How Do I Update the BIOS?

The process of updating the BIOS can be summarized in the following steps:

1. Determine your BIOS version.
2. Obtain the appropriate BIOS update.
3. Prepare a BIOS flash disk.
4. Flash the motherboard BIOS.

Now let's go through the process step by step.

Note

The term **flash** or **flashing** is used to describe the act of updating the BIOS.

Determining the BIOS Version

Before you update your BIOS, it's best to find out what version of BIOS you are currently using. If you already have the latest version, then there's no point in going through the process.

The display of the BIOS version number or ID varies from manufacturer to manufacturer.

However, it is most commonly the last two or four digits or letters at the end of the string that appears when you boot up the computer.

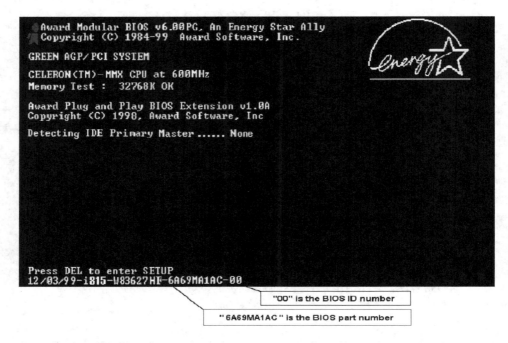

Award Modular BIOS v6.00PG, An Energy Star Ally
Copyright (C) 1984-99 Award Software, Inc.

GREEN AGP/PCI SYSTEM

CELERON(TM)-MMX CPU at 600MHz
Memory Test :   32768K OK

Award Plug and Play BIOS Extension v1.0A
Copyright (C) 1998, Award Software, Inc

Detecting IDE Primary Master ...... None

Press DEL to enter SETUP
12/03/99-i815-W83627HF-6A69MA1AC-00

"00" is the BIOS ID number

" 6A69MA1AC " is the BIOS part number

Determining the BIOS ID.
(Courtesy of ABIT Computer Corporation. Used with permission.)

Your motherboard manufacturer may use numbers or letters to represent the BIOS version or ID. The following is an example of the BIOS version or ID.

Because this string only appears for a few seconds when you start up the computer, you might want to turn on your monitor a few seconds before you start up your computer because some monitors take some time to initialize.

You can also use the Pause key to freeze the screen so that you can search for and identify the BIOS ID. Pressing any key after that will unfreeze the screen and allow the booting process to continue.

In the preceding example, the BIOS ID is a two-digit number (00). Other motherboards may use four digits or even letters instead of digits. Some even use a mix of letters and digits.

If the BIOS ID does not appear as it does in the example, please check the manual that came with your motherboard. Your motherboard manufacturer may have chosen to show the BIOS ID somewhere else.

Obtaining the BIOS Update

Now that you know your BIOS ID, it's time to check whether your motherboard manufacturer has a BIOS update for you.

BIOS updates are best obtained directly from the manufacturer's website instead of other distribution points like hardware sites and unofficial mirrors. This ensures that you have the very latest BIOS update available and reduces the risk of downloading a virus-infected copy.

So, head over to your motherboard manufacturer's website. The BIOS updates are usually listed in the Downloads or Support section of the website.

Please note that while different motherboard models may appear to have the same BIOS ID, you must download only the BIOS that was specifically meant for your motherboard. Flashing a BIOS update that was meant for another motherboard will likely cause your motherboard to fail.

After you have found the page listing the BIOS updates for your motherboard, there may be a long list of BIOS updates. For example, the adjacent figure shows a few of the BIOS updates for the ABIT KT7A-RAID-motherboard.

Although the number of BIOS updates may be confusing, don't worry! You don't have to download and flash all of them. All you need to do is download and flash the *latest* version.

However, you must first determine whether there is an update for your BIOS. Remember the BIOS ID? Compare it against the list of BIOS IDs.

Irrespective of how the BIOS ID appears, motherboard manufacturers always progressively label BIOS updates.

If your BIOS ID is a number, larger numbers always denote a newer BIOS. For example, a BIOS with an ID of 01 is newer than a BIOS with an ID of 00 but older than a BIOS with an ID of 02.

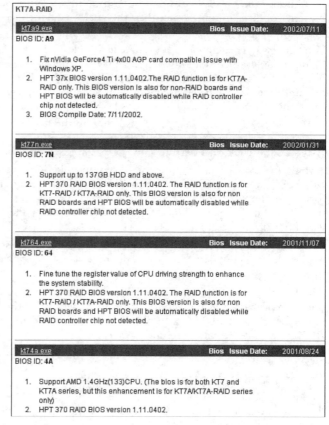

If the BIOS ID is made up of letters, letters lower in alphabetical order always denote a newer BIOS. For example, a BIOS with an ID of AB is newer than a BIOS with an ID of AA but older than a BIOS with an ID of AC.

List of BIOS updates for the ABIT KT7A-RAID motherboard. (Courtesy of ABIT Computer Corporation. Used with permission.)

The same goes even if your BIOS ID is a mix of letters and numbers, just like in the preceding KT7A-RAID example.

If your BIOS ID is the latest BIOS ID, then there's no need to proceed further with the BIOS flash. You already have the latest version. Just make sure you check back once in a while.

If there's a newer BIOS ID than your current BIOS ID, download the new BIOS image. It usually comes prepackaged with the flash utility in the form of a compressed ZIP file or a self-extracting compressed file.

Preparing a BIOS Flash Disk

Now that you have the compressed file containing the BIOS update, it's time to prepare a clean DOS boot disk. This is because most flash utilities require the use of real mode DOS. Also, to prevent conflicts, nothing other than the necessary boot files should be loaded into this boot disk.

You can easily create a clean boot disk in Windows. Even Windows XP, which does not support DOS, comes with a utility that allows you to create your own DOS boot disk. Just remember to use a reliable floppy disk. A defective disk may cause the BIOS update to be corrupted.

In Windows XP, all you need to do is bring up the floppy format utility. Just right-click on your floppy drive in Windows Explorer and click on **Format**. The Format 3 ½ screen appears.

Among the format options, there is an option called **Create an MS-DOS startup disk**. Check this option and click **Start** to format the floppy disk. Windows XP will then format your floppy disk, make it bootable and copy all the necessary files for it to boot up into real mode DOS.

After you have a clean DOS boot disk, all you need to do is extract the BIOS update file and the flash utility and copy them into the boot disk.

Creating a boot disk in Windows XP.

The BIOS update file or image usually has a *.bin* extension. Some come with a *.rom* extension. However, they are all the same; they are just BIOS image files. Write down the name of the BIOS image file. It will come in handy later.

Flashing the Motherboard BIOS

There are actually a few ways you can flash your BIOS. The traditional way is by a DOS boot disk. However these days, manufacturers are implementing newer methods.

For example, many BIOS now come with their own flash utility. Some manufacturers even provide you with a utility that allows you to flash the BIOS online!

For simplicity's sake, we will only touch on the common DOS flashing method using the AwardFlash software.

The AwardFlash software is probably the most common flash utility around. It is used to flash the BIOS of motherboards using the AwardBIOS. Please note that the AwardFlash utility is DOS-based. It cannot be used in a Windows-based environment. You must boot up using a DOS boot disk before using this utility.

The following is a screen capture of the available commands of the 8.23K version of the AwardFlash utility:

```
Command Prompt                                                      _ □ ×

AWDFLASH v8.23K (03/21) (C)Phoenix Technologies Ltd. 2003 All Rights Reserved

Usage:  AWDFLASH [FileName1] [FileName2] [/<sw>[/<sw>...]]
        FileName1 : New BIOS Name For Flash Programming
        FileName2 : BIOS File For Backing-up the Original BIOS
 <Swtches>    ?: Show Help Messages
     py: Program Flash Memory            pn: No Flash Programming
     sy: Backup Original BIOS To Disk File  sn: No Original BIOS Backup
     Sb: Skip BootBlock programming      Wb: Always Programming BootBlock
     cd: Clear DMI Data After Programming  cc: Clear CMOS Data After Programming
     cp: Clear PnP(ESCD) Data After Programming
     LD: Destroy CMOS Checksum And No System Halt For First Reboot
         After Programming              Tiny: Occupy lesser memory
     QI: Qualify flash part number with source file
      E: Return to DOS After Programming  R: RESET System After Programming
      F: Use Flash Routines in Original BIOS For Flash Programming
    cks: Show update Binfile checksum   cksXXXX: Compare Binfile CheckSum with XXXX

NVMAC:XXXXXXXXXXXX                NVGUID:XXXXXXXXXXXXXX
       Support nForce Input MAC,GUID Function,with "/wb" to update MAC and GUID.

Example: AWDFLASH 6A69R000.bin /py/sn/nvmac:xxxxxxxxxxxx/wb
```

AwardFlash utility commands..

As you can see, the utility is quite versatile. It provides numerous options. Of course, most of them are not necessary for our use. The manufacturer of our reference motherboard, ABIT, recommends the following parameters:

```
A:\>awdflash bios.bin /cc /cd /cp /py /sn /cks /r
```

This essentially tells the AwardFlash utility to do the following:

1. Skip back up of original BIOS image.
2. Show the bios.bin BIOS image file's checksum.
3. Program the Flash BIOS with the bios.bin BIOS image file.
4. Clear CMOS data after programming the Flash BIOS.
5. Clear DMI data after programming the Flash BIOS.
6. Clear PnP (ESCD) data after programming the Flash BIOS.
7. Automatically reset the computer after programming is complete.

Please consult your motherboard manufacturer for its recommended parameters. Different manufacturers may recommend different parameters even if they are all using the same AwardFlash utility.

If you run this command after booting up in DOS, the AwardFlash utility automatically updates the motherboard's Flash BIOS with the new BIOS image and clears the CMOS, DMI, and ESCD data before resetting the computer for the changes to take effect.

After the computer is rebooted, the new BIOS takes effect. Remember, because the CMOS data has been cleared during the flash process, the BIOS reverts to default settings. You should access the BIOS setup utility to set up the various parameters as well as optimize it.

Accessing the BIOS Setup Utility

The BIOS setup utility is only available for a few short seconds when you boot up your computer. If your operating system has already loaded up, you must reboot your computer before you can access the BIOS setup utility.

In motherboards using the AwardBIOS, the BIOS flashes the following message for a few seconds during the booting up process:

Press Del To Enter Setup

When you see that message, quickly press the **Del** (Delete) key. This halts the booting process and brings up the BIOS setup menu.

Please note that not all BIOS software use the **Del** key for access to the setup menu. Different BIOS vendors have different trigger keys. Alternatives to the Del key include:

- **Esc** (Escape) key
- **F2** key
- **Ctrl-Alt-Esc** key combination

Please consult your motherboard manual on the trigger key for your motherboard's BIOS setup utility.

The BIOS Setup Utility

The BIOS setup utility varies from motherboard to motherboard. Some have a graphical appearance while others have a simple menu system. The most common is the basic menu system. The top figure on the opposite page is an example of that menu system.

This is what greets you when you press the trigger key to access the BIOS setup utility. As you can see, the screen consists of nothing more than a list of available sub-menus on the left and some commands on the right.

The keyboard's cursor keys are used to navigate this menu system. Pressing the **Enter** key performs actions like opening up a sub-menu or activating one of the commands on the left menu.

Open up a sub-menu and the bottom figure on the opposite page is what you may see.

This sub-menu (**Advanced Chipset Features**) displays a list of available BIOS options or features. You can browse through the list using the cursor keys.

The values of those BIOS options can be modified using the + (plus) or − (minus) key in this BIOS. In other BIOS, you may use the **Page Up** and **Page Down** keys instead.

Optimizing the BIOS

This brings us to the crux of this book. Optimizing the BIOS is what this book is all about. Chapters 3 and 4 concentrate entirely on the numerous BIOS options you may encounter in your motherboard's BIOS setup utility.

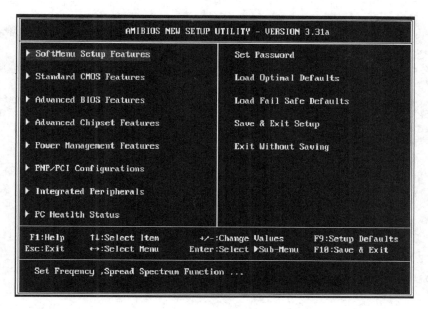

The ABIT SI7 BIOS setup utility.
(Courtesy of ABIT Computer Corporation. Used with permission.)

```
         AMIBIOS NEW SETUP UTILITY - VERSION 3.31a
  ┌──────────────────────────────────┬──────────────────────┐
  │  Advanced Chipset Features        │   [  Setup Help   ]  │
  │                                   │                      │
  │  === DRAM Relational Functions ===│                      │
  │  DRAM Data Integrity Mode   Non-ECC│                     │
  │  Synchronous Mode Select    Asynchronous                 │
  │  Channel Mode Select        Lock-Step(256×1)             │
  │  RAMBUS TDSEL Turbo Mode:   Enable │                     │
  │  RAMBUS RDSEL Turbo Mode:   Enable │                     │
  │  Cas Access Delay(tCAC)     Auto   │                     │
  │                                    │                     │
  │  === AGP Relational Functions ====│                      │
  │  Graphic Win Size           32M    │                     │
  │  AGP Fast Write             Disabled                     │
  │  Post Write Combine         Disabled                     │
  │  No Mask for SBA FE         Disabled                     │
  │                                    │                     │
  │  Hyper-Threading Technology Enabled│                     │
  │  APIC Select                Enabled│                     │
  │                                    │                     │
  │  MPS Revision               1.4    │                     │
  │  Auto Turn Off Pci Clock Pin Enabled                     │
  ├──────────────────────────────────┴──────────────────────┤
  │  F1:Help      ↑↓:Select Item   +/-:Change Values   F9:Setup Defaults│
  │  Esc:Previous Menu            Enter:Select ▶Sub-Menu  F10:Save & Exit│
  └──────────────────────────────────────────────────────────┘
```

A sub-menu in the ABIT SI7 BIOS setup utility.
(Courtesy of ABIT Computer Corporation. Used with permission.)

Chapters 3 and 4 offer two different levels of detail. Chapter 3 offers a quick guide to the various BIOS options and optimization recommendations. Chapter 4, on the other hand, delves into each BIOS option with much greater detail.

I hope you enjoy reading about the different BIOS options as much as I enjoyed researching and writing about them.

But before you head over to those chapters, be sure to read Chapter 2, which teaches you how to get out of trouble when something goes wrong during the optimization process. Remember to flip to Chapter 2 if you ever run into trouble!

Now, let's go optimize your BIOS!

Chapter 2
Special Topics

BIOS Emergencies

Although this book will help you optimize the BIOS, it cannot tell you just how far you should push your system. There are just too many possible permutations of hardware configurations to cover in this or any other book, for that matter.

If you are particularly adventurous, you will become very familiar with system crashes, spontaneous reboots, or an unresponsive system. Of course, rebooting the system and undoing the changes can correct all that.

However, occasionally, you may come face to face with emergencies like an unbootable computer or, even worse, a BIOS corruption! With such problems, the system is completely dead and you cannot access the BIOS.

Luckily, we have solutions for these problems. Let's take a look!

Unbootable System

This often happens when you set an excessively high clock speed while overclocking your processor or memory. It can also happen when you set certain BIOS options incorrectly.

In these cases, your system becomes completely unresponsive. When you power it up, it refuses to boot. Because the computer cannot be booted up, you cannot access the BIOS menu and correct the mistakes you made.

Fortunately, all you need to do is reset the BIOS. We cover four different methods here, in the order of simplicity.

Power Off-Power On

Certain motherboards have a built-in mechanism that protects the computer from being rendered unbootable due to incorrect BIOS settings.

In such motherboards, the BIOS automatically boots up using its default settings after several failures to boot. This allows you to access the BIOS and correct the BIOS settings.

You should check your motherboard manual to see whether your motherboard supports such a feature. Not all motherboards come with this feature.

If your motherboard supports this feature, all you need to do is power off your computer and power it on again. Sometimes, you need to do this four or five times before the mechanism kicks in.

After the motherboard boots up using its default settings, you should immediately access the BIOS and change the incorrect BIOS settings you made earlier.

Keyboard Reset

Some motherboards support the resetting of the BIOS using a keyboard shortcut. This allows you to reset the BIOS without opening your computer's case.

For specific instructions on how to do this, you should consult your motherboard manual. Different motherboard manufacturers have different implementations. However, no matter what key or key combination is used, they only work when the computer is booting up.

We will use the ABIT NF7-S motherboard as an example. In this motherboard, the **Insert** key is used as the BIOS reset key. Of course, it only works when the computer is powered up. After that, the **Insert** key functions normally.

To reset the BIOS, the system must be powered off first. Then, with the Insert key kept depressed, turn on the computer. This will force the motherboard to boot up with default settings.

After the motherboard boots up using its default settings, you should immediately access the BIOS and change the incorrect BIOS settings you made earlier.

CMOS Discharge Jumper

Every motherboard comes with a CMOS discharge jumper. This jumper allows you to discharge the CMOS and reset the BIOS to its default settings.

The position of this jumper varies between motherboard models. Please consult your motherboard manual for the location of the CMOS discharge jumper.

For the purpose of this discussion, we use the ABIT SI7 motherboard as an example. In this motherboard, the position of the CMOS discharge jumper is clearly shown in the opposite diagram (*from the ABIT SI7 manual*).

The diagram should give you a good idea of where to find the jumper.

To discharge the CMOS data, you should first power off the system. Please note that you should also turn off the main power to the computer. This cuts off the +5V standby power that can prevent the CMOS from discharging properly.

After ensuring the system is completely turned off, open up your computer case to gain access to the motherboard. Look for the CMOS discharge jumper as shown in the manual.

After you have located the CMOS discharge jumper, you will note some markings next to the header. In this example, the pins of the header are labeled 1, 2, and 3. By default, the CMOS discharge jumper shorts pins 1 and 2, thus allowing normal operation of the motherboard.

To flush the CMOS data in the ABIT SI7 motherboard, you just need to remove the jumper and use it to short pins 2 and 3. Leave the jumper there for 5 to 10 seconds. This flushes the CMOS data and restores the BIOS to its default settings.

You should then replace the jumper in its default position over pins 1 and 2. This allows the motherboard to boot up normally.

Now you can close up your computer's case and power on the system. Because the CMOS data has been erased, you should access the BIOS immediately and restore whatever customized settings you prefer.

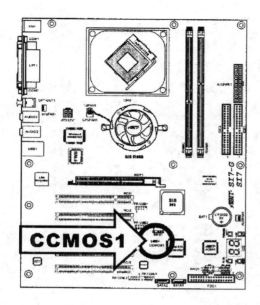
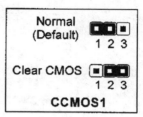

CMOS discharge jumper position, ABIT SI7 motherboard.
(Courtesy of ABIT Computer Corporation. Used with permission.)

CMOS Battery Removal

Every motherboard comes with a small battery, usually a 3V CR2032 battery. This battery provides the power necessary to keep the CMOS data intact when the computer is not powered.

If all other methods fail, removing the CMOS battery will erase the CMOS data. After the CMOS battery is removed, the CMOS will lose its data, resetting the BIOS to its default settings.

The position of the CMOS battery varies between motherboard models. Please consult your motherboard manual for the location of this battery in your motherboard.

For the purpose of this discussion, we will use the ABIT SI7 motherboard as an example. In the diagram on the opposite page, the position of the CMOS battery is circled.

After you have an idea of where to look for the CMOS battery, you can proceed.

1. Power off the computer.
2. Open up the computer case.
3. Locate the CMOS battery. Note the tensioned latch holding it in place.
4. Press the latch to release the battery and lift it out.
5. Wait for 5 to 10 seconds to allow the CMOS to discharge.
6. Replace the CMOS battery.
7. Close the computer case.
8. Power on the computer.

Because the CMOS data has been erased, you should access the BIOS immediately and restore whatever customized settings you prefer.

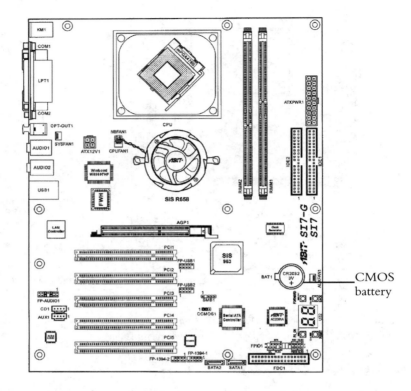

CMOS battery position, ABIT SI7 motherboard.
(Courtesy of ABIT Computer Corporation. Used with permission.)

Corrupted BIOS

Although the BIOS resides in a Flash ROM that protects it from data loss when power is not supplied, it is still susceptible to corruption. The BIOS can be corrupted by a variety of mechanisms—viruses, incomplete or bad BIOS flashes, flashing the wrong BIOS image, bugs in the BIOS itself, and so forth.

When such a corruption occurs, the BIOS either behaves abnormally or malfunctions, preventing the computer from booting up. As you can see, BIOS corruption is a big problem when it happens.

To prevent this, some manufacturers actually ship their motherboards with two BIOS chips. In the event that one BIOS chip gets corrupted for any reason, the user can easily switch to the alternate BIOS and repair the corrupted BIOS chip later by simply flashing it with a new BIOS image. Examples include Gigabyte's DualBIOS feature (shown in the picture on the opposite page) and Albatron's BIOS Mirror feature. In such motherboards, you can see two BIOS chips side by side.

However, most motherboards do not ship with two BIOS chips. For such motherboards, BIOS corruption usually means returning the motherboard to the manufacturer for repair or replacement. For the user, this means days to weeks of computer downtime.

The Gigabyte DualBIOS.
(Courtesy of Donovan Dennis Laoh. Used with permission.)

The more tech-savvy user can speed things up by requesting a replacement BIOS chip and replacing it herself. However, this is subject to the manufacturer's willingness to send the replacement chip. You will still have to wait a few days for the replacement chip to arrive.

A much quicker alternative is to **hot flash** the corrupted BIOS. However, this technique requires a moderate level of technical expertise and some experience working with hardware and flashing the BIOS.

The following is a short step-by-step guide on hot flashing for your reference. Please note that this is a dangerous procedure for the inexperienced. Do not attempt it unless you have experience working with hardware and flashing the BIOS.

Hot Flashing

No, hot flashing does not require you to heat up your BIOS nor does it have anything to do with heat. And no, it is certainly *not* related to the hot flashes that menopausal women experience!

Hot flashing is basically the same as a plain Jane BIOS flash—you use a BIOS flash utility to flash a BIOS image into the Flash ROM. However, there is a twist to it. Hot flashing requires you to swap BIOS chips while the system is running. That's what the word "**hot**" in hot flashing means—you swap the BIOS chip while your system is *hot*.

Now, why would anyone of sane mind do that? Obviously, messing around with any hardware while the system is running is an act that is often considered incredibly brave or incredibly stupid. Risk of electrocution aside, messing with your hardware while it is running can cause permanent damage to your hardware, not to mention the data in your computer.

However, the benefits of hot flashing may outweigh the risks. If your motherboard BIOS chip becomes corrupted, hot flashing allows you to revive the chip by replacing the corrupted BIOS software with a new BIOS image. Remember, when your BIOS becomes corrupted, you cannot boot up your computer. Therefore, the conventional BIOS flashing method cannot be used. If you cannot boot up the computer, you cannot load the BIOS flash utility.

This is where hot flashing comes in. Hot flashing circumvents the booting problem by using *another computer* to boot up. The corrupted BIOS chip is then transplanted into the computer (while it is still running) and updated with an uncorrupted BIOS image. This revives what was, for all intents and purposes, a dead BIOS chip. The BIOS chip can then be returned to the original motherboard to allow the computer to function once again.

Of course, you will need another system with a motherboard that supports the same BIOS chip. However, if you have access to such a computer and are not squeamish about swapping BIOS chips while the computer is running, you can save yourself a lot of time and money.

If you cannot hot flash your corrupted motherboard BIOS, you will have to send it back to the manufacturer or buy a replacement BIOS chip. Both alternatives are not particularly desirable because they cost money and you cannot use your computer until you get a replacement board or BIOS chip.

What Do I Need to Hot Flash a BIOS Chip?

If you want to hot flash a corrupted BIOS chip, you will need the following:

- A working computer with a motherboard that uses the same BIOS chip
- A suitable tool for removing BIOS chips
- The corrupted BIOS chip, of course
- A DOS boot disk containing the BIOS flash utility and the BIOS image for the corrupted BIOS chip

You also need to be experienced in flashing normal BIOS chips. Please do *not* attempt a hot flash unless you have prior experience in flashing the BIOS.

Okay, now that you have everything in place, let's proceed!

Step 1: Create a DOS Boot Disk

Because you are messing around with the system while it is still running, it is advisable to remove or at least disconnect all hard disks in the system and boot up using a DOS boot disk. So, you need to create a DOS boot disk.

Here is a refresher for those who have not created DOS boot disks in a while. Here are the steps to create a DOS boot disk in Windows XP:

1. Insert a blank floppy disk into the floppy drive.
2. Open Windows Explorer and right-click on the **3 ½ Floppy (A:)** drive.
3. Select the **Format...** option. The Format Floppy screen will pop up.

4. Tick the **Create an MS-DOS startup disk** checkbox.

5. Click the **Start** button and Windows XP will create a DOS boot disk.

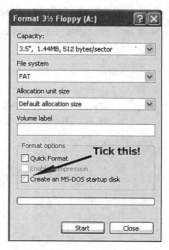

Next, you need to copy the BIOS image file for the corrupted BIOS chip as well as the BIOS flash utility into the DOS boot disk. You should get the latest BIOS image file from your motherboard manufacturer's website. BIOS image files usually have a *.bin* or *.rom* extension. Note the filename of the BIOS image file for future reference. You will need it later.

Manufacturers usually bundle these BIOS image files with the appropriate BIOS flash utility in a compressed ZIP file for easy downloading. All you need to do is download the zipped file and extract its contents into the DOS boot disk.

Step 2: Prepare a Hot Flash-Capable Computer

Creating a boot disk.

Not all computers can be used for hot flashing. For hot flashing purposes, the computer must use the same type of BIOS chip. BIOS chips come in either the form of a rectangular **DIP (Dual In-line Package)** or the square **PLCC (Plastic Leaded Chip Carrier)** package. The following are examples of PLCC BIOS chips:

Needless to say, you cannot use a motherboard with a DIP BIOS chip to hot flash a PLCC BIOS chip.

Please note that every BIOS chip has a notch on one corner. That notch tells you how to align the chip for proper insertion into the socket. It is very important to insert the BIOS chip the right way. Inserting it the wrong way may damage the BIOS chip as well as the motherboard.

After you have a system that is compatible with your corrupted BIOS chip, it is highly recommended that you remove or disconnect all unnecessary hardware, especially the hard disks. This prevents any possibility of data loss on the computer that is doing the hot flashing.

PLCC-type BIOS chips.
(Photo by author)

Step 3: Booting Up with the Boot Disk

Now, let's boot up the hot flash system using the DOS boot disk. Here is a refresher for those who have not done this in a long time:

1. Boot up and access the BIOS setup menu.
2. Set the BIOS to boot up using the floppy drive. Usually, this just involves setting the First Boot Device as Floppy.
3. Insert the DOS boot disk into the floppy drive.
4. Reboot the computer and allow it to boot up using the DOS boot disk.

Step 4: Swap the BIOS Chips

This is the time to swap the BIOS chips. You need to do so with the system still running.

The following is a picture of the good BIOS chip of the ABIT NF7-S, the motherboard I used to do the hot flash.

I only had tweezers to work with, so removing the BIOS chip with the system "hot" was rather dicey. First, I removed the BIOS chip with the system powered off. Then I seated the BIOS chip in its socket with just enough pressure to keep it in place *before* booting up. This allowed me to remove the BIOS chip with just a slight flick of a tweezer prong.

If you have a proper BIOS chip removal tool, you do not need to take the above precautions; you can just boot up and remove the BIOS chip.

If you are forced to use a metallic tool like a tweezer, please remember that you can cause a short circuit if you are not careful. To reduce the risk, you can cover the tip of your metallic tool with non-conductive tape like cellophane tape.

Good BIOS chip in its socket.
(Photo by author)

After the good BIOS chip has been removed, take the corrupted BIOS chip and insert it into the socket. Remember to align the notch in the BIOS chip's package with the notch in the socket before you insert the BIOS chip!

With the corrupted BIOS chip in place, all you need to do is flash it with a new BIOS image.

Step 5: Flash the Corrupted BIOS Chip

Now it's time to fire up the BIOS flash utility you have prepared in the DOS boot disk. If you have forgotten or did not write down the filename of the BIOS image file, you can check for it by running a dir command at the command prompt.

For the reference motherboard, the ABIT NF7-S, I used the following command (as recommended by ABIT):

```
A:\>awdflash bios.bin /cc /cd /cp /py /sn /cks /r
```

Please consult your motherboard manual for the proper commands for your motherboard. The commands may vary between motherboards.

After the BIOS flash utility completes flashing the BIOS image, it automatically reboots the computer. At this point in time, you should turn off the computer.

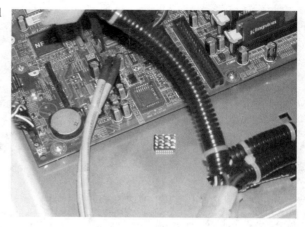

BIOS chip removed.
(Photo by author)

Inserting the corrupted BIOS chip.
(Photo by author)

Step 6: Swap the BIOS Chips Again

With the computer turned off, it is much easier to remove the revived BIOS chip and insert the original BIOS chip into the socket. Again, make sure the BIOS chip is aligned correctly before you insert it into the socket. Start up the system to make sure it didn't suffer any damage from the procedure.

You can now take the revived BIOS chip and insert it into its socket in the previously dead motherboard. Then press the Power button and watch your system boot up!

What If You Don't Have a Similar Motherboard?

Although it is advisable to use a similar motherboard to hot flash your dead BIOS chip, you can use a completely different motherboard model to do the hot flash. There are some things you need to consider before you do so, though.

First, you should find a working motherboard that supports the same BIOS chip as that of your dead motherboard. If your BIOS chip is of the square **PLCC** type, look for a working motherboard that also uses a PLCC BIOS chip. You can't hot flash a PLCC BIOS chip using a motherboard that uses a DIP BIOS chip!

And even if you find a motherboard that supports the same type of BIOS chip, you must make sure that it supports the same voltage. Older BIOS chips run at 5V while new ones only need 3.3V to run. Naturally, inserting a 3.3V BIOS chip into a 5V socket will burn up that 3.3V chip in no time at all.

So, check and make sure both the dead BIOS chip and the BIOS chip of the hot flash motherboard run at the same voltage. Because current motherboards all use 3.3V BIOS chips, this should only be a problem if you are attempting to use a very old motherboard to hot flash.

When you have everything ready, follow the steps we've gone through earlier. The only change at this point will be how to flash the dead BIOS chip.

Flashing with a Different Motherboard

Depending on the flash utility you use, it is possible to force the flash utility to flash the dead BIOS with your BIOS image file even if the flash utility detects it as the wrong BIOS image.

In this example, we will use the **8.23K** version of the AwardFlash utility. Let's look at the list of available options:

AwardFlash utility commands.

The manufacturer of my reference motherboard, ABIT, recommends the following command line parameters:

```
A:\>awdflash bios.bin /cc /cd /cp /py /sn /cks /r
```

To force the AwardFlash utility to flash the dead BIOS chip, you need to add a **/f** switch to the end of the command line. Thus, the command line should now be:

```
A:\>awdflash bios.bin /cc /cd /cp /py /sn /cks /r /f
```

That should force the AwardFlash utility to flash the dead BIOS chip with the BIOS image you prepared, even after booting up on a different motherboard with an incompatible BIOS.

If you are using a different flash utility, please consult your motherboard manufacturer for the correct force flash switch for that utility.

The Universal BIOS Flash Utility

If the preceding method fails, there is still a recourse. There is a BIOS flash utility that claims to be the universal BIOS flash utility! Behold—**UniFlash**!

Developed by **Ondrej Zary**, this utility has impressive lists of supported hardware and compatibility tests. Best of all, it appears to be updated regularly.

UniFlash is definitely worth checking out if you need to force flash a dead BIOS chip on a different motherboard. You can get the latest version of UniFlash at http://www.uniflash.org/.

Summary

When it comes to minor emergencies like an unbootable system, I have shown you a variety of ways to tackle the problem and restore the system. I have even listed them in order of preference (based on simplicity):

- Power Off-Power On
- Keyboard Reset
- CMOS Discharge Jumper
- CMOS Battery Removal

When it comes to a corrupted BIOS, it is usually the end of the road for the motherboard. You will have to send the motherboard back to the manufacturer or request a replacement BIOS chip.

Of course, I have shown you an alternative in the form of the hot flashing technique. As you have seen, the concept of hot flashing is pretty simple. It is the proper execution of the technique that is tricky.

If you are experienced in working with hardware and know how to flash the BIOS, then it should not be a difficult procedure even without the proper BIOS removal tool. You can use hot flashing to revive dead BIOS chips, thereby saving you money and keeping your computer's downtime to the absolute minimum.

However, if you have virtually no experience in hardware or flashing the BIOS, then hot flashing can be a rather dangerous endeavor. Failure to restore the dead BIOS chip would be the least of your worries. If you are unlucky or careless, you could damage the computer you are using to hot flash the dead BIOS chip.

Therefore, it is highly advisable that you do *not* attempt this procedure unless you are familiar with hardware and know how to flash BIOS.

I hope this section on hot flashing has helped you learn how to revive corrupted BIOS chips with minimal hassle and risk. If you are interested in more details on hot flashing, please feel free to check out *The ARP Hot Flashing Guide* (http://www.rojakpot.com/showar ticle.aspx?artno=62).

Chapter 3
Quick Reviews

Introduction

This chapter contains simplified explanations of each BIOS option as well as its recommended settings. This is the best chapter to consult if you need a quick overview of a BIOS option and its optimal settings.

You should also start with this chapter if you have only limited knowledge of computer hardware. This chapter offers simple explanations of the BIOS options, so you won't be confused by technical details.

The BIOS options are all arranged alphabetically with lettered tabs, so you can navigate quickly through the chapter. You can also use the Table of Contents and the Category Look-Up Table to quickly access the BIOS options you are interested in.

Note: Acronyms are not always spelled out, so a detailed list of acronyms is provided at the end of this book for your reference.

After you complete this chapter, you should head on to Chapter 4 for more details on the BIOS options covered in this chapter.

8-bit I/O Recovery Time

Common Options: NA, 8, 1, 2, 3, 4, 5, 6, 7

This BIOS feature allows you to add extra wait cycles between consecutive 8-bit PCI cycles to the ISA bus. This is used to correct timing issues between the PCI bus and ISA bus.

Please note that there is already a fixed minimum delay of 3.5 clock cycles. So whatever you set using this BIOS feature adds to that delay. Choosing **NA** sets the number of delay cycles to the minimum 3.5 clock cycles.

Most 8-bit ISA cards work fine with the minimum 3.5 delay cycles (**NA**). However, if your ISA card does not work properly, try increasing the number of additional delay cycles.

16-bit I/O Recovery Time

Common Options: NA, 4, 1, 2, 3

This BIOS feature allows you to add extra wait cycles between consecutive 16-bit PCI cycles to the ISA bus. This is used to correct timing issues between the PCI bus and ISA bus.

Please note that there is already a fixed minimum delay of 3.5 clock cycles. So whatever you set using this BIOS feature adds to that delay. Choosing **NA** sets the number of delay cycles to the minimum 3.5 clock cycles.

Most 16-bit ISA cards work fine with the minimum 3.5 delay cycles (**NA**). However, if your ISA card does not work properly, try increasing the number of additional delay cycles.

32-bit Disk Access

Common Options: Enabled, Disabled

This BIOS feature allows you to command the IDE controller to combine two 16-bit hard disk reads into a single 32-bit data transfer to the processor. This greatly improves the performance of the IDE controller as well as the PCI bus.

Therefore, it is highly advisable to enable 32-bit Disk Access. If you disable it, data transfers from the IDE controller to the processor will only occur in 16-bits chunks.

32-bit Transfer Mode

Common Options: On, Off

This BIOS feature allows you to command the IDE controller to combine two 16-bit hard disk reads into a single 32-bit data transfer to the processor. This greatly improves the performance of the IDE controller as well as the PCI bus.

Therefore, it is highly advisable to enable 32-bit Transfer Mode. If you disable it, data transfers from the IDE controller to the processor will only occur in 16-bit chunks.

Act Bank A to B CMD Delay

Common Options: 2 Cycles, 3 Cycles

This BIOS feature specifies the minimum amount of time between successive ACTIVATE commands to the *same* DDR device. The shorter the delay, the faster the next bank can be activated for read or write operations. However, because row activation requires a lot of current, using a short delay may cause excessive current surges.

For desktop PCs, a delay of **2 cycles** is recommended, as current surges aren't really important. The performance benefit of using the shorter 2-cycle delay is of far greater interest. The shorter delay means every back-to-back bank activation takes one clock cycle less to perform. This improves the DDR device's performance.

Switch to **3 cycles** only when there are stability problems with the 2-cycle setting.

AGP 2X Mode

Common Options: Enabled, Disabled

This BIOS feature is a toggle for the motherboard's AGP 2X support.

When **enabled**, it allows the AGP bus to make use of the AGP 2X transfer protocol to boost the AGP bus bandwidth. If it's **disabled**, then the AGP bus only uses the standard AGP1X transfer protocol.

The AGP 2X protocol must be supported by both the motherboard and graphics card for this feature to work. Of course, this feature only appears in your BIOS if your motherboard supports the AGP 2X transfer protocol!

So, all you need to do is make sure your graphics card supports AGP 2X transfers. If it does, **enable** AGP 2X Mode to take advantage of the faster transfer mode. **Disable** it only if you are facing stability issues or if you intend to overclock the AGP bus beyond 75MHz with **sidebanding support** enabled.

AGP 4X Drive Strength

Common Options: Auto, Manual

This BIOS feature allows you to set the AGP controller to dynamically adjust the AGP driving strength or allow manual configuration in the BIOS.

Normally, the recommended setting is **Auto**. The AGP Drive Strength values are provided by the auto-compensation circuitry. However, manual configuration of the AGP Drive Strength may be necessary to get certain AGP 4X cards to work properly.

To correct such compatibility problems, you should set the AGP 4X Drive Strength to **Manual**. This allows you to set a *higher* AGP Drive Strength value manually through the **AGP Drive Strength P Ctrl** and **AGP Drive Strength N Ctrl** options.

Please note that this feature is a little different from **AGP Driving Control,** because it usually comes with two to four different drive strength controls. The **AGP Driving Control** feature only comes with a single drive strength control.

AGP 4X Mode

Common Options: Enabled, Disabled

This BIOS feature is a toggle for the motherboard's AGP 4X support.

When **enabled**, it allows the AGP bus to make use of the AGP 4X transfer protocol to boost the AGP bus bandwidth. If it's **disabled**, then the AGP bus only uses the AGP 1X or AGP 2X transfer protocol.

The AGP 4X protocol must be supported by both the motherboard and graphics card for this feature to work. Of course, this feature only appears in your BIOS if your motherboard supports the AGP 4X transfer protocol!

So, all you need to do is make sure your graphics card supports AGP 4X transfers. If it does, **enable** AGP 4X Mode to take advantage of the faster transfer mode. You must **disable** it if your graphics card doesn't support AGP 4X transfers. The BIOS then reports that the maximum supported transfer mode is AGP 2X.

AGP 8X Mode

Common Options: Enabled, Disabled

This BIOS feature is a toggle for the motherboard's AGP 8X support.

When **enabled**, it allows the AGP bus to make use of the AGP 8X transfer protocol to boost the AGP bus bandwidth. If it's **disabled**, then the AGP bus is only allowed to use the AGP 4X transfer protocol.

The AGP 8X protocol must be supported by both the motherboard and graphics card for this feature to work. Of course, this feature only appears in your BIOS if your motherboard supports the AGP 8X transfer protocol!

So, all you need to do is make sure your graphics card supports AGP 8X transfers. If it does, **enable** AGP 8X Mode to take advantage of the faster transfer mode. You must **disable** it if your graphics card doesn't support AGP 8X transfers. The BIOS then reports that the maximum supported transfer mode is AGP 4X.

AGP Always Compensate

Common Options: Enabled, Disabled

This BIOS feature determines whether the AGP controller should be allowed to dynamically adjust the AGP driving strength or use preset drive strength values.

By default, it is set to automatically adjust the AGP drive strength once or at regular intervals. The circuitry can also be disabled or bypassed and a user setting used. However, this BIOS feature does not allow manual configuration.

When you **enable** AGP Always Compensate, the auto-compensation circuitry automatically adjusts the AGP Drive Strength *at regular intervals*. If you **disable** it, the circuitry only adjusts the drive strength *once* at boot-up. The drive strength values derived at boot-up remain until the system is rebooted.

It is recommended that you **enable** AGP Always Compensate, so the AGP controller can dynamically adjust the AGP driving strength at regular intervals.

AGP Aperture Size

Common Options: 4, 8, 16, 32, 64, 128, 256

This BIOS feature does two things: It selects the size of the AGP aperture, and it determines the size of the **GART (Graphics Address Relocation Table)**.

The aperture is a portion of the PCI memory address range that is dedicated for use as AGP memory address space, while the GART is a translation table that translates AGP memory addresses into actual memory addresses that are often fragmented. The GART allows the graphics card to see the memory region available to it as a contiguous piece of memory range.

Host cycles that hit the aperture range are forwarded to the AGP bus without need for translation. The aperture size also determines the maximum amount of system memory that can be allocated to the AGP graphics card for texture storage.

Please note that the AGP aperture is merely address space, *not* actual physical memory in use. Although it is very common to hear people recommending that the AGP aperture size should be *half* the size of system memory, this is *wrong*!

The requirement for AGP memory space *shrinks* as the graphics card's local memory increases in size. This is because the graphics card has more local memory to dedicate to texture storage. So, if you upgrade to a graphics card with more memory, you shouldn't be "deceived" into thinking you need even more AGP memory! On the contrary, a smaller AGP memory space is required.

It is recommended that you keep the AGP aperture around **64MB** to **128MB** in size, even if your graphics card has a lot of onboard memory. This allows flexibility in the event that you actually need extra memory for texture storage. It also keeps the GART within a reasonable size.

AGP Capability

Common Options: Auto, 1X Mode, 2X Mode, 4X Mode, 8X Mode

This BIOS feature is only found in AGP 8X-capable motherboards. AGP 8X is backward-compatible with earlier AGP standards. This BIOS feature allows you to set the motherboard's maximum supported AGP transfer protocol.

It is recommended that you leave this BIOS feature at its default setting of **Auto**. This allows the motherboard to set the appropriate AGP transfer protocol based on the graphics card's AGP support detected during boot up.

However, the other options are useful if your graphics card has problems using the detected AGP transfer protocol. You can manually select a slower AGP transfer protocol to solve the problem.

A

AGP Clock / CPU FSB Clock

Common Options: 1/1, 2/3, 1/2, 2/5

This BIOS feature allows you to set the ratio between the AGP clock speed and the CPU bus (*also known as front side bus or FSB*) clock speed. This allows you to keep the AGP bus speed within specifications (66MHz) while using a much faster CPU bus speed.

When the ratio is set to **1/1**, the AGP bus runs at the same speed as the CPU bus. This is meant for processors that use the 66MHz bus speed, such as the older Intel Celeron processors.

The **2/3** divider is used when you use a processor running with a bus speed of 100MHz. This divider cuts the AGP bus speed down to 66MHz.

The **1/2** divider is used when you use a processor running with a bus speed of 133MHz. This divider cuts the AGP bus speed down to 66MHz.

The **2/5** divider is used when you use a processor running with a bus speed of 166MHz. This divider cuts the AGP bus speed down to 66MHz.

Generally, you should set this feature according to the CPU bus speed you are using. This means using the **1/1** divider for 66MHz bus speed CPUs, the **2/3** divider for 100MHz bus speed CPUs, the **1/2** divider for 133MHz CPUs, and the **2/5** divider for 166MHz CPUs.

AGP Drive Strength

Common Options: Auto, Manual

This BIOS feature allows you to set the AGP controller to dynamically adjust the AGP driving strength or the BIOS to manually configure it.

Normally, the recommended setting is **Auto**. The AGP Drive Strength values are provided by the auto-compensation circuitry. However, manual configuration of the AGP Drive Strength may be necessary to get certain AGP 4X/8X cards to work properly.

To correct such compatibility problems, you should set the AGP Drive Strength to **Manual**. This allows you to manually set a *higher* AGP Drive Strength value through the **AGP Drive Strength P Ctrl** and **AGP Drive Strength N Ctrl** options.

Please note that this feature is a little different from **AGP Driving Control,** because it usually comes with two to four different drive strength controls. The **AGP Driving Control** feature only comes with a single drive strength control.

AGP Drive Strength N Ctrl

Common Options: 0 to F (Hex numbers), 0h to Fh

This BIOS feature only is activated if you set the **AGP Drive Strength** BIOS feature to **Manual**. It determines the N transistor drive strength of the AGP bus.

The drive strength is represented by Hex values from 0 to F (0 to 15 in decimal). The higher the drive strength, the greater the compensation for the motherboard's impedance on the AGP bus.

In conjunction with **AGP Drive Strength** and **AGP Drive Strength P Ctrl**, this function is used to bypass AGP dynamic compensation in cases where the auto-compensation circuitry cannot provide adequate compensation. Please check with your graphics card manufacturer if your card requires the N transistor drive strength to be set manually.

Incidentally, increasing the AGP drive strength does *not* improve the performance of the AGP bus. It is not a performance-enhancing feature, so you shouldn't increase the N transistor drive strength unless you need to.

AGP Drive Strength P Ctrl

Common Options: 0 to F (Hex numbers), 0h to Fh

This BIOS feature only is activated if you set the **AGP Drive Strength** BIOS feature to **Manual**. It determines the P transistor drive strength of the AGP bus.

The drive strength is represented by Hex values from 0 to F (0 to 15 in decimal). The higher the drive strength, the greater the compensation for the motherboard's impedance on the AGP bus.

In conjunction with **AGP Drive Strength** and **AGP Drive Strength N Ctrl**, this function is used to bypass AGP dynamic compensation in cases where the auto-compensation circuitry cannot provide adequate compensation. Please check with your graphics card manufacturer if your card requires the P transistor drive strength to be set manually.

Incidentally, increasing the AGP drive strength does *not* improve the performance of the AGP bus. It is not a performance-enhancing feature, so you shouldn't increase the P transistor drive strength unless you need to.

AGP Driving Control

Common Options: Auto, Manual

This BIOS feature allows you to set the AGP controller to dynamically adjust the AGP driving strength or allow manual configuration by the BIOS.

Normally, the recommended setting is **Auto**. The AGP drive strength values are provided by the auto-compensation circuitry. However, manual configuration of the AGP Drive Strength may be necessary to get certain AGP 4X/8X cards to work properly.

To correct such compatibility problems, you should set the AGP Drive Strength to **Manual**. This allows you to set a *higher* AGP Drive Strength value manually through the **AGP Driving Value** function.

Please note that this feature is a little different from **AGP 4X Drive Strength,** because it usually comes with a single drive strength control. The **AGP 4X Drive Strength** feature comes with two to four drive strength controls.

AGP Driving Value

Common Options: 00 to FF (Hex numbers), 00h to FFh

This BIOS feature is only activated if you set the **AGP Driving Control** BIOS feature to **Manual**. It determines the overall drive strength of the AGP bus.

The drive strength is represented by Hex values from 00 to FF (0 to 255 in decimal). The higher the drive strength, the greater the compensation for the motherboard's impedance on the AGP bus.

In conjunction with **AGP Drive Strength** and **AGP Drive Strength P Ctrl**, this function is used to bypass AGP dynamic compensation in cases where the auto-compensation circuitry cannot provide adequate compensation. If you are using an AGP card built around the NVIDIA GeForce 2 line of GPUs, then you should put **AGP Driving Control** into **Manual** mode and set the AGP Driving Value to **EA** (234). For other cards, please check with the manufacturer if your card requires the AGP driving strength to be set manually.

Incidentally, increasing the AGP drive strength does *not* improve the performance of the AGP bus. It is not a performance-enhancing feature, so you shouldn't increase the AGP drive strength unless you need to.

AGP Fast Write

Common Options: Enabled, Disabled

This BIOS feature controls the AGP bus Fast Write capability. Fast Write is a feature that accelerates memory write transactions from the chipset to the AGP device.

Fast Write allows the AGP device to act like a PCI device. This allows it to bypass the main memory and directly access the data, which improves AGP read performance. However, AGP write performance is not affected.

It is recommended that you **enable** AGP Fast Write for better AGP read performance, but **disable** it if any of your PCI cards start acting funny.

AGP ISA Aliasing

Common Options: Enabled, Disabled

This BIOS feature allows you to determine whether the system controller performs ISA Aliasing to prevent conflicts between ISA devices.

The default setting of **Enabled** forces the system controller to alias ISA addresses using address bits [15:10]. This restricts all 16-bit addressing devices to a maximum contiguous I/O space of 256 bytes.

When **disabled**, the system controller does not perform any ISA aliasing and all 16 address lines can be used for I/O address space decoding. This gives 16-bit addressing devices access to the full 64KB I/O space.

It is recommended that you **disable** AGP ISA Aliasing for optimal AGP (and PCI) performance. It also prevents your AGP or PCI card from conflicting with your ISA cards. **Enable** it only if you have ISA devices that are conflicting with each other.

AGP Master 1WS Read

Common Options: Enabled, Disabled

This BIOS feature allows you to reduce the time the AGP bus-mastering device has to wait before it can initiate a read command to only one wait state. This speeds up all reads that the AGP bus-master makes from the system memory.

So, for better AGP read performance, **enable** this feature. **Disable** it only if you notice visual anomalies or if your system hangs on running software that makes use of AGP texturing.

Curiously, some motherboards come with a default AGP master read latency of **0**! Enabling the AGP Master 1WS Read in such cases actually *increases* the latency by one wait state and reduces AGP read performance. Although it's quite unlikely that the default AGP master read latency would be zero, that's what their manuals say.

AGP Master 1WS Write

Common Options: Enabled, Disabled

This BIOS feature allows you to reduce the time the AGP bus-mastering device has to wait before it can initiate a write command to only one wait state. This speeds up all writes that the AGP bus-master makes to the system memory.

So, for better AGP read performance, **enable** this feature. **Disable** it only if you notice visual anomalies or if your system hangs on running software that makes use of AGP texturing.

Curiously, some motherboards come with a default AGP master write latency of **0**! Enabling the AGP Master 1WS Write in such cases actually *increases* the latency by one wait state and reduces AGP write performance. Although it's quite unlikely that the default AGP master write latency would be zero, that's what their manuals say.

AGP Prefetch

Common Options: Enabled, Disabled

This feature controls the system controller's AGP prefetch capability.

When **enabled**, the system controller prefetches data whenever the AGP device reads from the system memory. This speeds up AGP reads because it allows contiguous memory reads by the AGP device to proceed with minimal delay.

Therefore, it is recommended that you **enable** this feature for better AGP read performance.

AGP Secondary Lat Timer

Common Options: 00h, 20h, 40h, 60h, 80h, C0h, FFh

This BIOS feature controls how long the AGP bus can hold the PCI bus (via the PCI-to-PCI bridge) before another PCI device takes over. The longer the latency, the longer the AGP bus can retain control of the PCI bus before handing it over to another PCI device.

Normally, the AGP Secondary Latency Timer is set to **20h** (**32 clock cycles**). This means the AGP bus PCI-to-PCI bridge has to complete its transactions within 32 clock cycles or hand it over to the next PCI device.

For better AGP performance, a longer latency should be used. Try increasing it to **40h** (**64 cycles**) or even **80h** (**128 cycles**). The optimal value for every system is different. You should benchmark your AGP card's performance after each change to determine the optimal latency for your system.

If you set the AGP Secondary Latency Timer to a very large value like **80h** (**128 cycles**) or **C0h** (**192 cycles**), you should set the **PCI Latency Time** to **32 cycles**. This provides better access for your PCI devices that might be unnecessarily stalled if both the AGP and PCI buses have very long latencies.

In addition, some time-critical PCI devices may not agree with a long AGP latency. Such devices require priority access to the PCI bus, which may not be possible if the PCI bus is held up by the AGP bus for a long period. In such cases, it is recommended that you keep to the default latency of **20h** (**32 clock cycles**).

AGP Spread Spectrum

Common Options: 0.25%, 0.5%, Disabled

This BIOS feature allows you to reduce the EMI of the AGP bus by modulating the signals it generates so that the spikes are reduced to flatter curves. It achieves this by varying the frequency *slightly*, so the signal does not use any particular frequency for more than a moment.

The BIOS usually offers two levels of modulation—**0.25%** or **0.5%**. The greater the modulation, the greater the reduction of EMI. Therefore, if you need to significantly reduce the AGP bus EMI, a modulation of **0.5%** is recommended.

In most conditions, frequency modulation using this feature should not cause any problems. However, system stability may be compromised if you are overclocking the AGP bus. Of course, this depends on the amount of modulation, the extent of overclocking, and other factors such as temperature, and so forth. As such, the problem may not manifest itself immediately.

Therefore, it is recommended that you **disable** this feature if you are overclocking the AGP bus. The risk of crashing your system is not worth the reduction in EMI. Of course, if EMI reduction is important to you, **enable** this feature by all means. However, you should reduce the clock speed a little to provide a margin of safety.

If you are not overclocking, the decision to **enable** or **disable** this feature is really up to you. However, unless you have EMI problems or sensitive data that must be safeguarded from electronic eavesdropping, it is best to **disable** this feature to remove the possibility of instability.

AGP to DRAM Prefetch

Common Options: Enabled, Disabled

This feature controls the system controller's AGP prefetch capability.

When **enabled**, the system controller prefetches data whenever the AGP device reads from the system memory. This speeds up AGP reads because it allows contiguous memory reads by the AGP device to proceed with minimal delay.

Therefore, it is recommended that you **enable** this feature for better AGP read performance.

AGPCLK / CPUCLK

Common Options: 1/1, 2/3, 1/2, 2/5

This BIOS feature allows you to set the ratio between the AGP clock speed and the CPU bus (*also known as front side bus or FSB*) clock speed. This allows you to keep the AGP bus speed within specifications (66MHz) while using a much faster CPU bus speed.

When the ratio is set to **1/1**, the AGP bus runs at the same speed as the CPU bus. This is meant for processors that use the 66MHz bus speed, such as the older Intel Celeron processors.

The **2/3** divider is used when you use a processor running with a bus speed of 100MHz. This divider cuts the AGP bus speed down to 66MHz.

The **2/5** divider is used when you use a processor running with a bus speed of 166MHz. This divider cuts the AGP bus speed down to 66MHz.

Generally, you should set this feature according to the CPU bus speed you are using. This means using the **1/1** divider for 66MHz bus speed CPUs, the **2/3** divider for 100MHz bus speed CPUs, the **1/2** divider for 133MHz CPUs, and the **2/5** divider for 166MHz CPUs.

Anti-Virus Protection

Common Options: Enabled, Disabled, ChipAway

This BIOS feature controls the motherboard's virus protection features.

When **enabled**, the BIOS protects the boot sector and partition table by halting the system and flashing a warning message whenever there is an attempt to write to these areas.

This feature can cause problems with software that needs to access the boot sector, for example the installation routine of all versions of Microsoft Windows from Windows 95 onward. When **enabled**, this feature causes the installation routine to fail. You should **disable** this feature before running such software.

Alternatively, you can select the internal rule-based anti-virus code known as **ChipAway**. Enabling **ChipAway** provides better anti-virus protection by scanning for and detecting boot viruses before they have a chance to infect the boot sector of any hard disk. Note that this feature is useless for hard disks that run on external controllers with their own BIOS.

APIC Function

Common Options: Enabled, Disabled

This BIOS feature is used to enable or disable the motherboard's **APIC (Advanced Programmable Interrupt Controller)**. The APIC provides multiprocessor support, more IRQs, and faster interrupt handling.

However, it is only supported by newer operating systems such as Microsoft Windows NT, Windows 2000, and Windows XP. Older operating systems such as DOS or Windows 95/98 do not support this feature.

It is recommended that you **enable** this feature if you are using a newer operating system such as Windows XP. **Disable** it only if you are using an older operating system such as DOS or Windows 95/98.

Assign IRQ For USB

Common Options: Enabled, Disabled

This BIOS feature controls whether the BIOS should assign an IRQ to the USB controller.

When **enabled**, an IRQ is assigned to the USB controller, and you are able to connect your USB devices to it.

When **disabled**, the USB controller is not assigned an IRQ. This disables the USB controller but frees up an IRQ.

It is recommended that you **enable** this feature if you use USB peripherals.

Assign IRQ For VGA

Common Options: Enabled, Disabled

This BIOS feature controls whether the BIOS should assign an IRQ to the graphics card.

When **enabled**, an IRQ is assigned to the graphics card.

When **disabled**, the graphics card is not assigned an IRQ.

While there are some exceptions, most graphics cards require an IRQ to work properly. Therefore, it is recommended that you **enable** this feature for proper operation of your graphics card.

AT Bus Clock

Common Options: 7.16MHz, CLK/2, CLK/3, CLK/4, CLK/5, CLK/6

This BIOS feature allows you to select the ISA bus clock speed. The chipset actually generates the ISA bus clock by dividing the PCI clock. Hence, the available settings of **CLK/2**, **CLK/3**, **CLK/4, CLK/5,** and **CLK/6**.

The fixed speed of **7.16MHz** is derived by dividing the reference clock generator speed of **14.318MHz** by a factor of two.

A

As you can see, the setting of **CLK/4** yields an ISA bus speed of **8.33MHz**, which is the maximum speed allowed by the official ISA specifications. However, you can choose to overclock the ISA by selecting the settings **CLK/3** or **CLK/2**, which yield clock speeds of **11.11MHz** and **16.67MHz**, respectively.

Overclocking the ISA bus greatly improves its performance. Therefore, it is recommended that you try to use the faster settings if possible. However, while newer ISA cards are capable of running at this "out-of-spec" speed, older ones may not work properly at this speed.

If your ISA cards fail to work properly, then you should select the setting of **CLK/4** or **7.16MHz**. This keeps the ISA bus within specifications.

Please note that the aforementioned calculations and recommendations were based on a **33MHz** PCI bus clock. If you are overclocking your PCI bus, please take the increased PCI clock speed into account!

If this is confusing and you want to play it safe, select the setting of **7.16MHz**. This is the failsafe setting because it sets the ISA bus to run at a fixed speed of 7.16MHz, irrespective of the PCI bus speed.

ATA100RAID IDE Controller

Common Options: Enabled, Disabled

This BIOS feature enables or disables the motherboard's external UltraDMA/100 IDE RAID controller.

When **enabled**, the external UltraDMA/100 IDE RAID controller is enabled to provide an additional two IDE channels and RAID capabilities.

When **disabled**, the external UltraDMA/100 IDE RAID controller is disabled, freeing up two IRQs and speeding up system initialization.

It is recommended that you **enable** this feature if you require the use of the external UltraDMA/100 IDE RAID controller, but **disable** it if you don't use it.

Athlon 4 SSED Instruction

Common Options: Enabled, Disabled

Beginning with the Palomino core of the Athlon XP (and MP) family of processors, AMD started implementing Intel's SSE instruction set. AMD also added a status bit that tells any querying software that the Athlon XP/MP supports the full SSE instruction set. However, this status bit ends up causing some compatibility issues with the BeOS operating system and some graphics cards.

This is where the **Athlon 4 SSED Instruction** BIOS feature comes in. This BIOS feature is a simple toggle for the AMD Athlon XP/MP's SSE status bit.

When **enabled**, the BIOS enables the SSE status bit. Querying software will recognize the processor as a SSE-compatible processor. This allows the processor to take advantage of SSE-optimized software.

When **disabled**, the BIOS disables the SSE status bit. Querying software will *not* recognize the processor as a SSE-compatible processor. The processor can only take advantage of Enhanced 3DNow!-optimized software.

By default, this BIOS feature is set to **Enabled**, which allows for optimal performance with SSE-optimized software. It is highly recommended that you leave it at the default setting of **Enabled**.

You should **disable** this BIOS feature only if you are facing compatibility issues with the SSE status bit.

Auto Detect DIMM/PCI Clk

Common Options: Enabled, Disabled

This BIOS feature determines whether the BIOS should actively reduce **EMI (Electromagnetic Interference)** and reduce power consumption by turning off unoccupied or inactive expansion slots.

When **enabled**, the BIOS monitors AGP, PCI, and memory slots and turns off clock signals to all unoccupied and inactive slots.

When **disabled**, the BIOS does not monitor AGP, PCI, and memory slots. All clock signals remain active even to unoccupied or inactive slots.

It is recommended that you **enable** this feature to save power and reduce EMI.

Auto Turn Off PCI Clock Pin

Common Options: Enabled, Disabled

This BIOS feature determines whether the BIOS should actively reduce EMI and reduce power consumption by turning off unoccupied or inactive PCI slots.

When **enabled**, the BIOS monitors PCI slots and turns off clock signals to all unoccupied and inactive slots.

When **disabled**, the BIOS does not monitor PCI slots. All clock signals remain active even to unoccupied or inactive slots.

It is recommended that you **enable** this feature to save power and reduce EMI.

B

Boot Other Device

Common Options: Enabled, Disabled

This BIOS feature determines whether the BIOS attempts to load an operating system from the **Second Boot Device** or **Third Boot Device** if it fails to load one from the **First Boot Device**.

This feature is **enabled** by default, and it is recommended that you leave it as such.

Boot Sequence

Common Options: A, C, SCSI

C, A, SCSI

C, CD-ROM, A

CD-ROM, C, A

D, A, SCSI (only when you have at least 2 IDE hard disks)

E, A, SCSI (only when you have at least 3 IDE hard disks)

F, A, SCSI (only when you have 4 IDE hard disks)

SCSI, A, C

SCSI, C, A

A, SCSI, C

LS/ZIP, C

This BIOS feature enables you to set the sequence by which the BIOS searches for an operating system during the boot-up process. To ensure the shortest booting time possible, set the hard disk that contains your operating system as the first choice. Normally, this is drive **C** for IDE drives, but if you are using an SCSI hard disk, then select **SCSI**.

Some motherboards have an external (not part of the chipset) IDE controller. In such motherboards, the **SCSI** option is replaced with an **EXT** option. If you want to boot from an IDE hard disk running off the internal IDE controller, do *not* set the **Boot Sequence** to start with **EXT**. Please note that this feature works in conjunction with the **Boot Sequence EXT Means** feature.

Boot Sequence EXT Means

Common Options: IDE, SCSI

This BIOS feature determines whether the system boots from an IDE hard disk connected to an *external* IDE controller or an SCSI hard disk. However, it only has an effect if the **EXT** option had been selected in the **Boot Sequence** feature.

To boot from an IDE hard disk that's connected to the *external* IDE controller, you must set this feature to **IDE**.

To boot from an SCSI hard disk, you must set this feature to **SCSI**.

Boot To OS/2

Common Options: Yes, No

This is similar to the **OS Select For DRAM > 64M** BIOS feature.

This BIOS feature determines how systems with more than 64MB of memory are managed. A wrong setting can cause problems like erroneous memory detection.

If you are using an older version of the IBM OS/2 operating system, you should select **Yes**.

If you are using the IBM OS/2 Warp v3.0 or higher operating system, you should select **No**.

If you are using an older version of the IBM OS/2 operating system but have already installed all the relevant IBM FixPaks, you should select **No**.

Users of non-OS/2 operating systems (such as Microsoft Windows XP) should select the **No** option.

Boot Up Floppy Seek

Common Options: Enabled, Disabled

This BIOS feature determines whether the BIOS checks for a floppy drive during boot-up.

If **enabled**, the BIOS attempts to detect and initialize the floppy drive. If it cannot detect one, it flashes an error message. However, the system is still allowed to continue the boot process.

If this feature is **disabled**, the BIOS skips the floppy drive check. This speeds up the booting process by several seconds.

Because a floppy drive check is really pointless, it is recommended that you **disable** this feature for a faster booting process.

Boot Up NumLock Status

Common Options: On, Off

This BIOS feature sets the input mode of the numeric keypad at boot up.

If you turn this feature **on**, the BIOS sets the numeric keypad to function in the **numeric mode**.

If you set it to **Off**, the numeric keypad functions in the **cursor control mode** instead.

The numeric keypad's input mode can be switched to either numeric or cursor control mode and back again at any time after boot up.

The choice of initial keypad input mode is entirely up to your preference.

Byte Merge

B

Common Options: Enabled, Disabled

This BIOS feature is similar to the **PCI Dynamic Bursting** feature.

When **enabled**, the PCI write buffer accumulates and merges 8-bit and 16-bit writes into 32-bit writes. This increases the efficiency of the PCI bus and improves its bandwidth.

When **disabled**, the PCI write buffer does not accumulate or merge 8-bit or 16-bit writes. It just writes them to the PCI bus as soon as the bus is free. As such, there may be a loss of PCI bus efficiency when 8-bit or 16-bit data is written to the PCI bus.

Therefore, it is recommended that you **enable** Byte Merge for better performance.

However, please note that **Byte Merge** may be incompatible with certain PCI network interface cards (also known as NICs). So, if your NIC does not work properly, try **disabling** this feature.

C

Clock Throttle

Common Options: 12.5%, 25.0%, 37.5%, 50.0%, 62.5%, 75.0%, 87.5%

This BIOS feature allows manual configuration of the Thermal Control Circuit. Instead of allowing the TCC to automatically start with a duty cycle of **30–50%**, you can manually set the duty cycle.

Available options for this BIOS feature are set values of the processor's duty cycle when the Thermal Control Circuit gets activated. They range from a low of **12.5%** to a high of **87.5%**. Please note that these options reflect the processor's **duty cycle**, *not* its clock speed. The clock speed of the processor remains unchanged.

If you are looking for a Disabled option, there is no such option. You cannot turn off the Thermal Control Circuit. But if you keep your processor cool enough so that it never exceeds the maximum safe operating temperature, the Thermal Control Circuit will never get activated.

The default setting is usually **62.5%**. This means the Thermal Control Circuit will insert null cycles to allow the processor to "rest" **37.5%** of the time.

The choice of what you should set the Thermal Control Circuit to run at is really up to you. The lower the duty cycle, the slower your processor will perform, but it will take less time to cool down the processor enough to turn off the TCC. Using a higher duty cycle will not impair performance as much but it will take longer for your processor to cool down enough to turn off the TCC.

Compatible FPU OPCODE

Common Options: Enabled, Disabled

This BIOS feature determines how Pentium 4 and Xeon processors handle FOP codes using the FOP (final opcode) register.

When **enabled**, the Pentium 4 and Xeon engage the FOP code compatibility mode, which stores the FOP of the last non-transparent instruction in the FOP register.

When **disabled**, the Pentium 4 and Xeon turn off the FOP code compatibility mode and store only the FOP of the last non-transparent floating point instruction *that had an unmasked exception*. This allows for better FPU performance.

Therefore, it is recommended that you **disable** this feature for better FPU performance unless your software requires this feature to recover from FPU exceptions.

CPU/DRAM CLK Synch CTL

Common Options: Synchronous, Asynchronous, Auto

This BIOS feature allows a clear-cut way of controlling the memory controller's operating mode.

When set to **Synchronous**, the memory controller will set the memory clock to the same speed as the front side bus.

When set to **Asynchronous**, the memory controller will allow the memory clock to run at any speed.

When set to **Auto**, the operating mode of the memory controller will depend on the memory clock you set.

It is recommended that you select the **Synchronous** operating mode. This generally provides the best performance, even if your memory modules are capable of higher clock speeds.

CPU Drive Strength

Common Options: 0, 1, 2, 3

This BIOS feature allows you to manually set the drive strength of the CPU bus. The higher the value, the stronger the drive strength.

If you are facing stability problems with your processor, you might want to try boosting the CPU drive strength to a higher value. It helps correct any possible increase in impedance from the motherboard. Due to the nature of this BIOS feature, it is also possible to use it as an aid in overclocking the CPU.

However, this is *not* a surefire way of overclocking the CPU. Increasing it to the highest value does not necessarily mean that you can overclock the CPU more than you already can. In addition, it is important to note that increasing the CPU drive strength does *not* improve its performance. Contrary to popular opinion, it is *not* a performance-enhancing feature.

CPU Fast String

Common Options: Enabled, Disabled

This BIOS feature controls the processor's fast string feature.

When **enabled**, the processor operates on the string in a cache line when the "fast string" conditions are met.

When **disabled**, the processor does not operate on the string while it is in a cache line.

It is recommended that you **enable** CPU Fast String for better performance. There is currently no reason why you should disable CPU Fast String.

CPU Hyper-Threading

Common Options: Enabled, Disabled

This BIOS feature controls the functionality of the Intel Hyper-Threading Technology.

Intel Hyper-Threading Technology allows a single processor to execute *two or more* separate threads concurrently. When hyper-threading is enabled, multi-threaded software applications can execute their threads in parallel, thereby improving their performance.

The Intel Hyper-Threading Technology is only supported by the Intel Pentium 4 (officially only those 3.06GHz and faster) and the Intel Xeon processors. Please note that for Hyper-Threading to work, you should have the following:

- Intel processor that supports Hyper-Threading
- Motherboard with a chipset and BIOS that support Hyper-Threading
- Operating system that supports Hyper-Threading (Microsoft Windows XP or Linux 2.4.x)

Because it behaves like two separate processors with their own APICs, you should also enable **APIC Function** in the BIOS, which is required for multi-processing.

It is highly recommended that you **enable** CPU Hyper-Threading for improved processor performance.

CPU L2 Cache ECC Checking

Common Options: Enabled, Disabled

This BIOS feature enables or disables the **L2 (Level 2 or Secondary)** cache's **ECC (Error Checking and Correction)** function, if available.

Enabling this feature is recommended, because it detects and corrects single-bit errors in data stored in the L2 cache. As most data reads are satisfied by the L2 cache, the L2 cache's ECC function should catch and correct almost all single-bit errors in the memory subsystem.

It also detects double-bit errors, although it cannot correct them. However, this isn't such a big deal, because double-bit errors are *extremely* rare. For all practical purposes, the ECC check should be able to catch virtually all data errors. This is especially useful at overclocked speeds when errors are most likely to creep in.

So, for most intents and purposes, I recommend that you **enable** this feature for greater system stability and reliability.

Please note that the presence of this feature in the BIOS does *not* necessarily mean that your processor's L2 cache actually supports ECC checking. Many processors do not ship with ECC-capable L2 cache. In such cases, you still can enable this feature in the BIOS, but it will have *no effect*.

CPU Latency Timer

Common Options: Enabled, Disabled

This BIOS feature allows you to control how the processor should handle a deferrable processor operation when there is a new request for the processor. By default, it is **disabled**.

When **disabled**, the processor will *immediately* defer all deferrable operations when there is a new processor request.

When **enabled**, the processor will defer those operations only *after* they have been held in a Snoop Stall for **31 clock cycles** when the new processor request arrives.

It is recommended that you **enable** this BIOS feature to ensure that deferrable operations are given sufficient time to complete. This improves performance by allowing deferrable operations to be processed without excessive delay.

CPU Level 1 Cache

Common Options: Enabled, Disabled

This BIOS feature controls the functionality of the processor's Level 1 cache.

When **enabled**, the processor's Level 1 cache is allowed to function. This allows the best possible performance from the processor.

When **disabled**, the processor's Level 1 cache is disabled. The processor bypasses the Level 1 cache and relies only on the Level 2 and Level 3 (if available) caches. This reduces the performance of the processor.

The recommended setting is obviously **Enabled** because disabling it severely affects the processor's performance. However, the **Disabled** setting is useful as a troubleshooting tool, especially when you are overclocking your processor.

CPU Level 2 Cache

Common Options: Enabled, Disabled

This BIOS feature controls the functionality of the processor's Level 2 cache.

When **enabled**, the processor's Level 2 cache is allowed to function. This allows the best possible performance from the processor.

When **disabled**, the processor's Level 2 cache is disabled. The processor bypasses the Level 2 cache and relies only on the Level 1 and Level 3 (if available) caches. This reduces the performance of the processor.

The recommended setting is obviously **Enabled** because disabling it severely affects the processor's performance. However, the **Disabled** setting is useful as a troubleshooting tool, especially when you are overclocking your processor.

CPU Level 3 Cache

Common Options: Enabled, Disabled

This BIOS feature controls the functionality of the processor's Level 3 cache.

When **enabled**, the processor's Level 3 cache is allowed to function. This allows the best possible performance from the processor.

When **disabled**, the processor's Level 3 cache is disabled. The processor bypasses the Level 3 cache and relies only on the Level 1 and Level 2 caches. This reduces the performance of the processor.

The recommended setting is obviously **Enabled** because disabling it severely affects the processor's performance. However, the **Disabled** setting is useful as a troubleshooting tool, especially when you are overclocking your processor.

CPU Thermal-Throttling

Common Options: 12.5%, 25.0%, 37.5%, 50.0%, 62.5%, 75.0%, 87.5%

This BIOS feature allows manual configuration of the Thermal Control Circuit. Instead of allowing the TCC to automatically start with a duty cycle of **30-50%**, you can manually set the duty cycle.

Available options for this BIOS feature are set values of the processor's **duty cycle** when the Thermal Control Circuit gets activated. They range from a low of **12.5%** to a high of **87.5%**. Please note that these options reflect the processor's duty cycle, *not* its clock speed. The clock speed of the processor remains unchanged.

If you are looking for a Disabled option, there is no such option. You cannot turn off the Thermal Control Circuit. But if you keep your processor cool enough so that it never exceeds the maximum safe operating temperature, the Thermal Control Circuit will never get activated.

The default setting is usually **62.5%**. This means the Thermal Control Circuit will insert null cycles to allow the processor to "rest" **37.5%** of the time.

The choice of what you should set the Thermal Control Circuit to run at is really up to you. The lower the duty cycle, the slower your processor will perform, but it will take less time to cool down the processor enough to turn off the TCC. Using a higher duty cycle will not impair performance as much but it will take longer for your processor to cool down enough to turn off the TCC.

CPU to PCI Post Write

Common Options: Enabled, Disabled

This BIOS feature controls the chipset's CPU-to-PCI write buffer. It is used to store PCI writes from the processor before they are written to the PCI bus.

When **enabled**, all PCI writes from the processor go directly to the write buffer. This allows the processor to work on something else while the write buffer writes the data to the PCI bus on the next available PCI cycle.

When **disabled**, the processor bypasses the buffer and writes directly to the PCI bus. This ties up the processor for the entire length of the transaction.

It is recommended that you **enable** this BIOS feature for better performance.

CPU to PCI Write Buffer

Common Options: Enabled, Disabled

This BIOS feature controls the chipset's CPU-to-PCI write buffer. It is used to store PCI writes from the processor before they are written to the PCI bus.

When **enabled**, all PCI writes from the processor go directly to the write buffer. This allows the processor to work on something else while the write buffer writes the data to the PCI bus on the next available PCI cycle.

When **disabled**, the processor bypasses the buffer and writes directly to the PCI bus. This ties up the processor for the entire length of the transaction.

It is recommended that you **enable** this BIOS feature for better performance.

CPU VCore Voltage

Common Options: Std. Vcore, Raising

This is a BIOS feature so far seen only in the **ABIT NV7-series** of motherboards. It is used to give a small boost to the processor's core voltage.

When set to **Std. Vcore**, the motherboard supplies the processor with the default core voltage.

When set to **Raising**, the motherboard boosts the processor's core voltage by approximately **3%**. So, if your processor has a core voltage of **1.7 volts**, using the Raising option raises that voltage to about **1.75V**.

As you can see, the voltage boost courtesy of this BIOS feature is not remarkable. However, because it appears to be the only way to boost the processor's core voltage in NVIDIA nForce-based motherboards, this **3%** boost is better than nothing at all! It may not allow radical over-clocking, but it should allow a little more overclocking freedom.

If you are an overclocker, it is recommended that you select the **Raising** option. It should allow your processor to be a little more overclockable. At the very least, it improves its stability at overclocked speeds.

D

DBI Output for AGP Trans.

Common Options: Enabled, Disabled

The full name for this BIOS feature is **Dynamic Bus Inversion Output for AGP Transmitter**. It is an AGP 3.0-specific BIOS feature that only appears when you install an AGP 3.0-compliant graphics card.

When **enabled**, the AGP controller is allowed to use the Dynamic Bus Inversion scheme to reduce power consumption and signal noise.

When **disabled**, the AGP controller does not use the Dynamic Bus Inversion scheme to reduce power consumption and signal noise.

The AGP bus has 32 data lines divided into two sets. Sometimes, a large number of these data lines may switch together to the same polarity (either 1 or 0) and then switch back to the opposite polarity. This mass switching to the same polarity is called **simultaneous switching outputs** and it creates a lot of unwanted electrical noise at the AGP controller and GPU interfaces.

To avoid this, the AGP 3.0 specifications introduced a scheme called **Dynamic Bus Inversion** or **DBI**. It makes use of two new DBI lines—one for each 16-line set. These DBI lines are only supported by AGP 3.0-compliant graphics cards.

Dynamic Bus Inversion ensures that the data lines are limited to a maximum of **8 simultaneous** switchings or transitions per 16-line set. It does so by switching the DBI line instead of the data lines when the number of simultaneous transitions exceeds **8** or **50%** of the data lines. This ensures that electrical noise due to simultaneous switching outputs is minimized.

In short, DBI improves stability of the AGP interface by reducing signal noises that occur as a result of **simultaneous switching outputs**. It also reduces the AGP controller's power consumption.

Therefore, it is recommended that you **enable DBI Output for AGP Trans.** to save power as well as reduce signal noise from simultaneous switching outputs.

Delay DRAM Read Latch

Common Options: Auto, No Delay, 0.5ns, 1.0ns, 1.5ns

This feature is similar to the **DRAM Read Latch Delay** BIOS feature. It fine-tunes the DRAM timing parameters to adjust for different DRAM loadings.

The DRAM load changes with the number as well as the type of memory modules installed. DRAM loading increases as the number of memory modules increases. It also increases if you use double-sided modules instead of single-sided ones. In short, the more DRAM devices you use, the greater the DRAM loading.

With heavier DRAM loads, you may need to delay the moment when the memory controller latches onto the DRAM device during reads. Otherwise, the memory controller may fail to latch properly onto the desired DRAM device and read from it.

The **Auto** option allows the BIOS to select the optimal amount of delay from values preset by the manufacturer.

The **No Delay** option forces the memory controller to latch onto the DRAM device without delay, even if the BIOS presets indicate that a delay is required.

The three timing options (**0.5ns**, **1.0ns**, and **1.5ns**) give you manual control of the read latch delay.

Normally, you should let the BIOS select the optimal amount of delay from values preset by the manufacturer (using the **Auto** option). However, if you notice that your system has become unstable upon installation of additional memory modules, you should try setting the DRAM read latch delay yourself.

The amount of delay should be just enough to allow the memory controller to latch onto the DRAM device in your particular situation. Don't unnecessarily increase the delay. Start with **0.5ns** and work your way up until your system stabilizes.

If you have a light DRAM load, you can ensure optimal performance by manually using the **No Delay** option. If your system becomes unstable after using the **No Delay** option, simply revert back to the default value of **Auto** so that the BIOS can adjust the read latch delay to suit the DRAM load.

Delay IDE Initial

Common Options: 0 to 15

Motherboards are capable of booting up much faster these days. Therefore, initialization of IDE devices now takes place much earlier. Unfortunately, this also means that some older IDE drives are not be able to spin up in time to be initialized! When this happens, the BIOS is not able to detect that IDE drive and the drive is not accessible even though it is actually running just fine.

This is where the **Delay IDE Initial** BIOS feature comes in. It allows you to force the BIOS to delay the initialization of IDE devices for up to 15 seconds. The delay allows your IDE devices more time to spin up before the BIOS initializes them.

If you do not use old IDE drives and the BIOS has no problem initializing your IDE devices, it is recommended that you leave the delay at the default value of **0** for the shortest possible booting time. Most IDE devices manufactured in the last few years have no problem spinning up in time for initialization.

However, if one or more of your IDE devices fail to initialize during the boot up process, start with a delay of **1 second**. If that doesn't help, gradually increase the delay until all your IDE devices initialize properly during the boot up process.

Delay Prior To Thermal

Common Options: 4 Minutes, 8 Minutes, 16 Minutes, 32 Minutes

This BIOS feature is only valid for systems that are powered by 0.13μ Intel Pentium 4 processors with 512KB L2 cache. These processors come with a **Thermal Monitor** that actually consists of an on-die thermal sensor and a **Thermal Control Circuit** (**TCC**).

When the Thermal Monitor is in automatic mode and the thermal sensor detects that the processor has reached its maximum safe operating temperature, it activates the TCC. The TCC then modulates the clock cycles by inserting null cycles, typically at a rate of **50-70%** of the total number of clock cycles. This results in the processor "resting" 50-70% of the time.

As the die temperature drops, the TCC gradually reduces the number of null cycles until no more is required to keep the die temperature below the safe point. Then the thermal sensor turns the TCC off. This mechanism allows the processor to dynamically adjust its duty cycles to ensure its die temperature remains within safe limits.

The **Delay Prior To Thermal** BIOS feature controls the activation of the Thermal Monitor's automatic mode. It allows you to determine when the Pentium 4's Thermal Monitor should be activated in automatic mode after the system boots. For example, with the default value of **16 Minutes**, the BIOS activates the Thermal Monitor in automatic mode 16 minutes after the system starts booting up.

Generally, the Thermal Monitor should *not* be activated immediately upon booting because the processor is under a heavy load during the booting process. This causes a sharp rise in die temperature from its cold state. Because it takes time for the thermal output to radiate from the die to the heat sink, the thermal sensor registers the sudden spike in die temperature and prematurely activates the TCC. This unnecessarily reduces the processor's performance during the booting up process.

Therefore, to ensure optimal booting performance, the activation of the Thermal Monitor must be delayed for a set period of time.

It is recommended that you set this BIOS feature to the lowest value (in minutes) that exceeds the time it takes to fully boot up your computer. For example, if it takes 5 minutes to fully boot up your system, you should select **8 Minutes**.

You should *not* select a delay value that is unnecessarily long. Without the Thermal Monitor, your processor may heat up to a critical temperature (approximately **135°C**), at which point, the thermal sensor shuts down your processor by removing the core voltage within **0.5 seconds**.

Delayed Transaction

Common Options: Enabled, Disabled

To meet PCI 2.1 compliance, the PCI maximum target latency rule must be observed. According to this rule, a PCI 2.1-compliant device must service a read request within **16** PCI clock cycles for the *initial* read and **8** PCI clock cycles for each *subsequent* read.

If it cannot do so, the PCI bus terminates the transaction so that other PCI devices can access the bus. However, instead of rearbitrating for access (and failing to meet the minimum latency requirement again), the PCI 2.1-compliant device can make use of the **PCI Delayed Transaction** feature.

With **PCI Delayed Transaction** enabled, the target device can independently continue the read transaction. So, when the master device successfully gains control of the bus and reissues the read command, the target device has the data ready for immediate delivery. This ensures that the retried read transaction can be completed within the stipulated latency period.

If the delayed transaction is a write, the master device rearbitrates for bus access while the target device completes writing the data. When the master device regains control of the bus, it reissues the same write request. This time, the target device just sends the completion status to the master device to complete the transaction.

One advantage of using **PCI Delayed Transaction** is that it allows other PCI masters to use the bus while the transaction is being carried out on the target device. Otherwise, the bus is left idling while the target device completes the transaction.

PCI Delayed Transaction also allows write-posted data to remain in the buffer while the PCI bus initiates a non-postable transaction and yet still adheres to the PCI ordering rules. Without **PCI Delayed Transaction**, all write-posted data has to be flushed before another PCI transaction can occur.

It is highly recommended that you **enable** Delayed Transaction for better PCI performance and to meet PCI 2.1 specifications. **Disable** it only if your PCI cards cannot work properly with this feature enabled, or if you are using PCI cards that are *not* PCI 2.1-compliant.

Please note that while many manuals, and even earlier versions of the BIOS Optimization Guide, have stated that this is an ISA bus-specific BIOS feature that enables a 32-bit write-posted buffer for faster PCI-to-ISA writes, they are *incorrect*! This BIOS feature is *not* ISA bus-specific, and it does *not* control any write-posted buffers. It merely allows write-posting to continue while a non-postable PCI transaction is underway.

Differential Current

Common Options: 4x Iref, 5x Iref, 6x Iref, 7x Iref

This BIOS feature allows you to change the amount of differential current produced by the clock driver pairs, effectively changing the voltage swing of the system clocks.

When set to **4x Iref**, the current difference is four times that of **Iref**, the reference current source.

When set to **5x Iref**, the current difference is five times that of **Iref**, the reference current source.

When set to **6x Iref**, the current difference is six times that of **Iref**, the reference current source.

When set to **7x Iref**, the current difference is seven times that of **Iref**, the reference current source.

By default, this BIOS feature is set to **4x Iref**. Unfortunately, it is not known what that translates to in voltage. Not even the Iref value is known. However, the higher the differential current, the greater the voltage swing.

As a higher voltage swing improves integrity of the clock signals and overall system stability, it is recommended that you set this BIOS feature to **7x Iref** for a higher differential current. However, please note that this will increase the amount of **EMI (Electromagnetic Interference)** produced by the motherboard.

Disable Unused PCI Clock

Common Options: Enabled, Disabled

This BIOS feature determines whether the BIOS should actively reduce **EMI (Electromagnetic Interference)** and reduce power consumption by turning off unoccupied or inactive PCI slots.

When **enabled**, the BIOS monitors PCI slots and turns off clock signals to all unoccupied and inactive slots.

When **disabled**, the BIOS does not monitor PCI slots. All clock signals remain active even to unoccupied or inactive slots.

It is recommended that you **enable** this feature to save power and reduce EMI.

DOS Flat Mode

Common Options: Enabled, Disabled

This BIOS feature controls the BIOS' built-in extended memory manager.

When **enabled**, DOS programs can run in protected mode without the need of an extended memory manager.

When **disabled**, DOS programs require an extended memory manager to run in protected mode.

It is recommended that you **enable** this BIOS feature if you use the MS-DOS operating system and run protected mode DOS programs.

However, if you use a newer operating system that supports protected mode (for example, Windows XP), **disable** this BIOS feature.

DRAM Act to PreChrg CMD

Common Options: 5T, 6T, 7T, 8T, 9T

Like **SDRAM Tras Timing Value**, this BIOS feature controls the memory bank's minimum row active time (t_{RAS}). This constitutes the time when a row is activated until the time the same row can be deactivated. Hence, the name **DRAM Act to PreChrg CMD**, which is short for **DRAM Activate Command to Precharge Command**.

If the t_{RAS} period is too long, it can reduce performance by unnecessarily delaying the deactivation of active rows. Reducing the t_{RAS} period allows the active row to be deactivated earlier.

However, if the t_{RAS} period is too short, there may not be enough time to complete a burst transfer. This reduces performance and data may be lost or corrupted.

For optimal performance, use the lowest value you can. Usually, this should be **CAS latency + tRCD + 2 clock cycles.** For example, if you set the CAS latency to 2 clock cycles and the tRCD to 3 clock cycles, the optimum t_{RAS} value would be 7 clock cycles.

However, if you start getting memory errors or system crashes, increase the t_{RAS} value one clock cycle at a time until your system becomes stable.

DRAM Burst Length 8QW

Common Options: Enabled, Disabled

This BIOS feature allows you to control the length of a burst transaction.

When this feature is set to **Disabled**, a burst transaction can only be comprised of up to **four** quadword (QW) reads or writes.

When this feature is set to **Enabled**, a burst transaction can only be comprised of up to **eight** quadword (QW) reads or writes.

As the initial CAS latency is fixed for each burst transaction, a longer burst transaction allows more data to be read or written for less delay than a shorter burst transaction. Therefore, a burst length of 8 is faster than a burst length of 4.

Therefore, it is recommended that you **enable** this BIOS feature for better performance.

DRAM Data Integrity Mode

Common Options: ECC, Non-ECC

This BIOS feature controls the **ECC** feature of the memory controller.

ECC, which stands for **Error Checking and Correction**, enables the memory controller to detect and correct single-bit soft memory errors. The memory controller is also able to detect double-bit errors, although it is not able to correct them. This provides increased data integrity and system stability. However, this feature can only be enabled if you are using special ECC memory modules.

Because present day processors use 64-bit wide data paths, 72-bit (64-bit data + 8-bit ECC) ECC memory modules are required to implement ECC. Please note that the maximum data transfer rate of the **72-bit** ECC memory module is the same as the **64-bit** memory module. The extra 8-bits are only for the ECC code and do not carry any data. So, using 72-bit memory modules does *not* give you any boost in performance.

In fact, because the memory controller has to calculate the ECC code for *every* data word that is read or written, there is some performance degradation, roughly in the region of **3–5%**. This is one of the reasons why ECC memory modules are not popular among desktop users. Throw in the fact that ECC memory modules are both expensive and hard to come by, and you have the top three reasons why ECC memory modules will never be mainstream solutions.

If you are using standard 64-bit memory modules, you must select the **Non-ECC** option.

However, if you have already forked out the money for 72-bit ECC memory modules, you should enable the **ECC** feature, no matter what people say about losing some memory performance. It doesn't make sense to buy expensive ECC memory modules and then disable ECC! Remember, you are not really losing performance. You are just trading it for greater stability and data integrity.

DRAM Idle Timer

Common Options: 0T, 8T, 16T, 64T, Infinite, Auto

This BIOS feature sets the number of idle cycles allowed before the memory controller forces such open pages to close and precharge.

The premise behind this BIOS feature is the concept of **temporal locality**. According to this concept, the longer the open page is left idle, the less likely it will be accessed again before it needs to be precharged. Therefore, it is better to prematurely close and precharge the page, so it can be opened quickly when a data request comes along.

It can be set to a variety of clock cycles from **0T** to **64T**. This sets the number of clock cycles the open pages are allowed to idle before they are closed and precharged. An **Infinite** option is available as well as an **Auto** option.

If you select **0 Cycle**, then the memory controller immediately precharges the open pages as soon as there's an idle cycle.

If you select **Infinite**, the memory controller never precharges the open pages prematurely. The open pages are left activated until they have to be precharged.

If you select **Auto**, the memory controller uses the manufacturer's preset default setting.

Most manufacturers use a default value of **8T**, which allows the memory controller to precharge the open pages after eight idle cycles have passed.

For general desktop use, it is recommended that you choose the **Infinite** option, so precharging can be delayed for as long as possible. This reduces the number of refreshes and increases the effective memory bandwidth.

For applications (for example, servers) that perform a lot of random accesses, it is advisable that you select **0T** because subsequent data requests most likely will be fulfilled by other pages. Closing open pages to precharge prepares those pages for the next data request that hits them. Increased data integrity is an added benefit of having more frequent refreshes.

D

DRAM Interleave Time

Common Options: 0ms, 0.5ms

This BIOS feature determines the amount of *additional* delay between successive bank accesses when the **SDRAM Bank Interleave** feature has been enabled. Naturally, the shorter the delay, the faster the memory module can switch between banks and, consequently, increases performance.

Therefore, it is recommended that you set the **DRAM Interleave Time** as low as possible for better memory performance. In this case, it is **0ms**, which introduces *no* additional delay between bank accesses. Increase the **DRAM Interleave Time** to **0.5ms** only if you experience instability with the 0ms setting.

DRAM Page-Mode

Common Options: Enabled, Disabled

This BIOS feature controls the page mode operation of the memory subsystem.

When **enabled**, the activated row is held open to allow multiple memory accesses to the same memory row.

When **disabled**, the activated row is closed right after a single memory access. Subsequent memory accesses to that row will require re-activation of the row.

It is highly recommended that you **enable** this BIOS feature for much better memory performance.

DRAM PreChrg to Act CMD

Common Options: 2T, 3T, 4T

Like **SDRAM Trp Timing Value**, this BIOS feature controls the **RAS precharge time** (**tRP**). This constitutes the time it takes for the Precharge command to complete and the row to be available for activation. Hence, the name **DRAM PreChrg to Act CMD**, which is short for **DRAM Precharge Command to Activate Command**.

If the RAS precharge time is too long, it reduces performance by delaying all row activations. Reducing the precharge time to **2T** improves performance by allowing a new row to be activated earlier.

However, the short precharge time of 2T may be insufficient for some memory modules. In such cases, the active row may lose its contents before they can be returned to the memory bank and the row deactivated. This may cause data loss or corruption when the memory controller attempts to read from or write to the active row.

Therefore, it is recommended that you reduce the RAS precharge time to **2T** for better performance but increase it to **3T** or **4T** if you experience system stability issues after reducing the precharge time.

D

DRAM Ratio (CPU:DRAM)

Common Options: 1:1, 3:2, 3:4, 4:5, 5:4

The choice of options in this BIOS feature depends entirely on the setting of the **DRAM Ratio H/W Strap** or **N/B Strap CPU As** BIOS feature.

When **DRAM Ratio H/W Strap** has been set to **Low**, the available options are **1:1** and **3:4**.

When **DRAM Ratio H/W Strap** has been set to **High**, the available options are **1:1** and **4:5**.

When **N/B Strap CPU As** has been set to **PSB800**, the available options are **1:1**, **3.2**, and **5:4**.

When **N/B Strap CPU As** has been set to **PSB533**, the available options are **1:1** and **4:5**.

When **N/B Strap CPU As** has been set to **PSB400**, the only available option is **3:4**.

The options of **1:1**, **3:2**, **3:4**, and **4:5** refer to the available CPU-to-DRAM (or CPU:DRAM) ratios.

Please note that while the Pentium 4 processor is said to have a 400MHz, 533MHz, or 800MHz **FSB** (**front side bus**), the front side bus (also known as CPU bus) is actually only running at 100MHz, 133MHz, or 200MHz, respectively. This is because the Pentium 4 bus is a **Quad Data Rate** or **QDR** bus, which transfers four times as much data as a single data rate bus.

For marketing reasons, the Pentium 4 bus is labeled as running at 400MHz, 533MHz, or 800MHz when it is actually running at only 100MHz, 133MHz, and 200MHz, respectively. It is important to keep this in mind when setting this BIOS feature.

For example, if you set a **3:2** ratio with a 200MHz (800MHz QDR) CPU bus, the memory bus runs at (200MHz / 3) x 2 = **133MHz** or **266MHz DDR**.

By default, this BIOS feature is set to **By SPD**. This allows the chipset to query the **SPD** (**Serial Presence Detect**) chip on every memory module and use the appropriate ratio.

It is recommended that you select the ratio that allows you to maximize your memory modules' capabilities. However, bear in mind that a synchronous operation using the **1:1** ratio is also highly desirable because it allows a high throughput.

DRAM Ratio H/W Strap

Common Options: High, Low, By CPU

This BIOS feature allows you to circumvent the CPU-to-DRAM ratio limitation found in the newer Intel i845-series of chipsets. In those chipsets, Intel has chosen to limit the choices of available CPU-to-DRAM ratios.

When a **400MHz FSB** processor is installed, the choices of CPU-to-DRAM ratio are limited to **1:1** or **3:4**.

When a **533MHz FSB** processor is installed, the choices of CPU-to-DRAM ratio are limited to **1:1** or **4:5**.

Fortunately, this BIOS feature allows you to circumvent that limitation.

The **DRAM Ratio H/W Strap** BIOS feature actually controls the setting of the external hardware reset strap assigned to the **MCH** (**Memory Controller Hub**) of the chipset. By setting it **High** or **Low**, you can trick the chipset into thinking that the **400MHz FSB** or the **533MHz FSB** is being used.

When this BIOS feature is set to **High**, you are able to access the **533MHz** CPU-to-DRAM ratios of **1:1** and **4:5**.

When this BIOS feature is set to **Low**, you are able to access the **400MHz** CPU-to-DRAM ratios of **1:1** and **3:4**.

By default, this BIOS feature is set to **By CPU**, whereby the hardware strap is set according to the actual FSB rating of the processor.

Generally, you do not need to manually adjust the hardware strap setting. However, if you require access to the CPU-to-DRAM ratio that would normally not be available to you, then this BIOS feature would be very helpful indeed.

DRAM Read Latch Delay

Common Options: Enabled, Disabled

This BIOS feature is similar to the **Delay DRAM Read Latch** BIOS feature. It fine-tunes the DRAM timing parameters to adjust for different DRAM loadings.

The DRAM load changes with the number as well as the type of memory modules installed. DRAM loading increases as the number of memory modules increase. It also increases if you use double-sided modules instead of single-sided ones. In short, the more DRAM devices you use, the greater the DRAM loading.

With heavier DRAM loads, you may need to delay the moment when the memory controller latches onto the DRAM device during reads. Otherwise, the memory controller may fail to latch properly onto the desired DRAM device and read from it.

The **Auto** option allows the BIOS to select the optimal amount of delay from values preset by the manufacturer.

The **No Delay** option forces the memory controller to latch onto the DRAM device without delay, even if the BIOS presets indicate that a delay is required.

The three timing options (**0.5ns**, **1.0ns**, and **1.5ns**) give you manual control of the read latch delay.

Normally, you should let the BIOS select the optimal amount of delay from values preset by the manufacturer (using the **Auto** option). However, if you notice that your system has become unstable upon installation of additional memory modules, you should try setting the DRAM read latch delay yourself.

The amount of delay should be just enough to allow the memory controller to latch onto the DRAM device in your particular situation. Don't unnecessarily increase the delay. Start with **0.5ns** and work your way up until your system stabilizes.

If you have a light DRAM load, you can ensure optimal performance by manually using the **No Delay** option. If your system becomes unstable after using the **No Delay** option, simply revert back to the default value of **Auto** so that the BIOS can adjust the read latch delay to suit the DRAM load.

D

DRAM Refresh Rate

Common Options: 7.8 μsec, 15.6 μsec, 31.2 μsec, 64 μsec, 128 μsec, Auto

This BIOS feature allows you to set the refresh interval of the memory chips. There are three different settings as well as an **Auto** option. If the **Auto** option is selected, the BIOS queries the memory modules' SPD chips and uses the lowest setting found for maximum compatibility.

For better performance, you should consider increasing the **DRAM Refresh Rate** from the default values (15.6 μsec for 128Mbit or smaller memory chips and 7.8 μsec for 256Mbit or larger memory chips) up to **128 μsec**. Please note that if you increase the **DRAM Refresh Rate** too much, the memory cells may lose their contents.

Therefore, you should start with small increases in the **DRAM Refresh Rate** and test your system after each hike before increasing it further. If you face stability problems after increasing the refresh interval, reduce the refresh interval step by step until the system is stable.

Duplex Select

Common Options: Full-Duplex, Half-Duplex

This BIOS feature allows you to determine the transmission mode of the **IR** (**Infra-Red**) communications port.

Selecting **Full-Duplex** permits simultaneous two-way transmission, like a conversation over the phone.

Selecting **Half-Duplex**, on the other hand, only permits transmission in one direction at any one time, which is more like a conversation over a walkie-talkie.

Naturally, the **Full-Duplex** mode is the faster and more desirable choice. You should use **Full-Duplex** if possible.

Consult your IR peripheral's manual to determine whether it supports **Full-Duplex** transmission. The IR peripheral *must* support **Full-Duplex** for this option to work.

ECP Mode Use DMA

Common Options: Channel 1, Channel 3

This BIOS feature determines which DMA channel the parallel port should use when it is in ECP mode.

The ECP mode uses the DMA protocol to achieve data transfer rates of up to **2.5 Mbits/s** and provides symmetric bidirectional communications. For all this, it requires the use of a DMA channel.

By default, the parallel port uses DMA **Channel 3** when it is in ECP mode. This works fine in most situations.

This feature was provided just in case one of your add-on cards requires the use of DMA Channel 3. In such a case, you can use this BIOS feature to force the parallel port to use the alternate DMA **Channel 1**.

Please note that there is no performance advantage in choosing DMA Channel 3 over DMA Channel 1 or vice versa. As long as either Channel 3 or Channel 1 is available for your parallel port to use, the parallel port is able to function properly in ECP mode.

EPP Mode Select

Common Options: EPP 1.7, EPP 1.9

There are two versions of the EPP transfer protocol—**EPP 1.7** and **EPP 1.9**. This BIOS feature allows you to select the version of EPP that the parallel port should use.

Generally, **EPP 1.9** is the preferred setting because it supports the newer EPP 1.9 devices and most EPP 1.7 devices and offers advantages like support for longer cables. However, because certain EPP 1.7 devices cannot work properly with an EPP 1.9 port, this BIOS feature was implemented to allow you to set the EPP mode to **EPP 1.7** when such an issue crops up.

Therefore, it is recommended that you set this BIOS feature to **EPP 1.9**. However, if you have trouble connecting to your parallel port device, switch to **EPP 1.7**.

Fast R-W Turn Around

Common Options: Enabled, Disabled

When the memory controller receives a **write** command immediately after a **read** command, an additional period of delay is normally introduced before the write command is actually initiated.

As its name suggests, this BIOS feature allows you to skip that delay. This improves the write performance of the memory subsystem. Therefore, it is recommended that you **enable** this feature for faster read-to-write turnarounds.

However, not all memory modules can work with the tighter read-to-write turn-around. If your memory modules cannot handle the faster turn-around, the data that was written to the memory module may be lost or become corrupted. So, when you face stability issues, **disable** this feature to correct the problem.

Fast Write to Read Turnaround

Common Options: Enabled, Disabled

This BIOS feature controls the **Write Data In to Read Command Delay (tWTR)** memory timing. This constitutes the minimum number of clock cycles that must occur between the last valid *write* operation and the next *read* command to the **same** internal bank of the DDR device.

Enabling this BIOS feature naturally allows faster switching from writes to reads and consequently better read performance.

Disabling this BIOS feature reduces read performance but it will improve stability, especially at higher clock speeds. It may also allow the memory chips to run at a higher speed. In other words, increasing this delay may allow you to overclock the memory module higher than is normally possible.

It is recommended that you **enable** this BIOS feature for better memory read performance if you are using DDR266 or DDR333 memory modules. You can also try enabling it with DDR400 memory modules. But if you face stability issues, revert to the default setting of **Disabled**.

First Boot Device

Common Options: Floppy, LS/ZIP, HDD-0, SCSI, CDROM, HDD-1, HDD-2, HDD-3, LAN, Disabled

This BIOS feature allows you to select the *first* device from which the BIOS attempts to load an operating system. If the BIOS finds and loads an operating system from the device selected through this feature, it doesn't load another operating system, even if you have one on a different device.

By default, **Floppy** is the first boot device in practically all motherboards. Unless you boot often from the floppy drive, it is better to set your hard disk (usually **HDD-0**) as the first boot device. This shortens the booting process because the BIOS no longer needs to check the floppy drive for a bootable operating system.

To install operating systems that come on bootable CD-ROMs (for example, Microsoft Windows XP) in a new hard disk, you need to select **CDROM** as the first boot device. This enables you to boot directly from the CD-ROM and load the operating system's installation routine.

Flash BIOS Protection

Common Options: Enabled, Disabled

The **Flash BIOS Protection** feature is a software toggle that controls write access to the BIOS. When it is **enabled**, the BIOS code is write-protected and cannot be changed. This protects it from any attempt to modify it, including BIOS updates and virus attacks. Therefore, if you intend to update the BIOS, you'll need to **disable** this feature first.

It is highly recommended that you **enable** this feature at all times. You should only **disable** it when you intend to update the BIOS. After updating the BIOS, you should immediately re-enable it to protect the BIOS against viruses.

F

Floppy 3 Mode Support

Common Options: Disabled, Drive A, Drive B, Both

For reasons best known to the Japanese, their computers come with special 3 mode 3.5" floppy drives. While physically similar to the standard 3.5" floppy drives used by the rest of the world, these 3 mode floppy drives differ in the disk formats they support.

Unlike normal floppy drives, 3 mode floppy drives support three different floppy disk formats— 1.44MB, 1.2MB, and 720KB, hence, their name. They allow the system to support the Japanese 1.2MB floppy disk format as well as the standard 1.44MB and 720KB (obsolete) disk formats.

If you own a 3 mode floppy drive and need to use the Japanese 1.2MB disk format, you must enable this feature by selecting either **Drive A**, **Drive B**, or **Both** (if you have two 3 mode floppy drives). Otherwise, your 3 mode floppy drive won't be able to read the special 1.2MB format properly.

However, if you only have a standard floppy drive, **disable** this feature or your floppy drive may not function properly.

Floppy Disk Access Control

Common Options: R/W, Read Only

This BIOS feature controls write access to the floppy drive.

Setting this BIOS feature to **R/W** (**Read/Write**) allows full access to the floppy drive. You will be allowed to write to floppy disks as well as read from them.

Setting this BIOS feature to **Read Only** prevents write access to the floppy drive. You will be allowed to read from floppy disks but you cannot write to them.

It is recommended that you set this BIOS feature to **R/W**, so you have full access to the floppy drive. Set it to **Read Only** if you do not wish to provide write access to the floppy drive.

Force 4-Way Interleave

Common Options: Enabled, Disabled

This BIOS feature allows you to force the memory controller to use the 4-bank SDRAM interleave mode, which provides better performance than the 2-bank interleave mode. However, you must have at least 4 banks of memory in the system for this feature to work properly.

Normally, SDRAM modules that use **16Mbit** memory chips (usually **32MB** or smaller in size) have only two memory banks. So, if you are using such a small capacity DIMM, you should **disable** Force 4-Way Interleave. If you use two or more of such DIMMs, you can still **enable** Force-4-Way Interleave.

SDRAM modules that use **64Mbit** or larger memory chips are four-banked in nature. These modules are at least **64MB** in size. If you are using such four-banked modules, it no longer matters if you are using just one module or several of them. You can **enable** Force 4-Way Interleave without fear.

Therefore, it is recommended that you **enable** this BIOS feature if you are using *64MB or larger memory modules* or *at least two 32MB or smaller memory modules*. Otherwise, it is best to **disable** this BIOS feature.

For more information on memory bank interleaving, you should check out the details of the **SDRAM Bank Interleave** BIOS feature.

Force Update ESCD

Common Options: Enabled, Disabled

If you install a new piece of hardware or modify your computer's hardware configuration, the BIOS automatically detects the changes and reconfigures the **ESCD** (**Extended System Configuration Data**). Therefore, there is usually no need to manually force the BIOS to reconfigure the ESCD.

However, the occasion may arise where the BIOS may not be able to detect the hardware changes. A serious resource conflict may occur and the operating system may not even boot as a result. This is where the **Force Update ESCD** BIOS feature comes in.

This BIOS feature allows you to manually force the BIOS to clear the previously saved ESCD data and reconfigure the settings. All you need to do is **enable** this BIOS feature and then reboot your computer. The new ESCD should resolve the conflict and allow the operating system to load normally.

Please note that the BIOS automatically resets it to the default setting of **Disabled** after reconfiguring the new ESCD. So, there is no need for you to manually **disable** this feature after rebooting.

FPU OPCODE Compatible Mode

Common Options: Enabled, Disabled

This BIOS feature determines how Pentium 4 and Xeon processors handle FOP codes using the **FOP** (**final opcode**) register.

When **enabled**, the Pentium 4 and Xeon engage the FOP code compatibility mode, which stores the FOP of the last non-transparent instruction in the FOP register.

When **disabled**, the Pentium 4 and Xeon turn off the FOP code compatibility mode and store only the FOP of the last non-transparent floating point instruction *that had an unmasked exception*. This allows for better FPU performance.

Therefore, it is recommended that you **disable** this feature for better FPU performance unless your software requires this feature to recover from FPU exceptions.

Frame Buffer Size

Common Options: 1MB, 4MB, 8MB, 16MB, 32MB, 64MB

This BIOS feature controls the amount of system memory that is allocated to the integrated GPU.

The selection of memory sizes allows you to select how much system memory you want to allocate to the integrated GPU. The amount you allocate to the GPU is deducted from the amount of system memory available to your operating system and programs.

Please note that unlike the **AGP Aperture Size**, once the system memory is allocated to the GPU, it cannot be used by anything else. Even if the GPU does not make use of it, it is not available to the operating system.

Therefore, it is recommended that you select the absolute minimum amount of system memory that the GPU requires for your monitor. You can calculate it by multiplying the resolution and color depth that you are using.

For example, if you use a resolution of 1600×1200 and a color depth of 32-bit, the amount of memory your GPU requires will be $1600 \times 1200 \times 32\text{-bits} = 61,440,000$ bits, or 7.68MB. You should set this BIOS feature to **8MB** in this example.

F

FSB Spread Spectrum

Common Options: 0.5%, 1.0%, Disabled

This BIOS feature allows you to reduce the EMI of the **front side bus** (also known as the **FSB** or processor bus) by modulating the signals it generates, so the spikes are reduced to flatter curves. It achieves this by varying the frequency slightly, so the signal does not use any particular frequency for more than a moment.

The BIOS usually offers two levels of modulation—**0.5%** or **1.0%**. The greater the modulation, the greater the reduction of EMI. Therefore, if you need to significantly reduce the front side bus EMI, a modulation of **1.0%** is recommended.

In most conditions, frequency modulation through this feature should not cause any problems. However, system stability may be compromised if you are overclocking the front side bus. Of course, this depends on the amount of modulation, the extent of overclocking, and other factors like temperature, and so forth. As such, the problem may not manifest itself immediately.

Therefore, it is recommended that you **disable** this feature if you are overclocking the front side bus. The risk of crashing your system is not worth the reduction in EMI. Of course, if EMI reduction is important to you, **enable** this feature by all means. However, you should reduce the clock speed a little to provide a margin of safety.

If you are not overclocking, the decision to enable or disable this feature is really up to you. Unless you have EMI problems or sensitive data that must be safeguarded from electronic eavesdropping, it is best to **disable** this feature to remove the possibility of stability issues.

Full Screen Logo

Common Options: Enabled, Disabled

This BIOS feature determines whether the motherboard or system manufacturer's logo appears instead of the usual boot-up screen.

When it is **enabled**, the BIOS displays the full-screen logo during the boot-up sequence.

When it is **disabled**, the BIOS displays the usual boot-up screen instead of the full-screen logo.

Please note that enabling this BIOS feature often adds 2–3 seconds of delay to the booting sequence. This delay ensures that the logo is displayed for a sufficient amount of time.

Therefore, it is recommended that you **disable** this BIOS feature for a faster boot-up time.

G

Gate A20 Option

Common Options: Normal, Fast

This BIOS feature is used to determine the method by which Gate A20 is controlled. The **Normal** option forces the chipset to use the slow keyboard controller to do the switching. The **Fast** option, on the other hand, allows the chipset to use its own 0x92 port for faster switching. No candy for guessing which is the recommended setting!

Please note this feature is only important for operating systems that switch a lot between real mode and protected mode. These operating systems include 16-bit operating systems, such as MS-DOS and 16-bit/32-bit hybrid operating systems like Microsoft Windows 98.

This feature has no effect if the operating system only runs in real mode (no operating system currently in use does that, as far as I know!), or if the operating system operates entirely in protected mode (for example, Microsoft Windows XP). This is because if A20 mode switching is not required, then it does not matter at all if the switching was done by the slow keyboard controller or the faster 0x92 port.

With all that said and done, the recommended setting for this BIOS feature is still **Fast**, even with operating systems that don't do much mode switching. Although using the 0x92 port to control Gate A20 has been known to cause spontaneous reboots in very rare instances, there is really no reason why you should keep using the slow keyboard controller to turn A20 on or off.

Graphic Win Size

Common Options: 4, 8, 16, 32, 64, 128, 256

This BIOS feature does two things. It selects the size of the AGP aperture (hence, the name **Graphic Windows Size**), and it determines the size of the **GART** (**Graphics Address Relocation Table**).

The aperture is a portion of the PCI memory address range that is dedicated for use as AGP memory address space, while the GART is a translation table that translates AGP memory addresses into actual memory addresses, which are often fragmented. The GART allows the graphics card to see the memory region available to it as a contiguous piece of memory range.

Host cycles that hit the aperture range are forwarded to the AGP bus without need for translation. The aperture size also determines the maximum amount of system memory that can be allocated to the AGP graphics card for texture storage.

Please note that the AGP aperture is merely address space, *not* actual physical memory in use. Although it is very common to hear people recommending that the AGP aperture size should be *half* the size of system memory, that is *wrong*!

G

The requirement for AGP memory space *shrinks* as the graphics card's local memory increases in size. This is because the graphics card has more local memory to dedicate to texture storage. So, if you upgrade to a graphics card with more memory, you shouldn't be "deceived" into thinking that you need even more AGP memory! On the contrary, a smaller AGP memory space is required.

It is recommended that you keep the AGP aperture around **64MB** to **128MB** in size, even if your graphics card has a lot of onboard memory. This allows flexibility in the event that you actually need extra memory for texture storage. It also keeps the GART within a reasonable size.

Graphic Window WR Combin

Common Options: Enabled, Disabled

This BIOS feature allows you to control the **USWC (Uncached Speculative Write Combining)** write combine buffers. Somehow, they had to give it the badly mangled name of **Graphic Window WR Combin**.

If **enabled**, the write combine buffers will accumulate and combine partial or smaller graphics writes from the processor and write them to the graphics card as burst writes.

If **disabled**, the write combine buffers will be disabled. All graphics writes from the processor will be written to the graphics card directly.

It is highly recommended that you **enable** this feature for improved graphics and processor performance.

However, if you are using an older graphics card, it may not be compatible with this feature. Enabling this feature with such graphics cards will cause a host of problems, such as graphics artifacts, system crashes, and even the inability to boot up properly.

If you face such problems, you should **disable** this BIOS feature immediately.

Graphics Aperture Size

Common Options: 4, 8, 16, 32, 64, 128, 256

This BIOS feature does two things: It selects the size of the AGP aperture, and it determines the size of the **GART (Graphics Address Relocation Table)**.

The aperture is a portion of the PCI memory address range that is dedicated for use as AGP memory address space, whereas the GART is a translation table that translates AGP memory addresses into actual memory addresses, which are often fragmented. The GART allows the graphics card to see the memory region available to it as a contiguous piece of memory range.

Host cycles that hit the aperture range are forwarded to the AGP bus without need for translation. The aperture size also determines the maximum amount of system memory that can be allocated to the AGP graphics card for texture storage.

Please note that the AGP aperture is merely address space, *not* actual physical memory in use. Although it is very common to hear people recommending that the AGP aperture size should be *half* the size of system memory, that is *wrong*!

The requirement for AGP memory space *shrinks* as the graphics card's local memory increases in size. This is because the graphics card will have more local memory to dedicate to texture storage. So, if you upgrade to a graphics card with more memory, you shouldn't be "deceived" into thinking that you will need even more AGP memory! On the contrary, a smaller AGP memory space will be required.

It is recommended that you keep the AGP aperture around **64MB** to **128MB** in size, even if your graphics card has a lot of onboard memory. This allows flexibility in the event that you actually need extra memory for texture storage. It will also keep the GART (Graphics Address Relocation Table) within a reasonable size.

G

Hardware Reset Protect

Common Options: Enabled, Disabled

This BIOS feature is very useful for file servers and routers that need to be running 24 hours a day, 365 days a year. When it is **enabled**, the hardware reset button is *disabled*. This prevents the possibility of any accidental resets. When **disabled**, the reset button functions as normal.

If you are running a mission-critical server or have kids who just love to press little red buttons, it is highly recommended that you **enable** this feature. Otherwise, it is really up to your preference. Naturally, people using buggy operating systems or applications are advised to keep this feature **disabled** for more convenient reboots.

HDD S.M.A.R.T. Capability

Common Options: Enabled, Disabled

This BIOS feature controls support for the hard disk's **S.M.A.R.T. (Self Monitoring Analysis And Reporting Technology)** capability.

S.M.A.R.T. is supported by all current hard disks and it allows the early prediction and warning of impending hard disk disasters. You should **enable** it if you want to use S.M.A.R.T.-aware utilities to monitor the hard disk's condition. Enabling it also allows the monitoring of the hard disk's condition over a network.

Although S.M.A.R.T. looks like a really great safety feature, it isn't really that useful or even necessary for most users. For S.M.A.R.T. to work, it is not just a matter of enabling it in the BIOS. You must also keep a S.M.A.R.T.-aware hardware monitoring utility running in the background all the time.

That's quite alright if the hard disk you are using has a spotty reputation and you need advanced warning of any impending failure. However, hard disks these days are mostly reliable enough to make S.M.A.R.T. redundant. Unless you are running mission-critical applications, it is very unlikely that S.M.A.R.T. will be of any use at all.

With that said, S.M.A.R.T. is still useful in providing a modicum of data loss prevention by continuously monitoring hard disks for signs of impending failure. If you have critical or irreplaceable data, you should **enable** this BIOS feature and use a S.M.A.R.T.-aware hardware monitoring software. Just don't rely completely on it! Back up your data on a CD or DVD!

Please note that even if you do not use any S.M.A.R.T.-aware utility, enabling S.M.A.R.T. in the BIOS uses up some bandwidth because the hard disk continuously sends out data packets. So, if you do not use S.M.A.R.T.-aware utilities, or if you do not need that level of real-time reporting, **disable** HDD S.M.A.R.T. Capability for better overall performance.

Some of the newer BIOSes now come with S.M.A.R.T. monitoring support built-in. When you enable HDD S.M.A.R.T. Capability, these new BIOSes automatically check the hard disk's S.M.A.R.T. status at boot-up. However, such a feature has very limited utility because it can only tell you the status of the hard disk at boot-up. Therefore, it is still advisable for you to **disable** HDD S.M.A.R.T. Capability unless you use a proper S.M.A.R.T.-aware monitoring utility.

Host Bus In-Order Queue Depth

Common Options: 1, 4, 8, 12

This BIOS feature controls the use of the processor bus command queue. Normally, there are only two options available. Depending on the motherboard chipset, the options could be (**1** and **4**), (**1** and **8**), or (**1** and **12**).

The first queue depth option is always **1**, which prevents the processor bus pipeline from queuing any outstanding commands. If selected, each command only is issued after the processor has finished with the previous one. Therefore, every command incurs the maximum amount of latency. This varies from **4 clock cycles** for a 4-stage pipeline to **12 clock cycles** for pipelines with 12 stages.

In most cases, it is highly recommended that you enable command queuing by selecting the option of **4 / 8 / 12** or, in some cases, **Enabled**. This allows the processor bus pipeline to mask its latency by queuing outstanding commands. You can expect a significant boost in performance with this feature enabled.

Interestingly, this feature can also be used as an aid in overclocking the processor. Although the queuing of commands brings with it a big boost in performance, it may also make the processor unstable at overclocked speeds. To overclock beyond what's normally possible, you can try **disabling** command queuing.

But please note that the performance deficit associated with deeper pipelines (8 or 12 stages) may not be worth the increase in processor overclockability. This is because the deep processor bus pipelines have very long latencies. If they are not masked by command queuing, the processor may be stalled so badly that you end up with poorer performance, even if you are able to further overclock the processor. So, it is recommended that you **enable** command queuing for deep pipelines, even if it means reduced overclockability.

Hyper-Threading Technology

H

Common Options: Enabled, Disabled

This BIOS feature controls the functionality of the Intel Hyper-Threading Technology.

The **Intel Hyper-Threading Technology** allows a single processor to execute *two or more* separate threads concurrently. When hyper-threading is enabled, multi-threaded software applications can execute their threads in parallel, thereby improving their performance.

The Intel Hyper-Threading Technology is only supported by the Intel Pentium 4 (officially only those 3.06GHz and faster) and the Intel Xeon processors. Please note that for Hyper-Threading to work, you should have the following:

- An Intel processor that supports Hyper-Threading

■ A motherboard with a chipset and BIOS that support Hyper-Threading

■ An operating system that supports Hyper-Threading (Microsoft Windows XP or Linux 2.4.x)

Because it behaves like two separate processors with their own APICs, you should also enable **APIC Function** in the BIOS, which is required for multi-processing.

It is highly recommended that you **enable** Hyper-Threading Technology for improved processor performance.

H

I

IDE Bus Master Support

Common Options: Enabled, Disabled

This BIOS feature is a misnomer because it doesn't actually control the bus mastering ability of the onboard IDE controller. It is actually a toggle for the built-in driver that allows the onboard IDE controller to perform **DMA (Direct Memory Access)** transfers.

When this BIOS feature is **enabled**, the BIOS loads up the 16-bit busmastering driver for the onboard IDE controller. This allows the IDE controller to transfer data through DMA, resulting in greatly improved transfer rates and lower CPU utilization in real-mode DOS and during the loading of other operating systems.

When this BIOS feature is **disabled**, the BIOS will *not* load up the 16-bit busmastering driver for the onboard IDE controller. The IDE controller then transfers data through **PIO (Programmed Input/Output)**.

Therefore, it is recommended that you **enable** IDE Bus Master Support. This greatly improves the IDE transfer rate and reduces CPU utilization during the booting process or when you are using real-mode DOS. Users of DOS-based disk utilities, such as Norton Ghost, can expect to benefit a lot from this feature.

IDE HDD Block Mode

Common Options: Enabled, Disabled

This BIOS feature speeds up hard disk access by transferring multiple sectors of data per interrupt instead of using the usual single-sector transfer mode. This mode of transferring data is known as block transfers.

When you enable this feature, the BIOS automatically detects whether your hard disk supports block transfers and sets the proper block transfer settings for it. Depending on the IDE controller, up to **64KB** of data can be transferred per interrupt when block transfers are enabled. Because all current hard disks support block transfers, there is *usually* no reason why IDE HDD Block Mode should be disabled.

Please note that if you **disable** IDE HDD Block Mode, only **512 bytes** of data can transfer per interrupt. Needless to say, this significantly degrades performance.

Therefore, you should **disable** IDE HDD Block Mode *only* if you actually face the possibility of data corruption (with an unpatched version of Windows NT 4.0). Otherwise, it is highly recommended that you **enable** this BIOS feature for significantly better hard disk performance!

I

Init Display First

Common Options: AGP, PCI

This BIOS feature allows you to select whether to boot the system using the AGP graphics card or the PCI graphics card. This is particularly important if you have AGP and PCI graphics cards but only one monitor.

If you are only using a single graphics card, then the BIOS detects it as such and boots it up, irrespective of what you set the feature to. However, there may be a slight reduction in the time taken to detect and initialize the card if you select the proper setting for this BIOS feature. For example, if you only use an AGP graphics card, then setting **Init Display First** to **AGP** may speed up your system's booting-up process.

Therefore, if you are only using a single graphics card, it is recommended that you set the Init Display First feature to the proper setting for your system (**AGP** for a single AGP card and **PCI** for a single PCI card).

However, if you are using multiple graphics cards, it is up to you which card you want to use as your primary display card. It is recommended that you select the fastest graphics card as the primary display card.

In-Order Queue Depth

Common Options: 1, 4, 8, 12

This BIOS feature controls the use of the processor bus command queue. Normally, there are only two options available. Depending on the motherboard chipset, the options could be (**1** and **4**), (**1** and **8**), or (**1** and **12**).

The first queue depth option is always **1**, which prevents the processor bus pipeline from queuing any outstanding commands. If selected, each command only is issued after the processor has finished with the previous one. Therefore, every command incurs the maximum amount of latency. This varies from **4 clock cycles** for a 4-stage pipeline to **12 clock cycles** for pipelines with 12 stages.

In most cases, it is highly recommended that you enable command queuing by selecting the option of **4 / 8 / 12** or, in some cases, **Enabled**. This allows the processor bus pipeline to mask its latency by queuing outstanding commands. You can expect a significant boost in performance with this feature enabled.

Interestingly, this feature also can be used as an aid in overclocking the processor. Although the queuing of commands brings with it a big boost in performance, it may also make the processor unstable at overclocked speeds. To overclock beyond what's normally possible, you can try **disabling** command queuing.

However, please note that the performance deficit associated with deeper pipelines (8 or 12 stages) may not be worth the increase in processor overclockability. This is because the deep processor bus pipelines have very long latencies. If they are not masked by command queuing, the processor may be stalled so badly that you may end up with poorer performance even if you are able to further overclock the processor. So, it is recommended that you **enable** command queuing for deep pipelines, even if it means reduced overclockability.

Interrupt Mode

Common Options: PIC, APIC

This BIOS feature is used to enable or disable the motherboard's **APIC** (**Advanced Programmable Interrupt Controller**). The APIC provides multiprocessor support, more IRQs, and faster interrupt handling.

However, it is only supported by newer operating systems like Microsoft Windows NT, Windows 2000, and Windows XP. Older operating systems like DOS or Windows 95/98 do not support this feature.

It is recommended that you select **APIC** if you are using a newer operating system like Windows XP. Select **PIC** only if you are using an older operating system like DOS or Windows 95/98.

IOQD

Common Options: 1, 4, 8, 12

This BIOS feature controls the use of the processor bus command queue. Normally, there are only two options available. Depending on the motherboard chipset, the options could be (**1** and **4**), (**1** and **8**), or (**1** and **12**).

The first queue depth option is always **1**, which prevents the processor bus pipeline from queuing any outstanding commands. If selected, each command only is issued after the processor has finished with the previous one. Therefore, every command incurs the maximum amount of latency. This varies from **4 clock cycles** for a 4-stage pipeline to **12 clock cycles** for pipelines with 12 stages.

In most cases, it is highly recommended that you enable command queuing by selecting the option of **4 / 8 / 12** or, in some cases, **Enabled**. This allows the processor bus pipeline to mask its latency by queuing outstanding commands. You can expect a significant boost in performance with this feature enabled.

Interestingly, this feature also can be used as an aid in overclocking the processor. Although the queuing of commands brings with it a big boost in performance, it may also make the processor unstable at overclocked speeds. To overclock beyond what's normally possible, you can try **disabling** command queuing.

However, please note that the performance deficit associated with deeper pipelines (8 or 12 stages) may not be worth the increase in processor overclockability. This is because the deep processor bus pipelines have very long latencies. If they are not masked by command queuing, the processor may be stalled so badly that you may end up with poorer performance even if you are able to further overclock the processor. So, it is recommended that you **enable** command queuing for deep pipelines, even if it means reduced overclockability.

I

ISA 14.318MHz Clock

Common Options: Enabled, Disabled

This BIOS feature allows you to overclock the ISA bus using the reference clock generator speed of **14.318MHz**. This greatly improves the ISA bus speed by running the bus **72%** faster than normal. At this clock speed, 8-bit cards have a bandwidth of **7.16MB/s** while 16-bit cards have a bandwidth of **14.32MB/s**.

In most cases, it is recommended that you **enable** this feature to give the ISA bus a performance boost. Of course, this is only useful if you have ISA devices in your system. Otherwise, this feature is redundant.

Please note that while newer ISA cards are capable of running at this "out-of-spec" speed, older ones may not work properly at this speed. Therefore, if your ISA card fails to function properly, **disable** this feature.

ISA Enable Bit

Common Options: Enabled, Disabled

This BIOS feature allows you to determine if the system controller will perform ISA aliasing to prevent conflicts between ISA devices.

The default setting of **Enabled** forces the system controller to alias ISA addresses using address bits [15:10]. This restricts all 16-bit addressing devices to a maximum contiguous I/O space of 256 bytes.

When **disabled**, the system controller does not perform any ISA aliasing and all 16 address lines can be used for I/O address space decoding. This gives 16-bit addressing devices access to the full 64KB I/O space.

It is recommended that you **disable ISA Enable Bit** for optimal AGP (and PCI) performance. It also prevents your AGP or PCI cards from conflicting with your ISA cards. **Enable** it only if you have ISA devices that are conflicting with each other.

I

K7 CLK_CTL Select

Common Options: Default, Optimal

As the name suggests, this is an AMD-specific BIOS feature. It controls the **Clock Control (CLK_CTL) Model Specific Register (MSR)**, which is part of the AMD Athlon's power management control system.

Now, unlike the Intel Pentium 4 processor, the Athlon processor saves power by actually reducing its *internal* clock speed. The Athlon bus clock speed remains constant but by using an internal clock divider, the Athlon processor can reduce its internal clock speed to **1/64th** (Palomino cores and older) or **1/8th** (Thoroughbred cores and newer) of its nominal clock speed.

The older Athlons have a bug (Errata No. 11) called *PLL Overshoot on Wake-Up from Disconnect Causes Auto-Compensation Circuit to Fail.* What happens is the processor can sometimes overshoot the nominal clock speed when it ramps up after a power-saving session. This causes a reduction in the Athlon bus I/O drive strength levels, which the auto-compensation circuitry attempts to correct. However, because there is not enough time, the proper drive strengths cannot be attained before the processor reconnects to the system bus. This causes the system bus to fail, which results in a system hang.

This bug is particularly prominent in the older Athlons that use the 1/64 internal divider because they normally require a longer ramp-up time, which increases the chance for the processor to overshoot the nominal clock speed. Hence, a workaround for this bug was devised whereupon the BIOS manually reprograms the CLK_CTL register to *reduce* the ramp-up time.

By default, the BIOS programs the CLK_CTL register with a value of **6003_1223h** during the POST routine. To increase the ramp-up speed, the BIOS has to change the value to **2003_1223h**.

This is where the **K7 CLK_CTL Select** BIOS feature comes in. When set to **Default**, the BIOS programs the CLK_CTL register with a value of **6003_1223h**. Setting to **Optimal** causes the BIOS to program the CLK_CTL register with a value of **2003_1223h**.

If you are using an AMD Athlon processor with a *Palomino or older* core, it is recommended that you set **K7 CLK_CTL Select** to **Optimal**. This prevents Errata No. 11 from manifesting itself and may even provide a speed boost by allowing the processor to disconnect and connect to the system bus faster.

From the **Thoroughbred-A** core (CPUID 680) onward, AMD started using an internal clock divider of only **1/8** with the CLK_CTL value of **6003_1223h**. This neatly circumvents the Errata No. 11 problem, although AMD also corrected that bug. With such processors, the CLK_CTL should be set to the **Default** value of **6003_1223h**.

Unfortunately, AMD then did an about-face with the Thoroughbred-B core (CPUID 681) and changed the value associated with the **1/8** divider from **6003_1223h** to **2003_1223h**. Unless the BIOS was updated to recognize this difference, it probably would write the **6003_1223h** value used for the Thoroughbred-A core into the register instead of the correct **2003**_1223h required by the Thoroughbred-B core. When this happens, the processor may become unstable during transitions from sleep mode to active mode.

Therefore, for **Thoroughbred-B** cores and above, you should set the **K7 CLK_CTL Select** BIOS feature to the **Optimal** setting to ensure proper setting of the internal clock divider.

KBC Input Clock Select

Common Options: 8MHz, 12MHz, 16MHz

The PS/2 keyboard communicates with the keyboard controller on the motherboard through a serial data link. The speed of the data link depends on the clock signal generated by the keyboard controller. The higher the clock speed, the faster the keyboard interface. This translates into a more responsive keyboard, although not all keyboards can work with higher clock speeds.

This BIOS feature allows you to adjust the keyboard interface clock for a better response or to fix a keyboard problem. It is recommended that you select the **16MHz** option for a better keyboard response. However, if the keyboard performs erratically or fails to initialize, try a lower clock speed.

Keyboard Auto-Repeat Delay

Common Options: 1/4 Sec, 1/2 Sec, 3/4 Sec, 1 Sec

This BIOS feature determines how long, in fractions of a second, the keyboard controller waits before it starts repeating the keystroke that you have pressed continuously. The longer the delay, the longer the keyboard controller waits before it starts repeating the keystroke.

Generally, using a short delay is useful for people who type quickly and don't like to wait long for a keystroke to be repeated. On the other hand, a long delay is useful for users who tend to press the keys longer while typing. This prevents the keyboard controller from unnecessarily repeating keystrokes with such users.

Keyboard Auto-Repeat Rate

Common Options: 6/Sec, 8/Sec, 10/Sec, 12/Sec, 20/Sec, 24/Sec, 30/Sec

This BIOS feature determines the rate at which the keyboard repeats a keystroke if you press it continuously.

The available settings are in characters per second. Therefore, a typematic rate of **30/Sec** causes the keyboard to repeat the keystroke at a rate of 30 characters per second if you press a particular key continuously. The higher the typematic rate, the faster the keyboard repeats the keystroke.

The choice of what setting to use is entirely up to your personal preference. Please note that this typematic rate is only applicable in operating systems that communicate with the hardware through the BIOS, like **MS-DOS**. The typematic rate in operating systems like Windows XP is controlled by the keyboard driver's settings.

L

L3 Cache

Common Options: Enabled, Disabled

This BIOS feature controls the functionality of the processor's Level 3 cache.

When **enabled**, the processor's Level 3 cache is allowed to function. This allows the best possible performance from the processor.

When **disabled**, the processor's Level 3 cache is disabled. The processor bypasses the Level 3 cache and relies only on the Level 1 and Level 2 caches. This reduces the performance of the processor.

The recommended setting is obviously **Enabled** because disabling it severely affects the processor's performance. However, the **Disabled** setting is useful as a troubleshooting tool, especially when you are overclocking your processor.

LD-Off Dram RD/WR Cycles

Common Options: Delay 1T, Normal

This BIOS feature controls the lead-off time for the memory read and write cycles.

When set to **Delay 1T**, the memory controller issues the memory address first. The read or write command is issued only after a delay of one clock cycle.

When set to **Normal**, the memory controller issues both the memory address and read/write command simultaneously.

It is recommended that you select the **Normal** option for better performance. Select the **Delay 1T** option only if you have stability issues with your memory modules.

Level 2 Cache Latency

Common Options: Auto, 1 to 15

This BIOS feature enables you to change the latency of the processor's Level 2 cache. By default, this feature is set to **Auto**, which means that the processor's Level 2 cache is left to its default latency setting. This is the safest option.

You can also manually select the latency of the cache. For this purpose, this BIOS feature provides options ranging from **1** clock cycle to **15** clock cycles. Please note that setting the latency too low can cause the Level 2 cache to lose data integrity or fail altogether. This will manifest as a system crash or an inability to boot-up altogether.

Therefore, it is recommended that you start with a high latency and work your way down until you start to encounter stability issues. This allows you to figure out the lowest latency your processor's Level 2 cache can support. Select that latency for optimal performance without stability issues.

Please note that this is a processor-dependent feature. Not all processors support BIOS manipulation of the Level 2 cache latency. If the processor does not allow any manipulation of its Level 2 cache latency, this BIOS feature will not have any effect, irrespective of what was selected.

Master Drive PIO Mode

Common Options: Auto, 0, 1, 2, 3, 4

This BIOS feature allows you to set the **PIO (Programmed Input/Output)** mode for the Master IDE drive attached to that particular IDE channel.

Setting this BIOS feature to **Auto** lets the BIOS auto-detect the IDE drive's maximum supported PIO mode at boot-up.

Setting this BIOS feature to **0** forces the BIOS to use **PIO Mode 0** for the IDE drive.

Setting this BIOS feature to **1** forces the BIOS to use **PIO Mode 1** for the IDE drive.

Setting this BIOS feature to **2** forces the BIOS to use **PIO Mode 2** for the IDE drive.

Setting this BIOS feature to **3** forces the BIOS to use **PIO Mode 3** for the IDE drive.

Setting this BIOS feature to **4** forces the BIOS to use **PIO Mode 4** for the IDE drive.

Normally, you should leave it as **Auto** and let the BIOS auto-detect the IDE drive's PIO mode. You should only set it manually for the following reasons:

- If the BIOS cannot detect the correct PIO mode
- If you want to try forcing the IDE device to use a faster PIO mode than it was designed for
- If you want to force the IDE device to use a slower PIO mode if it cannot work properly with the current PIO mode (for example, when the PCI bus is overclocked)

Please note that forcing an IDE device to use a PIO transfer rate that is faster than what it is rated for can potentially cause data corruption.

Master Drive UltraDMA

Common Options: Auto, Disabled

This BIOS feature allows you to enable or disable **DMA (Direct Memory Access)** support (if available) for the Master IDE device attached to that particular IDE channel.

Setting this BIOS feature to **Auto** lets the BIOS auto-detect the IDE drive's maximum supported DMA mode at boot-up.

Setting this BIOS feature to **Disabled** forces the BIOS to disable DMA transfers for the IDE drive.

Normally, you should leave it as **Auto** and let the BIOS auto-detect the drive's DMA support. If the drive supports DMA transfers, the proper DMA transfer mode is enabled for that drive, allowing it to burst data at anywhere from 33MB/s to 133MB/s (depending on the transfer mode supported).

You should only **disable** it for troubleshooting purposes. For example, certain IDE devices may not run properly using DMA transfers when the PCI bus is overclocked. Disabling DMA support forces the drive to use the slower PIO transfer mode. This may allow the drive to work properly with the higher PCI bus speed.

Please note that setting this to **Auto** does *not* enable DMA transfers for IDE devices that do not support DMA transfers. If your drive does not support DMA transfers, the BIOS automatically sets the drive to do PIO transfers only.

Also note that this BIOS feature merely enables DMA transfers during the booting up process and for operating systems that do not load their own drivers for IDE functions. For operating systems that use their own IDE drivers (for example, Windows 9x/2000/XP), you have to enable DMA support for the drive within the operating system as well.

Master Priority Rotation

Common Options: 1 PCI, 2 PCI, 3 PCI

This BIOS feature controls the priority of the processor's accesses to the PCI bus.

If you choose **1 PCI**, the processor always grants access right after the **current** PCI bus master completes its transaction, irrespective of how many other PCI bus masters are on the queue.

If you choose **2 PCI**, the processor always grants access right after the **second** PCI bus master on the queue completes its transaction.

If you choose **3 PCI**, the processor always grants access right after the **third** PCI bus master on the queue completes its transaction.

No matter what you choose, the processor is guaranteed access to the PCI bus after a certain number of PCI bus master grants. It doesn't matter if there are numerous PCI bus masters on the queue or when the processor requests access to the PCI bus. The processor is always granted access after one PCI bus master transaction (**1 PCI**), two transactions (**2 PCI**), or three transactions (**3 PCI**).

For better overall performance, it is recommended that you select the **1 PCI** option as this allows the processor to access the PCI bus with minimal delay. However, if you wish to improve the performance of your PCI devices, you can try the **2 PCI** or **3 PCI** options. They ensure that your PCI cards receive greater PCI bus priority.

MD Driving Strength

Common Options: Hi, Lo / High, Low

This BIOS feature offers simplified control of the memory data bus driving strength.

The default value is **Lo** or **Low**. With heavy DRAM loads, you might want to set this feature to **Hi** or **High**.

Due to the nature of this BIOS feature, it is possible to use it as an aid in overclocking the memory bus. Your memory module may not overclock as well as you want it to. By raising the driving strength of the memory bus, it is possible to improve its stability at overclocked speeds.

However, this is not a surefire way of overclocking the memory bus. All you may get at the end of the day is increased EMI and power consumption.

Please note too that increasing the memory bus drive strength does *not* improve the perform-ance of your memory subsystem.

Therefore, it is recommended that you leave the MD Driving Strength at its default **Lo** or **Low** setting. Set it to **Hi** or **High** only if you have a heavy DRAM load or if you are trying to stabi-lize an overclocked memory module.

Memory Hole At 15M–16M

Common Options: Enabled, Disabled

Certain ISA cards require exclusive access to the 1MB block of memory, from the 15th to the 16th megabyte, to work properly. This BIOS feature allows you to reserve that 1MB block of memory for such cards to use.

If you **enable** this feature, 1MB of memory (the 15th MB) is reserved exclusively for the ISA card's use. This effectively reduces the total amount of memory available to the operating system by 1MB.

Please note that in certain motherboards, enabling this feature may actually render all memory above the 15th MB unavailable to the operating system!

If you **disable** this feature, the 15th MB of RAM is *not* reserved for the ISA card's use. The full range of memory is therefore available for the operating system to use. However, if your ISA card requires the use of that memory area, it may fail to work.

Because ISA cards are a thing of the past, it is highly recommended that you **disable** this fea-ture. Even if you have an ISA card that you absolutely have to use, you may *not* actually need to enable this feature.

Most ISA cards do *not* need exclusive access to this memory area. Make sure that your ISA card requires this memory area before enabling this feature. You should use this BIOS feature only in a last-ditch attempt to get a stubborn ISA card to work.

MP Capable Bit Identify

Common Options: Enabled, Disabled

This BIOS feature determines whether the BIOS should query the MP Capable bit to correctly identify an AMD Athlon MP processor.

When set to **Enabled**, the BIOS will query the MP Capable bit at boot-up. If it detects a MP Capable bit setting of **1**, it writes the Athlon MP processor string name into the appropriate registers.

When set to **Disabled**, the BIOS will not query the MP Capable bit at boot-up. The Athlon MP processor will be indistinguishable from the Athlon XP processor, as far as the processor identification is concerned.

If you are using an AMD Athlon MP processor, it is recommended that you **enable** this BIOS feature to allow proper identification of the processor. If you are using other Athlon processors, you should **disable** this BIOS feature as the BIOS does not need to query the MP Capable bit to detect the processor correctly.

MPS Control Version For OS

Common Options: 1.1, 1.4

This feature is only applicable to multiprocessor motherboards as it specifies the version of the **Multi-Processor Specification** (**MPS**) that the motherboard uses. The MPS is a specification by which PC manufacturers design and build Intel architecture systems with two or more processors.

MPS 1.1 was the original specification. MPS version 1.4 adds extended configuration tables for improved support of multiple PCI bus configurations and greater expandability in the future. In addition, MPS 1.4 introduces support for a secondary PCI bus without requiring a PCI bridge.

If your operating system comes with support for MPS 1.4, you should change the setting from the default of 1.1 to **1.4**. You also need to enable MPS 1.4 support if you need to make use of the secondary PCI bus on a motherboard that doesn't come with a PCI bridge.

You should only leave it as **1.1** if you are running an older operating system that only supports MPS 1.1.

As far as Microsoft operating systems are concerned, Windows NT/2000/XP support MPS 1.4.

However, users of the ABIT BP6 motherboard and Windows 2000 should take note of a possible problem with the MPS version set to 1.4. If you set the MPS version to 1.4 in the ABIT BP6 motherboard, Windows 2000 does *not* use the second processor. So, if you encounter this problem, set the MPS Version Control For OS to **1.1**.

MPS Revision

Common Options: 1.1, 1.4

This feature is only applicable to multiprocessor motherboards as it specifies the version of the **Multi-Processor Specification** (**MPS**) that the motherboard uses. The MPS is a specification by which PC manufacturers design and build Intel architecture systems with two or more processors.

MPS 1.1 was the original specification. MPS version 1.4 adds extended configuration tables for improved support of multiple PCI bus configurations and greater expandability in the future. In addition, MPS 1.4 introduces support for a secondary PCI bus without requiring a PCI bridge.

If your operating system comes with support for MPS 1.4, you should change the setting from the default of 1.1 to **1.4**. You also need to enable MPS 1.4 support if you need to make use of the secondary PCI bus on a motherboard that doesn't come with a PCI bridge.

You should only leave it as **1.1** if you are running an older operating system that only supports MPS 1.1.

As far as Microsoft operating systems are concerned, Windows NT/2000/XP support MPS 1.4.

However, users of the ABIT BP6 motherboard and Windows 2000 should take note of a possible problem with the MPS version set to 1.4. If you set the MPS version to 1.4 in the ABIT BP6 motherboard, Windows 2000 does *not* use the second processor. So, if you encounter this problem, set the MPS Revision to **1.1**.

Multi-Sector Transfers

Common Options: Disabled, 2 Sectors, 4 Sectors, 8 Sectors, 16 Sectors, 32 Sectors, Maximum

This BIOS feature speeds up hard disk access by transferring multiple sectors of data per interrupt instead of using the usual single-sector transfer mode. This mode of transferring data is known as block transfers.

There are a few available options, ranging from **Disabled** to Maximum, with a few different multiple sectors options between.

The **Disabled** option forces your IDE controller to transfer only a single sector (512 bytes) per interrupt. Needless to say, this will significantly degrade performance.

The selection of **2 Sectors** to **32 Sectors** allows you to manually select the number of sectors that the IDE controller is allowed to transfer per interrupt.

The **Maximum** option allows your IDE controller to transfer as many sectors per interrupt as the hard disk is able to support.

Since all current hard disks support block transfers, there is *usually* no reason why IDE HDD Block Mode should be disabled.

Therefore, you should **disable** IDE HDD Block Mode *only* if you actually face the possibility of data corruption (*with an unpatched version of Windows NT 4.0*). Otherwise, it is highly recommended that you select the **Maximum** option for significantly better hard disk performance.

The manual selection of 2 to 32 sectors is useful if you notice data corruption with the **Maximum** option. It allows you to scale back the multi-sector transfer feature to correct the problem without losing too much performance.

N

N/B Strap CPU As

Common Options: By CPU, PSB400, PSB533, PSB800

This BIOS feature allows you to circumvent the CPU-to-DRAM ratio limitation found in the newer Intel i865/i875-series of chipsets. In those chipsets, Intel has chosen to limit the choices of available CPU-to-DRAM ratios.

When a **400MHz FSB** processor is installed, the choice of CPU-to-DRAM ratio is limited to **3:4**.

When a **533MHz FSB** processor is installed, the choices of CPU-to-DRAM ratio are limited to **1:1** or **4:5**.

When a **800MHz FSB** processor is installed, the choices of CPU-to-DRAM ratio are limited to **1:1, 3:2,** or **5:4**.

Fortunately, this BIOS feature allows you to circumvent that limitation.

The **N/B Strap CPU As** BIOS feature actually controls the setting of the external hardware reset strap assigned to the **MCH (Memory Controller Hub)** of the chipset. By setting it to **PSB400, PSB533,** or **PSB800**, you can trick the chipset into thinking that the **400MHz FSB, 533MHz FSB,** or the **800MHz FSB** is being used.

When this BIOS feature is set to **PSB800**, you are able to access the **800MHz** CPU-to-DRAM ratios of **1:1, 3.2** and **5:4**.

When this BIOS feature is set to **PSB533**, you are able to access the **533MHz** CPU-to-DRAM ratios of **1:1** and **4:5**.

When this BIOS feature is set to **PSB400**, you are able to access the **400MHz** CPU-to-DRAM ratio of **3:4**.

By default, this BIOS feature is set to **By CPU**, whereby the hardware strap is set according to the actual FSB rating of the processor.

Generally, you do not need to manually adjust the hardware strap setting. However, if you require access to the CPU-to-DRAM ratio that normally would not be available to you, then this BIOS feature will be very helpful indeed.

No Mask of SBA FE

Common Options: Enabled, Disabled

This BIOS feature controls the masking of the signal used to calibrate the **SBA (Sideband Address)** port. It is used to fix compatibility issues with certain graphics cards.

When **enabled**, the chipset masks (*hides*) the SBA calibration signal, so the graphics chip does not initiate the SBA calibration cycle. Because the SBA port is never recalibrated, the issue of the graphics card hanging due to SBA recalibration is avoided.

When **disabled**, the graphics chip is allowed to initiate the SBA calibration cycle right after the AGP bus calibration cycle.

Users of ATI R3xx-based graphics cards (for example, Radeon 9700 Pro, Radeon 9800) are advised to **enable** this BIOS feature if the graphic card hangs or crashes during 3D benchmarking or gaming.

Users of other unaffected graphics cards are advised to **disable** this feature, so the chipset can dynamically calibrate the SBA port.

Onboard FDC Swap A & B

Common Options: No Swap, Swap AB

This BIOS feature is used to logically swap the mapping of drives A: and B:. Therefore, it is only useful if you have two floppy drives.

Normally, the sequence by which you connect the floppy drives to the cable determines which is drive A: and which is drive B:. If you attach the floppy drives the wrong way and obtain a drive mapping that is not to your satisfaction, the usual way of correcting this is to physically swap the floppy cable connectors.

This feature allows you to swap the logical arrangement of the floppy drives without the need to open up the case and physically swap the connectors.

When this BIOS feature is set to **Swap AB**, the floppy drive that originally was mapped to drive A: is remapped to drive B: and vice versa for the drive that was originally set as drive B:.

When this BIOS feature is set to **No Swap**, the floppy drive mapping remains as set by the drive connector arrangement.

Although this appears to be nothing more than a feature of convenience, it can be quite important if you are using two floppy drives of different form factors (3.5"and 5.25") and you need to boot from the second drive. Because the BIOS can only boot from drive A:, you have to physically swap the drive connections or use this BIOS feature to do it logically.

If your floppy drive mapping is correct or if you only have a single floppy drive, there is no need to set this feature to **Swap AB**. Leave it at the default setting of **No Swap**.

Onboard FDD Controller

Common Options: Enabled, Disabled

This BIOS feature allows you to enable or disable the onboard floppy drive controller.

When **enabled**, the motherboard's onboard floppy drive controller is enabled.

When **disabled**, the motherboard's onboard floppy drive controller is disabled. This frees up the IRQ used by the floppy drive controller.

If you are using a floppy drive connected to the motherboard's built-in floppy drive controller, select the **Enabled** option.

If you are using an add-on floppy drive controller card or if you are not using any floppy drive at all, set it to **Disabled** to save an IRQ that can be used by other devices.

Onboard IDE-1 Controller

Common Options: Enabled, Disabled

This BIOS feature is actually a misnomer because there is only one IDE controller integrated into current chipsets.

This single IDE controller comes with two IDE channels, each of which supports up to two IDE drives. Therefore, the IDE controller supports a total of four IDE devices through two IDE channels.

When **enabled**, the IDE channel is able to provide support for up to two IDE drives.

When **disabled**, the IDE channel is disabled. Any attached IDE drives is not accessible. However, this frees up an IRQ, which can be used by other devices. Disabling this IDE channel also speeds up the booting sequence a little as the BIOS does not need to query this channel for IDE devices when it boots up.

You should leave this **enabled** if you are using this IDE channel. Disabling it prevents any IDE devices attached to this channel from being accessed.

If you are not attaching any IDE devices to this IDE channel (or if you are using a SCSI/add-on IDE card), you can **disable** this IDE channel to free an IRQ and speed up the booting sequence.

Onboard IDE-2 Controller

Common Options: Enabled, Disabled

This BIOS feature is actually a misnomer because there is only one IDE controller integrated into current chipsets.

This single IDE controller comes with two IDE channels, each of which supports up to two IDE drives. Therefore, the IDE controller supports a total of four IDE devices through two IDE channels.

When **enabled**, the IDE channel is able to provide support for up to two IDE drives.

When **disabled**, the IDE channel is disabled. Any attached IDE drives are not accessible. However, this frees up an IRQ, which can be used by other devices. Disabling this IDE channel also speeds up the booting sequence a little as the BIOS does not need to query this channel for IDE devices when it boots up.

You should leave this **enabled** if you are using this IDE channel. Disabling it prevents any IDE devices attached to this channel from being accessed.

If you are not attaching any IDE devices to this IDE channel (or if you are using a SCSI/add-on IDE card), you can **disable** this IDE channel to free an IRQ and speed up the booting sequence.

Onboard IR Function

Common Options: IrDA (HPSIR) mode, ASK IR (Amplitude Shift Keyed IR) mode, Disabled

There are two different **IR** (**Infra-Red**) modes—**IrDA** and **ASK IR**.

You should select the IR mode that is supported by your external IR device. Choosing the wrong IR mode prevents your computer from communicating with the external IR device.

However, if there is a choice between IrDA and ASK IR, the natural choice is **IrDA**, of course! IrDA is faster and has a longer range.

Please note that such IR communications require an IR beam kit to be plugged into the IR header on the motherboard. Without the IR beam kit, this feature won't have any effect.

You should also note that enabling this IR function prevents the second serial port from being used by normal serial devices. Therefore, if you do not need to use the onboard IR function, **disable** this BIOS feature, so the second serial port can be used by normal serial devices.

Onboard Parallel Port

Common Options: 3BCh/IRQ7, 278h/IRQ5, 378h/IRQ7, Disabled

This BIOS feature allows you to select the I/O address and IRQ for the onboard parallel port.

The default I/O address of **378h** and IRQ of **7** should work well in most cases. Unless you have a problem with the parallel port, you should leave it at the default settings.

You should only select an alternative I/O address or IRQ if the default settings are causing a conflict with other devices.

You can also **disable** the onboard parallel port if you do not need to use it. Doing so frees up the I/O port and IRQ used by the parallel port. Those resources can then be reallocated for other devices to use.

Onboard Serial Port 1

Common Options: Auto, 3F8h/IRQ4, 2F8h/IRQ3, 3E8h/IRQ4, 2E8h/IRQ3, Disabled

This BIOS feature allows you to manually select the I/O address and IRQ for the first serial port.

It is recommended that you leave it as **Auto**, so the BIOS can select the best settings for it. If you need a particular I/O port or IRQ that has been taken up by this serial port, you can manually select an alternative I/O port or IRQ for it.

Please note that any I/O port or IRQ can be used for the serial port. There is no advantage or disadvantage in any of the options. As long as you do not select an I/O port or IRQ that has already been allocated to another device, any option will do.

You can also **disable** this serial port if you do not need to use it. Doing so frees up the I/O port and IRQ used by this serial port. Those resources then can be reallocated for other devices to use.

Onboard Serial Port 2

Common Options: Auto, 3F8h/IRQ4, 2F8h/IRQ3, 3E8h/IRQ4, 2E8h/IRQ3, Disabled

This BIOS feature allows you to manually select the I/O address and IRQ for the first serial port.

It is recommended that you leave it as **Auto**, so the BIOS can select the best settings for it. If you need a particular I/O port or IRQ that has been taken up by this serial port, you can manually select an alternative I/O port or IRQ for it.

Please note that any I/O port or IRQ can be used for the serial port. There is no advantage or disadvantage in any of the options. As long as you do not select an I/O port or IRQ that has already been allocated to another device, any option will do.

You can also **disable** this serial port if you do not need to use it. Doing so frees up the I/O port and IRQ used by this serial port. Those resources then can be reallocated for other devices to use.

Onboard USB Controller

Common Options: Enabled, Disabled

This BIOS feature enables or disables the motherboard's onboard USB controller.

It is recommended that you **enable** this feature, so you can use the onboard USB controller to communicate with your USB devices.

If you **disable** this feature, the USB controller is disabled and you are not able to use it to communicate with any USB device. This frees up an IRQ for other devices to use. This is useful when you have many devices that cannot share IRQs.

However, it is recommended that you do *not* disable this BIOS feature unless you do not use any USB device or if you are using a different USB controller for your USB needs.

OnChip VGA Mode Select

Common Options: 1MB, 4MB, 8MB, 16MB, 32MB, 64MB

This BIOS feature controls the amount of system memory that is allocated to the integrated GPU.

The selection of memory sizes allows you to select how much system memory you want to allocate to the integrated GPU. The amount you allocate to the GPU is deducted from the amount of system memory available to your operating system and programs.

Please note that unlike the **AGP Aperture Size**, once the system memory is allocated to the GPU, it cannot be used by anything else. Even if the GPU does not make use of it, it is not available to the operating system.

Therefore, it is recommended that you select the absolute minimum amount of system memory that the GPU requires for your monitor. You can calculate it by multiplying the resolution and color depth that you are using.

For example, if you use a resolution of 1600 × 1200 and a color depth of 32-bit, the amount of memory your GPU requires will be 1600 × 1200 × 32-bits = 61,440,000 bits or 7.68MB. You should set this BIOS feature to **8MB** in this example.

OS/2 Onboard Memory > 64M

Common Options: Enabled, Disabled

This is similar to the **OS Select For DRAM > 64M** BIOS feature.

This BIOS feature determines how systems with more than 64MB of memory are managed. A wrong setting can cause problems like erroneous memory detection.

If you are using an older version of the IBM OS/2 operating system, you should select **Yes**.

If you are using the IBM OS/2 Warp v3.0 or higher operating system, you should select **No**.

If you are using an older version of the IBM OS/2 operating system but have already installed all the relevant IBM FixPaks, you should select **No**.

Users of non-OS/2 operating systems (like Microsoft Windows XP) should select the **No** option.

OS Select For DRAM > 64MB

Common Options: OS/2, Non-OS/2

This BIOS feature determines how systems with more than 64MB of memory are managed. A wrong setting can cause problems like erroneous memory detection.

If you are using an older version of the IBM OS/2 operating system, you should select **OS/2**.

If you are using the IBM OS/2 Warp v3.0 or higher operating system, you should select **Non-OS/2**.

If you are using an older version of the IBM OS/2 operating system but have already installed all the relevant IBM FixPaks, you should select **Non-OS/2**.

Users of non-OS/2 operating systems (like Microsoft Windows XP) should select the **Non-OS/2** option.

P

P2C/C2P Concurrency

Common Options: Enabled, Disabled

The BIOS feature allows PCI-to-CPU and CPU-to-PCI traffic to occur concurrently. This means PCI traffic to the CPU and CPU traffic to the PCI bus can occur simultaneously.

This prevents the CPU from being "locked up" during PCI transfers. It also allows PCI traffic to the processor to occur without delay even when the processor is writing to the PCI bus. This may prevent performance issues with certain PCI cards.

Therefore, it is recommended that you **enable** this feature for better performance.

Parallel Port Mode

Common Options: Normal (SPP), ECP, EPP, ECP+EPP

By default, the parallel port is usually set to the **Normal (SPP)** mode. **SPP** stands for **Standard Parallel Port**. It is the original transfer protocol for the parallel port. Therefore, it works with all parallel port devices.

The **ECP (Extended Capabilities Port)** transfer mode uses the DMA protocol to achieve data transfer rates of up to **2MB/s** and provides *symmetric* bidirectional communication.

On the other hand, **EPP (Enhanced Parallel Port)**, now known as **IEEE 1284**, uses existing parallel port signals to provide *asymmetric* bidirectional communication. It was also designed for high-speed communications, offering transfer rates of up to **2MB/s**.

As you can see, SPP is a very slow transfer mode. It only should be selected when faster transfer modes cannot be used (for example, with old printers or scanners). With modern parallel port devices, the ECP and EPP modes are the transfer modes of choice.

Generally, because of its FIFOs and the DMA channel it uses, **ECP** is good at large data transfers. Therefore, it is the transfer mode that works best with scanners and printers. **EPP** is better with devices that switch between reads and writes frequently (like ZIP drives and hard disks).

However, you should check your parallel port device's documentation before you set the transfer mode. The manufacturer of your parallel port peripheral may have designated a preferred transfer mode for the device in question. In that case, it is best to follow their recommendation.

If the device documentation did not state any preferred transfer mode and you still do not know what mode to select, you can select the **ECP+EPP** mode. If you select this mode, the BIOS automatically determines the transfer mode to use for your device.

Passive Release

Common Options: Enabled, Disabled

This BIOS feature controls the passive release feature of the **CPU to PCI Write Buffer**. Therefore, if the write buffer is disabled, this BIOS feature does not have any effect. However, the reverse is not true. The **CPU to PCI Write Buffer** feature still works even if **Passive Release** is disabled.

When Passive Release is **enabled**, the write buffer independently writes the data to the PCI bus at the first available opportunity. It can do so even when the processor is busy doing something else.

When Passive Release is **disabled**, the write buffer waits until the processor reasserts (retries) the write request. Only then does it write to the PCI bus. This still improves performance because the processor does not need to resend the data. However, the write buffer still loses some of its effectiveness because it has to wait for the CPU to retry the transaction.

For best performance, it is highly recommended that you **enable** Passive Release. This dramatically reduces the effect of slow ISA devices hogging the PCI bus. However, some ISA cards may not work well with Passive Release. In such cases, **disable** Passive Release or better yet, throw the card away and get a PCI version instead!

If you don't use any ISA device, this feature should still be **enabled** because it allows the write buffer to offload its data to the PCI bus without waiting for the processor to retry the transaction. This improves the performance of the processor and PCI bus.

Please note again that this BIOS feature has no effect if you disable the **CPU to PCI Write Buffer**.

PCI#2 Access #1 Retry

Common Options: Enabled, Disabled

This BIOS feature is linked to **CPU to PCI Write Buffer**. Therefore, if the write buffer is disabled, this BIOS feature does not have any effect. However, the reverse is not true. The **CPU to PCI Write Buffer** feature still works even if **PCI#2 Access #1 Retry** is disabled.

When the buffer is enabled, the processor writes directly to the buffer instead of the PCI bus. The buffer then attempts to write the data to the PCI bus by **Passive Release**. This allows the processor to perform other tasks without waiting for its data to be written to the PCI bus.

However, the attempted buffer write to the PCI bus may fail because the PCI bus may still be occupied by another device. When that happens, this BIOS feature determines if the buffer write should be reattempted or sent back for arbitration.

If this BIOS feature is **enabled**, the buffer attempts to write to the PCI bus until it is successful.

If this BIOS feature is **disabled**, the buffer flushes its contents and registers the transaction as failed. The processor now has to write again to the write buffer.

Generally, it is recommended that you **enable** this feature because it improves the processor's performance.

However, if you have many PCI devices and their performance is more important, you may want to **disable** this feature. This prevents excessive generation of retries by the write buffer, which may severely tax the PCI bus. Disabling this feature improves the PCI bus performance, especially with slow PCI devices that hog the bus for long periods of time at a stretch.

Please note again that this BIOS feature has no effect if you disable the **CPU to PCI Write Buffer**.

PCI 2.1 Compliance

Common Options: Enabled, Disabled

To meet PCI 2.1 compliance, the PCI maximum target latency rule must be observed. According to this rule, a PCI 2.1-compliant device must service a read request within **16** PCI clock cycles for the *initial* read and **8** PCI clock cycles for each *subsequent* read.

If it cannot do so, the PCI bus terminates the transaction, so other PCI devices can access the bus. However, instead of rearbitrating for access (and failing to meet the minimum latency requirement again), the PCI 2.1-compliant device can make use of the **PCI Delayed Transaction** feature.

With **PCI Delayed Transaction** enabled, the target device can independently continue the read transaction. So, when the master device successfully gains control of the bus and reissues the read command, the target device has the data ready for immediate delivery. This ensures that the retried read transaction can be completed within the stipulated latency period.

If the delayed transaction is a *write*, the master device rearbitrates for bus access while the target device completes writing the data. When the master device regains control of the bus, it reissues the same write request. This time, the target device just sends the completion status to the master device to complete the transaction.

One advantage of using **PCI Delayed Transaction** is that it allows other PCI masters to use the bus while the transaction is being carried out on the target device. Otherwise, the bus is left idling while the target device completes the transaction.

PCI Delayed Transaction also allows write-posted data to remain in the buffer, while the PCI bus initiates a non-postable transaction, and yet still adhere to the PCI ordering rules. Without **PCI Delayed Transaction**, all write-posted data has to be flushed before another PCI transaction can occur.

It is highly recommended that you **enable** PCI 2.1 Compliance for better PCI performance and to meet PCI 2.1 specifications. **Disable** it only if your PCI cards cannot work properly with this feature enabled or if you are using PCI cards that are *not* PCI 2.1-compliant.

Please note that while many manuals and even earlier versions of the BIOS Optimization Guide have stated that this is an ISA bus-specific BIOS feature that enables a 32-bit write-posted buffer for faster PCI-to-ISA writes, they are *incorrect*! This BIOS feature is *not* ISA bus-specific, and it does *not* control any write-posted buffers. It merely allows write-posting to continue while a non-postable PCI transaction is underway.

PCI Chaining

Common Options: Enabled, Disabled

This BIOS feature is designed to speed up writes from the processor to the PCI bus by allowing write combining to occur at the PCI interface.

When PCI chaining is **enabled**, up to four quadwords of processor writes to *contiguous* PCI addresses are chained together and written to the PCI bus as a single PCI burst write.

When PCI chaining is **disabled**, each processor write to the PCI bus is handled as separate non-burstable writes.

Needless to say, writing four quadwords of data in a single PCI write is much faster than doing so in four separate non-burstable writes. A single PCI burst write also reduces the amount of time the processor has to wait while writing to the PCI bus.

Therefore, it is recommended that you **enable** this feature for better CPU to PCI write performance.

PCI Clock / CPU FSB Clock

Common Options: 1/2, 1/3, 1/4, 1/5, 1/6

This BIOS feature allows you to manually select the PCI bus clock divider. Because this divider determines the speed at which the PCI bus runs, manipulation of this feature allows you some control over the PCI bus speed.

It was meant to keep the PCI bus running within specifications when you overclock the processor bus, but you can also use it to overclock the PCI bus. With that said, you should keep in mind that the recommended safe limit for an overclocked PCI bus is **37.5MHz**. This is the speed at which practically all new PCI cards can run without breaking a sweat.

Selecting the clock divider of **1/2** makes the PCI bus run at half the processor bus speed. As such, this clock divider is useful for processor bus speeds of **66MHz to 75MHz**.

Selecting the clock divider of **1/3** makes the PCI bus run at a third of the processor bus speed. As such, this clock divider is useful for processor bus speeds of **100MHz to 112.5MHz**.

Selecting the clock divider of **1/4** makes the PCI bus run at a quarter of the processor bus speed. As such, this clock divider is useful for processor bus speeds of **133MHz to 150MHz**.

Selecting the clock divider of **1/5** makes the PCI bus run at a fifth of the processor bus speed. As such, this clock divider is useful for processor bus speeds of **166MHz to 187.5MHz**.

Selecting the clock divider of **1/6** makes the PCI bus run at a sixth of the processor bus speed. As such, this clock divider is useful for processor bus speeds of **200MHz to 225MHz**.

You are probably wondering about the gaps in the processor bus speeds listed above. For your convenience, only processor bus speeds that produce PCI clock speeds within the range of optimal PCI clock speeds (33MHz to 37.5MHz) are displayed above. The other processor bus speeds either produce a slow PCI bus or an excessively overclocked one.

Therefore, for optimal PCI bus performance, try to shoot for one of the processor bus speed-divider combinations shown above.

PCI Delay Transaction

Common Options: Enabled, Disabled

To meet PCI 2.1 compliance, the PCI maximum target latency rule must be observed. According to this rule, a PCI 2.1-compliant device must service a read request within **16** PCI clock cycles for the *initial* read and **8** PCI clock cycles for each *subsequent* read.

If it cannot do so, the PCI bus terminates the transaction, so other PCI devices can access the bus. However, instead of rearbitrating for access (and failing to meet the minimum latency requirement again), the PCI 2.1-compliant device can make use of the **PCI Delayed Transaction** feature.

With **PCI Delayed Transaction** enabled, the target device can independently continue the read transaction. So, when the master device successfully gains control of the bus and reissues the read command, the target device has the data ready for immediate delivery. This ensures that the retried read transaction can be completed within the stipulated latency period.

If the delayed transaction is a *write*, the master device rearbitrates for bus access while the target device completes writing the data. When the master device regains control of the bus, it reissues the same write request. This time, the target device just sends the completion status to the master device to complete the transaction.

One advantage of using **PCI Delayed Transaction** is that it allows other PCI masters to use the bus while the transaction is being carried out on the target device. Otherwise, the bus is left idling while the target device completes the transaction.

PCI Delayed Transaction also allows write-posted data to remain in the buffer, while the PCI bus initiates a non-postable transaction, and yet still adhere to the PCI ordering rules. Without **PCI Delayed Transaction**, all write-posted data has to be flushed before another PCI transaction can occur.

It is highly recommended that you **enable** PCI Delay Transaction for better PCI performance and to meet PCI 2.1 specifications. **Disable** it only if your PCI cards cannot work properly with this feature enabled or if you are using PCI cards that are *not* PCI 2.1-compliant.

Please note that while many manuals and even earlier versions of the BIOS Optimization Guide have stated that this is an ISA bus-specific BIOS feature that enables a 32-bit write-posted buffer for faster PCI-to-ISA writes, they are *incorrect*! This BIOS feature is *not* ISA bus-specific, and it does *not* control any write-posted buffers. It merely allows write-posting to continue while a non-postable PCI transaction is underway.

P

PCI Dynamic Bursting

Common Options: Enabled, Disabled

This BIOS feature is similar to the **Byte Merge** feature.

When **enabled**, the PCI write buffer accumulates and merges 8-bit and 16-bit writes into 32-bit writes. This increases the efficiency of the PCI bus and improves its bandwidth.

When **disabled**, the PCI write buffer does not accumulate or merge 8-bit or 16-bit writes. It just writes them to the PCI bus as soon as the bus is free. As such, there may be a loss of PCI bus efficiency when 8-bit or 16-bit data is written to the PCI bus.

Therefore, it is recommended that you **enable** PCI Dynamic Bursting for better performance.

However, please note that **PCI Dynamic Bursting** may be incompatible with certain PCI network interface cards (also known as NICs). So, if your NIC won't work properly, try **disabling** this feature.

PCI IDE Busmaster

Common Options: Enabled, Disabled

This BIOS feature is a misnomer because it doesn't actually control the bus mastering ability of the onboard IDE controller. It is actually a toggle for the built-in driver that allows the onboard IDE controller to perform **DMA** (**Direct Memory Access**) transfers.

When this BIOS feature is **enabled**, the BIOS loads up the 16-bit busmastering driver for the onboard IDE controller. This allows the IDE controller to transfer data through DMA, resulting in greatly improved transfer rates and lower CPU utilization in real-mode DOS and during the loading of other operating systems.

When this BIOS feature is **disabled**, the BIOS does *not* load up the 16-bit busmastering driver for the onboard IDE controller. The IDE controller then transfers data through **PIO** (**Programmed Input/Output**).

Therefore, it is recommended that you **enable** PCI IDE Busmaster. This greatly improves the IDE transfer rate and reduces the CPU utilization during the booting process or when you are using real-mode DOS. Users of DOS-based disk utilities like Norton Ghost can expect to benefit a lot from this feature.

PCI IRQ Activated By

Common Options: Edge, Level

This BIOS feature allows you to set the method by which the IRQs for your PCI devices are activated or triggered.

ISA and old PCI devices are **edge-triggered** (using a single voltage level) while newer PCI and AGP devices are **level-triggered** (using multiple voltage levels). This is important mainly because PCI devices must be level-triggered to share IRQs.

Because all PCI devices currently in the market are level-triggered, it is recommended that you set this BIOS feature to **Level**, so your PCI devices can share IRQs.

However, if you are still using old edge-triggered devices, select **Edge** to force the chipset to allow only edge-triggering of PCI devices. This may cause configuration problems if there are IRQ conflicts, but it prevents system lockups that can occur if the chipset erroneously attempts to level-trigger an edge-triggered PCI device.

PCI Latency Timer

Common Options: 0–255

This BIOS feature controls how long a PCI device can hold the PCI bus before another takes over. The longer the latency, the longer the PCI device can retain control of the bus before handing it over to another PCI device.

Normally, the PCI Latency Timer is set to **32 cycles**. This means the active PCI device has to complete its transactions within 32 clock cycles or hand it over to the next PCI device.

For better PCI performance, a longer latency should be used. Try increasing it to **64 cycles** or even **128 cycles**. The optimal value for every system is different. You should benchmark your PCI cards' performance after each change to determine the optimal PCI latency time for your system.

Please note that a longer PCI latency isn't necessarily better. A long latency can also reduce performance as the other PCI devices queuing up may be stalled for too long. This is especially true with systems with many PCI devices or PCI devices that continuously write short bursts of data to the PCI bus. Such systems work better with shorter PCI latencies because they allow rapid access to the PCI bus.

In addition, some time-critical PCI devices may not agree with a long latency. Such devices require priority access to the PCI bus, which may not be possible if the PCI bus is held up by another device for a long period. In such cases, it is recommended that you keep to the default PCI latency of **32 cycles**.

PCI Master 0 WS Read

Common Options: Enabled, Disabled

This BIOS feature determines whether the chipset inserts a delay before any reads from the PCI bus.

If **PCI Master 0 WS Read** is **enabled**, read requests to the PCI bus are executed immediately (with zero wait states), if the PCI bus is ready to send data.

If PCI Master 0 WS Read is **disabled**, every read request to the PCI bus is delayed by one wait state.

It is recommended that you **enable** this feature for better PCI read performance.

However, **disabling** it may be useful if you are attempting to stabilize an overclocked PCI bus. The delay generally improves the overclockability and stability of the PCI bus.

P

PCI Master 0 WS Write

Common Options: Enabled, Disabled

This BIOS feature determines whether the chipset inserts a delay before any writes from the PCI bus.

If **PCI Master 0 WS Write** is **enabled**, write requests to the PCI bus are executed immediately (with zero wait states), if the PCI bus is ready to send data.

If PCI Master 0 WS Write is **disabled**, every write request to the PCI bus is delayed by one wait state.

It is recommended that you **enable** this feature for better PCI write performance.

However, **disabling** it may be useful if you are attempting to stabilize an overclocked PCI bus. The delay generally improves the overclockability and stability of the PCI bus.

PCI Master Read Caching

Common Options: Enabled, Disabled

This is an AMD-specific BIOS feature. It determines whether the processor's L2 cache is used to cache PCI bus master reads.

If this feature is **enabled**, the processor's L2 cache is used to cache PCI bus master reads. This boosts the performance of PCI bus masters. On the other hand, it reduces the processor's performance because it uses up some of the precious L2 cache.

This is why motherboard manufacturers like ASUS recommend that only systems using AMD Athlon processors should **enable** this feature. Duron users should **disable** this feature because its small L2 cache is not able to cache the PCI reads without causing a massive hit to memory bandwidth.

Although the final word is still in the air, I recommend **disabling** this feature. The use of precious L2 cache to cache PCI bus masters is not worth the potential benefit in PCI bus performance.

PCI Pipelining

Common Options: Enabled, Disabled

This BIOS feature determines if PCI transactions to the memory subsystem are pipelined.

If the PCI pipeline feature is **enabled**, the memory controller allows PCI transactions to be pipelined. This masks the latency of each PCI transaction and improves the efficiency of the PCI bus.

If the PCI pipeline feature is **disabled**, the memory controller is forced to check for outstanding transactions from other devices to the same block address that each PCI transaction is targeting.

For better PCI performance, the PCI pipeline should be **enabled**. This allows the latency of the bus to be masked for consecutive transactions.

However, if your system constantly locks up for no apparent reason, try **disabling** this feature. Disabling PCI Pipelining reduces performance but ensures that data coherency is strictly maintained for maximum reliability.

PCI Prefetch

Common Options: Enabled, Disabled

This feature controls the system controller's PCI prefetch capability.

When **enabled**, the system controller prefetches data whenever the PCI device reads from the system memory. This speeds up PCI reads because it allows contiguous memory reads by the PCI device to proceed with minimal delay.

Therefore, it is recommended that you **enable** this feature for better PCI read performance.

PCI Target Latency

Common Options: Enabled, Disabled

This BIOS feature determines whether the system controller should conform to the PCI maximum target latency rule.

When this feature is **enabled**, the system controller disconnects the PCI bus master if it cannot service a read request within 32 PCI clock cycles for the initial read and 8 PCI clock cycles for subsequent reads. The PCI bus master then rearbitrates for access to the PCI bus.

When this feature is **disabled**, the PCI bus master is *not* disconnected if it cannot service a read request within the stipulated 32 PCI clock cycles for the initial read and 8 PCI clock cycles for subsequent reads. The PCI bus master is allowed to complete its transactions.

It is recommended that you **enable** this feature to enforce the PCI maximum target latency rule and prevent potential deadlocks.

PCI to DRAM Prefetch

Common Options: Enabled, Disabled

This feature controls the system controller's PCI prefetch capability.

When **enabled**, the system controller prefetches data whenever the PCI device reads from the system memory. This speeds up PCI reads because it allows contiguous memory reads by the PCI device to proceed with minimal delay.

Therefore, it is recommended that you **enable** this feature for better PCI read performance.

PCI/VGA Palette Snoop

Common Options: Enabled, Disabled

This BIOS feature determines whether your graphics card should allow VGA palette snooping by a fixed function display card. It is only useful if you use a fixed-function display card that requires a VGA-compatible graphics card to be present (for example, MPEG decoder card).

Such fixed-function display cards generally do not have their own VGA palette. So, they have to "snoop" VGA palette data from the graphics card to generate the proper colors. Normally, the graphics card's Feature Connector is used for this purpose.

When this feature is **enabled**, the graphics card does not respond to framebuffer writes. It forwards them to the fixed-function display card through its Feature Connector. The fixed-function display card then snoops the palette data and generates the proper colors.

When this feature is **disabled**, the graphics card displays all framebuffer writes.

It is recommended that you **disable** this feature if you do not use any fixed-function display card like an MPEG decoder card.

However, if you are using a fixed-function display card that requires palette snooping, enable this feature. Otherwise, the colors displayed may not be accurate and the monitor will blank out once you stop using the fixed-function display card.

P

PIO Mode

Common Options: Auto, 0, 1, 2, 3, 4

This BIOS feature allows you to set the **PIO (Programmed Input/Output)** mode for the IDE drive.

Setting this BIOS feature to **Auto** lets the BIOS auto-detect the IDE drive's maximum supported PIO mode at boot-up.

Setting this BIOS feature to **0** forces the BIOS to use **PIO Mode 0** for the IDE drive.

Setting this BIOS feature to **1** forces the BIOS to use **PIO Mode 1** for the IDE drive.

Setting this BIOS feature to **2** forces the BIOS to use **PIO Mode 2** for the IDE drive.

Setting this BIOS feature to **3** forces the BIOS to use **PIO Mode 3** for the IDE drive.

Setting this BIOS feature to **4** forces the BIOS to use **PIO Mode 4** for the IDE drive.

Normally, you should leave it as **Auto** and let the BIOS auto-detect the IDE drive's PIO mode. You should only set it manually for the following reasons:

- If the BIOS cannot detect the correct PIO mode.
- If you want to try forcing the IDE device to use a faster PIO mode than it was designed for.
- If you want to force the IDE device to use a slower PIO mode if it cannot work properly with the current PIO mode (for example, when the PCI bus is overclocked).

Please note that forcing an IDE device to use a PIO transfer rate that is faster than what it is rated for can potentially cause data corruption.

PIRQ x Use IRQ No.

Common Options: Auto, 3, 4, 5, 7, 9, 10, 11, 12, 14, 15

This BIOS feature allows you to manually set the IRQ for a particular device installed on the AGP and PCI buses.

It is especially useful when you are transferring a hard disk from one computer to another, and you don't want to reinstall your operating system to redetect the IRQ settings. By setting the IRQs to fit the original settings, you can circumvent a lot of configuration problems after installing the hard disk in a new system. However, this is only true for non-ACPI systems.

Here are some important notes from the reference motherboard (may vary between motherboards):

- If you specify a particular IRQ here, you can't specify the same IRQ for the ISA bus. If you do, you will cause a hardware conflict.
- Each PCI slot is capable of activating up to 4 interrupts: INT A, INT B, INT C and INT D.
- The AGP slot is capable of activating up to 2 interrupts: INT A and INT B.

Normally, each slot is allocated INT A. The other interrupts are reserves and used only when the PCI/AGP device requires more than one IRQ or if the IRQ requested has been used up.

The AGP slot and PCI slot #1 share the same IRQ.

PCI slot #4 and #5 share the same IRQs.

USB uses PIRQ_4.

The following table shows the relationship between PIRQ (Programmable Interrupt Request) signals and INT in the reference motherboard:

Signals	AGP Slot PCI Slot 1	PCI Slot 2	PCI Slot 3	PCI Slot 4 PCI Slot 5
PIRQ_0	**INT A**	INT D	INT C	INT B
PIRQ_1	INT B	**INT A**	INT D	INT C
PIRQ_2	INT C	INT B	**INT A**	INT D
PIRQ_3	INT D	INT C	INT B	**INT A**

You will notice that the interrupts are staggered, so conflicts do not happen easily.

Even then, you should try not to use up paired slots that share the same set of IRQs. In such cases, it is recommended that you use only one of the two slots.

In most cases, you should just leave the setting as **Auto**. This allows the motherboard to assign the IRQs automatically. However, if you need to assign a particular IRQ to a device on the AGP or PCI bus, here is how you can make use of this BIOS feature.

1. Determine the slot in which the device is located.

2. Check your motherboard's **PIRQ table** (in the manual) to determine the slot's primary PIRQ.

3. You then select the IRQ you want by assigning the IRQ to the appropriate PIRQ.

Just remember that the BIOS always tries to allocate the PIRQ linked to INT A for each slot. It is just a matter of linking the IRQ you want to the correct PIRQ for that slot.

Please note the table, notes, and INT details are only examples provided by the reference motherboard. They may vary between motherboards.

PNP OS Installed

Common Options: Yes, No

What this BIOS feature actually does is determine what devices are configured by the BIOS when the computer boots up and what are left to the operating system.

Non-ACPI BIOSes are found in older motherboards that do not support the new **ACPI** (**Advanced Configuration and Power Interface**) initiative. With such a BIOS, setting the PNP OS Installed feature to **No** allows the BIOS to configure all devices under the assumption that the operating system cannot do so. Therefore, all hardware settings are fixed by the BIOS at boot up and are not changed by the operating system.

On the other hand, if you set the feature to **Yes**, the BIOS only configures critical devices that are required to boot up the system. The other devices are then configured by the operating system. This allows the operating system some flexibility in shuffling system resources like IRQs and IO ports to avoid conflicts. It also gives you some degree of freedom when you want to manually assign system resources.

Of course, all current motherboards now ship with the new **ACPI BIOS**. If you are using an ACPI-compliant operating system (for example, Windows 98 and above) with an ACPI BIOS, then this PNP OS Installed feature is no longer relevant. This is because the operating system uses the ACPI BIOS interface to configure all devices as well as retrieve system information.

However, if your operating system does not support ACPI, then the BIOS falls back to PNP mode. In this situation, consider the BIOS as you would a **Non-ACPI BIOS**. If there is no need to configure any hardware manually, it is again recommended that you set this feature to **No**.

Linux is not really PnP-compatible, but most distributions use a software called ISAP-NPTOOLS to set up ISA cards. If PnP OS is set to **No**, the BIOS will attempt to configure the ISA cards, but that won't work with Linux. Worse, if ISAPNPTOOLS is used to configure the ISA cards as well, it may lead to conflicts between the two.

Therefore, it is recommended that you set PnP OS to **Yes** in Linux and allow ISAPNPTOOLS to handle the task instead.

As far as OS/2 is concerned, PnP OS should be set to **No**, especially in a multi-boot system. In addition, if you add or change hardware, you should enable full hardware detection during the initial boot sequence of OS/2.

To sum it all up, except for certain cases, it is highly recommended that you set this BIOS feature to **No**, irrespective of the operating system you actually use. Exceptions to this would be the inability of the BIOS to configure the devices properly in PnP mode and a specific need to manually configure one or more of the devices.

Post Write Combine

Common Options: Enabled, Disabled

This BIOS feature allows you to control the **USWC (Uncached Speculative Write Combining)** write combine buffers.

If **enabled**, the write combine buffers accumulate and combine partial or smaller graphics writes from the processor and write them to the graphics card as burst writes.

If **disabled**, the write combine buffers are disabled. All graphics writes from the processor are written to the graphics card directly.

It is highly recommended that you **enable** this feature for improved graphics and processor performance.

However, if you are using an older graphics card, it may not be compatible with this feature. Enabling this feature with such graphics cards causes a host of problems like graphics artifacts, system crashes, and even the inability to boot up properly.

If you face such problems, you should **disable** this BIOS feature immediately.

Power On Function

Common Options: Button Only, Keyboard 98, Hot Key, Mouse Left, Mouse Right

This BIOS feature allows you to select the method to turn on your computer.

By default, this feature is set to **Button Only**. This allows your computer to be started up only through the use of the power button or switch. Other available options:

A *Keyboard 98*-compatible keyboard (which comes with a wake-up button)

A keyboard hot key (for non-Keyboard 98 keyboards)

A mouse button (either the right or left button)

If you select the **Mouse Left** option, the left button of the mouse is used to start up the system. The **Mouse Right** option selects the right mouse button as the power on button instead.

Please note that only PS/2 mice support the **Mouse Left** or **Mouse Right** options. Mice using serial or USB connections do not support this power on function.

The **Keyboard 98** option only works if you are using Windows 98 or better and have the appropriate keyboard. Then you can use the keyboard's wake-up or power-on button to start up the computer.

Older keyboards that do not conform to the *Keyboard 98* standard, and therefore do not have the special wake-up button, can use the **Hot Key** option instead. There are 12 hot keys available: **Ctrl-F1** through **Ctrl-F12**. Select the hot key you want and you are able to start up the computer using that hot key.

There is no performance advantage in choosing any of the options above. So, choose the option that you are most comfortable with.

Primary Graphics Adapter

Common Options: AGP, PCI

This BIOS feature allows you to select whether to boot the system using the AGP graphics card or the PCI graphics card. This is particularly important if you have AGP and PCI graphics cards but only one monitor.

If you are only using a single graphics card, then the BIOS detects it as such and boots it up, irrespective of what you set the feature to. However, there may be a slight reduction in the time taken to detect and initialize the card if you select the proper setting for this BIOS feature. For example, if you only use an AGP graphics card, then setting Primary Graphics Adapter to **AGP** may speed up your system's booting-up process.

Therefore, if you are only using a single graphics card, it is recommended that you set the Primary Graphics Adapter feature to the proper setting for your system (**AGP** for a single AGP card and **PCI** for a single PCI card).

However, if you are using multiple graphics cards, it is up to you which card you want to use as your primary display card. It is recommended that you select the fastest graphics card as the primary display card.

Primary VGA BIOS

Common Options: AGP VGA Card, PCI VGA Card

This BIOS feature allows you to select whether to boot the system using the AGP graphics card or the PCI graphics card. This is particularly important if you have AGP and PCI graphics cards but only one monitor.

If you are only using a single graphics card, then the BIOS detects it as such and boots it up, irrespective of what you set the feature to. However, there may be a slight reduction in the time taken to detect and initialize the card if you select the proper setting for this BIOS feature. For example, if you only use an AGP graphics card, then setting Primary VGA BIOS to **AGP VGA Card** may speed up your system's booting-up process.

Therefore, if you are only using a single graphics card, it is recommended that you set the Primary VGA BIOS feature to the proper setting for your system (**AGP VGA Card** for a single AGP card and **PCI VGA Card** for a single PCI card).

However, if you are using multiple graphics cards, it is up to you which card you want to use as your primary display card. It is recommended that you select the fastest graphics card as the primary display card.

Processor Number Feature

Common Options: Enabled, Disabled

This BIOS feature allows you to control the use of the processor's embedded **unique identification number**. Therefore, it is only valid if you are using a processor that features such a feature.

This infamous "feature" debuted in the Intel Pentium III processor and is mainly found only in that processor. The Transmeta Crusoe processor also supports this feature. But most manufacturers have refrained from integrating such a feature in their processors. Even Intel has declined to add this feature to the Intel Pentium 4 processors.

If **enabled**, the processor's identification number can be read by external programs. It used to be required for certain secure transactions. However, this is no longer true because the initiative has long been abandoned.

If **disabled**, the processor's identification number cannot be read by external programs.

It is highly advisable that you **disable** this feature because it no longer has a use. Even worse, it can actually be misused to track your online activities. Disabling this feature safeguards your privacy by preventing the identification of your computer by the processor's identification number.

PS/2 Mouse Function Control

Common Options: Enabled, Auto

IRQ12 is the interrupt usually reserved for the PS/2 mouse's use. This BIOS feature determines whether the BIOS should reserve IRQ12 for the PS/2 mouse or allow other devices to make use of this IRQ.

Setting this BIOS feature to **Auto** allows the BIOS to allocate IRQ12 to the PS/2 mouse if the mouse is detected at startup. Otherwise, IRQ12 is released for use by other devices in the system.

Setting this BIOS feature to **Enabled** forces the BIOS to reserve IRQ12 even if a PS/2 mouse was not detected at startup.

It is recommended that you leave this BIOS feature at its default setting of **Auto**. This allows your BIOS to release IRQ12 for other devices to use if it doesn't detect the presence of a PS/2 mouse during startup.

P

Q

Quick Boot

Common Options: Enabled, Disabled

This BIOS feature allows you to decrease the time it takes to boot up the computer by shortening or skipping certain standard booting procedures.

If **enabled**, the BIOS shortens the booting process by skipping some tests and shortening others. In addition, it also performs the following tricks to further speed up the booting process:

- Spin up the hard disks as soon as power is supplied (or as soon as possible)
- Initialize only critical parts of the chipset
- Read memory size from the **SPD** (**Serial Presence Detect**) chip on the memory modules
- Eliminate logo delays (inserted by many manufacturers)

If **disabled**, the BIOS runs the whole gamut of boot-up tests.

It is recommended that you **disable** this feature when you boot up a new computer for the first time or whenever you install a new piece of hardware. This allows the BIOS to run full diagnostic tests to detect any problems that may slip past Quick Boot's abbreviated testing scheme.

After a few error-free test runs, you should **enable** this feature for much faster booting.

Quick Power On Self Test

Common Options: Enabled, Disabled

This BIOS feature allows you to decrease the time it takes to boot up the computer by shortening or skipping certain standard booting procedures.

If **enabled**, the BIOS shortens the booting process by skipping some tests and shortening others.

If **disabled**, the BIOS runs the whole gamut of boot-up tests.

It is recommended that you **disable** this feature when you boot up a new computer for the first time or whenever you install a new piece of hardware. This allows the BIOS to run full diagnostic tests to detect any problems that may slip past the abbreviated testing scheme.

After a few error-free test runs, you should **enable** this feature for much faster booting.

R

Rank Interleave

Common Options: Enabled, Disabled

This BIOS feature is similar to **SDRAM Bank Interleave**. Interleaving allows banks of SDRAM to alternate their refresh and access cycles. One bank undergoes its refresh cycle while another is being accessed. This improves memory performance by masking the refresh cycles of each memory bank. The only difference is that **Rank Interleave** works between different physical banks or, as they are called now, **ranks**.

Because a minimum of two ranks are required for interleaving to be supported, double-sided memory modules are a must if you wish to enable Rank Interleave. Enabling Rank Interleave with single-sided memory modules does not result in any performance boost.

It is highly recommended that you **enable** Rank Interleave for better memory performance. You can also **enable** Rank Interleave if you are using a mixture of single- and double-sided memory modules. However, if you are using only single-sided memory modules, it's advisable to **disable** Rank Interleave.

Read-Around-Write

Common Options: Enabled, Disabled

This BIOS feature allows the processor to execute read commands out of order as if they are independent from the write commands. It does this by using a **Read-Around-Write** buffer.

If this BIOS feature is **enabled**, all processor writes to memory are first accumulated in that buffer. This allows the processor to execute read commands without waiting for the write commands to be completed.

The buffer then combines the writes and writes them to memory as burst transfers. This reduces the number of writes to memory and boosts the processor's write performance.

If this BIOS feature is **disabled**, the processor writes directly to the memory controller. This reduces the processor's read performance.

Therefore, it is highly recommended that you **enable** this feature for better processor read and write performance.

Read Wait State

Common Options: 0 Cycle, 1 Cycle

This BIOS feature determines how long the memory controller should wait before sending read data to the data requester (for example, processor, graphics card, and so forth).

If this feature is set to **1 Cycle**, the memory controller imposes a delay of **one clock cycle** before the data is sent to the requester. This reduces memory read performance because the memory controller delays the transfer of each piece of requested data by one clock cycle.

If this feature is set to **0 Cycle**, the memory controller transfers read data to the data requester without any delay.

Therefore, it is recommended that you set the Read Wait State to **0 Cycle** for better memory read and write performance.

Please note that this may cause system instabilities in certain configurations. When that happens, just reset the value to **1 Cycle**.

Refresh Interval

Common Options: 7.8 μsec, 15.6 μsec, 31.2 μsec, 64 μsec, 128 μsec, Auto

This BIOS feature allows you to set the refresh interval of the memory chips. There are three different settings as well as an **Auto** option. If the **Auto** option is selected, the BIOS queries the memory modules' SPD chips and uses the lowest setting found for maximum compatibility.

For better performance, you should consider increasing the **Refresh Interval** from the default values (15.6 μsec for 128Mbit or smaller memory chips and 7.8 μsec for 256Mbit or larger memory chips) up to **128 μsec**. Please note that if you increase the **Refresh Interval** too much, the memory cells may lose their contents.

Therefore, you should start with small increases in the **Refresh Interval** and test your system after each hike before increasing it further. If you face stability problems upon increasing the refresh interval, reduce the refresh interval step by step until the system is stable.

Refresh Mode Select

Common Options: 7.8 μsec, 15.6 μsec, 31.2 μsec, 64 μsec, 128 μsec, Auto

This BIOS feature allows you to set the refresh interval of the memory chips. There are three different settings as well as an **Auto** option. If the **Auto** option is selected, the BIOS queries the memory modules' SPD chips and uses the lowest setting found for maximum compatibility.

For better performance, you should consider increasing the **Refresh Mode Select** from the default values (15.6 μsec for 128Mbit or smaller memory chips and 7.8 μsec for 256Mbit or larger memory chips) up to **128 μsec**. Please note that if you increase the **Refresh Mode Select** too much, the memory cells may lose their contents.

Therefore, you should start with small increases in the **Refresh Mode Select** and test your system after each hike before increasing it further. If you face stability problems upon increasing the refresh interval, reduce the refresh interval step by step until the system is stable.

Report No FDD For Win95

Common Options: Enabled, Disabled

This BIOS feature allows you to set whether the BIOS should report the absence of a floppy disk drive to Windows 95.

For some reason, the Microsoft Windows 95 operating system requires a floppy disk drive to be present. However, in an age of USB flash media and CD/DVD writers, not all computers come with a floppy disk drive. Such computers fail to boot up Windows 95 without a floppy disk drive.

If this feature is **enabled**, the BIOS assigns IRQ 6 to another device. This allows computers with no floppy disk drives to boot into Windows 95 normally.

If this feature is **disabled**, Windows 95 detects the absence of the floppy disk drive and halts the system with an error message.

If you are using Windows 95 *without* a floppy disk drive, you have to **enable** this feature to allow Windows 95 to boot up normally.

If you are using Windows 95 *with* a floppy disk drive, you can **enable** or **disable** this feature. Windows 95 boots up normally either way.

Please note that this BIOS feature has no relevance in other operating systems. Only Windows 95 is affected. It does not matter what you set this BIOS option to if you are using other operating systems.

Reset Configuration Data

Common Options: Enabled, Disabled

If you install a new piece of hardware or modify your computer's hardware configuration, the BIOS automatically detects the changes and reconfigures the **ESCD (Extended System Configuration Data)**. Therefore, there is usually no need to manually force the BIOS to reconfigure the ESCD.

However, the occasion may arise where the BIOS may not be able to detect the hardware changes. A serious resource conflict may occur and the operating system may not even boot as a result. This is where the **Reset Configuration Data** BIOS feature comes in.

This BIOS feature allows you to manually force the BIOS to clear the previously saved ESCD data and reconfigure the settings. All you need to do is **enable** this BIOS feature and then reboot your computer. The new ESCD should resolve the conflict and allow the operating system to load normally.

Please note that the BIOS automatically resets it to the default setting of **Disabled** after reconfiguring the new ESCD. So, there is no need for you to manually **disable** this feature after rebooting.

Resource Controlled By

Common Options: Auto, Manual

This BIOS feature determines whether the BIOS should automatically configure IRQ and DMA resources.

The BIOS is generally capable of automatically configuring IRQ and DMA resources for the devices in your computer. Therefore, it is advisable that you set this feature to **Auto**.

However, if the BIOS has problems assigning the resources properly, you can select the **Manual** option to reveal the IRQ and DMA assignment fields. You can then assign each IRQ or DMA channel to either **Legacy ISA** or **PCI/ISA PnP** devices.

Legacy ISA devices are compliant with the original PC AT bus specification and require a specific interrupt or DMA channel to function properly. **PCI/ISA PnP** devices, on the other hand, adhere to the Plug and Play standard and can use any interrupt or DMA channel.

RxD, TxD Active

Common Options: Hi, Hi or Lo, Lo or Hi, Lo or Lo, Hi

This BIOS feature allows you to set the infra-red reception (**RxD**) and transmission (**TxD**) polarity.

It is usually found under the **Onboard Serial Port 2** BIOS feature and is linked to the second serial port. So, if you disable that port, this feature disappears from the screen or appears grayed out.

There are four options available based on combinations of Hi and Lo. You'll need to consult your IR peripheral's documentation to determine the correct polarity. Choosing the wrong polarity prevents a proper IR connection from being established with the IR peripheral.

S

S2K Bus Driving Strength

Common Options: Auto, Manual

This BIOS feature determines whether the motherboard chipset should automatically adjust the drive strength of the Athlon processor bus or allow manual configuration.

If you set this feature to **Auto**, the chipset is allowed to dynamically adjust the S2K bus strength or use values pre-set by the manufacturer.

If you set this feature to **Manual**, the chipset's dynamic compensation circuitry for the S2K bus is turned off. You then can manually set the S2K bus strength.

Generally, it is recommended that you set this feature to **Auto**, so the S2K bus strength can be dynamically adjusted by the chipset. However, there may be occasions when manual configuration of the S2K bus driving strength may be desirable.

It is possible to make use of this feature for overclocking purposes. Increasing the drive strength increases the stability of the S2K bus. However, please be very circumspect when you increase the S2K bus drive strength with an overclocked processor because you may irreversibly damage the processor!

If you wish to manually configure the S2K bus driving strength, you must set the S2K Bus Driving Strength to **Manual**. This allows you to manually set the S2K bus driving strength value through the **S2K Strobe P Control** and **S2K Strobe N Control** BIOS features.

S2K Strobe N Control

Common Options: 0 to F (Hex numbers), 0h to Fh

This BIOS feature determines the N transistor drive strength of the S2K bus.

The N transistor drive strength is represented by Hex values from **0** to **F** (**0** to **15** in decimal). The default N transistor drive strength differs between motherboards. However, the higher the drive strength, the greater the compensation for the motherboard's impedance on the S2K bus.

Due to the nature of this BIOS feature, it is possible to use it as an aid in overclocking the S2K bus. A higher N (and P) transistor drive strength may be just what you need to overclock the S2K bus higher than is normally possible. By raising the drive strength of the S2K bus, you can improve its stability at overclocked speeds.

Please be very circumspect when you increase the S2K drive strength with an overclocked processor because you may irreversibly damage the processor!

Also, contrary to popular opinion, increasing the S2K drive strength does *not* improve the performance of your AMD processor. It is not a performance-enhancing feature, so you should not increase the N transistor drive strength unnecessarily.

S2K Strobe P Control

Common Options: 0 to F (Hex numbers), 0h to Fh

This BIOS feature determines the P transistor drive strength of the S2K bus.

The P transistor drive strength is represented by Hex values from **0** to **F** (**0** to **15** in decimal). The default P transistor drive strength differs between motherboards. However, the higher the drive strength, the greater the compensation for the motherboard's impedance on the S2K bus.

Due to the nature of this BIOS feature, it is possible to use it as an aid in overclocking the S2K bus. A higher P (and N) transistor drive strength may be just what you need to overclock the S2K bus higher than is normally possible. By raising the drive strength of the S2K bus, you can improve its stability at overclocked speeds.

Please be very circumspect when you increase the S2K drive strength with an overclocked processor because you may irreversibly damage the processor!

Also, contrary to popular opinion, increasing the S2K drive strength does *not* improve the performance of your AMD processor. It is not a performance-enhancing feature, so you should not increase the P transistor drive strength unnecessarily.

SDRAM 1T Command

Common Options: Enabled, Disabled, Auto

This BIOS feature allows you to select the delay between the assertion of the Chip Select signal until the time the memory controller starts sending commands to the memory bank. The lower the value, the sooner the memory controller can send commands out to the activated memory bank.

When this feature is **enabled**, the memory controller only inserts a command delay of one clock cycle or 1T.

When this feature is **disabled**, the memory controller inserts a command delay of two clock cycles or 2T.

The **Auto** option allows the memory controller to use the memory module's SPD value for command delay.

If the SDRAM command delay is too long, it can reduce performance by unnecessarily preventing the memory controller from issuing the commands sooner.

However, if the SDRAM command delay is too short, the memory controller may not be able to translate the addresses in time and the "bad commands" that result cause data loss and corruption.

It is recommended that you **enable** SDRAM 1T Command for better memory performance. However, if you face stability issues, disable this BIOS feature.

SDRAM 1T Command Control

Common Options: Enabled, Disabled, Auto

This BIOS feature allows you to select the delay between the assertion of the Chip Select signal until the time the memory controller starts sending commands to the memory bank. The lower the value, the sooner the memory controller can send commands out to the activated memory bank.

When this feature is **enabled**, the memory controller inserts a command delay of only one clock cycle or 1T.

When this feature is **disabled**, the memory controller inserts a command delay of two clock cycles or 2T.

The **Auto** option allows the memory controller to use the memory module's SPD value for command delay.

If the SDRAM command delay is too long, it can reduce performance by unnecessarily preventing the memory controller from issuing the commands sooner.

However, if the SDRAM command delay is too short, the memory controller may not be able to translate the addresses in time and the "bad commands" that result cause data loss and corruption.

It is recommended that you **enable** SDRAM 1T Command Control for better memory performance. However, if you face stability issues, disable this BIOS feature.

SDRAM Active to Precharge Delay

Common Options: 4, 5, 6, 7, 8, 9

Like **DRAM Act to PreChrg CMD**, this BIOS feature controls the memory bank's minimum row active time (**tRAS**). This constitutes the time when a row is activated until the time the same row can be deactivated.

If the tRAS period is too long, it can reduce performance by unnecessarily delaying the deactivation of active rows. Reducing the tRAS period allows the active row to be deactivated earlier.

However, if the tRAS period is too short, there may not be enough time to complete a burst transfer. This reduces performance, and data may be lost or corrupted.

For optimal performance, use the lowest value you can. Usually, this should be **CAS latency + tRCD + 2 clock cycles**. For example, if you set the CAS latency to 2 clock cycles and the tRCD to 3 clock cycles, the optimum tRAS value would be 7 clock cycles.

But if you start getting memory errors or system crashes, increase the tRAS value one clock cycle at a time until your system becomes stable.

SDRAM Bank Interleave

Common Options: 2-Bank, 4-Bank, Disabled

This BIOS feature enables you to set the interleave mode of the SDRAM interface.

Interleaving allows banks of SDRAM to alternate their refresh and access cycles. One bank undergoes its refresh cycle while another is being accessed. This improves memory performance by masking the refresh cycles of each memory bank. A close examination reveals that, because the refresh cycles of all the memory banks are staggered, this produces a kind of pipelining effect.

However, bank interleaving only works if the addresses requested consecutively are not in the same bank. If they are in the same memory bank, then the data transactions behave as if the banks were not interleaved. The processor has to wait until the first data transaction clears and that memory bank refreshes before it can send another address to that bank.

Each SDRAM module is internally divided into either **two** or **four** banks of memory. Double-banked SDRAM modules generally use **16Mbit** SDRAM chips and are usually **32MB** or smaller in size. Quad-banked SDRAM modules, on the other hand, usually use higher density (**64Mbit-256Mbit**) SDRAM chips. All SDRAM modules of at least **64MB** in size are quad-banked in nature.

If you are using a *single* double-banked SDRAM module, set this feature to **2-Bank**. This is the only option available for the single double-banked SDRAM module.

If you are using at least *two* double-banked SDRAM modules, you can use the **4-Bank** option as well as the **2-Bank** option. Of course, it is recommended that you select **4-Bank** for better interleaving performance.

If you are using quad-banked SDRAM modules, you can use either interleave options. Of course, it is recommended that you select **4-Bank** for better interleaving performance.

Because a 4-bank interleave always allows for better interleaving performance, it is highly recommended that you select the **4-Bank** option if your system supports it. Use the **2-Bank** option only if you are using a single double-banked SDRAM module.

Please note that **Award** (now part of **Phoenix Technologies**) recommends that SDRAM bank interleaving be **disabled** if **16Mbit** SDRAM modules are used. This is because early 16Mbit SDRAM modules have stability problems with bank interleaving. The good news is all current SDRAM modules support bank interleaving.

SDRAM Bank-to-Bank Delay

Common Options: 2 cycles, 3 cycles

This BIOS feature specifies the minimum amount of time between successive ACTIVATE commands to the **same** DDR device. The shorter the delay, the faster the next bank can be activated for read or write operations. However, because row activation requires a lot of current, using a short delay may cause excessive current surges.

For desktop PCs, a delay of **2 cycles** is recommended because current surges aren't really important. The performance benefit of using the shorter 2 cycles delay is of far greater interest. The shorter delay means every back-to-back bank activation take one clock cycle less to perform. This improves the DDR device's read and write performance.

Switch to **3 cycles** only when there are stability problems with the 2 cycles setting.

SDRAM Burst Len

Common Options: 4, 8

This BIOS feature allows you to control the length of a burst transaction.

When this feature is set to **4**, a burst transaction can only be comprised of up to **four** reads or **four** writes.

When this feature is set to **8**, a burst transaction can only be comprised of up to **eight** reads or **eight** writes.

As the initial CAS latency is fixed for each burst transaction, a longer burst transaction allows more data to be read or written for less delay than a shorter burst transaction. Therefore, a burst length of 8 is faster than a burst length of 4.

Therefore, it is recommended that you select the longer burst length of **8** for better performance.

SDRAM Burst Length

Common Options: 4, 8

This BIOS feature allows you to control the length of a burst transaction.

When this feature is set to **4**, a burst transaction can only be comprised of up to **four** reads or **four** writes.

When this feature is set to **8**, a burst transaction can only be comprised of up to **eight** reads or **eight** writes.

As the initial CAS latency is fixed for each burst transaction, a longer burst transaction allows more data to be read or written for less delay than a shorter burst transaction. Therefore, a burst length of 8 is faster than a burst length of 4.

Therefore, it is recommended that you select the longer burst length of **8** for better performance.

SDRAM CAS Latency Time

S

Common Options: 2, 3 (SDR memory) or 1.5, 2, 2.5, 3 (DDR memory)

This BIOS feature controls the delay (in clock cycles) between the assertion of the CAS signal and the availability of the data from the target memory cell. It also determines the number of clock cycles required for the completion of the first part of a burst transfer. In other words, the lower the CAS latency, the faster memory reads or writes can occur.

Please note that some memory modules may not be able to handle the lower latency and may lose data. Therefore, while it is recommended that you reduce the **SDRAM CAS Latency Time** to 2 or 2.5 clock cycles for better memory performance, you should increase it if your system becomes unstable.

Interestingly, increasing the CAS latency time often allows the memory module to run at a higher clock speed. So, if you hit a snag while overclocking your SDRAM modules, try increasing the CAS latency time.

SDRAM Command Leadoff Time

Common Options: 3, 4

By definition, the command leadoff time is the period between the assertion of the address/command lines and the activation of the target memory bank. This BIOS feature allows you to adjust the command leadoff time to meet timing variances of the motherboard as well as the memory module.

The shorter the leadoff time, the earlier the target bank can be activated. This allows faster access to the data in the memory module. Therefore, it is recommended that you set the SDRAM Command Leadoff Time to **3 clock cycles** for better memory performance.

However, your motherboard and memory combination may not be able to support the tighter command leadoff time of 3 clock cycles. If your system becomes unstable with a command leadoff time of 3 clock cycles, revert to the slower command leadoff time of **4** clock cycles.

SDRAM Command Rate

Common Options: 1T, 2T

This BIOS feature allows you to select the delay between the assertion of the Chip Select signal until the time the memory controller starts sending commands to the memory bank. The lower the value, the sooner the memory controller can send commands out to the activated memory bank.

If the SDRAM command delay is too long, it can reduce performance by unnecessarily preventing the memory controller from issuing the commands sooner.

However, if the SDRAM command delay is too short, the memory controller may not be able to translate the addresses in time and the "bad commands" that result cause data loss and corruption.

It is recommended that you try the 1T command delay for better memory performance. However, if you face stability issues, increase the command delay to 2T.

SDRAM Cycle Length

Common Options: 2, 3 (SDR memory) or 1.5, 2, 2.5, 3 (DDR memory)

This BIOS feature is the same as the **SDRAM CAS Latency Time** BIOS feature. It controls the delay (in clock cycles) between the assertion of the CAS signal and the availability of the data from the target memory cell. It also determines the number of clock cycles required for the completion of the first part of a burst transfer. In other words, the lower the CAS latency, the faster memory reads or writes can occur.

Please note that some memory modules may not be able to handle the lower latency and may lose data. Therefore, while it is recommended that you reduce the **SDRAM CAS Latency Time** to **2** or **2.5** clock cycles for better memory performance, you should increase it if your system becomes unstable.

Interestingly, increasing the CAS latency time often allows the memory module to run at a higher clock speed. So, if you hit a snag while overclocking your SDRAM modules, try increasing the CAS latency time.

SDRAM Cycle Time Tras/Trc

Common Options: 5/6, 6/8

This BIOS feature determines the **tRAS** and the **tRC** parameters of the SDRAM memory module.

tRAS refers to the SDRAM **Row Active Time**, which is the length of time the row remains open for data transfers.

tRC, on the other hand, refers to the SDRAM **Row Cycle Time**, which determines the minimum number of clock cycles a memory row takes to complete a full cycle, from row activation up to the precharging of the active row.

The default setting is **6/8**, which is more stable and slower than **5/6**. The **5/6** setting cycles faster, but it may not leave the row open long enough for burst transactions to complete. When this happens, data may be lost and the contents of the memory cells may be corrupted.

For better memory performance, you should try the **5/6** setting. However, increase it to **6/8** if your system becomes unstable.

SDRAM ECC Setting

Common Options: Disabled, Check Only, Correct Errors, Correct+Scrub

This BIOS feature is the extended version of the **DRAM Data Integrity Mode** BIOS feature. It is found in newer chipsets that support more than just simple **ECC** (**Error Checking and Correction**).

The first mode is **Disabled**, which disables the memory controller's ECC capabilities. If you are *not* using ECC memory modules, you must select this option.

The **Check Only** mode forces the memory controller to only check for errors. The memory controller detects and reports single- and double-bit errors, but it does *not* correct them. This mode offers minimal performance degradation but doesn't improve data integrity at all.

If you select the **Correct Errors** mode, the memory controller not only checks for and detects single- and double-bit errors, it also corrects single-bit errors. This mode has a higher overhead. The plus side is it improves data integrity by seamlessly correcting single-bit errors.

The final ECC mode is **Correct+Scrub**. With this mode enabled, the memory controller not only detects multiple-bit errors and correct single-bit errors, it also writes the corrected single-bit value back into memory! However, the scrubbing operation results in even more overhead.

Generally speaking, the **Check Only** mode isn't particularly useful because it only offers error checking and reporting. Users of ECC memory modules should focus mainly on the **Correct Errors** and **Correct+Scrub** modes because they actually improve data integrity by correcting single-bit errors. Of course, if you are using normal, non-ECC memory modules, you must select the **Disabled** mode!

For more information on how ECC works, please refer the **DRAM Data Integrity Mode** BIOS feature.

SDRAM Idle Limit

Common Options: Disabled, 0 Cycle, 8 Cycles, 12 Cycles, 16 Cycles, 24 Cycles, 32 Cycles, 48 Cycles

This BIOS feature sets the number of idle cycles allowed before the memory controller forces such open pages to close and precharge.

The premise behind this BIOS feature is the concept of **temporal locality**. According to this concept, the longer the open page is left idle, the less likely it will be accessed again before it needs to be precharged. Therefore, it is better to prematurely close and precharge the page, so it can be opened quickly when a data request comes along.

It can be set to a variety of clock cycles from **0 Cycle** to **48 Cycles**. This sets the number of clock cycles the open pages are allowed to idle before they are closed and precharged. There's also a **Disabled** option.

If you select **0 Cycle**, then the memory controller immediately precharges the open pages as soon as there's an idle cycle.

If you select **Disabled**, the memory controller never precharges the open pages prematurely. The open pages are left activated until they have to be precharged.

The default value is **8 cycles**, which allows the memory controller to precharge the open pages once eight idle cycles have passed.

For general desktop use, it is recommended that you **disable** this feature, so precharging can be delayed for as long as possible. This reduces the number of refreshes and increases the effective memory bandwidth.

For applications (for example, servers) that perform a lot of random accesses, it is advisable that you select **0 Cycle** as subsequent data requests are most likely fulfilled by other pages. Closing open pages to precharge prepares those pages for the next data request that hits them. There's also the added benefit of increased data integrity due to more frequent refreshes.

SDRAM Leadoff Command

Common Options: 3, 4

This BIOS feature is actually a misnomer. It should actually be called the **SDRAM Command Leadoff Time**.

By definition, the **command leadoff time** is the period between the assertion of the address/command lines and the activation of the target memory bank. This BIOS feature allows you to adjust the command leadoff time to meet timing variances of the motherboard as well as the memory module.

The shorter the leadoff time, the earlier the target bank can be activated. This allows faster access to the data in the memory module. Therefore, it is recommended that you set the SDRAM Leadoff Command to **3 clock cycles** for better memory performance.

However, your motherboard and memory combination may not be able to support the tighter command leadoff time of 3 clock cycles. If your system becomes unstable with a command leadoff time of 3 clock cycles, revert to the slower command leadoff time of **4** clock cycles.

SDRAM Page Closing Policy

Common Options: One Bank, All Banks

This BIOS feature is similar to **SDRAM Precharge Control**.

This BIOS feature determines whether the chipset should try to leave the pages open (by closing just one open page) or try to keep them closed (by closing all open pages) whenever there is a page miss.

The **One Bank** setting forces the memory controller to close only one page whenever a page miss occurs. This allows the other open pages to be accessed at the cost of only one clock cycle.

However, when a page miss occurs, there is a chance that subsequent data requests result in page misses as well. In long memory reads that cannot be satisfied by any of the open pages, this may cause up to *four* full latency reads to occur.

The **All Banks** setting, on the other hand, forces the memory controller to send an **All Banks Precharge Command** to the SDRAM interface whenever there is a page miss. This causes all the open pages to close (precharge). Therefore, subsequent reads only need to activate the necessary memory bank. This is useful in cases where subsequent data requests also result in page misses.

As you can see, both settings have their advantages and disadvantages. However, you should see better performance with the **One Bank** setting because the open pages allow very fast accesses. The **All Banks** setting, however, has the advantage of keeping the memory contents refreshed more often. This improves data integrity, although it is only useful if you have chosen a SDRAM **refresh interval** that is longer than the standard 64 msec.

Therefore, it is recommended that you select the **One Bank** setting for better memory performance. The **All Banks** setting can improve data integrity, but if you are keeping the SDRAM refresh interval within specification, then it is of little use.

SDRAM Page Hit Limit

Common Options: 1 Cycle, 4 Cycles, 8 Cycles, 16 Cycles, 32 Cycles

This BIOS feature is designed to reduce the data starvation that occurs when pending non-page hit requests are unduly delayed. It does so by limiting the number of consecutive **page hit** requests that are processed by the memory controller before attending to a **non-page hit** request.

Generally, the default value of **8 Cycles** should provide a balance between performance and fair memory access to all devices. However, you can try using a higher value (**16 Cycles**) for better memory performance by giving priority to a larger number of consecutive page hit requests. A lower value is not advisable because this normally results in a higher number of page interruptions.

SDRAM PH Limit

Common Options: 1 Cycle, 4 Cycles, 8 Cycles, 16 Cycles, 32 Cycles

This BIOS feature is designed to reduce the data starvation that occurs when pending non-page hit requests are unduly delayed. It does so by limiting the number of consecutive **page hit** requests that are processed by the memory controller before attending to a **non-page hit** request.

Generally, the default value of **8 Cycles** should provide a balance between performance and fair memory access to all devices. However, you can try using a higher value (**16 Cycles**) for better memory performance by giving priority to a larger number of consecutive page hit requests. A lower value is not advisable because this normally results in a higher number of page interruptions.

SDRAM Precharge Control

Common Options: Enabled, Disabled

This BIOS feature is similar to **SDRAM Page Closing Policy**.

This BIOS feature determines whether the chipset should try to leave the pages open (by closing just one open page) or try to keep them closed (by closing all open pages) whenever there is a page miss.

When **enabled**, the memory controller only closes one page whenever a page miss occurs. This allows the other open pages to be accessed at the cost of only one clock cycle.

However, when a page miss occurs, there is a chance that subsequent data requests result in page misses as well. In long memory reads that cannot be satisfied by any of the open pages, this may cause up to *four* full latency reads to occur.

When **disabled**, the memory controller sends an **All Banks Precharge Command** to the SDRAM interface whenever there is a page miss. This causes all the open pages to close (precharge). Therefore, subsequent reads only need to activate the necessary memory bank. This is useful in cases where subsequent data requests also result in page misses.

As you can see, both settings have their advantages and disadvantages. However, you should see better performance with this feature **enabled** because the open pages allow very fast accesses. **Disabling** this feature, however, has the advantage of keeping the memory contents refreshed more often. This improves data integrity, although it is only useful if you have chosen a SDRAM **refresh interval** that is longer than the standard 64 msec.

Therefore, it is recommended that you **enable** this feature for better memory performance. **Disabling** this feature can improve data integrity, but if you are keeping the SDRAM refresh interval within specification, then it is of little use.

SDRAM RAS Precharge Delay

Common Options: 2, 3, 4, 5

This BIOS feature sets the number of cycles required for the RAS to accumulate its charge before another row can be activated. If the RAS Precharge Time is too long, it will reduce performance by delaying all row activations. Reducing the precharge time to **2** improves performance by allowing a new row to be activated earlier.

However, the short precharge time of 2 may be insufficient for some memory modules. In such cases, the active row may lose its contents before they can be returned to the memory bank and the row deactivated. This may cause data loss or corruption when the memory controller attempts to read from the active row or write to it.

Therefore, it is recommended that you reduce the SDRAM RAS Precharge Delay to **2** for better performance, but increase it to **3** or **4** if you experience system stability issues after reducing the precharge time.

SDRAM RAS Precharge Time

Common Options: 2, 3, 4

This BIOS feature sets the number of cycles required for the RAS to accumulate its charge before another row can be activated. If the RAS Precharge Time is too long, it reduces performance by delaying all row activations. Reducing the precharge time to **2** improves performance by allowing a new row to be activated earlier.

However, the short precharge time of 2 may be insufficient for some memory modules. In such cases, the active row may lose its contents before they can be returned to the memory bank and the row deactivated. This may cause data loss or corruption when the memory controller attempts to read from the active row or write to it.

Therefore, it is recommended that you reduce the SDRAM RAS Precharge Time to **2** for better performance, but increase it to 3 or 4 if you experience system stability issues after reducing the precharge time.

SDRAM RAS Pulse Width

Common Options: 4, 5, 6, 7, 8, 9

Like **DRAM Act to PreChrg CMD**, this BIOS feature controls the memory bank's minimum row active time (tRAS). This constitutes the time when a row is activated until the time the same row can be deactivated.

If the tRAS period is too long, it can reduce performance by unnecessarily delaying the deactivation of active rows. Reducing the tRAS period allows the active row to be deactivated earlier.

However, if the tRAS period is too short, there may not be enough time to complete a burst transfer. This reduces performance and data may be lost or corrupted.

For optimal performance, use the lowest value you can. Usually, this should be CAS latency + tRCD + 2 clock cycles. For example, if you set the CAS latency to 2 clock cycles and the tRCD to 3 clock cycles, the optimum tRAS value would be 7 clock cycles.

However, if you start getting memory errors or system crashes, increase the tRCD value one clock cycle at a time until your system becomes stable.

S

SDRAM RAS-to-CAS Delay

Common Options: 2, 3, 4

This BIOS feature allows you to set the delay between the RAS and CAS signals. The appropriate delay for your memory module is reflected in its rated timings. In JEDEC specifications, it is the *second* number in the three or four number sequence.

Because this delay occurs whenever the row is refreshed or a new row is activated, reducing the delay improves performance. Therefore, it is recommended that you reduce the delay to **3** or **2** for better memory performance.

Please note that if you use a value that is too low for your memory module, this can cause the system to be unstable. If your system becomes unstable after you reduce the RAS-to-CAS delay, you should increase the delay or reset it to the rated delay.

Interestingly, increasing the RAS-to-CAS delay may allow the memory module to run at a higher clock speed. So, if you hit a snag while overclocking your SDRAM modules, you can try increasing the RAS-to-CAS delay.

SDRAM Row Active Time

Common Options: 4, 5, 6, 7, 8, 9

Like **DRAM Act to PreChrg CMD**, this BIOS feature controls the memory bank's minimum row active time (tRAS). This constitutes the time when a row is activated until the time the same row can be deactivated.

If the tRAS period is too long, it can reduce performance by unnecessarily delaying the deactivation of active rows. Reducing the tRAS period allows the active row to be deactivated earlier.

However, if the tRAS period is too short, there may not be enough time to complete a burst transfer. This reduces performance and data may be lost or corrupted.

For optimal performance, use the lowest value you can. Usually, this should be CAS latency + tRCD + 2 clock cycles. For example, if you set the CAS latency to 2 clock cycles and the tRCD to 3 clock cycles, the optimum tRAS value is 7 clock cycles.

However, if you start getting memory errors or system crashes, increase the tRAS value one clock cycle at a time until your system becomes stable.

SDRAM Row Cycle Time

Common Options: 7, 8, 9, 10, 11, 12, 13

This BIOS feature controls the memory module's Row Cycle Time or tRC. The row cycle time determines the minimum number of clock cycles a memory row takes to complete a full cycle, from row activation up to the precharging of the active row.

Formula-wise, the row cycle time (**tRC**) = minimum row active time (**tRAS**) + row precharge time (**tRP**). Therefore, it is important to find out what the tRAS and tRP parameters are before setting the row cycle time.

If the row cycle time is too long, it can reduce performance by unnecessarily delaying the activation of a new row after a completed cycle. Reducing the row cycle time allows a new cycle to begin earlier.

However, if the row cycle time is too short, a new cycle may be initiated before the active row is sufficiently precharged. When this happens, there may be data loss or corruption.

For optimal performance, use the lowest value you can, according to the tRC = tRAS + tRP formula. For example, if your memory module's tRAS is 7 clock cycles and its tRP is 4 clock cycles, then the row cycle time or tRC should be 11 clock cycles.

SDRAM Tras Timing Value

Common Options: 4, 5, 6, 7, 8, 9

Like **DRAM Act to PreChrg CMD**, this BIOS feature controls the memory bank's minimum row active time (tRAS). This constitutes the time when a row is activated until the time the same row can be deactivated.

If the tRAS period is too long, it can reduce performance by unnecessarily delaying the deactivation of active rows. Reducing the tRAS period allows the active row to be deactivated earlier.

However, if the tRAS period is too short, there may not be enough time to complete a burst transfer. This reduces performance and data may be lost or corrupted.

For optimal performance, use the lowest value you can. Usually, this should be CAS latency + tRCD + 2 clock cycles. For example, if you set the CAS latency to 2 clock cycles and the tRCD to 3 clock cycles, the optimum tRAS value would be 7 clock cycles.

However, if you start getting memory errors or system crashes, increase the tRAS value one clock cycle at a time until your system becomes stable.

SDRAM Trc Timing Value

Common Options: 7, 8, 9, 10, 11, 12, 13

This BIOS feature controls the memory module's Row Cycle Time or tRC. The row cycle time determines the minimum number of clock cycles a memory row takes to complete a full cycle, from row activation up to the precharging of the active row.

Formula-wise, the row cycle time (**tRC**) = minimum row active time (**tRAS**) + row precharge time (**tRP**). Therefore, it is important to find out what the tRAS and tRP parameters are before setting the row cycle time.

If the row cycle time is too long, it can reduce performance by unnecessarily delaying the activation of a new row after a completed cycle. Reducing the row cycle time allows a new cycle to begin earlier.

However, if the row cycle time is too short, a new cycle may be initiated before the active row is sufficiently precharged. When this happens, there may be data loss or corruption.

For optimal performance, use the lowest value you can, according to the tRC = tRAS + tRP formula. For example, if your memory module's tRAS is 7 clock cycles and its tRP is 4 clock cycles, then the row cycle time or tRC should be 11 clock cycles.

S

SDRAM Trcd Timing Value

Common Options: 2, 3, 4

This BIOS feature allows you to set the delay between the RAS and CAS signals. The appropriate delay for your memory module is reflected in its rated timings. In JEDEC specifications, it is the *second* number in the three- or four-number sequence.

Because this delay occurs whenever the row is refreshed or a new row is activated, reducing the delay improves performance. Therefore, it is recommended that you reduce the delay to **3** or **2** for better memory performance.

Please note that if you use a value that is too low for your memory module, this can cause the system to be unstable. If your system becomes unstable after you reduce the tRCD timing value, you should increase the delay or reset it to the rated delay.

Interestingly, increasing the tRCD timing value may allow the memory module to run at a higher clock speed. So, if you hit a snag while overclocking your SDRAM modules, you can try increasing the tRCD timing value.

SDRAM Trp Timing Value

Common Options: 2, 3, 4

This BIOS feature sets the number of cycles required for the RAS to accumulate its charge before another row can be activated. If the tRP timing value is too long, it reduces performance by delaying all row activations. Reducing the precharge time to **2** improves performance by allowing a new row to be activated earlier.

However, the short precharge time of 2 may be insufficient for some memory modules. In such cases, the active row may lose its contents before they can be returned to the memory bank and the row deactivated. This may cause data loss or corruption when the memory controller attempts to read from the active row or write to it.

Therefore, it is recommended that you reduce the SDRAM tRP timing value to **2** for better performance, but increase it to 3 or 4 if you experience system stability issues after reducing the precharge time.

SDRAM Bank-to-Bank Delay

Common Options: 2 cycles, 3 cycles

This BIOS feature specifies the minimum amount of time between successive ACTIVATE commands to the **same** DDR device. The shorter the delay, the faster the next bank can be activated for read or write operations. However, because row activation requires a lot of current, using a short delay may cause excessive current surges.

For desktop PCs, a delay of **2 cycles** is recommended as current surges aren't really important. The performance benefit of using the shorter 2 cycles delay is of far greater interest. The shorter delay means every back-to-back bank activation takes one clock cycle less to perform. This improves the DDR device's read and write performance.

Switch to **3 cycles** only when there are stability problems with the 2 cycles setting.

SDRAM Trrd Timing Value

Common Options: 2 cycles, 3 cycles

This BIOS feature specifies the minimum amount of time between successive ACTIVATE commands to the **same** DDR device. The shorter the delay, the faster the next bank can be activated for read or write operations. However, because row activation requires a lot of current, using a short delay may cause excessive current surges.

For desktop PCs, a delay of **2 cycles** is recommended as current surges aren't really important. The performance benefit of using the shorter 2 cycles delay is of far greater interest. The shorter delay means every back-to-back bank activation takes one clock cycle less to perform. This improves the DDR device's read and write performance.

Switch to **3 cycles** only when there are stability problems with the 2 cycles setting.

SDRAM Write Recovery Time

Common Options: 1 Cycle, 2 Cycles, 3 Cycles

This BIOS feature controls the **Write Recovery Time (tWR)** of the memory modules.

It specifies the amount of delay (in clock cycles) that must elapse after the completion of a valid write operation before an active bank can be precharged. This delay is required to guarantee that data in the write buffers can be written to the memory cells before precharge occurs.

The shorter the delay, the earlier the bank can be precharged for another read/write operation. This improves performance but runs the risk of corrupting data written to the memory cells.

It is recommended that you select **2 Cycles** if you are using DDR200 or DDR266 memory modules and **3 Cycles** if you are using DDR333 or DDR 400 memory modules. You can try using a shorter delay for better memory performance, but if you face stability issues, revert to the specified delay to correct the problem.

SDRAM Write to Read Command Delay

Common Options: 1 Cycle, 2 Cycles

This BIOS feature controls the **Write Data In to Read Command Delay (tWTR)** memory timing. This constitutes the minimum number of clock cycles that must occur between the last valid *write* operation and the next *read* command to the *same* internal bank of the DDR device.

The **1 Cycle** option naturally offers faster switching from writes to reads and, consequently, better read performance.

The **2 Cycles** option reduces read performance, but it improves stability, especially at higher clock speeds. It may also allow the memory chips to run at a higher speed. In other words, increasing this delay may allow you to overclock the memory module higher than is normally possible.

It is recommended that you select the **1 Cycle** option for better memory read performance if you are using DDR266 or DDR333 memory modules. You can also try using the **1 Cycle** option with DDR400 memory modules. However, if you face stability issues, revert to the default setting of **2 Cycles**.

Second Boot Device

Common Options: Floppy, LS/ZIP, HDD-0, SCSI, CDROM, HDD-1, HDD-2, HDD-3, LAN, Disabled

This BIOS feature allows you to select the **second** device from which the BIOS attempts to load an operating system. If the BIOS finds and loads an operating system from the device selected through this feature, it doesn't load another operating system, even if you have one on a different device.

By default, **HDD-0** is the second boot device in practically all motherboards. However, unless you boot often from the floppy drive (which is often the first boot device), it is better to set your hard disk (**HDD-0**) as the first boot device. This shortens the boot process because the BIOS no longer needs to check the floppy drive for a bootable operating system.

More importantly, doing so prevents the BIOS from loading the wrong operating system in case you forgot to remove the boot disk from the floppy drive! This also indirectly prevents the loading of any virus-infected floppy disk that was left in the drive during booting.

Security Setup

Common Options: System, Setup

This BIOS feature controls the application of the BIOS' password protection. It only works after you have created a password through the **Password Setting** option in the main BIOS screen.

Selecting the **System** option forces the BIOS to ask for the password every time the system boots up.

If you choose **Setup**, then the password is only required for access to the BIOS. This option is useful for system administrators or computer resellers who need to keep novice users from messing around with the BIOS.:

Shadowing Address Ranges

Common Options: C8000-CBFFF, CC000-CFFFF, D0000-D3FF, D4000-D7FFF, D8000-DBFFF, DC000-DFFFF, Disabled

This BIOS feature allows you to cordon off specific memory blocks (xxxx-xxxx) to shadow the BIOS of certain add-on cards. This improves the performance of cards that are accessed and controlled through their BIOS, as opposed to drivers. Currently, this is mostly limited to bootable network cards.

For most users, there is absolutely no need for this feature because modern operating systems directly access hardware through drivers. Shadowing your device's BIOS just wastes memory. Therefore, it is recommended that you **disable** this feature.

Share Memory Size

Common Options: 1MB, 4MB, 8MB, 16MB, 32MB, 64MB

This BIOS feature controls the amount of system memory that is allocated to the integrated GPU.

The selection of memory sizes allows you to select how much system memory you want to allocate to the integrated GPU. The amount you allocate to the GPU is deducted from the amount of system memory available to your operating system and programs.

Please note that unlike the **AGP Aperture Size**, once the system memory is allocated to the GPU, it cannot be used by anything else. Even if the GPU does not make use of it, it is not available to the operating system.

Therefore, it is recommended that you select the absolute minimum amount of system memory that the GPU requires for your monitor. You can calculate it by multiplying the resolution and color depth that you are using.

For example, if you use a resolution of 1600×1200 and a color depth of 32-bit, the amount of memory your GPU requires will be $1600 \times 1200 \times 32\text{-bits} = 61,440,000$ bits or 7.68MB. You should set this BIOS feature to **8MB** in this example.

Slave Drive PIO Mode

Common Options: Auto, 0, 1, 2, 3, 4

This BIOS feature allows you to set the **PIO (Programmed Input/Output)** mode for the Slave IDE drive attached to that particular IDE channel.

Setting this BIOS feature to **Auto** lets the BIOS auto-detect the IDE drive's maximum supported PIO mode at boot-up.

Setting this BIOS feature to **0** forces the BIOS to use **PIO Mode 0** for the IDE drive.

Setting this BIOS feature to **1** forces the BIOS to use **PIO Mode 1** for the IDE drive.

Setting this BIOS feature to **2** forces the BIOS to use **PIO Mode 2** for the IDE drive.

Setting this BIOS feature to **3** forces the BIOS to use **PIO Mode 3** for the IDE drive.

Setting this BIOS feature to **4** forces the BIOS to use **PIO Mode 4** for the IDE drive.

Normally, you should leave it as **Auto** and let the BIOS auto-detect the IDE drive's PIO mode. You should only set it manually for the following reasons:

- If the BIOS cannot detect the correct PIO mode.
- If you want to try forcing the IDE device to use a faster PIO mode than it was designed for.
- If you want to force the IDE device to use a slower PIO mode if it cannot work properly with the current PIO mode (for example, when the PCI bus is overclocked).

Please note that forcing an IDE device to use a PIO transfer rate that is faster than what it is rated for can potentially cause data corruption.

S

Slave Drive UltraDMA

Common Options: Auto, Disabled

This BIOS feature allows you to enable or disable **DMA (Direct Memory Access)** support (if available) for the Slave IDE device attached to that particular IDE channel.

Setting this BIOS feature to **Auto** lets the BIOS auto-detect the IDE drive's maximum supported DMA mode at boot-up.

Setting this BIOS feature to **Disabled** forces the BIOS to disable DMA transfers for the IDE drive.

Normally, you should leave it as **Auto** and let the BIOS auto-detect the drive's DMA support. If the drive supports DMA transfers, the proper DMA transfer mode is enabled for that drive, allowing it to burst data at anywhere from 33MB/s to 133MB/s (depending on the transfer mode supported).

You should only **disable** it for troubleshooting purposes. For example, certain IDE devices may not run properly using DMA transfers when the PCI bus is overclocked. Disabling DMA support forces the drive to use the slower PIO transfer mode. This may allow the drive to work properly with the higher PCI bus speed.

Please note that setting this to **Auto** does *not* enable DMA transfers for IDE devices that do not support DMA transfers. If your drive does not support DMA transfers, the BIOS automatically sets the drive to do PIO transfers only.

Also note that this BIOS feature merely enables DMA transfers during the booting up process and for operating systems that do not load their own drivers for IDE functions. For operating systems that use their own IDE drivers (for example, Windows 9x/2000/XP), you have to enable DMA support for the drive within the operating system as well.

Speed Error Hold

Common Options: Enabled, Disabled

This BIOS feature prevents accidental overclocking by preventing the system from booting up if the processor clock speed was not properly set.

When **enabled**, the BIOS checks the processor clock speed at boot up and halts the boot process if the clock speed is different from that imprinted in the processor ID. It also displays an error message to warn you that the processor is running at the wrong speed.

If you are thinking of overclocking the processor, you must **disable** this feature because it prevents the motherboard from booting up with an overclocked processor. When **disabled**, the BIOS does *not* check the processor clock speed at boot up. It allows the system to boot with the clock speed set in the BIOS, even if it does not match the processor's rated clock speed (as imprinted in the processor ID).

Although this may seem really obvious, I have seen countless overclocking initiates puzzling over the error message whenever they try to overclock their processors. So, before you start pulling your hair out and screaming hysterically that Intel or AMD has finally implemented a clock speed lock on their processors, try **disabling** this feature.

Split Lock Operations

Common Options: Enabled, Disabled

This is a debug feature specific to the Intel Pentium 4 and the Intel Pentium 4 Xeon processors. It allows you to prevent the processor from issuing split lock cycles to the processor bus if such operations cause problems.

Split lock cycles can potentially cause problems in certain situations. For example, the **Split Lock Cycles** bug in the Intel 82860 MCH.

Usually, it is recommended that you leave Split Lock Operation at its default setting of **Enabled**. This allows the processor to issue split lock cycles to the processor bus. However, if you are using a motherboard based on the Intel 82860 chipset, you should **disable** this feature.

There may be other situations where split lock cycles can cause problems. If your system hangs or crashes for no apparent reason, you can try disabling this feature and see if it solves the problem. Otherwise, leave it **Enabled**.

Spread Spectrum

Common Options: 0.25%, 0.5%, Smart Clock, Disabled

This BIOS feature allows you to reduce the EMI of your motherboard by modulating the signals it generates, so the spikes are reduced to flatter curves. It achieves this by varying the frequency *slightly*, so the signal does not use any particular frequency for more than a moment.

The BIOS usually offers two levels of modulation—**0.25%** or **0.5%**. The greater the modulation, the greater the reduction of EMI. Therefore, if you need to significantly reduce your motherboard's EMI, a modulation of **0.5%** is recommended.

In most conditions, frequency modulation through this feature does not cause any problems. However, system stability may be slightly compromised in certain situations. For example, this BIOS feature may cause improper functioning of timing-critical devices, such as clock-sensitive SCSI devices.

Spread Spectrum can also cause problems with overclocked systems, especially those that have been taken to extremes. Even a slight modulation of frequency may cause the processor or any other overclocked components of the system to fail, leading to very predictable consequences.

Therefore, it is recommended that you **disable** this feature if you are overclocking your system. The risk of crashing your system is not worth the reduction in EMI. Of course, if EMI reduction is important to you, **enable** this feature by all means. However, you should reduce the clock speed a little to provide a margin of safety.

Some BIOSes also offer a **Smart Clock** option. Instead of modulating the frequency of signals over time, Smart Clock turns off the AGP, PCI, and SDRAM clock signals that are not in use. Therefore, EMI can be reduced *without* compromising system stability. As a bonus, using Smart Clock also helps reduce power consumption. The degree of EMI and power reduction depend on the number of empty AGP, PCI, and SDRAM slots. However, generally, Smart Clock is unable to reduce EMI as effectively as simple frequency modulation.

With that said, it is recommended that you enable **Smart Clock**, instead of the **0.25%** or **5%** options, if the option is available to you. It allows you to reduce some EMI without any risk of compromising your computer's stability.

Super Bypass Mode

Common Options: Enabled, Disabled

This BIOS feature basically allows the **memory request organizer** (**MRO**) of the memory controller to skip certain pipeline stages while transferring data to and from the memory subsystem.

This improves memory performance by allowing lower latency accesses to the memory subsystem. However, this feature can only be safely enabled if the following conditions are true:

- The system only has a single processor present. Systems using dual-processor motherboards can enable this feature if only one processor is present.
- The processor clock speed multiplier must be 4 or greater. This means the processor must be running at least four times faster than its bus speed.

For better memory performance, it is recommended that you **enable** this feature. However, you must make sure that you are only using a single processor that is running at least four times faster than the processor bus. You should **disable** this feature if your system does not meet the two requirements stated above.

Super Bypass Wait State

Common Options: 0 Cycle, 1 Cycle

This BIOS feature is used to fine-tune the **Super Bypass** feature to correct for internal timing variations.

When set to **0 Cycle**, the memory controller initiates all super bypass requests without delay.

When set to **1 Cycle**, the memory controller forces a wait state delay for all super bypass requests.

Official documents recommend that a wait state be added for a 133MHz (266MHz DDR) memory bus. Systems using a 100MHz (200MHz DDR) memory bus do not need this delay.

Forcing a wait state on all super bypass requests reduces the effectiveness of the **Super Bypass** feature. Therefore, it is recommended that you try using the **0 Cycle** setting for maximum performance.

However, if you experience system stability issues after using this **0 Cycle** setting, set this feature to **1 Cycle**. This slows down super bypass transactions but allows your system to use the **Super Bypass** feature at higher clock speeds.

SuperStability Mode

Common Options: Enabled, Disabled

This is a **NVIDIA nForce** chipset-specific BIOS feature. It controls the hitherto hidden "feature" of the nForce chipset, which *locks* the memory clock at **200MHz** instead of the rated **266MHz** when it detects a memory module that is not compatible with the motherboard. This allows the use of substandard or incompatible memory modules, albeit at reduced performance.

The chipset only allows the memory clock to be set at 266MHz when it is satisfied that each and every memory module installed has met its standard. If even a single module fails to meet the standard, the chipset locks the memory clock at 200MHz, irrespective of the clock speed at which it was set to run.

While NVIDIA claims that this feature allows nForce motherboards to work with substandard or incompatible memory modules that would otherwise be unusable, there have been reports that even compatible memory modules are being locked down to 200MHz. Apparently, loading the second slot (Slot B) of the second memory controller with a **double-sided** DIMM also causes SuperStability to kick in.

After this feature was discovered by Chris Connolly of GamePC, the BIOS was revised to include this **SuperStability Mode** feature. This allows you to switch the SuperStability feature on or off.

When left at the default setting of **Enabled**, the nForce chipset locks the memory clock at 200MHz if it detects an incompatible memory module or if Slot B of the second memory controller is filled with a double-sided memory module.

When **disabled**, the nForce chipset does not check the memory modules for incompatibility or Slot B of the second memory controller for a double-sided memory module. The memory modules are allowed to run at the clock speed you set.

It is highly recommended that you **disable** SuperStability Mode for better SDRAM performance, especially if you use all three DIMM slots. There is really no need to enable it because you can lower the memory clock speed yourself or increase their timings in order to use incompatible memory modules.

Swap Floppy Drive

Common Options: Enabled, Disabled

This BIOS feature is used to logically swap the mapping of drives A: and B:. Therefore, it is only useful if you have two floppy drives.

Normally, the sequence by which you connect the floppy drives to the cable determines which is drive A: and which is drive B:. If you attach the floppy drives the wrong way and obtain a drive mapping that is not to your satisfaction, the usual way of correcting this is to physically swap the floppy cable connectors.

This feature allows you to swap the logical arrangement of the floppy drives without the need to open up the case and physically swap the connectors.

When this BIOS feature is **enabled**, the floppy drive that originally was mapped to drive A: is remapped to drive B: and vice-versa for the drive that was originally set as drive B:.

When this BIOS feature is **disabled**, the floppy drive mapping remains as that set by the drive connector arrangement.

Although this appears to be nothing more than a feature of convenience, it can be quite important if you are using two floppy drives of different form factors (3.5" and 5.25") and you need to boot from the second drive. Because the BIOS can only boot from drive A:, you have to physically swap the drive connections or use this feature to do it logically.

If your floppy drive mapping is correct or if you only have a single floppy drive, there is no need to enable this feature. Leave it at the default setting of **disabled**.

S

Synchronous Mode Select

Common Options: Synchronous, Asynchronous

This BIOS feature controls the signal synchronization of the DRAM-CPU interface.

When set to **Synchronous**, the chipset synchronizes the signals from the DRAM controller with signals from the CPU bus (or front side bus). Please note that for the signals to be synchronous, the DRAM controller and the CPU bus must run at the same clock speed.

When set to **Asynchronous**, the chipset decouples the DRAM controller from the CPU bus. This allows the DRAM controller and the CPU bus to run at different clock speeds.

Generally, it is advisable to use the **Synchronous** setting because a synchronized interface allows data transfers to occur without delay. This results in a much higher throughput between the CPU bus and the DRAM controller.

System BIOS Cacheable

Common Options: Enabled, Disabled

Enabling this feature allows the caching of the motherboard BIOS ROM from **F0000h** to **FFFFFh** by the processor's **Level 2 cache**. This greatly speeds up accesses to the BIOS.

However, this does not translate into better system performance because modern operating systems like Microsoft Windows XP do not need to communicate with the hardware through the BIOS. Current operating systems make use of drivers to access the hardware directly.

Therefore, it is a waste of the Level 2 cache's bandwidth if the motherboard BIOS was cached instead of data that are more critical to the system's performance.

In addition, if any errant program writes into this memory area, it results in a system crash. Therefore, it is highly recommended that you **disable** this feature for better system performance.

S

T

Third Boot Device

Common Options: Floppy, LS/ZIP, HDD-0, SCSI, CDROM, HDD-1, HDD-2, HDD-3, LAN, Disabled

This BIOS feature allows you to select the **third** device from which the BIOS attempts to load an operating system. If the BIOS finds and loads an operating system from the device selected through this feature, it won't load another operating system, even if you have one on a different device.

By default, **LS/ZIP** is the third boot device in practically all motherboards. Because the third boot device is only tried after no bootable operating system can be found in the first two boot devices, it is of little consequence what you set here. Therefore, the choice of boot device for this BIOS feature is entirely up to your personal preference.

TX, RX Inverting Enable

Common Options: No-No, No-Yes, Yes-No, Yes-Yes

This BIOS feature allows you to set the infra-red reception (**RxD**) and transmission (**TxD**) polarity.

It is usually found under the **Onboard Serial Port 2** BIOS feature and is linked to the second serial port. So, if you disable that port, this feature disappears from the screen or appears grayed out.

There are four options available based on combinations of **Yes** (read as **High**) and **No** (read as **Low**). You'll need to consult your IR peripheral's documentation to determine the correct polarity. Choosing the wrong polarity prevents a proper IR connection from being established with the IR peripheral.

Typematic Rate

Common Options: 6, 8, 10, 12, 15, 20, 24, 30

This BIOS feature only works if the **Typematic Rate Setting** feature has been **enabled**.

This feature determines the rate at which the keyboard repeats a keystroke if you press it continuously.

The available settings are in characters per second. Therefore, a typematic rate of **30** causes the keyboard to repeat the keystroke at a rate of 30 characters per second if you press a particular key continuously. The higher the typematic rate, the faster the keyboard repeats the keystroke.

The choice of what setting to use is entirely up to your personal preference. However, note that this typematic rate is only applicable in operating systems that communicate with the hardware through the BIOS, like **MS-DOS**. The typematic rate in operating systems like Windows XP are controlled by the keyboard driver's settings.

Typematic Rate Delay

Common Options: 250, 500, 750, 1000

This BIOS setting only works if the **Typematic Rate Setting** feature has been enabled.

This feature determines how long, in **milliseconds** (thousandths of a second), the keyboard controller waits before it starts repeating the keystroke that you have pressed continuously. The longer the delay, the longer the keyboard controller waits before it starts repeating the keystroke.

Generally, using a short delay is useful for people who type quickly and don't like to wait long for a keystroke to be repeated. On the other hand, a long delay is useful for users who tend to press the keys longer while typing. This prevents the keyboard controller from unnecessarily repeating keystrokes with such users.

Typematic Rate Setting

Common Options: Enabled, Disabled

This BIOS feature allows you to gain manual control of the keystroke repeat feature.

When **enabled**, you are given access to these two typematic controls:

- Typematic Rate
- Typematic Rate Delay

They allow you to manually adjust the **Typematic Rate** and the **Typematic Rate Delay**.

If you **disable** this feature, the two typematic controls are disabled and grayed out. The keyboard controller thereby uses the default typematic rate and typematic rate delay.

T

U

Ultra DMA Mode

Common Options: Disabled, 0, 1, 2, 3, 4, 5, 6, Auto

This BIOS feature allows you to enable or disable **DMA (Direct Memory Access)** support (if available) for the IDE device.

Setting this BIOS feature to **Disabled** forces the BIOS to disable DMA transfers for the IDE drive.

Setting this BIOS feature to **0** forces the BIOS to use **DMA Mode 0** for DMA transfers.

Setting this BIOS feature to **1** forces the BIOS to use **DMA Mode 1** for DMA transfers.

Setting this BIOS feature to **2** forces the BIOS to use **DMA Mode 2** for DMA transfers.

Setting this BIOS feature to **3** forces the BIOS to use **UltraDMA 33** for DMA transfers.

Setting this BIOS feature to **4** forces the BIOS to use **UltraDMA 66** for DMA transfers.

Setting this BIOS feature to **5** forces the BIOS to use **UltraDMA 100** for DMA transfers.

Setting this BIOS feature to **6** forces the BIOS to use **UltraDMA 133** for DMA transfers.

Setting this BIOS feature to **Auto** lets the BIOS auto-detect the IDE drive's maximum supported DMA mode at boot-up.

Normally, you should leave it as **Auto** and let the BIOS auto-detect the drive's DMA support. If the drive supports DMA transfers, the proper DMA transfer mode is enabled for that drive, allowing it to burst data from anywhere between 33MB/s to 133MB/s (depending on the transfer mode supported).

You should only **disable** it for troubleshooting purposes. For example, certain IDE devices may not run properly using DMA transfers when the PCI bus is overclocked. Disabling DMA support force the drive to use the slower PIO transfer mode. This may allow the drive to work properly with the higher PCI bus speed.

UltraDMA-100 IDE Controller

Common Options: Enabled, Disabled

This BIOS feature is only found in certain motherboards that come with an additional built-in IDE controller. It allows you to enable or disable the function of that IDE controller.

If you want to attach one or more IDE devices to the external UltraDMA/100 controller, you should **enable** this feature. You should only **disable** this BIOS feature for the following reasons:

■ If you do not have any IDE device attached to the external UltraDMA/100 controller
■ For troubleshooting purposes

Disabling the external IDE controller frees up two IRQs, which can be used by other devices in the system. It also speeds up the boot-up sequence because the external IDE controller's BIOS no longer needs to be loaded. Your system is also able to skip the external controller's long boot-up check and initialization sequence.

Therefore, if you do not use the external IDE controller, it is recommended that you **disable** it for a much faster booting process.

UltraDMA-133 IDE Controller

Common Options: Enabled, Disabled

This BIOS feature is only found in certain motherboards that come with an additional built-in IDE controller. It allows you to enable or disable the function of that IDE controller.

If you want to attach one or more IDE devices to the external UltraDMA/133 controller, you should **enable** this feature. You should only **disable** this BIOS feature for the following reasons:

- If you do not have any IDE device attached to the external UltraDMA/133 controller
- For troubleshooting purposes

Disabling the external IDE controller frees up two IRQs, which can be used by other devices in the system. It also speeds up the boot-up sequence because the external IDE controller's BIOS no longer needs to be loaded. Your system also is able to skip the external controller's long boot-up check and initialization sequence.

Therefore, if you do not use the external IDE controller, it is recommended that you **disable** it for a much faster booting process.

UltraDMA-66 IDE Controller

Common Options: Enabled, Disabled

This BIOS feature is only found in certain motherboards that come with an additional built-in IDE controller. It allows you to enable or disable the function of that IDE controller.

If you want to attach one or more IDE devices to the external UltraDMA/66 controller, you should **enable** this feature. You should only **disable** this BIOS feature for the following reasons:

- If you do not have any IDE device attached to the external UltraDMA/66 controller
- For troubleshooting purposes

Disabling the external IDE controller frees up two IRQs, which can be used by other devices in the system. It also speeds up the boot-up sequence because the external IDE controller's BIOS no longer needs to be loaded. Your system also is able to skip the external controller's long boot-up check and initialization sequence.

Therefore, if you do not use the external IDE controller, it is recommended that you **disable** it for a much faster booting process.

USB Controller

Common Options: Enabled, Disabled

This BIOS feature enables or disables the motherboard's onboard USB controller.

It is recommend that you **enable** this feature, so you can use the onboard USB controller to communicate with your USB devices.

If you **disable** this feature, the USB controller is disabled and you are unable to use it to communicate with any USB device. This frees up an IRQ for other devices to use. This is useful when you have many devices that cannot share IRQs.

However, it is recommended that you do *not* disable this BIOS feature unless you do not use any USB device or you are using a different USB controller for your USB needs.

USB Keyboard Support

Common Options: OS, BIOS

This BIOS feature determines whether support for the USB keyboard should be provided by the operating system or the BIOS. Therefore, it only affects those who are using USB keyboards.

If your operating system offers native support for USB keyboards, you should select the **OS** option. This provides much greater functionality. However, if you are using DOS or operating systems that do not offer support for USB keyboards, then using the OS option essentially disables the keyboard because these operating systems cannot detect or work with USB keyboards.

This is where the **BIOS** option comes in. When selected, the BIOS provides support for the USB keyboard. You are able to use the keyboard with both operating systems that do not support USB keyboards and those that do.

However, the BIOS option offers only rudimentary support for the USB keyboard, so using it strips the keyboard of all except basic functions. Therefore, you should *not* select this option if you are using an operating system that supports USB keyboards. It is recommended that you select the **OS** option if you are using a current operating system like Windows XP.

However don't forget to switch from the **OS** option to the **BIOS** option whenever you want to boot up using a DOS boot disk. Even if the boot disk was created by a USB-aware operating system like Windows XP, it does *not* support the USB keyboard.

USB Mouse Support

Common Options: OS, BIOS

This BIOS feature determines whether support for the USB mouse should be provided by the operating system or the BIOS. Therefore, it only affects those who are using USB mice.

If your operating system offers native support for USB mice, you should select the **OS** option. This provides much greater functionality. However, if you are using DOS or operating systems that do not offer support for USB mice, then using the OS option essentially disables the mouse because these operating systems cannot detect or work with USB mice.

This is where the **BIOS** option comes in. When selected, the BIOS provides support for the USB mouse. You are able to use the mouse with both operating systems that do not support USB mice and those that do.

However, the BIOS option offers only rudimentary support for the USB mouse, so using it strips the mouse of all except basic functions. Therefore, you should *not* select this option if you are using an operating system that supports USB mice. It is recommended that you select the **OS** option if you are using a current operating system like Windows XP.

However don't forget to switch from the **OS** option to the **BIOS** option whenever you want to boot up using a DOS boot disk. Even if the boot disk was created by a USB-aware operating system like Windows XP, it does *not* support the USB mouse.

USWC Write Posting

Common Options: Enabled, Disabled

This BIOS feature allows you to control the **USWC (Uncached Speculative Write Combining)** write combine buffers.

If **enabled**, the write combine buffers accumulate and combine partial or smaller graphics writes from the processor and write them to the graphics card as burst writes.

If **disabled**, the write combine buffers are disabled. All graphics writes from the processor are written to the graphics card directly.

It is highly recommended that you **enable** this feature for improved graphics and processor performance.

However, if you are using an older graphics card, it may not be compatible with this feature. Enabling this feature with such graphics cards causes a host of problems like graphics artifacts, system crashes, and even the inability to boot up properly.

If you face such problems, you should **disable** this BIOS feature immediately.

V

Video BIOS Cacheable

Common Options: Enabled, Disabled

This BIOS feature aims to further boost the performance of a shadowed video BIOS by caching it using the processor's Level 2 cache. It works in conjunction with **Video BIOS Shadowing** and is only valid when the **Video BIOS Shadowing** feature is enabled.

If this BIOS feature is **enabled**, a 32KB block of the video BIOS from **C0000h–C7FFFh** is cached by the processor's Level 2 cache. This greatly speeds up *subsequent consecutive* accesses to the video BIOS.

If this BIOS feature is **disabled**, the video BIOS is not cached. The video BIOS is read from the system memory (if it has been shadowed) or directly from the BIOS chip.

However, caching the video BIOS does not necessarily translate into better system performance. First of all, modern operating systems like Microsoft Windows XP do not need to use the video BIOS. They bypass the BIOS completely and use the graphics card's driver instead. Therefore, absolutely no benefit can be realized by caching the BIOS.

Unlike system memory, which can be a gigabyte or more, the processor's L2 cache is a limited resource. Diverting such a large portion of the L2 cache for the purpose of caching the video BIOS deprives the processor of L2 cache for its own data. Consequently, there is a significant deterioration in processor performance whenever the video BIOS is cached.

As with the **Video BIOS Shadowing** feature, Flash ROM upgrades should not be attempted if the video BIOS is cached. If the video BIOS is cached, any attempt at flashing the video BIOS will likely result in a system crash. Worst of all, because only 32KB of the video BIOS is cached, the end result is usually a corrupted video BIOS.

Of course, caching the video BIOS theoretically provides a significant boost in real-mode DOS games or certain operating systems in fail-safe mode. However, the loss of the processor's L2 cache negates any performance advantage gained by caching the video BIOS.

Therefore, it is recommended that you **disable** Video BIOS Caching, even if you play a lot of real-mode DOS games or work with operating systems running in fail-safe mode.

Video BIOS Shadowing

Common Options: Enabled, Disabled

This BIOS feature allows faster access to the video BIOS by *shadowing* or making a copy of it in the system memory. This appears quite an attractive feature because it results in at least a thousand-fold improvement in video BIOS performance, and the only price you pay is losing the small amount of system memory used to mirror the video BIOS. Unfortunately, the truth is not so simple.

Modern operating systems do not even use the video BIOS. They bypass the BIOS completely and use the graphics card's driver instead. Therefore, absolutely no benefit can be realized by shadowing the BIOS.

In addition, shadowing the video BIOS can sometimes cause conflicts to occur. There is always a risk of certain software writing to the RAM region used to shadow the video BIOS. When this happens, a conflict occurs and the system crashes.

What could be a bigger issue would be the shadowing of just a portion of the video BIOS. Newer video BIOSes are generally much larger than 32KB in size. However, most motherboards shadow only a 32KB block from **C0000** to **C7FFF**. If only this region of the video BIOS is shadowed and the rest left unshadowed, applications may have trouble accessing the video BIOS properly.

Finally, all graphics cards now use Flash ROM, which allows easy upgrading of the firmware by a simple BIOS flash. However, if the video BIOS is shadowed, any attempt at flashing the video BIOS will likely result in a system crash. It could be even worse if only a *portion* of the video BIOS had been shadowed when the video BIOS upgrade was attempted.

With all that said, there may still be a use or two for this BIOS feature. For one thing, most real-mode DOS games use the video BIOS's VGA functions because they cannot directly access the graphics processor. Such games benefit from the shadowing of the video BIOS.

Shadowing of the video BIOS also provides performance benefits when it comes to the fail-safe mode of certain operating systems (for example, Safe Mode in Microsoft Windows XP). These operating systems fall back on the video BIOS because all video BIOSes contain the same, standardized VGA functions.

If this BIOS feature is **enabled**, the video BIOS is shadowed in system memory. This improves graphics rendering performance if the VGA functions of the video BIOS are used.

If this BIOS feature is **disabled**, the video BIOS is *no* shadowed in system memory. Any access to the video BIOS must go through the XT or LPC bus.

Because drivers have replaced the video BIOS as the interface between the graphics hardware and the operating system, it is recommended that you **disable** Video BIOS Shadowing. The risk of crashes and BIOS corruptions due to this BIOS feature is not worth the benefits it provides in certain circumstances.

However, if you do play a lot of old real-mode DOS games or work a lot in safe-mode Windows, then you should shadow the video BIOS for improved performance.

Video Memory Cache Mode

Common Options: USWC, UC

This is yet another BIOS feature with a misleading name. It does not cache the video memory or even graphics data (such data is uncacheable anyway).

This BIOS feature allows you to control the **USWC (Uncached Speculative Write Combining)** write combine buffers.

If **enabled**, the write combine buffers accumulates and combines partial or smaller graphics writes from the processor and writes them to the graphics card as burst writes.

If **disabled**, the write combine buffers are disabled. All graphics writes from the processor are written to the graphics card directly.

It is highly recommended that you **enable** this feature for improved graphics and processor performance.

However, if you are using an older graphics card, it may not be compatible with this feature. Enabling this feature with such graphics cards causes a host of problems like graphics artifacts, system crashes, and even the inability to boot up properly.

If you face such problems, you should **disable** this BIOS feature immediately.

Video RAM Cacheable

Common Options: Enabled, Disabled

This BIOS feature aims to boost VGA graphics performance by using the processor's Level 2 cache to cache the 64KB VGA graphics memory area from **A0000h** to **AFFFFh**.

If this BIOS feature is **enabled**, the VGA graphics memory area is cached by the processor's **Level 2 cache**. This speeds up accesses to the VGA graphics memory area.

If this BIOS feature is **disabled**, the VGA graphics memory area is *not* cached by the processor's **Level 2 cache**.

From what we have discussed so far, it sounds like caching the VGA graphics memory area is logically the way to go. Caching the VGA graphics memory area definitely speeds up VGA graphics performance by caching accesses to the graphics memory area.

However, reality is far less ideal. For one thing, VGA modes are hardly used at all these days. For compatibility reason, VGA is still used in Windows XP's **Safe Mode**. It is also used in real mode DOS, if you still use that. Other than that, there is no more use for VGA modes. If VGA graphics modes are not used, no benefit can possibly be realized by enabling this BIOS feature.

Even if you use DOS modes a lot, is there even a point in caching the VGA graphics memory area for better performance? Even the slowest computer today is more than capable of handling VGA graphics with ease. In short, caching the VGA graphics memory area does not bring any noticeable advantage.

On the other hand, caching this memory area costs you some processor performance. Because some of the processor's Level 2 cache is being diverted to cache the VGA graphics memory area, there is less to keep the processor supplied with data. Consequently, the processor's performance suffers.

Therefore, it is highly recommended that you **disable** this BIOS feature. There is no reason to enable it even if you use real mode DOS a lot or work a lot in Windows Safe Mode.

Virus Warning

Common Options: Enabled, Disabled

This BIOS feature provides rudimentary anti-virus protection by monitoring writes to the boot sector and partition table.

If this feature is **enabled**, the BIOS halts the system and flashes a warning message whenever it detects an attempt to write to the boot sector or the partition table.

If this feature is **disabled**, the BIOS does not monitor writes to the boot sector and partition table.

This feature can cause problems with software that need to access the boot sector. One good example is the installation routine of all versions of Microsoft Windows from Windows 95 onward. When **enabled**, this feature causes the installation routine to fail. You should **disable** this feature before running such software.

VLink 8X Support

Common Options: Enabled, Disabled

The **VLink 8X Support** BIOS feature is used to toggle the V-Link bus mode between the original V-Link and the newer and faster 8X V-Link.

If this feature is **enabled**, the quad-pumped 8-bit V-Link bus switches to the new 8X V-Link mode, which runs at 133MHz and delivers a bandwidth of 533MB/s.

If this feature is **disabled**, the V-Link bus uses a clock speed of 66MHz, essentially reverting to the original V-Link standard. It then delivers a bandwidth of 266MB/s.

This BIOS feature was most likely included for troubleshooting purposes. It is highly recommended that you **enable** this BIOS feature for better performance.

Watchdog Timer

Common Options: Enabled, Disabled

This BIOS feature controls the operation of the chipset's Watchdog Timer.

When **enabled**, the Watchdog Timer monitors the time taken for each task performed by the operating system. Any timeout will cause it to initiate corrective actions like generate a non-maskable interrupt or reboot the computer.

When **disabled**, the Watchdog Timer does not monitor the time taken for each task performed by the operating system. Even if the system locks up, the Watchdog Timer does not initiate any corrective action.

It is recommended that you **enable** the Watchdog Timer to automatically detect hardware and software errors that lock up the computer. While it may do nothing more than automatically reboot or shut down the computer when an irresolvable error occurs, there is a chance it may allow the correction of the problem and allow the computer to function normally.

Write Data In to Read Delay

Common Options: 1 Cycle, 2 Cycles

This BIOS feature controls the **Write Data In to Read Command Delay (tWTR)** memory timing. This constitutes the minimum number of clock cycles that must occur between the last valid *write* operation and the next *read* command to the *same* internal bank of the DDR device.

The **1 Cycle** option naturally offers faster switching from writes to reads and, consequently, better read performance.

The **2 Cycles** option reduces read performance but it improves stability, especially at higher clock speeds. It may also allow the memory chips to run at a higher speed. In other words, increasing this delay may allow you to overclock the memory module higher than is normally possible.

It is recommended that you select the **1 Cycle** option for better memory read performance if you are using DDR266 or DDR333 memory modules. You can also try using the **1 Cycle** option with DDR400 memory modules. However, if you face stability issues, revert to the default setting of **2 Cycles**.

Write Recovery Time

Common Options: 1 Cycle, 2 Cycles, 3 Cycles

This BIOS feature controls the **Write Recovery Time (tWR)** of the memory modules.

It specifies the amount of delay (in clock cycles) that must elapse after the completion of a valid write operation before an active bank can be precharged. This delay is required to guarantee that data in the write buffers can be written to the memory cells before precharge occurs.

The shorter the delay, the earlier the bank can be precharged for another read/write operation. This improves performance but runs the risk of corrupting data written to the memory cells.

It is recommended that you select **2 Cycles** if you are using DDR200 or DDR266 memory modules and **3 Cycles** if you are using DDR333 or DDR 400 memory modules. You can try using a shorter delay for better memory performance, but if you face stability issues, revert to the specified delay to correct the problem.

Chapter 4
Detailed Descriptions

Introduction

This chapter contains in-depth explanations of each BIOS option and discusses how I arrived at the recommended settings.

If you already have a moderate level of hardware knowledge, this is the best chapter to read because it allows you to achieve a greater understanding of the various BIOS options and the logic behind their recommended settings.

The BIOS options are all arranged alphabetically on separate pages. Lettered tabs are provided to help you navigate quickly through the chapter. You can also use the Table of Contents and the Category Look-Up Table to quickly access the BIOS option you are interested in.

You should start with Chapter 3 before starting with this chapter if you have only limited knowledge of computer hardware or if you need a quick reference on BIOS options.

8-bit I/O Recovery Time

Common Options: NA, 8, 1, 2, 3, 4, 5, 6, 7

The PCI bus runs at a much higher clock speed than the ISA bus. So, for ISA cards to work properly with I/O cycles from the PCI bus, additional bus clock cycles must be inserted between each consecutive PCI-originated I/O cycle to the ISA bus.

By default, the bus recovery mechanism inserts 3.5 clock cycles between each consecutive 8-bit I/O cycle to the ISA bus. This feature enables you to insert even more clock cycles between each consecutive 8-bit I/O cycle to the ISA bus. For example, if you choose **3** cycles, the bus recovery mechanism inserts a total of 3.5 cycles + 3 cycles = 6.5 cycles between each consecutive 8-bit I/O cycle. Choosing **NA** sets the number of delay cycles to the minimum 3.5 clock cycles.

Most 8-bit ISA cards work fine with the minimum 3.5 delay cycles. However, some ISA cards may require additional delay cycles. Keep increasing the number of additional delay cycles until the card works properly. You might also need to increase the number of delay cycles if you are overclocking the PCI bus. If possible, set the 8-bit I/O Recovery Time to **NA** for optimal ISA bus performance. Increase the I/O Recovery Time only if you are having problems with your 8-bit ISA cards.

Note that this feature is only valid if you are using 8-bit ISA cards. It has no effect if there are no 8-bit ISA devices in the system.

16-bit I/O Recovery Time

Common Options: NA, 4, 1, 2, 3

The PCI bus runs at a much higher clock speed than the ISA bus. So, for ISA cards to work properly with I/O cycles from the PCI bus, additional bus clock cycles must be inserted between each consecutive PCI-originated I/O cycle to the ISA bus.

By default, the bus recovery mechanism inserts 3.5 clock cycles between each consecutive 16-bit I/O cycle to the ISA bus. This feature enables you to insert even more clock cycles between each consecutive 16-bit I/O cycle to the ISA bus. For example, if you choose **3** cycles, the bus recovery mechanism inserts a total of 3.5 cycles + 3 cycles = 6.5 cycles between each consecutive 16-bit I/O cycle. Choosing **NA** sets the number of delay cycles to the minimum 3.5 clock cycles.

Most 16-bit ISA cards work fine with the minimum 3.5 delay cycles. However, some ISA cards may require additional delay cycles. Keep increasing the number of additional delay cycles until the card works properly. You might also need to increase the number of delay cycles if you are overclocking the PCI bus. If possible, set the 16-bit I/O Recovery Time to **NA** for optimal ISA bus performance. Increase the I/O Recovery Time only if you are having problems with your 16-bit ISA cards.

Note that this feature is only valid if you are using 16-bit ISA cards. It has no effect if there are no 16-bit ISA devices in the system.

32-bit Disk Access

Common Options: Enabled, Disabled

The name **32-bit Disk Access** is actually a misnomer because it doesn't really allow 32-bit access to the hard disk. The IDE interface is always 16-bits in width even when the IDE controller is on the 32-bit PCI bus. What this feature actually does is command the IDE controller to combine two 16-bit reads from the hard disk into a single 32-bit double word transfer to the processor. This allows the PCI bus to be used more efficiently as the number of transactions required for a particular amount of data is effectively *halved*!

However, according to a Microsoft article (*Enhanced IDE Operation Under Windows NT 4.0*), 32-bit disk access can cause data corruption under Windows NT in some cases. Therefore, Microsoft recommends that Windows NT 4.0 users **disable** 32-bit Disk Access.

Microsoft took a serious view of the issue and corrected it in the Windows NT 4.0 Service Pack 2. Therefore, it is safe to **enable** 32-bit Disk Access in a Windows NT 4.0 system, so long as it has been upgraded with Service Pack 2.

It is highly advisable to **enable** 32-bit Disk Access because it realizes the performance potential of the 32-bit IDE controller and improves the efficiency of the PCI bus. If you **disable** it, data transfers from the IDE controller to the processor only occur in 16-bits chunks. Naturally, this degrades the performance of the IDE controller as well as the PCI bus. As such, you should **disable** this feature *only* if you actually face the possibility of data corruption (with an unpatched version of Windows NT 4.0).

You can also find more information on the Windows NT issue in the details of the **IDE HDD Block Mode** feature.

32-bit Transfer Mode

Common Options: On, Off

This BIOS feature is similar to the **32-bit Disk Access** BIOS feature.

The name **32-bit Transfer Mode** is actually a misnomer because it doesn't really allow 32-bit transfers on the IDE bus. The IDE interface is always 16-bits in width even when the IDE controller is on the 32-bit PCI bus. What this feature actually does is command the IDE controller to combine two 16-bit reads from the hard disk into a single 32-bit double word transfer to the processor. This allows the PCI bus to be used more efficiently as the number of transactions required for a particular amount of data is effectively *halved*!

However, according to a Microsoft article (*Enhanced IDE Operation Under Windows NT 4.0*), 32-bit disk access can cause data corruption under Windows NT in some cases. Therefore, Microsoft recommends that Windows NT 4.0 users **disable** 32-bit Disk Access.

Microsoft took a serious view of the issue and corrected it in the Windows NT 4.0 Service Pack 2. Therefore, it is safe to **enable** 32-bit Disk Access in a Windows NT 4.0 system, so long as it has been upgraded with Service Pack 2.

It is highly advisable to **enable** 32-bit Transfer Mode because it realizes the performance poten-tial of the 32-bit IDE controller and improves the efficiency of the PCI bus. If you **disable** it, data transfers from the IDE controller to the processor only occur in 16-bits chunks. Naturally, this degrades the performance of the IDE controller as well as the PCI bus. As such, you should **disable** this feature *only* if you actually face the possibility of data corruption (with an unpatched version of Windows NT 4.0).

You can also find more information on the Windows NT issue in the details of the **IDE HDD Block Mode** feature.

A

Act Bank A to B CMD Delay

Common Options: 2 Cycles, 3 Cycles

Act Bank A to B CMD Delay (short for **Activate Bank A to Activate Bank B Command Delay**) or **tRRD** is a DDR timing parameter. It specifies the minimum amount of time between successive ACTIVATE commands to the *same* DDR device, even to *different* internal banks. The shorter the delay, the faster the next bank can be activated for read or write operations. However, because row activation requires a lot of current, using a short delay may cause excessive current surges.

Because this timing parameter is DDR device-specific, it may differ from one DDR device to another. DDR DRAM manufacturers typically specify the tRRD parameter based on the row ACTIVATE activity to limit current surges within the device. If you let the BIOS automatically configure your DRAM parameters, it retrieves the manufacturer-set tRRD value from the **SPD** (**Serial Presence Detect**) chip. However, you may want to manually set the tRRD parameter to suit your requirements.

For desktop PCs, a delay of **2 cycles** is recommended because current surges aren't really important. This is because the desktop PC essentially has an unlimited power supply, and even the most basic desktop cooling solution is sufficient to dispel any extra thermal load the current surges may impose. The performance benefit of using the shorter 2-cycle delay is of far greater interest. The shorter delay means every back-to-back bank activation takes one clock cycle less to perform. This improves the DDR device's performance.

Note that the shorter delay of **2 cycles** works with most DDR DIMMs, even at 133MHz (266MHz DDR). However, DDR DIMMs running beyond 133MHz (266MHz DDR) may need to introduce a delay of **3 cycles** between each successive bank activation. Select **2 cycles** whenever possible for optimal DDR DRAM performance. Switch to **3 cycles** only when there are stability problems with the 2-cycle setting.

In mobile devices like laptops, however, it is advisable to use the longer delay of **3 cycles**. Doing so limits the current surges that accompany row activations. This reduces the DDR device's power consumption and thermal output, both of which should be of great interest to the road warrior.

AGP 2X Mode

Common Options: Enabled, Disabled

This BIOS feature is found on AGP 2X-capable motherboards. When **enabled**, it allows the AGP bus to make use of the AGP 2X transfer protocol to boost the AGP bus bandwidth. If it's **disabled**, then the AGP bus only uses the standard AGP 1X transfer protocol.

The baseline AGP 1X protocol only makes use of the rising edge of the AGP signal for data transfer. This translates into a bandwidth of 264MB/s. However, enabling AGP 2X Mode doubles that bandwidth by transferring data on *both* the rising and falling edges of the signal. Through this method, the effective bandwidth of the AGP bus is doubled, even though the AGP clock speed remains at the standard 66MHz. This is the same method by which UltraDMA/33 derives its performance boost.

The AGP 2X protocol must be supported by both the motherboard and graphics card for this feature to work. Of course, this feature only appears in your BIOS if your motherboard supports the AGP 2X transfer protocol. So, all you need to do is make sure your graphics card supports AGP 2X transfers. If it does, **enable** AGP 2X Mode to take advantage of the faster transfer mode. **Disable** it only if you are facing stability issues or if you intend to overclock the AGP bus beyond 75MHz with **sidebanding support** enabled.

Please note that doubling the AGP bus bandwidth through the AGP 2X transfer protocol won't double the performance of your AGP graphics card. The performance of the graphics card relies on far more than the bandwidth of the AGP bus. The performance boost is most apparent when the AGP bus is really stressed (for example, during a texture-intensive game).

AGP 4X Drive Strength

Common Options: Auto, Manual

This BIOS feature is similar to **AGP Driving Control**. It allows you to set whether the AGP controller should dynamically adjust the AGP driving strength or allow manual configuration in the BIOS.

Because of the tighter tolerances of the AGP 4X bus, the AGP 4X controller features auto-compensation circuitry that compensates for the motherboard's impedance on the AGP bus. It does this by dynamically adjusting the drive strength of the I/O pads over a range of temperature and voltages when AGP 4X mode is selected.

The auto-compensation circuitry has two operating modes. By default, it is set to automatically compensate for the impedance once, or at regular intervals, by dynamically adjusting the AGP Drive Strength. The circuitry can also be disabled or bypassed. In this case, it is up to the user (through the BIOS) to write the desired drive strength value to the AGP I/O pads.

When you set this BIOS feature to **Auto**, the AGP Drive Strength values are obtained from the auto-compensation circuitry. Normally, this is the *recommended* setting as it allows the AGP controller to dynamically adjust for motherboard impedance changes. However, **Manual** configuration of the AGP Drive Strength may be necessary.

Some AGP 4X cards were not designed according to published AGP 4X signal impedance and routing guidelines. Therefore, these cards may not work reliably with the default drive strengths issued by the compensation circuit. To correct this problem, you can bypass the compensation circuit and force the AGP I/O pads to use a particular drive strength. Usually, this is a higher than normal drive strength.

You can also make use of this feature for overclocking purposes. Increasing the drive strength increases the stability of the AGP bus by reducing the impedance from the motherboard and boosting the signal strength. However, be very circumspect when you increase the AGP Drive Strength on an overclocked AGP bus because your AGP card may be irreversibly damaged in the process!

For troubleshooting or overclocking purposes, you should set the AGP 4X Drive Strength to **Manual**. This allows you to manually set the AGP Drive Strength value through the **AGP Drive Strength P Ctrl** and **AGP Drive Strength N Ctrl** options.

Please note that this feature is a little different from **AGP Driving Control** because it usually comes with two to four different drive strength controls. The **AGP Driving Control** feature only comes with a single drive strength control.

AGP 4X Mode

A

Common Options: Enabled, Disabled

This BIOS feature is only found on AGP 4X-capable motherboards. When **enabled**, it allows the AGP bus to make use of the AGP 4X transfer protocol to boost the AGP bus bandwidth. If it's **disabled**, then the AGP bus is only allowed to use the AGP 1X or AGP 2X transfer protocol.

The baseline AGP 1X protocol only makes use of the rising edge of the AGP signal for data transfer. This translates into a bandwidth of 264MB/s. The AGP 2X protocol doubles that by utilizing the falling edge of the AGP signal for data transfer as well.

However, the AGP 4X protocol uses four strobe signals to further double the bandwidth to just over 1GB/s. The four strobes can be used either as four separate signals (with data transferred only on the falling edge) or they can be used as two differential pairs, transferring data on both edges of the signals. Either way, the AGP bandwidth is quadrupled over that of the AGP 1X transfer protocol.

The AGP 4X protocol must be supported by both the motherboard and graphics card for this feature to work. Of course, this feature only appears in your BIOS if your motherboard supports the AGP 4X transfer protocol. So, all you need to do is make sure your graphics card supports AGP 4X transfers. If it does, **enable** AGP 4X Mode to take advantage of the faster transfer mode. You must **disable** it if your graphics card doesn't support AGP 4X transfers. The BIOS then reports that the maximum supported transfer mode is AGP 2X.

By default, many motherboards come with the AGP 4X transfer mode **disabled**. This is because not everyone uses AGP 4X-capable graphic cards. When cards capable of only AGP 1X or 2X operation are installed, this feature *must* be **disabled** for the cards to function properly. To prevent complications with uninformed users, most manufacturers simply disable AGP 4X mode by default.

However, this means that users of AGP 4X cards unnecessarily lose out on the greater amount of bandwidth available through the AGP 4X transfer mode. So, if you are using an AGP 4X-capable graphics card, it's recommended that you **enable** this feature for better AGP bus performance.

Please note that quadrupling the AGP bus bandwidth through the AGP 4X transfer protocol doesn't really quadruple the performance of your AGP graphics card. The performance of the graphics card relies on far more than the bandwidth of the AGP bus. The performance boost is most apparent when the AGP bus is really stressed (for example, during a texture-intensive game).

AGP 8X Mode

Common Options: Enabled, Disabled

This BIOS feature is only found on AGP 8X-capable motherboards. When **enabled**, it allows the AGP bus to make use of the AGP 8X transfer protocol to boost the AGP bus bandwidth. If it's **disabled**, then the AGP bus is only allowed to use the AGP 4X transfer protocol.

The baseline AGP 1X protocol only makes use of the rising edge of the AGP signal for data transfer. This translates into a bandwidth of 264MB/s. The AGP 2X protocol doubles that by utilizing the falling edge of the AGP signal for data transfer as well. The AGP 4X protocol uses four strobe signals to further double the bandwidth to just over 1GB/s.

To double the transfer again, the new AGP 8X protocol now strobes the source synchronous signals at 8 times the reference frequency of 66MHz. This allows AGP 8X to boast a bandwidth of 2.1GB/s!

The AGP 8X protocol also boasts the following new features:

- New terminated signaling scheme with a lower voltage swing
- Dynamic calibration cycle
- Isochronous Transactions support
- Dynamic Bus Inversion support
- Support for multiple AGP ports
- Support for multiple GART page sizes

The AGP 8X protocol must be supported by both the motherboard and graphics card for this feature to work. Of course, this feature only appears in your BIOS if your motherboard supports the AGP 8X transfer protocol! So, all you need to do is make sure your graphics card supports AGP 8X transfers. If it does, **enable** AGP 8X Mode to take advantage of the faster transfer mode. You must **disable** it if your graphics card doesn't support AGP 8X transfers. The BIOS then reports that the maximum supported transfer mode is AGP 4X.

By default, many motherboards come with the AGP 8X transfer mode **disabled**. This is because not everyone uses AGP 8X-capable graphic cards. When cards capable of only AGP 4X operation are installed, this feature *must* be **disabled** for the cards to function properly. To prevent complications with uninformed users, most manufacturers simply disable AGP 8X mode by default.

However, this means that users of AGP 8X cards unnecessarily lose out on the greater amount of bandwidth available through the AGP 8X transfer mode. So, if you are using an AGP 8X-capable graphics card, it's recommended that you **enable** this feature for better AGP bus performance.

Please note that quadrupling the AGP bus bandwidth through the AGP 8X transfer protocol doesn't quadruple the performance of your AGP graphics card. The performance of the graphics card relies on far more than the bandwidth of the AGP bus. The performance boost is most apparent when the AGP bus is really stressed (for example, during a texture-intensive game).

AGP Always Compensate

Common Options: Enabled, Disabled

This feature is somewhat similar to the **AGP Drive Strength** feature. It determines whether the AGP controller should be allowed to dynamically adjust the AGP driving strength or use preset drive strength values.

Due to the tighter tolerances of the AGP 4X/8X bus, the AGP controller features auto-compensation circuitry that compensate for the motherboard's impedance on the AGP bus. It does this by dynamically adjusting the drive strength of the I/O pads over a range of temperatures and voltages.

The auto-compensation circuitry has two operating modes. By default, it is set to automatically compensate for the impedance once, or at regular intervals, by dynamically adjusting the AGP Drive Strength. The circuitry also can be disabled or bypassed. In this case, it is up to the user (through the BIOS) to write the desired drive strength value to the AGP I/O pads.

This is where **AGP Always Compensate** differs from the **AGP Drive Strength** feature. While AGP Drive Strength allows you to switch to manual configuration by the user, AGP Always Compensate does not. It only allows you to change the auto-compensation mode.

When you **enable** AGP Always Compensate, the auto-compensation circuitry dynamically compensates for changes in the impedance *at regular intervals*. If you **disable** it, the circuitry only compensates for the impedance *once* at boot-up. The drive strength values derived at boot-up remain until the system is rebooted.

It is recommended that you **enable** AGP Always Compensate, so the AGP controller can initiate dynamic compensation at regular intervals. This allows it to compensate for any changes in the impedance.

AGP Aperture Size

Common Options: 4, 8, 16, 32, 64, 128, 256

This BIOS feature does two things. It selects the size of the AGP aperture and it determines the size of the **GART (Graphics Address Relocation Table)**.

The aperture is a portion of the PCI memory address range dedicated for use as AGP memory address space, while the GART is a translation table that translates AGP memory addresses into actual memory addresses that are often fragmented. The GART allows the graphics card to see the memory region available to it as a contiguous piece of memory range.

Host cycles that hit the aperture address range are forwarded to the AGP bus without need for translation. The aperture size also determines the maximum amount of system memory that can be allocated to the AGP graphics card for texture storage.

The AGP aperture size is calculated using this formula:

AGP Aperture Size = (Maximum usable AGP memory size × 2) + 12MB

As you can see, the actual available AGP memory space is less than half the AGP aperture size set in the BIOS. This is because the AGP controller needs a **write combined memory area** equal in size to the actual AGP memory area (uncached), plus an additional 12MB for **virtual addressing**.

Therefore, it isn't simply a matter of determining how much AGP memory space you need. You also need to calculate the final aperture size by doubling the amount of AGP memory space desired and adding 12MB to the total.

Please note that the AGP aperture is merely address space, not actual physical memory in use. It doesn't lock up any of your system memory. The physical memory is allocated and released as needed whenever Direct3D makes a create non-local surface call.

Windows 95 (with VGARTD.VXD), and later versions of Microsoft Windows, use a waterfall method of memory allocation. Surfaces are first created in the graphics card's local memory. When that memory is full, surface creation spills over into AGP memory and then system memory. So, memory usage is automatically optimized for each application. AGP and system memory are not used unless absolutely necessary.

Unfortunately, it is very common to hear people recommending that the AGP aperture size should be half the size of system memory. However, this is wrong for the same reason swapfile size should not be fixed at 1/4 of system memory. Like the swapfile, the requirement for AGP memory space shrinks as the graphics card's local memory increases in size. This is because the graphics card has more local memory to use for texture storage!

This reduces the need for AGP memory. Therefore, when you upgrade to a graphics card with more memory, you shouldn't be deceived into thinking that you need even more AGP memory! On the contrary, a smaller AGP memory space is required.

If your graphics card has very little graphics memory (4MB–16MB), you may need to create a large AGP aperture, up to half the size of the system memory. The graphics card's local memory and the AGP aperture size combined should be roughly around **64MB**. Please note that the size of the aperture does not correspond to performance! Increasing it to gargantuan proportions does not improve performance.

Still, it is recommended that you keep the AGP aperture size around **64MB** to **128MB**. Now, why should we use such a large aperture size when most graphics cards come with large amounts of local memory? Shouldn't we set it to the absolute minimum to save system memory?

1. First of all, setting it to a lower memory *won't* save you memory! Don't forget that all the AGP aperture size does is limit the amount of system memory the AGP bus can appropriate whenever it needs more memory. It is *not* used unless absolutely necessary. So, setting the AGP aperture size to 64MB doesn't mean that 64MB of your system memory is appropriated and reserved for the AGP bus use. What it does is limit the AGP bus to a maximum of 64MB of system memory when the need arises.

2. Next, most graphics cards require an AGP aperture of at least 16MB in size to work properly. Many new graphics cards require even more. This is probably because the virtual addressing space is already 12MB in size. So, setting the AGP aperture size to 4MB or 8MB is a big no-no.

3. We should also remember that many software have AGP aperture size and texture storage requirements that are mostly unspecified. Some applications will not work with AGP apertures that are too small. And some games use so much texture that a large AGP aperture is needed even with graphics cards with large memory buffers.

4. Finally, you should remember that the actual available AGP memory space is less than half the size of the AGP aperture size you set. If you want just 15MB of AGP memory for texture storage, the AGP aperture has to be at least 42MB in size. Therefore, it makes sense to set a large AGP aperture size to cater to all eventualities.

Now, while increasing the AGP aperture size beyond 128MB doesn't take up system memory, it still is best to keep the aperture size in the **64MB–128MB** range, so the GART won't become too big. The larger the GART gets, the longer it takes to scan through the GART to find the translated address for each AGP memory address request.

With local memory on graphics cards increasing to incredible sizes and texture compression commonplace, there's really not much need for the AGP aperture size to grow beyond 64MB. Therefore, it is recommended that you set the AGP Aperture Size to **64MB** or at most, **128MB**.

A

AGP Capability

Common Options: Auto, 1X Mode, 2X Mode, 4X Mode, 8X Mode

This BIOS feature is only found in AGP 8X-capable motherboards. AGP 8X is backward-compatible with earlier AGP standards. This BIOS feature allows you to set the motherboard's maximum supported AGP transfer protocol.

When this BIOS feature is set to **Auto**, the motherboard automatically selects the appropriate AGP transfer protocol after detecting the capabilities of the AGP graphics card.

When this BIOS feature is set to **1X Mode**, the motherboard forces the AGP bus to use the AGP 1X transfer protocol. AGP 1X allows a maximum transfer rate of **266MB/s**.

When this BIOS feature is set to **2X Mode**, the motherboard forces the AGP bus to use the AGP 2X transfer protocol. AGP 2X allows a maximum transfer rate of **533MB/s**.

When this BIOS feature is set to **4X Mode**, the motherboard forces the AGP bus to use the AGP 4X transfer protocol. AGP 4X allows a maximum transfer rate of **1GB/s**.

When this BIOS feature is set to **8X Mode**, the motherboard forces the AGP bus to use the AGP 2X transfer protocol. AGP 8X allows a maximum transfer rate of **2.1GB/s**.

It is recommended that you leave this BIOS feature at its default setting of **Auto**. This allows the motherboard to set the appropriate AGP transfer protocol based on the graphics card's AGP support detected during the boot up process.

However, the other options are useful if your graphics card has problems using the detected AGP transfer protocol. You can manually select a slower AGP transfer protocol to solve the problem.

Please note that manually setting the AGP Capabilities BIOS feature to **8X Mode** does not enable AGP 8X transfers if your graphics card supports only AGP 4X. The AGP bus makes use of the fastest AGP transfer protocol supported by both motherboard and graphics card.

AGP Clock / CPU FSB Clock

Common Options: 1/1, 2/3, 1/2, 2/5

The AGP bus clock speed is referenced from the CPU bus clock speed. However, the AGP bus was only designed to run at 66MHz while the CPU bus runs anywhere from 66MHz to 133MHz. Therefore, a suitable AGP bus to CPU bus clock speed ratio or divider must be select-ed to ensure that the AGP bus does not run way beyond 66MHz.

When the ratio is set to **1/1**, the AGP bus runs at the same speed as the CPU bus. This is meant for processors that use the 66MHz bus speed, like the older Intel Celeron processors.

A

The **2/3** divider is used when you use a processor running with a bus speed of 100MHz. This divider cuts the AGP bus speed down to 66MHz.

The **1/2** divider was introduced with motherboards that provide 133MHz bus speed support. Such motherboards need the **1/2** divider to make the AGP bus run at the standard 66MHz. Without this divider, the AGP bus would have to run at 89MHz, which is more than what most AGP cards can withstand.

The **2/5** divider was introduced with motherboards that provide 166MHz bus speed support. Such motherboards need the **2/5** divider to make the AGP bus run at the standard 66MHz. Without this divider, the AGP bus would have to run at 83MHz, which is more than what most AGP cards can withstand.

Generally, you should set this feature according to the CPU bus speed you are using. This means using the **1/1** divider for 66MHz bus speed CPUs, the **2/3** divider for 100MHz bus speed CPUs, the **1/2** divider for 133MHz CPUs, and the **2/5** divider for 166MHz CPUs.

If you are overclocking the CPU bus, you are supposed to reduce the divider to ensure that the AGP bus speed remains within specifications. However, most AGP cards can run with the AGP bus overclocked to 75MHz. Some even happily run at 83MHz! However, anything above 83MHz is a little iffy.

In most cases, you can stick with the original AGP bus/CPU bus clock divider when you overclock the CPU. This means that the AGP bus is overclocked as well. As long as the AGP card can work at the higher clock speed, it shouldn't be a problem. In fact, you can expect a linear increase in AGP bus performance.

Be warned, though—overclocking the AGP bus *can* potentially damage your AGP card. So, be circumspect when you overclock the AGP bus. 75MHz is normally the safe limit for most AGP cards.

AGP Drive Strength

Common Options: Auto, Manual

This BIOS feature is similar to **AGP Driving Control**. It allows you to set whether to allow the AGP controller to dynamically adjust the AGP driving strength or to allow manual configuration by the BIOS.

Due to the tighter tolerances of the AGP 4X/8X bus, the AGP controller features auto-compensation circuitry that compensate for the motherboard's impedance on the AGP bus. It does this by dynamically adjusting the drive strength of the I/O pads over a range of temperatures and voltages.

The auto-compensation circuitry has two operating modes. By default, it is set to automatically compensate for the impedance once or at regular intervals by dynamically adjusting the AGP Drive Strength. The circuitry can also be disabled or bypassed. In this case, it is up to the user (through the BIOS) to write the desired drive strength value to the AGP I/O pads.

When you set this BIOS feature to **Auto**, the AGP Drive Strength values are obtained from the auto-compensation circuitry. Normally, this is the *recommended* setting as it allows the AGP controller to dynamically adjust for motherboard impedance changes. However, manual configuration of the AGP Drive Strength may be necessary.

Some AGP 4X/8X cards were not designed according to published AGP 4X/8X signal impedance and routing guidelines. Therefore, these cards may not work reliably with the default drive
strengths issued by the compensation circuit. To correct this problem, you can bypass the compensation circuit and force the AGP I/O pads to use a particular drive strength. Usually, this will
be a higher than normal drive strength.

You can also make use of this feature for overclocking purposes. Increasing the drive strength
increases the stability of the AGP bus by reducing the impedance from the motherboard and
boosting the signal strength. But be very, very circumspect when you increase the AGP Drive
Strength on an overclocked AGP bus as your AGP card may be irreversibly damaged in the
process!

Therefore, for troubleshooting or overclocking purposes, you should set the AGP Drive Strength
to **Manual**. This allows you to manually set the AGP Drive Strength value through the **AGP
Drive Strength P Ctrl** and **AGP Drive Strength N Ctrl** options.

Please note that this feature is a little different from **AGP Driving Control** because it usually
comes with two to four different drive strength controls. The **AGP Driving Control** feature
only comes with a single drive strength control.

AGP Drive Strength N Ctrl

Common Options: 0 to F (Hex numbers), 0h to Fh

This is one of the functions slaved to the **AGP Drive Strength** feature. If you set the AGP
Drive Strength to **Auto**, then the value you choose doesn't have any effect. For this function to
have any effect, you need to set the AGP Drive Strength to **Manual**.

This function determines the N transistor drive strength of the AGP bus. The drive strength is
represented by Hex values from 0 to F (0 to 15 in decimal). The default N transistor drive
strength differs from motherboard to motherboard. But the higher the drive strength, the greater
the compensation for the motherboard's impedance on the AGP bus.

In conjunction with **AGP Drive Strength** and **AGP Drive Strength P Ctrl**, this function is
used to bypass AGP dynamic compensation in cases where the auto-compensation circuitry
cannot provide adequate compensation. This is mainly seen when the AGP graphics card was
not designed according to the AGP 4X/8X impedance and routing guidelines. Please check
with your graphics card manufacturer if your card requires the N transistor drive strength to be
manually set.

Due to the nature of this BIOS function, it is possible to use it as an aid in overclocking the
AGP bus. The AGP bus is sensitive to overclocking, especially in AGP 4X/8X mode, with sideband and Fast Write support enabled. A higher N (and P) transistor drive strength may be just
what you need to overclock the AGP bus higher than is normally possible. By raising the drive
strength of the AGP bus, you can improve its stability at overclocked speeds.

Please be very circumspect when you increase the AGP Drive Strength on an overclocked AGP
bus because your AGP card may be irreversibly damaged in the process! Also, contrary to popular opinion, increasing the AGP Drive Strength does *not* improve the performance of the AGP
bus. It is not a performance-enhancing feature, so you shouldn't increase the N transistor drive
strength unless you need to.

AGP Drive Strength P Ctrl

Common Options: 0 to F (Hex numbers), 0h to Fh

This is one of the functions slaved to the **AGP Drive Strength** feature. If you set the AGP Drive Strength to **Auto**, then the value you choose doesn't have any effect. For this function to have any effect, you need to set the AGP Drive Strength to **Manual**.

This function determines the P transistor drive strength of the AGP bus. The drive strength is represented by Hex values from 0 to F (0 to 15 in decimal). The default P transistor drive strength differs from motherboard to motherboard. But the higher the drive strength, the greater the compensation for the motherboard's impedance on the AGP bus.

In conjunction with **AGP Drive Strength** and **AGP Drive Strength N Ctrl**, this function is used to bypass AGP dynamic compensation in cases where the auto-compensation circuitry cannot provide adequate compensation. This is mainly seen when the AGP graphics card was not designed according to the AGP 4X/8X impedance and routing guidelines. Please check with your graphics card manufacturer if your card requires the P transistor drive strength to be manually set.

Due to the nature of this BIOS function, it is possible to use it as an aid in overclocking the AGP bus. The AGP bus is sensitive to overclocking, especially in AGP 4X/8X mode, with side-band and Fast Write support enabled. A higher P (and N) transistor drive strength may be just what you need to overclock the AGP bus higher than is normally possible. By raising the drive strength of the AGP bus, you can improve its stability at overclocked speeds.

Please be very circumspect when you increase the AGP Drive Strength on an overclocked AGP bus because your AGP card may be irreversibly damaged in the process! Also, contrary to popular opinion, increasing the AGP Drive Strength does *not* improve the performance of the AGP bus. It is not a performance-enhancing feature, so you shouldn't increase the P transistor drive strength unless you need to.

AGP Driving Control

Common Options: Auto, Manual

This feature is similar to **AGP 4X Drive Strength**. It allows you to set whether the AGP controller should dynamically adjust the AGP driving strength or allow manual configuration by the BIOS.

Due to the tighter tolerances of the AGP 4X/8X bus, the AGP controller features auto-compensation circuitry that compensates for the motherboard's impedance on the AGP bus. It does this by dynamically adjusting the drive strength of the I/O pads over a range of temperatures and voltages when AGP 4X/8X mode is selected.

The auto-compensation circuitry has two operating modes. By default, it is set to automatically compensate for the impedance once or at regular intervals by dynamically adjusting the AGP Drive Strength. The circuitry can also be disabled or bypassed. In this case, it is up to the user (through the BIOS) to write the desired drive strength value to the AGP I/O pads.

When you set this BIOS feature to **Auto**, the AGP Drive Strength values are obtained from the auto-compensation circuitry. Normally, this is the *recommended* setting because it allows the AGP controller to dynamically adjust for motherboard impedance changes. However, manual configuration of the AGP Drive Strength may be necessary.

Some AGP 4X/8X cards were not designed according to published AGP 4X/8X signal impedance and routing guidelines. Therefore, these cards may not work reliably with the default drive strengths issued by the compensation circuit. To correct this problem, you can bypass the compensation circuit and force the AGP I/O pads to use a particular drive strength. Usually, this is a higher than normal drive strength.

You can also make use of this feature for overclocking purposes. Increasing the drive strength increases the stability of the AGP bus by reducing the impedance from the motherboard and boosting the signal strength. However, be very circumspect when you increase the AGP Drive Strength on an overclocked AGP bus because your AGP card may be irreversibly damaged in the process!

Therefore, for troubleshooting or overclocking purposes, you should set the AGP Driving Control to **Manual**. This allows you to manually set the AGP Drive Strength value through the **AGP Driving Value** function.

Please note that this feature is a little different from **AGP 4X Drive Strength** because it usually comes with a single drive strength control. The **AGP 4X Drive Strength** feature comes with two to four drive strength controls.

AGP Driving Value

Common Options: 00 to FF (Hex numbers), 00h to FFh

This function is slaved to **AGP Driving Control**. If you set the AGP Driving Control to **Auto**, then the value you set here won't have any effect. In order for this function to have any effect, you need to set the AGP Driving Control to **Manual**.

This function determines the overall drive strength of the AGP bus. The drive strength is represented by Hex values from 00 to FF (0 to 255 in decimal). The default AGP Drive Strength differs from motherboard to motherboard. But the higher the drive strength, the greater the compensation for the motherboard's impedance on the AGP bus. On the reference motherboard, the default drive strength was C5 (197).

In conjunction with **AGP Driving Control**, this function is used to bypass AGP dynamic compensation in cases where the auto-compensation circuitry cannot provide adequate compensation. This is mainly seen when the AGP graphics card was not designed according to the AGP 4X/8X impedance and routing guidelines. If you are using an AGP card built around the NVIDIA GeForce 2 line of GPUs, then it is recommended that you put **AGP Driving Control** into **Manual** mode and set the AGP Driving Value to **EA** (234). For other cards, please check with the manufacturer if your card requires the AGP driving strength to be set manually.

Due to the nature of this BIOS function, it is possible to use it as an aid in overclocking the AGP bus. The AGP bus is sensitive to overclocking, especially in AGP 4X/8X mode, with sideband and Fast Write support enabled. A higher AGP Drive Strength may be just what you need to overclock the AGP bus higher than is normally possible. By raising the drive strength of the AGP bus, you can improve its stability at overclocked speeds.

Please be very circumspect when you increase the AGP Drive Strength on an overclocked AGP bus because your AGP card may be irreversibly damaged in the process! Also, contrary to popular opinion, increasing the AGP Drive Strength does *not* improve the performance of the AGP bus. It is not a performance-enhancing feature, so you shouldn't increase the AGP Drive Strength unless you need to.

AGP Fast Write

Common Options: Enabled, Disabled

This BIOS feature controls the chipset's **AGP Fast Write** capability. Fast Write is a feature that accelerates memory write transactions from the chipset to the AGP device.

Normally, any data meant for the AGP device must be written to the main memory for the AGP device to read. Fast Write allows the AGP device to bypass the main memory and directly access the data. To do so, the AGP device acts as a PCI device whenever the chipset attempts to write to it. This allows the data to be written directly to the AGP device (*like other PCI devices*), instead of being written to the main memory first.

As you can see, bypassing the main memory saves time and improves the AGP read performance. However, AGP writes (to the chipset) do *not* benefit from Fast Writes because it follows normal AGP protocol and writes to the main memory.

In addition, while PCI signals are used for Fast Write transactions, the behavior of those PCI signals has been modified, so they do not follow PCI specifications. Therefore, this feature may cause problems with some PCI cards.

Therefore, it is recommended that you **enable** AGP Fast Write for better AGP read performance, but **disable** it if any of your PCI cards start acting funny.

Please note that for AGP Fast Write to work, both motherboard chipset and graphics card must support the Fast Write protocol, and the data transfer rate must be AGP2X or faster.

AGP ISA Aliasing

Common Options: Enabled, Disabled

The origin of this feature can be traced back all the way to the original IBM PC. When the IBM PC was designed, it only had 10 address lines (**10-bits**) for I/O space allocation. Therefore, the I/O space back in those days was only **1KB**, or 1024 bytes in size. Out of those 1024 available addresses, the first **256 addresses** were reserved exclusively for the motherboard's use, leaving the last **768 addresses** for use by add-in devices. This would eventually become a critical factor.

Later, motherboards began to utilize *16* address lines for I/O space allocation. This was supposed to create a contiguous I/O space of 64KB in size. Unfortunately, many ISA devices were only capable of doing 10-bit decodes. This was because they were designed for computers based on the original IBM design, which only supported 10 address lines.

To circumvent this problem, they fragmented the 64KB I/O space into **1KB** chunks. Unfortunately, because the first 256 addresses must be reserved exclusively for the motherboard, this meant that only the first (*or lower*) 256 bytes of each 1KB chunk could be decoded in full 16-bits. All 10-bits-decoding ISA devices are, therefore, restricted to the last (or top) 768 bytes of the 1KB chunk of I/O space.

As a result, such ISA devices only have 768 I/O locations to use. Because there were so many ISA devices back then, this limitation created a lot of compatibility problems because the chances of two ISA cards using the same I/O space were high. When that happened, one or both of the cards would not work. Although they tried to reduce the chance of such conflicts by standardizing the I/O locations used by different classes of ISA devices, it was still not good enough.

Eventually, they came up with a workaround. Instead of giving each ISA device all the I/O space it wants in the 10-bit range, they gave each ISA device a much smaller number of I/O locations and made up for the difference by "borrowing" them from the 16-bit I/O space! Here's how they did it.

The ISA device take up a small number of I/O locations in the 10-bit range. It then extends its I/O space by using **16-bit aliases** of the few 10-bit I/O locations taken up earlier. Because each I/O location in the 10-bit decode area has **sixty-three** 16-bit aliases, the total number of I/O locations expands from just 768 locations to a maximum of 49,152 locations!

More importantly, each ISA card now requires very few I/O locations in the 10-bit range. This drastically reduced the chances of two ISA cards conflicting with each other in the limited 10-bit I/O space. This workaround became known as **ISA Aliasing**.

Now, that's all well and good for ISA devices. Unfortunately, the 10-bit limitation of ISA devices becomes a liability to devices that require 16-bit addressing; AGP and PCI devices come to mind. As noted earlier, only the first 256 addresses of the 1KB chunks support 16-bit addressing. What that really means is all 16-bit addressing devices are limited to only 256 bytes of *contiguous* I/O space.

When a 16-bit addressing device requires a larger contiguous I/O space, it has to encroach on the 10-bit ISA I/O space. For example, if an AGP card requires 8KB of contiguous I/O space, it takes up *eight* of the 1KB I/O chunks (*which comprise of eight 16-bit areas and eight 10-bit areas!*). Because ISA devices are using ISA Aliasing to extend their I/O space, there is a high chance of I/O space conflicts between ISA devices and the AGP card. When that happens, the affected cards generally fail to work.

There are two ways out of this mess. Obviously, you can limit the AGP card to a maximum of 256 bytes of contiguous I/O space. Of course, this is not an acceptable solution.

The second, and the preferred method, is to throw away the restriction and provide the AGP card with all the contiguous I/O space it wants.

Here's where the **AGP ISA Aliasing** BIOS feature comes in. The default setting of **Enabled** forces the system controller to alias ISA addresses using address bits [15:10]—the last 6-bits. Only the first 10-bits (address bits 0 to 9) are used for decoding. This restricts all 16-bit addressing devices to a maximum contiguous I/O space of 256 bytes.

When **disabled**, the system controller does not perform any ISA aliasing and all 16 address lines can be used for I/O address space decoding. This gives 16-bit addressing devices access to the full 64KB I/O space.

It is recommended that you **disable** AGP ISA Aliasing for optimal AGP (and PCI) performance. It also prevents your AGP or PCI cards from conflicting with your ISA cards. **Enable** it only if you have ISA devices that are conflicting with each other.

AGP Master 1WS Read

Common Options: Enabled, Disabled

In most motherboards, the AGP bus-mastering device has to wait for at least two wait states (AGP clock cycles) before it can initiate a read command. This BIOS feature allows you to reduce that delay to only one wait state. This speeds up all reads that the AGP bus-master makes from the system memory.

So, for better AGP read performance, **enable** this feature. **Disable** it only if you notice visual anomalies like wireframe effects and pixel artifacts, or if your system depends on running software that makes use of AGP texturing.

Curiously, some motherboards come with a default AGP master read latency of **0**! Enabling the AGP Master 1WS Read in such cases actually *increases* the latency by one wait state and reduces AGP read performance. Although it's quite unlikely that the default AGP master read latency would be zero, that's what their manuals say.

So, check your motherboard manual to see if your motherboard's manufacturer implemented the first (and more common) interpretation of the AGP Master 1WS Read feature or the second one. Either way, the lower the AGP master read latency, the higher the read performance of the AGP bus.

AGP Master 1WS Write

Common Options: Enabled, Disabled

In most motherboards, the AGP bus-mastering device has to wait for at least two wait states (AGP clock cycles) before it can initiate a write command. This BIOS feature allows you to reduce that delay to only one wait state. This speeds up all writes that the AGP bus-master makes to the system memory.

So, for better AGP write performance, **enable** this feature. **Disable** it only if you notice visual anomalies like wireframe effects and pixel artifacts, or if your system depends on running software that makes use of AGP texturing.

Curiously, some motherboards come with a default AGP master write latency of **0**! Enabling the AGP Master 1WS Write in such cases actually *increases* the latency by one wait state and reduces AGP write performance. Although it's quite unlikely that the default AGP master write latency would be zero, that's what their manuals say.

So, check your motherboard manual to see if your motherboard's manufacturer implemented the first (and more common) interpretation of the AGP Master 1WS Write feature or the second one. Either way, the lower the AGP master write latency, the higher the write performance of the AGP bus.

AGP Prefetch

Common Options: Enabled, Disabled

This feature controls the system controller's AGP prefetch capability. When **enabled**, the system controller prefetches data whenever the AGP device reads from the system memory. Here's how it works.

Whenever the system controller reads AGP-requested data from the system memory, it also reads the subsequent chunk of data. This is done on the assumption that the AGP device requests the subsequent chunk of data. When the AGP device actually initiates a read command for that chunk of data, the system controller can immediately send it to the AGP device.

This speeds up AGP reads because the AGP device doesn't need to wait for the system controller to read from the system memory. As such, AGP Prefetch allows contiguous memory reads by the AGP device to proceed with minimal delay.

Therefore, it is recommended that you **enable** this feature for better AGP read performance. Please note that AGP writes to the system memory do not benefit from this feature.

AGP Secondary Lat Timer

Common Options: 00h, 20h, 40h, 60h, 80h, C0h, FFh

A bridge is a device that connects a primary bus (which connects to the host) with one or more logical secondary buses. The AGP bus is therefore a secondary bus connected to the PCI bus through a PCI-to-PCI bridge.

This BIOS feature is similar to the **PCI Latency Timer** BIOS feature. The only difference is this latency timer only applies to the AGP bus, which is a secondary bus connected to the PCI bus through a PCI-to-PCI bridge.

However, it is unknown why they named this BIOS feature **AGP Secondary Lat Timer** instead of the more appropriate AGP Latency Timer, or even PCI Secondary Latency Timer. The name is both misleading and inaccurate because the AGP bus does not have a secondary latency timer.

This BIOS feature controls how long the AGP bus can hold the PCI bus (through the PCI-to-PCI bridge) before another PCI device takes over. The longer the latency, the longer the AGP bus can retain control of the PCI bus before handing it over to another PCI device.

Because a bridge device introduces an additional delay to every transaction, a short latency further reduces the amount of time the AGP bus has access to the PCI bus. A longer latency allows the AGP bus more time to transact on the PCI bus. This speeds up AGP-to-PCI transactions.

The available options range is usually stated in terms of hexadecimal numbers. Here is a translation of those numbers into actual latencies:

Option (Hex)	Actual Latency
00h	0
20h	32
40h	64
60h	96
80h	128
C0h	192
FFh	255

Normally, the AGP Secondary Latency Timer is set to **20h** (**32 clock cycles**). This means the AGP bus PCI-to-PCI bridge has to complete its transactions within 32 clock cycles or hand it over to the next PCI device.

For better AGP performance, a longer latency should be used. Try increasing it to **40h** (**64 cycles**) or even **80h** (**128 cycles**). The optimal value for every system is different. You should benchmark your AGP card's performance after each change to determine the optimal latency for your system.

Please note that a longer latency isn't necessarily better. A long latency can reduce performance because the other PCI devices queuing up may be stalled for too long. This is especially true with systems with many PCI devices or PCI devices that continuously write short bursts of data to the PCI bus. Such systems work better with shorter latencies because they allow quicker access to the PCI bus.

Therefore, if you set the AGP Secondary Latency Timer to a very large value like **80h** (**128 cycles**) or **C0h** (**192 cycles**), it is recommended that you set the **PCI Latency Time** to **32 cycles**. This provides better access for your PCI devices that might be unnecessarily stalled if both the AGP and PCI buses have very long latencies.

In addition, some time-critical PCI devices may not agree with a long AGP latency. Such devices require priority access to the PCI bus, which may not be possible if the PCI bus is held up by the AGP bus for a long period. In such cases, it is recommended that you keep to the default latency of **20h** (**32 clock cycles**).

AGP Spread Spectrum

Common Options: 0.25%, 0.5%, Disabled

When the motherboard's clock generator pulses, the extreme values (*spikes*) of these signals generated create **EMI** (**Electromagnetic Interference**). This EMI interferes with other electronics in the area. There are also claims that it may allow electronic eavesdropping of the data that is being transmitted.

This BIOS feature allows you to reduce the EMI of the AGP bus by modulating the signals it generates, so the spikes are reduced to flatter curves. It achieves this by varying the frequency *slightly*, so the signal does not use any particular frequency for more than a moment. This reduces the amount of EMI generated by the motherboard.

The BIOS usually offers two levels of modulation: **0.25%** or **0.5%**. They denote the amount of modulation or jitter from the baseline signal. The greater the modulation, the greater the reduction of EMI. Therefore, if you need to significantly reduce the AGP bus EMI, a modulation of **0.5%** is recommended.

In most conditions, frequency modulation through this feature should not cause any problems. However, system stability may be compromised if you are overclocking the AGP bus. Of course, this depends on the amount of modulation, the extent of overclocking, and other factors like temperature, and so forth. As such, the problem may not manifest itself immediately.

Therefore, it is recommended that you **disable** this feature if you are overclocking the AGP bus. The risk of crashing your system is not worth the reduction in EMI. Of course, if EMI reduction is important to you, **enable** this feature by all means. But you should reduce the clock speed a little to provide a margin of safety.

If you are not overclocking, the decision to enable or disable this feature is really up to you. But unless you have EMI problems or sensitive data that must be safeguarded from electronic eavesdropping, it is best to **disable** this feature to remove the possibility of instability.

AGP to DRAM Prefetch

Common Options: Enabled, Disabled

This feature controls the system controller's AGP prefetch capability. When **enabled**, the system controller prefetches data whenever the AGP device reads from the system memory. Here's how it works.

When the system controller reads AGP-requested data from the system memory, it also reads the subsequent chunk of data. This is done on the assumption that the AGP device will request the subsequent chunk of data. When the AGP device actually initiates a read command for that chunk of data, the system controller can immediately send it to the AGP device.

This speeds up AGP reads because the AGP device doesn't need to wait for the system controller to read from the system memory. As such, AGP to DRAM Prefetch allows contiguous memory reads by the AGP device to proceed with minimal delay.

Therefore, it is recommended that you **enable** this feature for better AGP read performance. Please note that AGP writes to the system memory do not benefit from this feature.

AGPCLK / CPUCLK

Common Options: 1/1, 2/3, 1/2, 2/5

The AGP bus clock speed is referenced from the CPU bus clock speed. However, the AGP bus was only designed to run at 66MHz while the CPU bus runs anywhere from 66MHz to 133MHz. Therefore, a suitable AGP bus to CPU bus clock speed ratio or divider must be selected to ensure that the AGP bus doesn't run way beyond 66MHz.

When the ratio is set to **1/1**, the AGP bus runs at the same speed as the CPU bus. This is meant for processors that use the 66MHz bus speed, like the older Intel Celeron processors.

The **2/3** divider is used when you use a processor running with a bus speed of 100MHz. This divider cuts the AGP bus speed down to 66MHz.

The **1/2** divider was introduced with motherboards that provide 133MHz bus speed support. Such motherboards need the **1/2** divider to make the AGP bus run at the standard 66MHz. Without this divider, the AGP bus would have to run at 89MHz, which is more than what most AGP cards can withstand.

The **2/5** divider was introduced with motherboards that provide 166MHz bus speed support. Such motherboards need the **2/5** divider to make the AGP bus run at the standard 66MHz. Without this divider, the AGP bus would have to run at 83MHz, which is more than what most AGP cards can withstand.

Generally, you should set this feature according to the CPU bus speed you are using. This means using the **1/1** divider for 66MHz bus speed CPUs, the **2/3** divider for 100MHz bus speed CPUs, the **1/2** divider for 133MHz CPUs, and the **2/5** divider for 166MHz CPUs.

If you are overclocking the CPU bus, you are supposed to reduce the divider to ensure that the AGP bus speed remains within specifications. However, most AGP cards can run with the AGP bus overclocked to 75MHz. Some even happily run at 83MHz! However, anything above 83MHz is a little iffy.

A

In most cases, you can still stick with the original AGP bus/CPU bus clock divider when you overclock the CPU. This means that the AGP bus is overclocked as well. However, as long as the AGP card can work at the higher clock speed, it shouldn't be a problem. In fact, you can expect a linear increase in AGP bus performance.

Be warned, though—overclocking the AGP bus potentially *can* damage your AGP card. So, be circumspect when you overclock the AGP bus. 75MHz is normally the safe limit for most AGP cards.

Anti-Virus Protection

Common Options: Enabled, Disabled, ChipAway

The Anti-Virus Protection feature is actually an enhanced version of the **Virus Warning** feature. Besides the standard boot sector or partition table protection, this BIOS feature also offers more comprehensive anti-virus protection through built-in, rule-based, anti-virus code such as **ChipAway**.

When you **enable** this feature, the BIOS halts the system and flashes a warning message whenever there's an attempt to write to the boot sector or the partition table. Note that this only protects the boot sector and the partition table, not the entire hard disk.

This feature can cause problems with software that needs to access the boot sector. One good example is the installation routine of all versions of Microsoft Windows from Windows 95 onward. When **enabled**, this feature causes the installation routine to fail. Also, many disk diagnostic utilities that access the boot sector can also trigger the system halt and error message as well. Therefore, you should **disable** this feature before running such software.

Alternatively, you can select the internal rule-based, anti-virus code. The software used in the reference motherboard is called **ChipAway**. Enabling **ChipAway** provides better anti-virus protection by scanning for and detecting boot viruses before they have a chance to infect the boot sector of any hard disk.

Note that this feature is useless for hard disks that run on external controllers with their own BIOS. Boot sector viruses bypass the system BIOS with its anti-virus protection features and write directly to the hard disks. Such controllers include additional IDE or SCSI controllers that are either built into the motherboard or available through add-on cards.

APIC Function

Common Options: Enabled, Disabled

The **APIC Function** BIOS feature is used to enable or disable the motherboard's **APIC (Advanced Programmable Interrupt Controller)**. The APIC is a new distributed set of devices that make up an interrupt controller. In current implementations, it consists of three parts: a local APIC, an I/O APIC, and an APIC bus.

The local APIC delivers interrupts to a specific processor, so each processor in a system has to have its own local APIC. Therefore, a dual processor system must have two local APICs. Because a local APIC has been integrated into every processor since the debut of the original Intel Pentium P54C processor, there's no need to worry about the number of local APICs.

The I/O APIC is the replacement for the old chained **8259 PIC** (**Programmable Interrupt Controller**) still in use in many motherboards. It collects interrupt signals from I/O devices and sends messages to the local APICs through the APIC bus, which connects it to the local APICs.

There can be up to eight I/O APICs in a system, each supporting anywhere from 24 (usually) to 64 interrupt lines. As you can see, this allows a lot more IRQs than is currently possible with the 8259 PIC. Note that without at least one I/O APIC, the local APIC is useless and the system functions as if it's based on the 8259 PIC.

To sum it up, APIC provides multiprocessor support, more IRQs, and faster interrupt handling, which is not possible with the old 8259 PIC. Although they can be used in single-processor boards, you are more likely to find them in multi-processor motherboards. This is because APIC is only supported in Windows NT, 2000, and XP. It is not supported in operating systems that are required to support MS-DOS device drivers, for example Windows 95/98. However, as users transition to Windows XP, you can expect more manufacturers to ship single-processor boards with I/O APICs.

If your single-processor motherboard supports APIC and you are using a Win32 operating system (Windows NT, 2000, and XP), it's recommended that you **enable** this feature to allow faster and better IRQ handling. If you are using a multiprocessor motherboard, you must **enable** this feature because it's required for IRQ handling in multiprocessor systems.

However, if you are running Windows 95/98 or a DOS-based operating system on a single-processor motherboard, you must **disable** this feature. This is because MS-DOS drivers assume they can write directly to the 8259 PIC (APIC did not exist yet in those days) and its associated IDT entries. Disabling this feature forces the APIC to revert to the legacy 8259 PIC mode.

Assign IRQ For USB

Common Options: Enabled, Disabled

This BIOS feature is somewhat similar to **Onboard USB Controller**. It enables or disables the motherboard's onboard USB controller by determining whether it should be assigned an IRQ. **Enable** this feature if you want to attach your USB devices to the onboard USB controller.

If you **disable** this feature, the USB controller is not assigned an IRQ. This disables the controller and you aren't able to connect any USB devices to it. However, if you don't use any USB devices, this frees up an IRQ for other devices to use. This is particularly useful when you have many devices that can't share IRQs.

Disabling this feature may not be necessary with **APIC**-capable motherboards because they come with more IRQs.

Assign IRQ For VGA

Common Options: Enabled, Disabled

Many graphics cards require an IRQ to function properly. Disabling an IRQ assignment for such cards causes improper operation and poor performance. Therefore, it is recommended that you **enable** this feature. Doing so allows the BIOS to assign an IRQ to the graphics card.

Some graphics cards may not need an IRQ to work. These cards are usually the low-end cards that provide basic video functions. Check your graphics card's documentation to confirm whether it requires an IRQ to work.

If your graphics card doesn't require an IRQ, then you can **disable** this feature to release an IRQ for other devices to use. This is particularly useful when you have many devices that can't share IRQs. Disabling this feature may not be necessary with **APIC**-capable motherboards because they come with more IRQs.

When in doubt, it's often best to leave it **enabled** as graphics cards generally function better with an IRQ. This is true even for cards that *don't* require IRQs.

AT Bus Clock

Common Options: 7.16MHz, CLK/2, CLK/3, CLK/4, CLK/5, CLK/6

The AT bus is nothing more than another name for the ISA bus. The ISA bus was originally an **8-bit** bus running at just **4.77MHz**. It was then expanded to include a 16-bit bus running initially at 6MHz and later at 8MHz. Eventually, the ISA bus was standardized to run at a maximum speed of **8.33MHz**.

Because each ISA data transfer takes anywhere from two to eight clock cycles to complete, this yields a maximum bandwidth of only **4.77MB/s** for 8-bit cards and **8.33MB/s** for 16-bit cards.

Maximum bandwidth for the 8-bit ISA bus = 8.33MHz × 1 byte (8-bits) ÷ 2 clock cycles per transfer = 4.77MB/s

Maximum bandwidth for the 16-bit ISA bus = 8.33MHz × 2 bytes (16-bits) ÷ 2 clock cycles per transfer = 8.33MB/s

This BIOS feature allows you to select the ISA bus clock speed. The chipset actually generates the ISA bus clock by dividing the PCI clock. Hence, the available settings of **CLK/2**, **CLK/3**, **CLK/4**, **CLK/5**, and **CLK/6**. Assuming that the PCI clock is set to **33MHz**, these settings yield the following clock speeds and bandwidth with a 16-bit ISA bus:

Setting	Clock Speed	Bandwidth
CLK/2	16.67 MHz	16.67 MB/s
CLK/3	11.11 MHz	11.11 MB/s
CLK/4	8.33 MHz	8.33 MB/s
CLK/5	6.67 MHz	6.67 MB/s
CLK/6	5.56 MHz	5.56 MB/s

There is also the fixed speed of **7.16MHz**, which is derived by dividing the reference clock generator speed of **14.318MHz** by a factor of two.

As you can see, the setting of **CLK/4** yields an ISA bus speed of **8.33MHz**, which is the maximum speed allowed by the official ISA specifications. However, you can choose to overclock the ISA by selecting the settings **CLK/3** or **CLK/2**, which yield clock speeds of **11.11MHz** and **16.67MHz**, respectively.

Overclocking the ISA bus greatly improves its performance. Therefore, it is recommended that you try to use the faster settings if possible. However, while newer ISA cards are capable of running at this "out-of-spec" speed, older ones may not work properly at this speed.

If your ISA cards fail to work properly, then you should select the setting of **CLK/4** or **7.16MHz**. This keeps the ISA bus within specifications.

Please note that the previous calculations and recommendations were based on a 33MHz PCI bus clock. If you are overclocking your PCI bus, please take the increased PCI clock speed into account!

For example, with an **overclocked** PCI bus speed of 37.5MHz, the available settings of **CLK/2**, **CLK/3**, **CLK/4**, **CLK/5**, and **CLK/6** yields the following clock speeds and bandwidth with a 16-bit ISA bus:

A

Setting	Clock Speed	Bandwidth
CLK/2	18.75 MHz	18.75 MB/s
CLK/3	12.50 MHz	12.50 MB/s
CLK/4	9.38 MHz	9.38 MB/s
CLK/5	7.50 MHz	7.50 MB/s
CLK/6	6.25 MHz	6.25 MB/s

With a 37.5MHz PCI bus, all ISA bus speed dividers yield increased clock speeds. Only the settings of **CLK/5**, **CLK/6**, and **7.16MHz** remain within ISA specifications. So, if you overclock your PCI bus, keep that in mind when you select the ISA bus speed divider.

If all this is confusing and you want to play safe, select the setting of **7.16MHz**. That is the failsafe setting because it will set the ISA bus to run at a fixed speed of 7.16MHz, irrespective of the PCI bus speed.

ATA100RAID IDE Controller

Common Options: Enabled, Disabled

This feature is only found on certain motherboards that come with an extra UltraDMA/100 IDE controller with RAID support. It allows you to enable or disable the function of that controller.

Please note that the IDE controller covered by this BIOS feature is different from the chipset's built-in IDE controller. This extra UltraDMA/100 IDE controller is often added to provide UltraDMA/100 and RAID support in motherboards whose chipset does not offer UltraDMA/100 or RAID support. Even if the chipset's built-in IDE controller supports UltraDMA/100 as well as RAID, it is not controlled by this BIOS feature. This feature is only used for the extra IDE controller.

For the purpose of avoiding confusion, I shall hence refer to the built-in IDE controller as an **internal** IDE controller while the add-on IDE controller will be known as an **external** IDE controller.

If you want to attach one or more IDE devices to the external UltraDMA/100 RAID controller, you should enable this feature. You should only disable it for the following reasons:

- If you don't have any IDE device attached to the external UltraDMA/100 RAID controller

- For troubleshooting purposes

Disabling the external IDE controller frees up two IRQs and speeds up system booting. This is because the IDE controller's BIOS doesn't have to be loaded and the external controller's often long boot-up check and initialization sequence is skipped. So, if you don't use the external IDE controller, it is recommended that you **disable** it.

Athlon 4 SSED Instruction

Common Options: Enabled, Disabled

The AMD Athlon originally came with AMD's **Enhanced 3DNow!** Technology, which was a collection of **19** new SIMD instructions. These instructions were similar to Intel's **SSE (Streaming SIMD Extensions)** instruction set, which debuted in the Intel Pentium III processor. Intel's SSE was, however, more complete in the sense that it consisted of **70** SIMD instructions.

Eventually, AMD was forced to concede that the Intel SSE was far more popular with software developers. So, beginning with the Palomino core of the Athlon XP (and MP) family of processors, AMD started implementing Intel's SSE instruction set.

Since 18 of the original Enhanced 3DNow! instruction sets were identical to those in Intel's SSE, all AMD needed to do was add another 52 instructions to make a complete implementation of Intel's SSE instruction set. Of course, that didn't stop AMD from calling it the **3DNow! Professional**, even though it was really just Intel's SSE instruction set!

AMD also added a status bit that tells any querying software that the Athlon XP/MP supports the full SSE instruction set. This was meant to allow the Athlon XP/MP to immediately take advantage of SSE-optimized software. However, this status bit ends up causing some compatibility issues.

The BeOS operating system was probably the biggest victim. The SSE status bit actually *fooled* BeOS' kernel into thinking that the Athlon XP/MP processor was an Intel processor. This caused the kernel to send the wrong instructions to the Athlon XP/MP processor, causing it to crash and reboot.

There were also compatibility issues with other software, all due to the SSE status bit. For example, some graphics cards (for example, Matrox G450) cannot run Quake III under Windows NT 4.0 with the SSE status bit enabled.

This is where the **Athlon 4 SSED Instruction** BIOS feature comes in. This BIOS feature is a simple toggle for the AMD Athlon XP/MP's SSE status bit.

When **enabled**, the BIOS enables the SSE status bit. Querying software will recognize the processor as an SSE-compatible processor. This allows the processor to take advantage of SSE-optimized software.

When **disabled**, the BIOS disables the SSE status bit. Querying software will *not* recognize the processor as an SSE-compatible processor. The processor can only take advantage of Enhanced 3DNow!-optimized software.

By default, this BIOS feature is set to **Enabled**, which allows for optimal performance with SSE-optimized software. It is highly recommended that you leave it at the default setting of **Enabled**.

You should **disable** this BIOS feature only if you are facing compatibility issues with the SSE status bit.

A

Auto Detect DIMM/PCI Clk

Common Options: Enabled, Disabled

When the motherboard's clock generator pulses, the extreme values (spikes) of the pulses creates **EMI (Electromagnetic Interference)**. This causes interference with other electronics in the area. To reduce this problem, the BIOS can either modulate the pulses (to make them flatter) or turn off unused AGP, PCI, or memory clock signals.

This feature is similar to the **Smart Clock** option of the **Spread Spectrum** feature, which acts by the second method. If you enable it, the BIOS monitors the AGP, PCI, and memory slots. The clock signals of unoccupied slots are automatically turned off. The clock signals to *occupied* AGP, PCI, or memory slots are also turned off whenever there's no activity.

Theoretically, EMI can be reduced this way without compromising system stability. This also allows the computer to reduce power consumption because only components that are running use power, and then only when they are actually doing work.

The choice of whether to enable or disable this feature is really up to your personal preference. However, because this feature reduces EMI and power consumption without compromising system stability, it is recommended that you **enable** it.

Auto Turn Off PCI Clock Pin

Common Options: Enabled, Disabled

When the motherboard's clock generator pulses, the extreme values (spikes) of the pulses creates **EMI (Electromagnetic Interference)**. This causes interference with other electronics in the area. To reduce this problem, the BIOS can either modulate the pulses (to make them flatter) or turn off the unused clock signals.

This feature is a subset of the **Auto Detect DIMM/PCI Clk** feature. If you **enable** it, the BIOS monitors the PCI slots for activity. The clock signals of unoccupied slots are automatically turned off. The clock signals to *occupied* PCI slots are also turned off whenever there's no activity.

Theoretically, EMI can be reduced this way without compromising system stability. This also allows the computer to reduce power consumption because only components that are running use power, and then only when they are actually doing work.

The choice of whether to enable or disable this feature is really up to your personal preference. However, because this feature reduces EMI and power consumption without compromising system stability, it is recommended that you **enable** it.

B

Boot Other Device

Common Options: Enabled, Disabled

This feature determines whether the BIOS attempts to load an operating system from the **Second Boot Device** or **Third Boot Device** if it fails to load one from the **First Boot Device**. This feature is **enabled** by default, and it is recommended that you leave it as such.

This allows the BIOS to check the second and third boot devices for operating systems after failing to find one on the first boot device. Otherwise, the BIOS simply halts the booting process with the error message: **No Operating System Found**, even if there is an operating system on the second or third boot device.

Boot Sequence

Common Options: A, C, SCSI

C, A, SCSI

C, CD-ROM, A

CD-ROM, C, A

D, A, SCSI (only when you have at least 2 IDE hard disks)

E, A, SCSI (only when you have at least 3 IDE hard disks)

F, A, SCSI (only when you have 4 IDE hard disks)

SCSI, A, C

SCSI, C, A

A, SCSI, C

LS/ZIP, C

This feature enables you to set the sequence by which the BIOS searches for an operating system during the boot-up process.

To ensure the shortest booting time possible, set the hard disk that contains your operating system as the first choice. Normally, this would be drive **C** for IDE drives but if you are using a SCSI hard disk, then select **SCSI**.

Some motherboards have an external (not part of the chipset) IDE controller. In such motherboards, the **SCSI** option is replaced with an **EXT** option. This allows the computer to either boot from an IDE hard disk connected to the external IDE controller or an SCSI hard disk.

If you want to boot from an IDE hard disk running off the internal IDE controller, do *not* set the **Boot Sequence** to start with **EXT**. Please note that this feature works in conjunction with the **Boot Sequence EXT Means** feature.

Boot Sequence EXT Means

Common Options: IDE, SCSI

This BIOS feature determines whether the system boots from an IDE hard disk connected to the *external* IDE controller or an SCSI hard disk. However, it only has an effect if the **EXT** option has been selected in the **Boot Sequence** feature.

To boot from an IDE hard disk that's connected to the *external* IDE controller, you must first set the **Boot Sequence** feature to start with the **EXT** option. For example, the **EXT, C, A** setting. Then, you have to set the **Boot Sequence EXT Means** feature to **IDE**.

To boot from an SCSI hard disk, set the **Boot Sequence** feature to start with the **EXT** option. For example, the **EXT, C, A** setting. Then, you have to set the **Boot Sequence EXT Means** feature to **SCSI**.

B

Boot To OS/2

Common Options: Yes, No

This is similar to the **OS Select For DRAM > 64M** BIOS feature.

When there is more than 64MB of memory in a computer, older versions of IBM's OS/2 operating system differ from other operating systems in the way it manages memory. It is different from the conventional way of memory management. Therefore, a BIOS option was created to provide compatibility for such OS/2 systems.

If you are running an old, unpatched version of OS/2, you must select the Yes option. However, please note that this is only true for older versions of OS/2 that haven't been upgraded using IBM's FixPaks.

Starting with the OS/2 Warp v3.0, IBM changed the memory management system to the more conventional method. IBM also issued FixPaks to address this issue with older versions of OS/2.

Therefore, if you are using OS/2 Warp v3.0 or higher, you should select **No**. You should also select **No** if you have upgraded an older version of OS/2 with the FixPaks that IBM has been releasing over the years.

If you select the **Yes** option with a newer or updated version (v3.0 or higher) of OS/2, it causes erroneous memory detection. For example, if you have 64MB of memory, it may only register as 16MB. Or, if you have more than 64MB of memory, it may register as only 64MB of memory.

Users of non–OS/2 operating systems (such as Microsoft Windows XP) should select the **No** option. Doing otherwise causes memory errors if you have more than 64MB of memory in your system.

In conclusion:

- If you are using an older version of the IBM OS/2 operating system, you should select **Yes**.

- If you are using the IBM OS/2 Warp v3.0 or higher operating system, you should select **No**.

- If you are using an older version of the IBM OS/2 operating system but have already installed all the relevant IBM FixPaks, you should select **No**.

- Users of non–OS/2 operating systems (such as Microsoft Windows XP) should select the **No** option.

Boot Up Floppy Seek

Common Options: Enabled, Disabled

This BIOS feature determines if the BIOS checks for a floppy drive during boot-up.

If **enabled**, the BIOS attempts to detect and initialize the floppy drive. If it cannot detect one (due to improper configuration or physical unavailability), it flashes an error message. However, the system still is allowed to continue the boot process.

If the floppy drive is present, the BIOS queries the drive to find out if it supports 40 tracks or 80 tracks operation. Because all floppy drives in use today only support 80 tracks operation, this check is, frankly, redundant.

If this feature is **disabled**, the BIOS skips the floppy drive check. This speeds up the booting process by several seconds.

Because a floppy drive check is really pointless, it is recommended that you **disable** this feature for a faster booting process.

Boot Up NumLock Status

Common Options: On, Off

This BIOS feature sets the input mode of the numeric keypad at boot up.

If you turn this feature **on**, the BIOS sets the numeric keypad to function in the **numeric mode** (for typing out numbers).

If you set it to **Off**, the numeric keypad functions in the **cursor control mode** (for controlling the cursor) instead.

The numeric keypad's input mode can be switched to either numeric or cursor control mode and back again at any time after boot up. This feature merely sets the initial input mode of the keypad at boot up.

The choice of initial keypad input mode is entirely up to your preference.

Byte Merge

Common Options: Enabled, Disabled

This BIOS feature is similar to the **PCI Dynamic Bursting** feature.

If you have already read about the **CPU to PCI Write Buffer** feature, you should know that the chipset has an integrated PCI write buffer that allows the CPU to immediately write up to **four words** (or 64-bits) of PCI writes to it. This frees up the CPU to work on other tasks while the PCI write buffer writes them to the PCI bus.

Now, the CPU doesn't always write 32-bit data to the PCI bus. 8-bit and 16-bit writes can also take place. However, while the CPU may only write 8-bits of data to the PCI bus, it is still considered a single PCI transaction. This makes it equivalent to a 16-bit or 32-bit write in terms of PCI bandwidth. This reduces the effective PCI bandwidth, especially if there are many 8-bit or 16-bit CPU-to-PCI writes.

To solve this problem, the write buffer can be programmed to accumulate and merge 8-bit and 16-bit writes into 32-bit writes. The buffer then writes the merged data to the PCI bus. As you can see, merging the smaller 8-bit or 16-bit writes into a few large 32-bit writes reduces the number of PCI transactions required. This increases the efficiency of the PCI bus and improves its bandwidth.

This is where the **Byte Merge** BIOS feature comes in. It controls the byte merging capability of the PCI write buffer.

If it is **enabled**, every write transaction goes straight to the write buffer. They are accumulated until there is enough to be written to the PCI bus in a single burst. This improves the PCI bus performance.

If you **disable** byte merging, all writes still go to the PCI write buffer (if the **CPU to PCI Write Buffer** feature has been enabled). However, the buffer does not accumulate and merge the data. The data is written to the PCI bus as soon as the bus becomes free. This reduces PCI bus efficiency, particularly when 8-bit or 16-bit data is written to the PCI bus.

Therefore, it is recommended that you **enable** Byte Merge for better performance.

However, please note that Byte Merge may be incompatible with certain PCI network interface cards (also known as NICs). For example, 3Com's 3C905-series of NICs won't work properly with Byte Merge enabled.

So, if your NIC (Network Interface Card) won't work properly, try **disabling** Byte Merge. Otherwise, you should **enable** Byte Merge for better performance.

B

C

Clock Throttle

Common Options: 12.5%, 25.0%, 37.5%, 50.0%, 62.5%, 75.0%, 87.5%

This BIOS feature is only valid for systems that are powered by 0.13μ Intel Pentium 4 processors with 512KB L2 cache. These processors come with a **Thermal Monitor** that actually consists of an on-die thermal sensor and a **Thermal Control Circuit** (**TCC**). Because the thermal sensor is on-die and placed at the hottest part of the die—near the integer ALU units—it is able to closely monitor the processor's die temperature.

When the Thermal Monitor is in automatic mode and the thermal sensor detects that the processor has reached its maximum safe operating temperature, it will send a PROCHOT# (Processor Hot) signal, which activates the TCC. The TCC will then modulate the clock cycles by inserting null cycles, typically at a rate of **50-70%** of the total number of clock cycles. Note that the operating frequency of the processor remains unchanged. The TCC only inserts null cycles that result in the processor "resting" 50-70% of the time.

As the die temperature drops, the TCC will gradually reduce the number of null cycles until no more is required to keep the die temperature below the safe point. Then the thermal sensor stops sending the PROCHOT# signal, thereby turning off the TCC. This mechanism allows the processor to dynamically adjust its duty cycles to ensure its die temperature remains within safe limits.

This BIOS feature allows manual configuration of the Thermal Control Circuit. Instead of allowing the TCC to automatically start with a duty cycle of **30-50%**, you can manually set the duty cycle.

Available options for this BIOS feature are set values of the processo's **duty cycle** when the Thermal Control Circuit gets activated. They range from a low of **12.5%** to a high of **87.5%**. Please note that these options reflect the processor's duty cycle, *not* its clock speed. The clock speed of the processor remains unchanged.

If you are looking for a Disabled option, there is no such option. You cannot turn off the Thermal Control Circuit. But if you keep your processor cool enough so that it never exceeds the maximum safe operating temperature, the Thermal Control Circuit will never get activated.

The default setting is usually **62.5%**. This means the Thermal Control Circuit will insert null cycles to allow the processor to "rest" **37.5%** of the time.

The choice of what you should set the Thermal Control Circuit to run at is really up to you. The lower the duty cycle, the slower your processor will perform, but it will take less time to cool down the processor enough to turn off the TCC. Using a higher duty cycle will not impair performance as much but it will take longer for your processor to cool down enough to turn off the TCC.

Compatible FPU OPCODE

Common Options: Enabled, Disabled

In Intel IA-32 (P6 family, Pentium 4, and so forth) processors, the x87 FPU stores the opcode of the last executed non-control instruction (also known as the **fopcode** or **FOP code**) in an 11-bit register. This is to provide state information for exception handlers.

Because the first 5 bits of the first opcode byte are the same for all FPU opcodes, only the last 3 bits of the first opcode byte are stored in the register. The second opcode byte provides the remaining 8-bits of data.

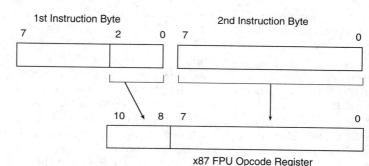

(Courtesy of Intel Corporation)

In previous implementations, the final opcode (or FOP) stored in the FOP register was always the FOP of the last non-transparent floating point instruction executed before an FSAVE, FSTENV, or FXSAVE instruction.

However, to improve FPU performance, the Pentium 4 and Xeon processors only store the FOP of the last non-transparent floating point instruction that have an unmasked exception. For backward compatibility, the Pentium 4 and Xeon processors allow programmable control of the FOP register. This is where the **Compatible FPU OPCODE** BIOS feature comes in.

When **enabled**, the processor reverts to the FOP code compatibility mode and stores the last non-transparent floating point instruction in the 11-bit FOP register. Intel recommends that this feature should only be **enabled** if the software was designed to use the fopcode to analyze program performance or to restart the program after an exception has been handled.

When **disabled**, the processor turns off the FOP code compatibility mode and only stores the FOP of the last non-transparent floating point instruction that had an unmasked exception. This allows for better FPU performance.

Therefore, it is recommended that you **disable** this feature. This allows for better FPU performance, although some older programs may require you to **enable** this feature to allow recovery from FPU exceptions.

CPU Drive Strength

Common Options: 0, 1, 2, 3

The system controller has auto-compensation circuitry that automatically compensates for impedance variations in motherboard designs. However, because the motherboard impedance is more or less fixed for each motherboard design, some manufacturers may choose to pre-calculate the optimal drive strength for a particular design and use it instead. Either way, the motherboard's impedance on the processor bus is compensated for.

However, when the auto-compensation logic is bypassed and a fixed drive strength is used, the amount of impedance compensation may not be sufficient sometimes. Hence the need for this BIOS feature. This BIOS feature allows you to manually set the processor bus drive strength. The higher the value, the stronger the drive strength.

So, if you are facing stability problems with your processor, you might want to try boosting the CPU drive strength to a higher value. It will help to correct any possible increase in impedance from the motherboard.

Due to the nature of this BIOS feature, it is also possible to use it as an aid in overclocking the CPU. By raising the **CPU Drive Strength**, it is possible to improve its stability at overclocked speeds. So, try the higher values of **2** or **3** if your CPU just won't go the extra mile.

However, this is *not* a surefire way of overclocking the CPU. Increasing it to the highest value does not necessarily mean that you can overclock the CPU more than you already can. In addition, it is important to note that increasing the CPU drive strength does *not* improve its performance. Contrary to popular opinion, it is *not* a performance-enhancing feature.

Although little else is known about this feature, the downside to a high CPU drive strength is increased **EMI (Electromagnetic Interference)**, power consumption, and thermal output. Therefore, unless you need to boost the processor bus drive strength (for troubleshooting or overclocking purposes), it is recommended that you leave it at the default setting.

CPU Fast String

Common Options: Enabled, Disabled

The Pentium 4, Xeon, and P6 family of processors can actually modify their operation during **string store** operations to maximize performance. This ability is called **fast string processing**.

If certain "fast string" conditions are met, the processor can actually operate *directly* on the string in a cache-line using the cache-line mode. The string data is then written back to the cache-line after modification by the processor.

This BIOS feature controls the processor's fast string feature.

When **enabled**, the processor operates on the string in a cache line when the "fast string" conditions are met.

When **disabled**, the processor does not operate on the string while it is in a cache line.

It is recommended that you **enable** CPU Fast String for better performance. There is currently no reason why you should disable CPU Fast String.

CPU Hyper-Threading

Common Options: Enabled, Disabled

The **Intel Hyper-Threading Technology** is an extension to the IA-32 architecture, which allows a single processor to execute *two or more* separate threads concurrently. When hyper-threading is enabled, multi-threaded software applications can execute their threads in parallel, thereby improving the processor's performance.

The current implementation involves *two* logical processors sharing the processor's execution engine and its bus interface. Each logical processor, however, comes with its own APIC. The other features of the processor are either shared or duplicated in each logical processor.

Here is a list of the features duplicated in each logical processor:

- General registers (EAX, EBX, ECX, EDX, ESI, EDI, ESP, and EBP)
- Segment registers (CS, DS, SS, ES, FS, and GS)
- EFLAGS and EIP registers
- x87 FPU registers (ST0 to ST7, status word, control word, tag word, data operand pointer, and instruction pointer)
- MMX registers (MM0 to MM7)
- XMM registers (XMM0 to XMM7)
- MXCSR register
- Control registers (CR0, CR2, CR3, CR4)
- System table pointer registers (GDTR, LDTR, IDTR, task register)
- Debug registers (DR0, DR1, DR2, DR3, DR6, DR7)
- Debug control MSR (IA32_DEBUGCTL)
- Machine check global status MSR (IA32_MCG_STATUS)
- Machine check capability MSR (IA32_MCG_CAP)
- Thermal clock modulation and ACPI power management control MSRs
- Time stamp counter MSRs
- Most of the other MSR registers including Page Attribute Table (PAT)
- Local APIC registers

Here are the features shared by the two logical processors:

- IA32_MISC_ENABLE MSR
- Memory type range registers (MTRRs)

And the following are features that can be duplicated or shared according to requirements:

- Machine check architecture (MCA) MSRs
- Performance monitoring control and counter MSRs

The Intel Hyper-Threading Technology is only supported by the Intel Pentium 4 (officially only those 3.06GHz and faster) and the Intel Xeon processors. Please note that for Hyper-Threading to work, you should have the following:

- An Intel processor that supports Hyper-Threading
- A motherboard with a chipset and BIOS that support Hyper-Threading
- An operating system that supports Hyper-Threading (Microsoft Windows XP or Linux 2.4.x)

Because it behaves like two separate processors with their own APICs, you should also enable **APIC Function** in the BIOS, which is required for multi-processing.

It is highly recommended that you **enable** CPU Hyper-Threading for improved processor performance.

CPU L2 Cache ECC Checking

Common Options: Enabled, Disabled

This BIOS feature enables or disables the **L2 (Level 2 or Secondary)** cache's **ECC (Error Checking and Correction)** function, if available.

Enabling this feature is recommended because it detects and corrects single-bit errors in data stored in the L2 cache. As most data reads are satisfied by the L2 cache, the L2 cache's ECC function should catch and correct almost all single-bit errors in the memory subsystem.

It also detects double-bit errors, although it cannot correct them. However, this isn't such a big deal because double-bit errors are *extremely* rare. For all practical purposes, the ECC check should be able to catch virtually all data errors. This is especially useful at overclocked speeds when errors are most likely to creep in.

There are those who advocate **disabling** ECC checking because it reduces performance. True, ECC checking doesn't come free. You can expect some performance degradation with ECC checking enabled. However, unlike ECC checking of DRAM modules, the performance degradation associated with L2 cache ECC checking is comparatively small.

Balance that against the increased stability and reliability achieved through L2 cache ECC checking and the minimal reduction in performance seems rather cheap, doesn't it? Of course, if you don't do any serious work with your system and want a little speed boost for your games, **disable** CPU L2 Cache ECC Checking by all means.

However, if you are overclocking your processor, ECC checking may enable you to overclock higher than originally possible. This is because any single-bit errors that occur as a result of overclocking are corrected by the L2 cache's ECC function. So, for most intents and purposes, I recommend that you **enable** this feature for greater system stability and reliability.

Please note that the presence of this feature in the BIOS does *not* necessarily mean that your processor's L2 cache actually supports ECC checking. Many processors do not ship with ECC-capable L2 cache. In such cases, you still can enable this feature in the BIOS, but it has *no effect*.

CPU Level 1 Cache

Common Options: Enabled, Disabled

The modern processor is a very fast piece of silicon. Unfortunately, RAM development has lagged so far behind that the processor would be fatally stalled by slow memory accesses if it has to rely entirely on current RAM technology.

To alleviate this problem, processors now come with a small amount of ultra-fast **SRAM (Static RAM)** within its core. This small amount of SRAM is used to cache instructions and data, so the processor can access them instantaneously.

Because this is the first cache that the processor checks when it needs data, it is known as the **Level 1 cache** or **L1 cache**. It is also known by some as the **primary cache**. In current processor designs, the Level 1 cache can range from 32KB to 128KB in size.

If the processor cannot find what it wants in the Level 1 cache, it checks the **Level 2 cache** before proceeding to the **Level 3 cache** (in some cases). In the worst-case scenario, all the caches are unable to fulfill the processor's request. When this happens, the processor has to access the RAM itself.

Naturally, the processor is severely stalled when it has to retrieve information from the much slower memory. Fortunately, the combination of fast caches is often able to satisfy the processor's data requests most of the time. In fact, the caches are so efficient that they make the entire memory subsystem appear almost as fast as they are!

This is where the **CPU Level 1 Cache** BIOS feature comes in. It controls the functionality of the processor's Level 1 cache.

When **enabled**, the processor's Level 1 cache is allowed to function. This allows the best possible performance from the processor.

When **disabled**, the processor's Level 1 cache is disabled. The processor bypasses the Level 1 cache and relies only on the Level 2 and Level 3 (if available) caches. This reduces the performance of the processor.

The recommended setting is obviously **Enabled** because disabling it severely affects the processor's performance. However, the **Disabled** setting is useful as a troubleshooting tool, especially when you are overclocking your processor.

For example, if your processor cannot reach 2GHz, you can try to find out if the cause is the Level 1 cache by **disabling** this BIOS feature. If this allows your processor to run at 2GHz and beyond, then the Level 1 cache is the cause of your processor's failure to run at 2GHz. However, if your processor still cannot run at 2GHz even with the Level 1 cache disabled, then the problem lies elsewhere.

Please note that disabling the Level 1 cache in order to increase the overclockability of the CPU is a *very bad* idea. If the Level 1 cache is disabled, the processor will stall frequently because the memory subsystem just isn't fast enough to continuously feed data to the processor by itself!

Therefore, except for troubleshooting purposes, this feature should always be left **enabled**.

CPU Level 2 Cache

Common Options: Enabled, Disabled

The modern processor is a very fast piece of silicon. Unfortunately, RAM development has lagged so far behind that the processor would be fatally stalled by slow memory accesses if it has to rely entirely on current RAM technology.

To alleviate this problem, processors now come with a small amount of ultra-fast **SRAM** (**Static RAM**) within its core. This small amount of SRAM is used to cache instructions and data, so the processor can access them instantaneously. This is known as the **Level 1 cache** or **L1 cache**. In current processor designs, the Level 1 cache can range from 32KB to 128KB in size.

If the processor cannot find what it wants in the Level 1 cache, it checks the **Level 2 cache** before proceeding to the **Level 3 cache** (in some cases). In the worst-case scenario, all the caches are unable to fulfill the processor's request. When this happens, the processor has to access the RAM itself.

Naturally, the processor is severely stalled when it has to retrieve information from the much slower memory. Fortunately, the combination of fast caches is often able to satisfy the processor's data requests most of the time. In fact, the caches are so efficient that they make the entire memory subsystem appear almost as fast as they are!

As mentioned above, the processor not only has a Level 1 cache but, by necessity, a **Level 2 cache** or **L2 cache** as well. This cache is also known by some as the **secondary cache**.

This Level 2 cache is designed to handle data requests that the Level 1 cache fails to satisfy. Although slower than the Level 1 cache, the Level 2 cache compensates by being much larger in size. While the largest Level 1 cache at this time is only 128KB, Level 2 caches can be as large as 1MB!

Irrespective of the actual numbers, the larger size of the Level 2 cache allows it to store a lot more data than the Level 1 cache. This gives it a high probability of satisfying *cache misses* from the Level 1 cache. In fact, the two caches working together are actually capable of satisfying the processor's data request *90-95%* of the time! This greatly reduces the need for the processor to access the much slower RAM.

This is where the **CPU Level 2 Cache** BIOS feature comes in. It controls the functionality of the processor's Level 2 cache.

When **enabled**, the processor's Level 2 cache is allowed to function. This allows the best possible performance from the processor.

When **disabled**, the processor's Level 2 cache is disabled. The processor bypasses the Level 2 cache and relies only on the Level 1 and Level 3 (if available) caches. This reduces the performance of the processor.

The recommended setting is obviously **Enabled** because disabling it severely affects the processor's performance. However, the **Disabled** setting is useful as a troubleshooting tool, especially when you are overclocking your processor.

For example, if your processor cannot reach 2GHz, you can try to find out if the cause is the Level 2 cache by **disabling** this BIOS feature. If this allows your processor to run at 2GHz and beyond, then the Level 2 cache is the cause of your processor's failure to run at 2GHz. However, if your processor still cannot run at 2GHz even with the Level 2 cache disabled, then the problem lies elsewhere.

Please note that disabling the Level 2 cache in order to increase the overclockability of the CPU is a *very bad* idea. If the Level 2 cache is disabled, the processor will stall frequently because the memory subsystem just isn't fast enough to continuously feed data to the processor by itself!

Therefore, except for troubleshooting purposes, this feature should always be left **enabled**.

CPU Level 3 Cache

Common Options: Enabled, Disabled

In addition to the Level 1 and Level 2 caches, some processors come with an additional cache called **Level 3 cache** or **L3 cache**.

This Level 3 cache is designed to handle data requests that the Level 1 and Level 2 caches fail to satisfy. Although slower than the Level 2 cache, the Level 3 cache compensates by being much larger in size. While the largest Level 2 cache at this time is only 512KB, Level 3 caches can be as large as 4MB!

Irrespective of the actual numbers, the larger size of the Level 3 cache allows it to store a lot more data than the Level 2 cache. This gives it a high probability of satisfying *cache misses* from the Level 2 cache. With three caches working together, the chance of the processor stalling due to the need to access the much slower RAM is very small.

This is where the **CPU Level 3 Cache** BIOS feature comes in. It controls the functionality of the processor's Level 3 cache.

Currently, this is an Intel Xeon MP-specific BIOS feature. The Intel Xeon MP processor features an on-die Level 3 cache that can be 512KB, 1MB or 2MB in size. It is an 8-way set associative sectored cache with 64-byte cache lines.

When **enabled**, the processor's Level 3 cache is allowed to function. This allows the best possible performance from the processor.

When **disabled**, the processor's Level 3 cache is disabled. The processor bypasses the Level 3 cache and relies only on the Level 1 and Level 2 caches. This reduces the performance of the processor.

The recommended setting is obviously **Enabled** because disabling it severely affects the processor's performance. However, the **Disabled** setting is useful as a troubleshooting tool, especially when you are overclocking your processor.

For example, if your processor cannot reach 2GHz, you can try to find out if the cause is the Level 3 cache by **disabling** this BIOS feature. If this allows your processor to run at 2GHz and beyond, then the Level 3 cache is the cause of your processor's failure to run at 2GHz. However, if your processor still cannot run at 2GHz even with the Level 3 cache disabled, then the problem lies elsewhere.

Please note that disabling the Level 3 cache in order to increase the overclockability of the CPU is a *very bad* idea. If the Level 3 cache is disabled, the processor may stall frequently, especially when the system is running memory-intensive applications.

Therefore, except for troubleshooting purposes, this feature should always be left **enabled**.

C

CPU Thermal-Throttling

Common Options: 12.5%, 25.0%, 37.5%, 50.0%, 62.5%, 75.0%, 87.5%

This BIOS feature is only valid for systems that are powered by 0.13μ Intel Pentium 4 processors with 512KB L2 cache. These processors come with a **Thermal Monitor**, which actually consists of an on-die thermal sensor and a **Thermal Control Circuit** (**TCC**). Because the thermal sensor is on-die and placed at the hottest part of the die[md]near the integer ALU units—it is able to closely monitor the processor's die temperature.

When the Thermal Monitor is in automatic mode and the thermal sensor detects that the processor has reached its maximum safe operating temperature, it will send a **PROCHOT#** (Processor Hot) signal, which activates the TCC. The TCC will then modulate the clock cycles by inserting null cycles, typically at a rate of **50-70%** of the total number of clock cycles. Note that the operating frequency of the processor remains unchanged. The TCC only inserts null cycles that result in the processor "resting" 50-70% of the time.

As the die temperature drops, the TCC will gradually reduce the number of null cycles until no more is required to keep the die temperature below the safe point. Then the thermal sensor stops sending the PROCHOT# signal, thereby turning off the TCC. This mechanism allows the processor to dynamically adjust its duty cycles to ensure its die temperature remains within safe limits.

This BIOS feature allows manual configuration of the Thermal Control Circuit. Instead of allowing the TCC to automatically start with a duty cycle of **30-50%**, you can manually set the duty cycle.

Available options for this BIOS feature are set values of the processor's **duty cycle** when the Thermal Control Circuit gets activated. They range from a low of **12.5%** to a high of **87.5%**. Please note that these options reflect the processor's duty cycle, *not* its clock speed. The clock speed of the processor remains unchanged.

If you are looking for a Disabled option, there is no such option. You cannot turn off the Thermal Control Circuit. But if you keep your processor cool enough so that it never exceeds the maximum safe operating temperature, the Thermal Control Circuit will never get activated.

The default setting is usually **62.5%**. This means the Thermal Control Circuit will insert null cycles to allow the processor to "rest" **37.5%** of the time.

The choice of what you should set the Thermal Control Circuit to run at is really up to you. The lower the duty cycle, the slower your processor will perform, but it will take less time to cool down the processor enough to turn off the TCC. Using a higher duty cycle will not impair performance as much but it will take longer for your processor to cool down enough to turn off the TCC.

CPU to PCI Post Write

Common Options: Enabled, Disabled

This BIOS feature controls the chipset's CPU-to-PCI write buffer. It is used to store PCI writes from the processor before they are written to the PCI bus.

If this buffer is **disabled**, the processor bypasses the buffer and writes directly to the PCI bus. Although this may seem like the faster and better method, it really isn't so.

When the processor wants to write to the PCI bus, it has to arbitrate for control of the PCI bus. This takes time, especially when there are other devices requesting access to the PCI bus as well. During this time, the processor cannot do anything else but wait for its turn.

Even when it gets control of the PCI bus, the processor still has to wait until the PCI bus is free. Because the processor bus (which can be as fast as 533MHz) is many times faster than the PCI bus (at only 33MHz), the processor wastes many clock cycles just waiting for the PCI bus. And it hasn't even begun writing to the PCI bus yet! The entire transaction, therefore, puts the processor out of commission for many clock cycles.

This is where the CPU-to-PCI write buffer comes in. It is a small memory buffer built into the chipset. The actual size of the buffer varies from chipset to chipset. But in most cases, it is big enough for **four words** or **64-bits** worth of data.

When this write buffer is **enabled**, all PCI writes from the processor go straight into it, instead of the PCI bus. This is virtually instantaneous because the processor does not have to arbitrate or wait for the PCI bus. That task is now left to the chipset and its write buffer. The processor is thus free to work on something else.

It is important to note that the write buffer isn't able to write the data to the PCI bus any faster than the processor can. This is because the write buffer still has to arbitrate and wait for control of the PCI bus! However, the difference here is that the entire transaction can be carried out without tying up the processor.

To sum it all up, enabling the CPU to PCI write buffer frees up CPU cycles that would normally be wasted waiting for the PCI bus. Therefore, it is recommended that you **enable** this feature for better performance.

CPU to PCI Write Buffer

Common Options: Enabled, Disabled

This BIOS feature controls the chipset's CPU-to-PCI write buffer. It is used to store PCI writes from the processor before they are written to the PCI bus.

If this buffer is **disabled**, the processor bypasses the buffer and writes directly to the PCI bus. Although this may seem like the faster and better method, it really isn't so.

When the processor wants to write to the PCI bus, it has to arbitrate for control of the PCI bus. This takes time, especially when there are other devices requesting access to the PCI bus as well. During this time, the processor cannot do anything else but wait for its turn.

Even when it gets control of the PCI bus, the processor still has to wait until the PCI bus is free. Because the processor bus (which can be as fast as 533MHz) is many times faster than the PCI bus (at only 33MHz), the processor wastes many clock cycles just waiting for the PCI bus. And it hasn't even begun writing to the PCI bus yet! The entire transaction, therefore, puts the processor out of commission for many clock cycles.

This is where the CPU-to-PCI write buffer comes in. It is a small memory buffer built into the chipset. The actual size of the buffer varies from chipset to chipset. But in most cases, it is big enough for **four words** or **64-bits** worth of data.

When this write buffer is **enabled**, all PCI writes from the processor go straight into it, instead of the PCI bus. This is virtually instantaneous because the processor does not have to arbitrate or wait for the PCI bus. That task is now left to the chipset and its write buffer. The processor is thus free to work on something else.

It is important to note that the write buffer isn't able to write the data to the PCI bus any faster than the processor can. This is because the write buffer still has to arbitrate and wait for control of the PCI bus! However, the difference here is that the entire transaction can be carried out without tying up the processor.

To sum it all up, enabling the CPU to PCI write buffer frees up CPU cycles that would normally be wasted waiting for the PCI bus. Therefore, it is recommended that you **enable** this feature for better performance.

CPU VCore Voltage

Common Options: Std. Vcore, Raising

This is a BIOS feature so far seen only in the **ABIT NV7-series** of motherboards. It is used to give a small boost to the processor's core voltage.

When set to **Std. Vcore**, the motherboard supplies the processor with the default core voltage.

When set to **Raising**, the motherboard boosts the processor's core voltage by approximately **3%**. So, if your processor has a core voltage of **1.7 volts**, using the Raising option raises that voltage to about **1.75V**.

As you can see, the voltage boost courtesy of this BIOS feature is not remarkable. In fact, this "boosted" voltage is still within the processor's specified voltage limits!

However, because it appears to be the only way to boost the processor's core voltage in NVIDIA nForce-based motherboards, this **3%** boost is better than nothing at all! It may not allow radical overclocking, but it should allow a little more overclocking freedom.

If you are an overclocker, it is recommended that you select the **Raising** option. It should allow your processor to be a little more overclockable. At the very least, it improves its stability at overclocked speeds.

If you are not an overclocker, the choice of whether to enable or disable this BIOS feature is really up to you. You can enable it to ensure a more stable processor or you can disable it to save power and reduce the thermal output.

D

DBI Output for AGP Trans.

Common Options: Enabled, Disabled

The full name for this BIOS feature is **Dynamic Bus Inversion Output for AGP Transmitter**. It is an AGP 3.0-specific BIOS feature that only appears when you install an AGP 3.0-compliant graphics card.

The AGP bus has 32 data lines divided into two sets. In each set, there are 16 data lines that individually switch to either a high (1) or low (0) as it sends out data. Sometimes, a large number of these data lines may switch together to the same polarity (either 1 or 0) and then switch back to the opposite polarity. This mass switching to the same polarity is called **simultaneous switching outputs** and it creates a lot of unwanted electrical noise at the AGP controller and GPU interfaces. This is only significant if the number of lines simultaneously switching to the same polarity exceeds **50%** of the data lines.

To avoid this, the AGP 3.0 specifications introduced a scheme called **Dynamic Bus Inversion** or **DBI**. It makes use of two new DBI lines—one for each 16-line set. These DBI lines are only supported by AGP 3.0-compliant graphics cards.

When **enabled**, it ensures that the data lines are limited to a maximum of **8 simultaneous** switchings or transitions per 16-line set. When the number of simultaneous transitions exceeds **8** or **50%** of the data lines, the AGP controller switches the polarity of the DBI line instead. The data lines that were supposed to switch en masse to the opposite polarity remain at the same polarity.

When **disabled**, there are no restrictions to the number of simultaneous switchings that the data lines can perform.

At the receiving end however, the data is reproduced exactly as it was meant to. This is because the DBI line actually serves as a reference signal for the AGP data signals. Although the data signals may have been inverted on the transmitter end, the inverted DBI signal corrects it at the receiving end.

However, because only one, instead of 9 or more, data lines switched to the opposite polarity, the amount of electrical noise generated is significantly reduced. In short, DBI improves stability of the AGP interface by reducing signal noises that occur as a result of **simultaneous switching outputs**. It also reduces the AGP controller's power consumption.

Therefore, it is recommended that you **enable DBI Output for AGP Trans.** to save power as well as reduce signal noise from simultaneous switching outputs.

Delay DRAM Read Latch

Common Options: Auto, No Delay, 0.5ns, 1.0ns, 1.5ns

This feature is similar to the **DRAM Read Latch Delay** BIOS feature. It fine-tunes the DRAM timing parameters to adjust for different DRAM loadings.

The DRAM load changes with the number as well as the type of memory modules installed. DRAM loading increases as the number of memory modules increases. It also increases if you use double-sided modules instead of single-sided ones. In short, the more DRAM devices you use, the greater the DRAM loading. As such, a lone single-sided memory module provides the lowest DRAM load possible.

With heavier DRAM loads, you may need to delay the moment when the memory controller latches onto the DRAM device during reads. Otherwise, the memory controller may fail to latch properly onto the desired DRAM device and read from it.

The **Auto** option allows the BIOS to select the optimal amount of delay from values preset by the manufacturer.

The **No Delay** option forces the memory controller to latch onto the DRAM device without delay, even if the BIOS presets indicate that a delay is required.

The three timing options (**0.5ns**, **1.0ns**, and **1.5ns**) give you manual control of the read latch delay.

Normally, you should let the BIOS select the optimal amount of delay from values preset by the manufacturer (using the **Auto** option). However, if you notice that your system has become unstable upon installation of additional memory modules, you should try setting the DRAM read latch delay yourself.

The longer the delay, the poorer the read performance of your memory modules. However, the stability of your memory modules won't increase together with the length of the delay. Remember, the purpose of the feature is to ensure that the memory controller is able to latch onto the DRAM device with all sorts of DRAM loadings.

The amount of delay should be just enough to allow the memory controller to latch onto the DRAM device in your particular situation. Don't unnecessarily increase the delay. It isn't going to increase stability. In fact, it may just make things worse! So, start with **0.5ns** and work your way up until your system stabilizes.

If you have a light DRAM load, you can ensure optimal performance by manually using the **No Delay** option. This forces the memory controller to latch onto the DRAM devices *without delay*, even if the BIOS presets indicate that a delay is required. Naturally, this can potentially cause stability problems if you actually have a heavy DRAM load. Therefore, if your system becomes unstable after using the **No Delay** option, simply revert back to the default value of **Auto** so that the BIOS can adjust the read latch delay to suit the DRAM load.

Delay IDE Initial

Common Options: 0 to 15

Regardless of its shortcomings, the IDE standard is remarkably backward-compatible. Every upgrade of the standard was designed to be fully compatible with older IDE devices. So, you can actually use the old 40MB hard disk that came with your ancient 386 system in your spanking new Athlon XP system! However, even backward compatibility cannot account for the slower motors used in the older drives.

Motherboards are capable of booting up much faster these days. Therefore, initialization of IDE devices now take place much earlier. Unfortunately, this also means that some older IDE drives are not be able to spin up in time to be initialized! When this happens, the BIOS is unable to detect that IDE drive and the drive is not accessible even though it is actually running just fine.

This is where the **Delay IDE Initial** BIOS feature comes in. It allows you to force the BIOS to delay the initialization of IDE devices for up to 15 seconds. The delay allows your IDE devices more time to spin up before the BIOS initializes them.

If you do not use old IDE drives and the BIOS has no problem initializing your IDE devices, it is recommended that you leave the delay at the default value of **0** for the shortest possible booting time. Most IDE devices manufactured in the last few years have no problem spinning up in time for initialization.

However, if one or more of your IDE devices fail to initialize during the boot up process, start with a delay of **1 second**. If that doesn't help, gradually increase the delay until all your IDE devices initialize properly during the boot up process.

Delay Prior To Thermal

Common Options: 4 Minutes, 8 Minutes, 16 Minutes, 32 Minutes

This BIOS feature is only valid for systems that are powered by 0.13μ Intel Pentium 4 processors with 512KB L2 cache. These processors come with a **Thermal Monitor** that actually consists of an on-die thermal sensor and a **Thermal Control Circuit** (**TCC**). Because the thermal sensor is on-die and placed at the hottest part of the die—near the integer ALU units, it is able to closely monitor the processor's die temperature.

When the Thermal Monitor is in automatic mode and the thermal sensor detects that the processor has reached its maximum safe operating temperature, it sends a **PROCHOT#** (**Processor Hot**) signal that activates the TCC. The TCC then modulates the clock cycles by inserting null cycles, typically at a rate of **50–70%** of the total number of clock cycles. Note that the operating frequency of the processor remains unchanged. The TCC only inserts null cycles that result in the processor "resting" 50–70% of the time.

As the die temperature drops, the TCC gradually reduces the number of null cycles until no more is required to keep the die temperature below the safe point. Then the thermal sensor stops sending the PROCHOT# signal, thereby turning off the TCC. This mechanism allows the processor to dynamically adjust its duty cycles to ensure its die temperature remains within safe limits.

The **Delay Prior To Thermal** BIOS feature controls the activation of the Thermal Monitor's automatic mode. It allows you to determine when the Pentium 4's Thermal Monitor should be activated in automatic mode after the system boots. For example, with the default value of **16 Minutes**, the BIOS activates the Thermal Monitor in automatic mode 16 minutes after the system starts booting up.

It also allows the watchdog timer to generate a **System Management Interrupt** (**SMI**), thereby presenting the BIOS with an opportunity to enable the Thermal Monitor when running non-ACPI-compliant operating systems.

Generally, the Thermal Monitor should *not* be activated immediately after booting because the processor is under a heavy load during the booting process. This causes a sharp rise in die temperature from its cold state. Because it takes time for the thermal output to radiate from the die to the heat sink, the thermal sensor registers the sudden spike in die temperature and prematurely activates the TCC. This unnecessarily reduces the processor's performance during the booting up process.

Therefore, to ensure optimal booting performance, the activation of the Thermal Monitor must be delayed for a set period of time. This allows the processor to operate at maximum performance without interference from the Thermal Monitor. It also prevents the unnecessary activation of the TCC and the subsequent modulation of processor cycles by allowing the die to stabilize to its true temperature before Thermal Monitor is activated.

It is recommended that you set this BIOS feature to the lowest value (in minutes) that exceeds the time it takes to fully boot up your computer. For example, if it takes 5 minutes to fully boot up your system, you should select **8 Minutes**.

You should *not* select a delay value that is unnecessarily long. Without the Thermal Monitor, your processor may heat up to a critical temperature (approximately **135°C**), at which point the **THERMTRIP#** signal is asserted. This shuts down your processor by removing the core voltage within **0.5 seconds**. While this measure saves the processor from permanent damage, you have to reset the system before the processor will start working again.

Delayed Transaction

Common Options: Enabled, Disabled

On the PCI bus, there are many devices that may not meet the PCI target latency rule. Such devices include I/O controllers and bridges (for example, PCI-to-PCI and PCI-to-ISA bridges). To meet PCI 2.1 compliance, the PCI maximum target latency rule must be observed.

According to this rule, a PCI 2.1-compliant device must service a read request within **16** PCI clock cycles (**32** clock cycles for a host bus bridge) for the *initial* read and **8** PCI clock cycles for each *subsequent* read. If it cannot do so, the PCI bus terminates the transaction, so other PCI devices can access the bus. However, instead of rearbitrating for access (and failing to meet the minimum latency requirement again), the PCI 2.1-compliant device can make use of the **PCI Delayed Transaction** feature.

When a master device reads from a target device on the PCI bus but fails to meet the latency requirements, the transaction is terminated with a Retry command. The master device then has to rearbitrate for bus access. However, if **PCI Delayed Transaction** is enabled, the target device can independently continue the read transaction. So, when the master device successfully gains control of the bus and reissues the read command, the target device has the data ready for immediate delivery. This ensures that the retried read transaction can be completed within the stipulated latency period.

If the delayed transaction is a write, the target device latches on the data and terminates the transaction if it cannot be completed within the target latency period. The master device then rearbitrates for bus access while the target device completes writing the data. When the master device regains control of the bus, it reissues the same write request. This time, instead of returning data (in the case of a read transaction), the target device sends the completion status to the master device to complete the transaction.

One advantage of using **PCI Delayed Transaction** is that it allows other PCI masters to use the bus while the transaction is being carried out on the target device. Otherwise, the bus is left idling while the target device completes the transaction.

PCI Delayed Transaction also allows write-posted data to remain in the buffer while the PCI bus initiates a non-postable transaction and yet still adheres to the PCI ordering rules. The write-posted data is written to memory while the target device is working on the non-postable transaction and flushed before the transaction is completed on the master device. Without **PCI**

Delayed Transaction, all write-posted data has to be flushed before another PCI transaction can occur.

As you can see, the **PCI Delayed Transaction** feature allows for more efficient use of the PCI bus as well as better PCI performance by allowing write-posting to occur concurrently with non-postable transactions. In this BIOS, the **Delayed Transaction** option allows you to enable or disable the **PCI Delayed Transaction** feature.

It is highly recommended that you **enable** Delayed Transaction for better PCI performance and to meet PCI 2.1 specifications. **Disable** it only if your PCI cards cannot work properly with this feature enabled or if you are using PCI cards that are *not* PCI 2.1-compliant.

Please note that while many manuals, and even earlier versions of the BIOS Optimization Guide, have stated that this is an ISA bus-specific BIOS feature that enables a 32-bit write-posted buffer for faster PCI-to-ISA writes, they are *incorrect!* This BIOS feature is not ISA bus-specific, and it does not control any write-posted buffers. It merely allows write-posting to continue while a non-postable PCI transaction is underway.

Disable Unused PCI Clock

Common Options: Enabled, Disabled

When the motherboard's clock generator pulses, the extreme values (spikes) of the pulses creates **EMI (Electromagnetic Interference)**. This causes interference with other electronics in the area. To reduce this problem, the BIOS can either modulate the pulses (to make them flatter) or turn off the unused clock signals.

This feature is a subset of the **Auto Detect DIMM/PCI Clk** feature. If you **enable** it, the BIOS monitors the PCI slots for activity. The clock signals of unoccupied slots are automatically turned off. The clock signals to *occupied* PCI slots are also turned off whenever there is no activity.

Theoretically, EMI can be reduced this way without compromising system stability. This also allows the computer to reduce power consumption because only components that are running use power and only when they are actually doing work.

The choice of whether to enable or disable this feature is really up to your personal preference. However, because this feature reduces EMI and power consumption without compromising system stability, it is recommended that you **enable** it.

DRAM Act to PreChrg CMD

Common Options: 5T, 6T, 7T, 8T, 9T

Whenever a read command is issued, a memory row is activated using the **RAS (Row Address Strobe)**. Then, to read data from the target memory cell, the appropriate column is activated using the **CAS (Column Address Strobe)**. Multiple cells can be read from the same active row by applying the appropriate CAS signals.

However, when data has to be read from a different row, the active row has to be deactivated. The row cannot be deactivated until the Minimum Row Active Time or tRAS has elapsed.

The appropriate delay for your memory module is reflected in its rated timings. In JEDEC specifications, it is the *fourth* number in the four number sequence. For example, if your memory module has the rated timings of 2-3-4-**7**, its rated tRAS delay would be 7 clock cycles.

Like **SDRAM Tras Timing Value**, this BIOS feature controls the memory bank's minimum row active time (**tRAS**). This constitutes the time when a row is activated until the time the same row can be deactivated. Hence, the name **DRAM Act to PreChrg CMD**, which is short for **DRAM Activate Command to Precharge Command**. It is also the length of time the row remains open for data transfers.

If the tRAS period is too long, it can reduce performance by unnecessarily delaying the deactivation of active rows. Reducing the tRAS period allows the active row to be deactivated earlier.

However, if the tRAS period is too short, there may not be enough time to complete a burst transfer. This reduces performance and data may be lost or corrupted.

For optimal performance, use the lowest value you can. Usually, this should be **CAS latency + tRCD + 2 clock cycles**. For example, if you set the CAS latency to 2 clock cycles and the tRCD to 3 clock cycles, the optimum tRAS value would be 7 clock cycles.

However, if you start getting memory errors or system crashes, increase the tRAS value one clock cycle at a time until your system becomes stable.

DRAM Burst Length 8QW

Common Options: Enabled, Disabled

Burst transactions improve SDRAM performance by allowing the reading or writing of whole "blocks" of contiguous data with only one column address.

In a burst sequence, only the *first* read or write transfer incurs the initial latency of activating the column. The subsequent reads or writes in that burst sequence can then follow behind without any further delay. This allows blocks of data to be read or written with far less delay than non-burst transactions.

For example, a burst transaction of four writes can incur the following latencies: **4-1-1-1**. In this example, the total time it takes to transact the four writes is merely **7** clock cycles.

In contrast, if the four writes are not written by burst transaction, they incur the following latencies: **4-4-4-4**. The time it takes to transact the four writes becomes **16** clock cycles, which is 9 clock cycles longer, or more than twice as slow as a burst transaction.

This is where the **DRAM Burst Length 8QW** BIOS feature comes in. It is a BIOS feature that allows you to control the length of a burst transaction.

When this feature is set to **Disabled**, a burst transaction can only be comprised of up to **four** quadword (QW) reads or writes.

When this feature is set to **Enabled**, a burst transaction can only be comprised of up to **eight** quadword (QW) reads or writes.

As the initial CAS latency is fixed for each burst transaction, a longer burst transaction allows more data to be read or written for less delay than a shorter burst transaction. Therefore, a burst length of 8 is faster than a burst length of 4.

For example, if the memory controller wants to write a block of contiguous data eight units long to memory, it can do it as a *single* burst transaction 8 units long or *two* burst transactions, each 4 units in length. The hypothetical latencies incurred by the single 8-unit long transaction would be **4-1-1-1-1-1-1-1** with a total time of **11** clock cycles for the entire transaction.

However, if the eight writes are written to memory as two burst transactions of 4 units in length, the hypothetical latencies incurred would be **4-1-1-1-4-1-1-1**. The time taken for the two transactions to complete would be **14** clock cycles. As you can see, this is slower than a single transaction, which is 8 units long.

Therefore, it is recommended that you **enable** this BIOS feature for better performance.

DRAM Data Integrity Mode

Common Options: ECC, Non-ECC

This BIOS feature controls the **ECC** feature of the memory controller.

ECC, which stands for **Error Checking and Correction**, enables the memory controller to detect and correct single-bit soft memory errors. The memory controller also is able to detect double-bit errors, although it is not able to correct them. This provides increased data integrity and system stability. However, this feature can only be enabled if you are using special ECC memory modules.

Now, this type of memory module is special (and more expensive!) because it comes with extra memory chips and a wider path. This is because the chipset needs to append a certain number of extra ECC bits (called **ECC code**) to each data word that is written to the memory module. When the data word is read back, the memory controller recalculates the ECC code of the read data word and compares it to the original ECC code that was written to memory earlier. If the codes are identical, then the data is valid.

However, if there's a single-bit error in the data word, the memory controller can identify the defective bit by analyzing the differences in the two ECC codes. That bit then can be corrected by simply flipping it to the opposite state (from **0** to **1**, and vice versa).

Here is a list of ECC code length required for various data path widths using the current Hamming code ECC algorithm:

Data Path Width	ECC Code Length
8-bit	5 ECC bits
16-bit	6 ECC bits
32-bit	7 ECC bits
64-bit	8 ECC bits
128-bit	9 ECC bits

Because present day processors use 64-bit wide data paths, 72-bit (64-bit data + 8-bit ECC) ECC memory modules are required to implement ECC. Please note that the maximum data transfer rate of the **72-bit** ECC memory module is the same as the **64-bit** memory module. The extra 8-bits are only for the ECC code and do not carry any data. So, using 72-bit memory modules does *not* give you any boost in performance.

In fact, because the memory controller has to calculate the ECC code for *every* data word that is read or written, there is some performance degradation, roughly in the region of **3–5%**. This is one of the reasons why ECC memory modules are not popular among desktop users. Throw in the fact that ECC memory modules are both expensive and hard to come by, and you have the top three reasons why ECC memory modules will never be mainstream solutions.

However, if data integrity is of utmost importance to you, and you can't afford to have your data corrupted or your system is down due to errant cosmic rays or radiation from DRAM packaging, ECC memory is the way to go. The loss of **3–5%** in memory performance is really nothing compared to the peace of mind that ECC can give. In any case, the matter of this BIOS feature is much easier to settle.

If you are using standard 64-bit memory modules, you must select the **Non-ECC** option.

However, if you have already forked out the money for 72-bit ECC memory modules, you should enable the **ECC** feature, no matter what people say about losing some memory performance. It doesn't make sense to buy expensive ECC memory modules and then disable ECC! Remember, you are not really losing performance. You are just trading it for greater stability and data integrity.

DRAM Idle Timer

Common Options: 0T, 8T, 16T, 64T, Infinite, Auto

The memory controller allows a number of memory pages to remain open. If a processor cycle to the SDRAM falls within those open pages, it can be satisfied without delay. This naturally improves performance.

However, these pages can only remain open for so long. They eventually have to be closed and precharged. If the page closes when the memory controller attempts to read from it, then the read operation is stalled until the page is activated again. Such a page miss is expensive in terms of clock cycles.

This is where the **SDRAM Idle Limit** BIOS feature comes in. This feature sets the number of idle cycles allowed before the memory controller forces such open pages to close and precharge.

The premise behind this BIOS feature is the concept of **temporal locality**. According to this concept, the longer the open page is left idle, the less likely it will be accessed again before it needs to be precharged. Therefore, it is better to prematurely close and precharge the page, so it can be opened quickly when a data request comes along.

It can be set to a variety of clock cycles from **0T** to **64T**. This sets the number of clock cycles the open pages are allowed to idle before they are closed and precharged. There's also an **Infinite** option as well as an **Auto** option.

If you select **0 Cycle**, then the memory controller immediately precharges the open pages as soon as there's an idle cycle.

If you select **Infinite**, the memory controller never precharges the open pages prematurely. The open pages are left activated until they have to be precharged.

If you select **Auto**, the memory controller uses the manufacturer's preset default setting.

Most manufacturers use a default value of **8T**, which allows the memory controller to precharge the open pages after eight idle cycles have passed.

Increasing the SDRAM Idle Limit to more than the default of **8T** allows the SDRAM bank to delay recharging longer during times of no activity so that if a read or write command comes along, it can be instantly satisfied.

However, this is limited by the refresh cycle already set by the BIOS. That means the open page refreshes when it needs to be recharged whether the number of idle cycles have reached the SDRAM Idle Limit or not. So, the SDRAM Idle Limit setting can only be used to force the refreshing of the SDRAM bank *before* the set refresh cycle but not to actually delay the refresh cycle.

Reducing the number of cycles from the default of 8 cycles to **0T** forces the memory controller to close all open pages after no valid requests are sent to the memory controller. In short, the open pages are refreshed as soon as data requests stop coming. Theoretically, this *may* increase the efficiency of the memory subsystem as the effects of refreshing the open pages are masked by precharging during idle cycles. However, any data requests that comes along after the page is closed have to wait until it is refreshed and activated before they can be satisfied.

Because refreshes do not occur that often (usually only about once every 64 msec), the impact of refreshes on memory performance is really quite minimal. The apparent benefits of masking the refreshes during idle cycles is not noticeable, especially since memory systems these days already use bank interleaving to mask refreshes.

With a **0T** setting, data requests are also likely to get stalled because even a single idle cycle causes the memory controller to close **all** open pages! In desktop applications, most memory reads favor the **spatial locality** concept whereby if one data bit is read, chances are high that the next data bit also needs to be read. That's why closing open pages prematurely using SDRAM Idle Limit usually causes reduced performance in desktop applications.

On the other hand, using a 0 or 8 idle cycles limit ensures that all memory contents are refreshed more often, thereby preventing the loss of data due to insufficiently refreshed memory cells. Forcing the memory controller to precharge open pages more often also ensures that in the event of a very long read, the pages can be opened long enough to fulfill the data request.

For general desktop use, it is recommended that you choose the **Infinite** option, so precharging can be delayed for as long as possible. This reduces the number of refreshes and increases the effective memory bandwidth.

For applications (for example, servers) that perform a lot of random accesses, it is advisable that you select **0T** because subsequent data requests are most likely fulfilled by other pages. Closing open pages to precharge prepares those pages for the next data request that hits them. Increased data integrity is an added benefit of having more frequent refreshes.

Alternatively, you can greatly increase the value of the **Refresh Interval** or **Refresh Mode Select** feature to boost bandwidth and use this BIOS feature to maintain the data integrity of the memory cells. As ultra-long refresh intervals (for example, 64 or 128 μsec) can cause memory cells to lose their contents, setting a low SDRAM Idle Limit like **0T** or **8T** allows the memory cells to be refreshed more often, with a high chance of those refreshes being done during idle cycles. This appears to combine the best of both worlds—a long bank active period when the memory controller is being stressed and more refreshes when the memory controller is idle.

In reality, however, this is not a reliable way of ensuring sufficient refresh cycles because it depends on the vagaries of memory usage to provide sufficient idle cycles to trigger the refreshes. If your memory subsystem is under extended load, there may not be any idle cycle to trigger an early refresh. This may cause the memory cells to lose their contents.

Therefore, it is recommended that you maintain a proper refresh interval and select the **Infinite** option (for desktops). This allows you to boost memory bandwidth by delaying refreshes for as long as possible and still maintain the data integrity of the memory cells through regular and reliable refresh cycles.

For servers, it is recommended that you maintain a proper refresh interval and use the **0T** setting. This precharges all open pages whenever there's an idle cycle.

D

DRAM Interleave Time

Common Options: 0ms, 0.5ms

This BIOS feature determines the amount of *additional* delay between successive bank accesses when the **SDRAM Bank Interleave** feature has been enabled. Naturally, the shorter the delay, the faster the memory module can switch between banks and, consequently, increases performance.

Therefore, it is recommended that you set the **DRAM Interleave Time** as low as possible for better memory performance. In this case, it would be **0ms**, which introduces *no* additional delay between bank accesses. Increase the **DRAM Interleave Time** to **0.5ms** only if you experience instability with the 0ms setting.

DRAM PreChrg to Act CMD

Common Options: 2T, 3T, 4T

Whenever a read command is issued, a memory row is activated using the **RAS (Row Address Strobe)**. Then, to read data from the target memory cell, the appropriate column is activated using the **CAS (Column Address Strobe)**. Multiple cells can be read from the same active row by applying the appropriate CAS signals.

But when data has to be read from a different row, the active row has to be deactivated. This introduces a short delay before the another row can be activated. This delay is known as the RAS Precharge Time **or tRP.**

The appropriate delay for your memory module is reflected in its rated timings. In JEDEC specifications, it is the *third* number in the three or four number sequence. For example, if your memory module has the rated timings of 2-3-4-7, its rated tRP delay would be 4 clock cycles.

Like **SDRAM Trp Timing Value**, this BIOS feature controls the RAS precharge time (tRP). This constitutes the time it takes for the Precharge command to complete and the row to be available for activation. Hence, the name **DRAM PreChrg to Act CMD**, which is short for **DRAM Precharge Command to Activate Command**.

If the RAS precharge time is too long, it reduces performance by delaying all row activations. Reducing the precharge time to **2T** improves performance by allowing a new row to be activated earlier.

However, the short precharge time of 2T may be insufficient for some memory modules. In such cases, the active row may lose its contents before they can be returned to the memory bank and the row deactivated. This may cause data loss or corruption when the memory controller attempts to read from or write to the active row.

Therefore, it is recommended that you reduce the RAS precharge time to **2T** for better performance but increase it to **3T** or **4T** if you experience system stability issues after reducing the precharge time.

DRAM Ratio (CPU:DRAM)

Common Options: 1:1, 3:2, 3:4, 4:5, 5:4

The choice of options in this BIOS feature depends entirely on the setting of the **DRAM Ratio H/W Strap** or **N/B Strap CPU As** BIOS feature.

When **DRAM Ratio H/W Strap** has been set to **Low**, the available options are **1:1** and **3:4**.

When **DRAM Ratio H/W Strap** has been set to **High**, the available options are **1:1** and **4:5**.

When **N/B Strap CPU As** has been set to **PSB800**, the available options are **1:1**, **3.2**, and **5:4**.

When **N/B Strap CPU As** has been set to **PSB533**, the available options are **1:1** and **4:5**.

When **N/B Strap CPU As** has been set to **PSB400**, the only available option is **3:4**.

The options of **1:1**, **3:2**, **3:4**, and **4:5** refer to the available CPU-to-DRAM (or CPU:DRAM) ratios.

Please note that while the Pentium 4 processor is said to have a 400MHz, 533MHz, or 800MHz **FSB** (**front side bus**), the front side bus (also known as CPU bus) is actually only running at 100MHz, 133MHz, or 200MHz, respectively. This is because the Pentium 4 bus is a **Quad Data Rate** or **QDR** bus, which transfers four times as much data as a single data rate bus.

For marketing reasons, the Pentium 4 bus is labeled as running at 400MHz, 533MHz, or 800MHz when it is actually running at only 100MHz, 133MHz, and 200MHz, respectively. It is important to keep this in mind when setting this BIOS feature.

For example, if you set a **3:2** ratio with a 200MHz (*800MHz QDR*) CPU bus, the memory bus will run at (200MHz / 3) × 2 = **133MHz** or **266MHz DDR**. Below are other examples.

If you use a **100MHz** (*400MHz QDR*) CPU bus with a:

- **3:2** ratio, the DRAM controller runs at **66MHz** (*or 133MHz DDR*)
- **5:4** ratio, the DRAM controller runs at **80MHz** (*or 160MHz DDR*)
- **1:1** ratio, the DRAM controller runs at **100MHz** (*or 200MHz DDR*)
- **4:5** ratio, the DRAM controller runs at **125MHz** (*or 250MHz DDR*)
- **3:4** ratio, the DRAM controller runs at **133MHz** (*or 266MHz DDR*)

If you use a **133MHz** (*533MHz QDR*) CPU bus with:

- **3:2** ratio, the DRAM controller runs at **89MHz** (*or 178MHz DDR*)
- **5:4** ratio, the DRAM controller runs at **106MHz** (*or 213MHz DDR*)
- **1:1** ratio, the DRAM controller runs at **133MHz** (*or 266MHz DDR*)
- **4:5** ratio, the DRAM controller runs at **166MHz** (*or 333MHz DDR*)
- **3:4** ratio, the DRAM controller runs at **177MHz** (*or 354MHz DDR*)

If you use a **200MHz** (*800MHz QDR*) CPU bus with:

- **3:2** ratio, the DRAM controller runs at **133MHz** (*or 266MHz DDR*)
- **5:4** ratio, the DRAM controller runs at **160MHz** (*or 320MHz DDR*)
- **1:1** ratio, the DRAM controller runs at **200MHz** (*or 400MHz DDR*)
- **4:5** ratio, the DRAM controller runs at **250MHz** (*or 500MHz DDR*)
- **3:4** ratio, the DRAM controller runs at **266MHz** (*or 533MHz DDR*)

D

By default, this BIOS feature is set to **By SPD**. This allows the chipset to query the SPD (**Serial Presence Detect**) chip on every memory module and use the appropriate ratio.

It is recommended that you select the ratio that allows you to maximize your memory modules' capabilities. However, bear in mind that synchronous operation using the **1:1** ratio is also highly desirable because it allows a high throughput.

DRAM Ratio H/W Strap

Common Options: High, Low, By CPU

This BIOS feature allows you to circumvent the CPU-to-DRAM ratio limitation found in the Intel i845-series of chipsets. In those chipsets, Intel has chosen to limit the choices of available CPU-to-DRAM ratios according to the clock speed of the CPU bus (also known as front side bus or FSB).

When a **400MHz FSB** processor is installed, the choices of CPU-to-DRAM ratio are limited to **1:1** or **3:4**.

When a **533MHz FSB** processor is installed, the choices of CPU-to-DRAM ratio are limited to **1:1** or **4:5**.

As you can see, this greatly limits the flexibility in selecting the best CPU-to-DRAM ratio for your system. Fortunately, this BIOS feature allows you to circumvent that limitation.

The **DRAM Ratio H/W Strap** BIOS feature actually controls the setting of the external hardware reset strap assigned to the **MCH** (**Memory Controller Hub**) of the chipset. By setting it **High** or **Low**, you can trick the chipset into thinking that the **400MHz FSB** or the **533MHz FSB** is being used.

When this BIOS feature is set to **High**, you are able to access the **533MHz** CPU-to-DRAM ratios of **1:1** and **4:5**.

When this BIOS feature is set to **Low**, you are able to access the **400MHz** CPU-to-DRAM ratios of **1:1** and **3:4**.

By default, this BIOS feature is set to **By CPU**, whereby the hardware strap is set according to the actual FSB rating of the processor.

Generally, you do not need to manually adjust the hardware strap setting. However, if you require access to the CPU-to-DRAM ratio that would normally not be available to you, then this BIOS feature would be very helpful indeed.

DRAM Read Latch Delay

Common Options: Enabled, Disabled

This feature is similar to the **Delay DRAM Read Latch** BIOS feature. It fine-tunes the DRAM timing parameters to adjust for different DRAM loadings.

The DRAM load changes with the number as well as the type of memory modules installed. DRAM loading increases as the number of memory modules increase. It also increases if you use double-sided modules instead of single-sided ones. In short, the more DRAM devices you use, the greater the DRAM loading. As such, a lone, single-sided memory module provides the lowest DRAM load possible.

With heavier DRAM loads, you may need to delay the moment when the memory controller latches onto the DRAM device during reads. Otherwise, the memory controller may fail to latch properly onto the desired DRAM device and read from it.

The **Auto** option allows the BIOS to select the optimal amount of delay from values preset by the manufacturer.

The **No Delay** option forces the memory controller to latch onto the DRAM device without delay, even if the BIOS presets indicate that a delay is required.

The three timing options (**0.5ns**, **1.0ns**, and **1.5ns**) give you manual control of the read latch delay.

Normally, you should let the BIOS select the optimal amount of delay from values preset by the manufacturer (using the **Auto** option). However, if you notice that your system has become unstable upon installation of additional memory modules, you should try setting the DRAM read latch delay yourself.

The longer the delay, the poorer the read performance of your memory modules. However, the stability of your memory modules won't increase together with the length of the delay. Remember, the purpose of the feature is only to ensure that the memory controller able to latch onto the DRAM device with all sorts of DRAM loadings.

The amount of delay should just be enough to allow the memory controller to latch onto the DRAM device in your particular situation. Don't unnecessarily increase the delay. It isn't going to increase stability. In fact, it may just make things worse! So, start with **0.5ns** and work your way up until your system stabilizes.

If you have a light DRAM load, you can ensure optimal performance by manually using the **No Delay** option. This forces the memory controller to latch onto the DRAM devices *without delay*, even if the BIOS presets indicate that a delay is required. Naturally, this can potentially cause stability problems if you actually have a heavy DRAM load. Therefore, if your system becomes unstable after using the **No Delay** option, simply revert back to the default value of **Auto**, so the BIOS can adjust the read latch delay to suit the DRAM load.

DRAM Refresh Rate

Common Options: 7.8 μsec, 15.6 μsec, 31.2 μsec, 64 μsec, 128 μsec, Auto

Memory cells normally need to be refreshed every 64 msec. However, simultaneously refreshing all the rows in a typical memory chip causes a big surge in power requirements. In addition, a simultaneous refresh causes all data requests to stall, which greatly impacts performance.

To avoid both problems, refreshes are normally staggered according to the number of rows. Because a typical memory chip contains 4096 rows, the memory controller usually refreshes a different row every **15.6 μsec** (64,000 μsec / 4096 rows = 15.6 μsec). This reduces the amount of current used during each refresh, and it allows data to be accessed from rows that are not being refreshed.

Usually, memory modules that use **128Mbit** or smaller memory chips have **4096 rows** while memory chips with higher capacity (256Mbit and above) have **8192 rows**. For memory chips that come with 8192 rows, the refresh interval needs to be halved to **7.8 μsec** because there are now twice as many rows to be serviced within the stipulated 64 msec for the entire chip.

Therefore, the typical refresh interval for 128Mbit (not MB!) or smaller memory chips is **15.6 μsec** while those for 256Mbit or larger memory chips is **7.8 μsec**. Please note that if you are using a mix of 128Mbit and 256Mbit memory modules, the fail-safe DRAM Refresh Rate is 7.8 μsec, **not** 15.6 μsec.

Although JEDEC standards call for a **64 msec** refresh cycle, memory chips these days can actually hold data for longer than that. So, using a longer refresh cycle is quite possible. With a longer refresh cycle, the memory chips are refreshed less often, reducing both the amount of bandwidth wasted on refreshes and the amount of power consumed (which is great for laptops and other portable devices).

This BIOS feature allows you to set the refresh interval of the memory chips. There are three different settings as well as an **Auto** option. If the **Auto** option is selected, the BIOS queries the memory modules' SPD chips and uses the lowest setting found for maximum compatibility.

For better performance, you should consider increasing the **DRAM Refresh Rate** from the default values (15.6 μsec for 128Mbit or smaller memory chips and 7.8 μsec for 256Mbit or larger memory chips) up to **128 μsec**. Please note that if you increase the **DRAM Refresh Rate** too much, the memory cells may lose their contents.

Therefore, you should start with small increases in the **DRAM Refresh Rate** and test your system after each hike before increasing it further. If you face stability problems upon increasing the refresh interval, reduce the refresh interval step by step until the system is stable.

D

Duplex Select

Common Options: Full-Duplex, Half-Duplex

The **Duplex Select** option is usually found under the **Onboard Serial Port 2** BIOS feature. It is slaved to the second serial port, so if you disable that serial port, this option disappears from the screen or appears grayed out.

This BIOS feature allows you to determine the transmission mode of the IR (Infra-Red) communications port.

Selecting **Full-Duplex** permits simultaneous two-way transmission, like a conversation over the phone.

Selecting **Half-Duplex**, on the other hand, only permits transmission in one direction at any one time, which is more like a conversation over a walkie-talkie.

Naturally, the **Full-Duplex** mode is the faster and more desirable choice. You should use **Full-Duplex** if possible.

Consult your IR peripheral's manual to determine if it supports **Full-Duplex** transmission. The IR peripheral *must* support **Full-Duplex** for this option to work.

E

ECP Mode Use DMA

Common Options: Channel 1, Channel 3

This BIOS feature is usually found under the **Parallel Port Mode** feature. It is slaved to the **ECP (Extended Capabilities Port)** option. Therefore, if you do not enable either **ECP** or **ECP+EPP**, this feature disappears from the screen or appears grayed out.

This BIOS feature determines which DMA channel the parallel port should use when it is in ECP mode.

The ECP mode uses the DMA protocol to achieve data transfer rates of up to **2.5 Mbits/s** and provides symmetric bidirectional communications. For all this, it requires the use of a DMA channel.

By default, the parallel port uses DMA **Channel 3** when it is in ECP mode. This works fine in most situations.

This feature was provided just in case one of your add-on cards requires the use of DMA Channel 3. In such a case, you can use this BIOS feature to force the parallel port to use the alternate DMA **Channel 1**.

Please note that there is no performance advantage in choosing DMA Channel 3 over DMA Channel 1 or vice versa. As long as either Channel 3 or Channel 1 is available for your parallel port to use, the parallel port is able to function properly in ECP mode.

EPP Mode Select

Common Options: EPP 1.7, EPP 1.9

This BIOS feature is usually found under the **Parallel Port Mode** feature. It's slaved to the **EPP (Enhanced Parallel Port)** option. Therefore, if you do not enable either **EPP** or **ECP+EPP**, this feature disappears from the screen or appears grayed out.

There are two versions of the EPP transfer protocol—**EPP 1.7** and **EPP 1.9**. This BIOS feature allows you to select the version of EPP that the parallel port should use.

In both versions of the EPP protocol, the port asserts a Request strobe, which tells the connected device that the port wishes to read or write data. The data is then written to or read from the device. At this point, the connected device returns an Acknowledge strobe.

Once the transaction is complete, the port negates the Request strobe while the connected device negates its Acknowledge strobe. The port and device is now ready for the next transaction.

The difference between EPP 1.7 and EPP 1.9 lies in their handling of the connected device's Acknowledge strobe.

An EPP 1.7 port won't bother checking if the connected device has actually negated its acknowledge strobe to show that it is ready for the next transaction. It just assumes that the device is ready for a new transaction after a delay of 125ns.

However, this creates problems with long cables because the delay may not be sufficient for the device to note the cessation of the Request strobe from the port and prepare for a new transaction.

An EPP 1.9 port does not have this problem because it actually waits for the connected device to negate the Acknowledge strobe before it begins a new cycle. This allows the use of longer cables.

Generally, **EPP 1.9** is the preferred setting because it supports the newer EPP 1.9 devices and most EPP 1.7 devices, and it offers advantages like support for longer cables. However, because certain EPP 1.7 devices cannot work properly with an EPP 1.9 port, this BIOS feature was implemented to allow you to set the EPP mode to **EPP 1.7** when such an issue crops up.

F

Fast R-W Turn Around

Common Options: Enabled, Disabled

When the memory controller receives a **write** command immediately after a **read** command, an additional period of delay is normally introduced before the write command is actually initiated.

Please note that this extra delay is only introduced when there is a switch from reads to writes. Switching from writes to reads does *not* suffer from such a delay.

As its name suggests, this BIOS feature allows you to skip that delay, so the memory controller can switch or "turn around" from reads to writes faster than normal. This improves the write performance of the memory subsystem. Therefore, it is recommended that you **enable** this feature for faster read-to-write turnarounds.

However, not all memory modules can work with the tighter read-to-write turn-around. If your memory modules cannot handle the faster turn-around, the data that was written to the memory module may be lost or become corrupted. So, when you face stability issues, **disable** this feature to correct the problem.

Fast Write to Read Turnaround

Common Options: Enabled, Disabled

This BIOS feature controls the **Write Data In to Read Command Delay (tWTR)** memory timing. This constitutes the minimum number of clock cycles that must occur between the last valid **write** operation and the next **read** command to the *same* internal bank of the DDR device.

Please note that this is only applicable for read commands that follow a write operation. Consecutive read operations or writes that follow reads are not affected.

If this BIOS feature is **enabled**, every read command that follows a write operation is delayed **one clock cycle** before it is issued.

If this BIOS feature is **disabled**, every read command that follows a write operation is delayed **two clock cycles** before it is issued.

Enabling this BIOS feature naturally allows faster switching from writes to reads and, consequently, improves performance.

Disabling this BIOS feature reduces read performance but it improves stability, especially at higher clock speeds. It may also allow the memory chips to run at a higher speed. In other words, increasing this delay may allow you to overclock the memory module higher than is normally possible.

By default, this BIOS feature is **disabled**. This meets JEDEC's specification of 2 clock cycles for write-to-read command delay in DDR400 memory modules. DDR266 and DDR333 memory modules require a write-to-read command delay of only 1 clock cycle.

It is recommended that you **enable** this BIOS feature for better memory read performance if you are using DDR266 or DDR333 memory modules. You can also try enabling it with DDR400 memory modules. However, if you face stability issues, revert to the default setting of **Disabled**.

First Boot Device

Common Options: Floppy, LS/ZIP, HDD-0, SCSI, CDROM, HDD-1, HDD-2, HDD-3, LAN, Disabled

This BIOS feature allows you to select the **first** device from which the BIOS attempts to load an operating system. If the BIOS finds and loads an operating system from the device selected through this feature, it doesn't load another operating system, even if you have one on a different device.

For example, if you set **Floppy** as the first boot device, the BIOS ignores the Windows XP installation on your hard disk and loads up the DOS 3.3 boot disk, which you have placed in the floppy drive instead. In short, this feature allows you to choose the first device from which to boot. This is particularly useful when you need to load a boot disk for troubleshooting purposes or for installing a new operating system.

By default, **Floppy** is the first boot device in practically all motherboards. Unless you boot often from the floppy drive, it is better to set your hard disk (usually **HDD-0**) as the first boot device. This shortens the booting process because the BIOS no longer needs to check the floppy drive for a bootable operating system.

More importantly, doing so prevents the BIOS from loading the wrong operating system in case you forgot to remove the boot disk from the floppy drive! This also indirectly prevents the loading of any virus-infected floppy disk that was left in the drive during booting.

To install operating systems that come on bootable CD-ROMs (for example, Microsoft Windows XP) in a new hard disk, you need to select **CDROM** as the first boot device. This enables you to boot directly from the CD-ROM and load the operating system's installation routine.

Flash BIOS Protection

Common Options: Enabled, Disabled

One frustrating problem faced by many users and motherboard manufacturers is the corruption of the BIOS by viruses or failed BIOS updates. This has been a problem since motherboards started shipping with Flash BIOS ROMs instead of static BIOS ROMs.

Because such an issue could potentially mean high numbers of really needless RMAs, many manufacturers now write-protect the BIOS code and only allow write access to the Flash ROM when the user specifically toggles a switch. The switch can be physical (a jumper or DIP switch) or it can be software-based (BIOS option).

The **Flash BIOS Protection** feature is a software toggle that controls write access to the BIOS. When it is **enabled**, the BIOS code is write-protected and cannot be changed. This protects it from any attempt to modify it, including BIOS updates and virus attacks. Therefore, if you intend to update the BIOS, you need to **disable** this feature first.

It is highly recommended that you **enable** this feature at all times. You should only **disable** it when you intend to update the BIOS. After updating the BIOS, you should immediately re-enable it to protect the BIOS against viruses.

Floppy 3 Mode Support

Common Options: Disabled, Drive A, Drive B, Both

For reasons best known to the Japanese, their computers come with special 3 mode 3.5" floppy drives. While physically similar to the standard 3.5" floppy drives used by the rest of the world, these 3 mode floppy drives differ in the disk formats they support.

Unlike normal floppy drives, 3 mode floppy drives support three different floppy disk formats— 1.44MB, 1.2MB, and 720KB, hence, their name. They allow the system to support the Japanese 1.2MB floppy disk format as well as the standard 1.44MB and 720KB (obsolete) disk formats.

If you own a 3 mode floppy drive and need to use the Japanese 1.2MB disk format, you must enable this feature by selecting either **Drive A**, **Drive B**, or **Both** (if you have two 3 mode floppy drives). Otherwise, your 3 mode floppy drive won't be able to read the special 1.2MB format properly.

However, if you only have a standard floppy drive, **disable** this feature or your floppy drive may not function properly.

Floppy Disk Access Control

Common Options: R/W, Read Only

This BIOS feature controls write access to the floppy drive.

Setting this BIOS feature to **R/W (Read/Write)** allows full access to the floppy drive. You will be allowed to write to floppy disks as well as read from them.

Setting this BIOS feature to **Read Only** prevents write access to the floppy drive. You will be allowed to read from floppy disks but you cannot write to them.

This BIOS feature is useful if you wish to prevent anyone from copying data out from a system that is only equipped with a floppy drive.

It is recommended that you set this BIOS feature to **R/W**, so you have full access to the floppy drive. Set it to **Read Only** if you do not wish to provide write access to the floppy drive.

F

Force 4-Way Interleave

Common Options: Enabled, Disabled

This BIOS feature allows you to force the memory controller to use the 4-bank SDRAM interleave mode, which provides better performance than the 2-bank interleave mode. However, you must have at least 4 banks of memory in the system for this feature to work properly.

Please note that we are talking about memory banks here, *not* the number of memory modules. A SDRAM module is internally made up of one or more memory banks that can be accessed simultaneously.

Normally, SDRAM modules that use **16Mbit** memory chips (usually **32MB** or smaller in size) have only two memory banks. So, if you are using such a small capacity DIMM, you should **disable** Force 4-Way Interleave.

However, if you use two or more of such DIMMs, you can still **enable** Force-4-Way Interleave. Just two DIMMs is sufficient to provide the four memory banks required for the four-bank interleave mode to work.

SDRAM modules that use **64Mbit** or larger memory chips are four-banked in nature. These modules are at least **64MB** in size. If you are using such four-banked modules, it no longer matters if you are using just one module or several of them. You can **enable** Force 4-Way Interleave without fear.

Therefore, it is recommended that you **enable** this BIOS feature if you are using *64MB or larger memory modules* or *at least two 32MB or smaller memory modules*. Otherwise, it is best to **disable** this BIOS feature.

For more information on memory bank interleaving, you should check out the details of the **SDRAM Bank Interleave** BIOS feature.

Force Update ESCD

Common Options: Enabled, Disabled

The **ESCD** (**Extended System Configuration Data**) is a feature of the Plug and Play BIOS that allows the BIOS to re-use system configuration data.

Whenever the BIOS boots up, it needs to configure the ISA, PCI, and AGP devices in the system (Plug and Play-capable or otherwise). However, because the installed devices are unlikely to change from one booting to another, the system configuration data actually remains the same. Therefore, if it can be stored and re-used, the BIOS can skip configuring the same devices every time you boot up the system.

This is where the ESCD feature comes in. It stores the IRQ, DMA, I/O and memory configurations of your system's devices in a special area of the BIOS Flash ROM. The BIOS snoops and re-uses the stored configuration data when it boots up the system. As long as there are no hardware changes, the BIOS does not need to reconfigure the ESCD.

If you install a new piece of hardware or modify your computer's hardware configuration, the BIOS automatically detects the changes and reconfigures the ESCD. Therefore, there is usually no need to manually force the BIOS to reconfigure the ESCD.

However, the occasion may arise where the BIOS may not be able to detect the hardware changes. A serious resource conflict may occur and the operating system may not even boot as a result. This is where the **Force Update ESCD** BIOS feature comes in.

This BIOS feature allows you to manually force the BIOS to clear the previously saved ESCD data and reconfigure the settings. All you need to do is **enable** this BIOS feature and then reboot your computer. The new ESCD should resolve the conflict and allow the operating system to load normally.

Please note that the BIOS automatically resets it to the default setting of **Disabled** after reconfiguring the new ESCD. So, there is no need for you to manually **disable** this feature after rebooting.

FPU OPCODE Compatible Mode

Common Options: Enabled, Disabled

In Intel IA-32 (P6 family, Pentium 4, and so forth) processors, the x87 FPU stores the opcode of the last executed non-control instruction (also known as the **fopcode** or **FOP code**) in an 11-bit register. This is to provide state information for exception handlers.

Because the first 5 bits of the first opcode byte are the same for all FPU opcodes, only the last 3 bits of the first opcode byte are stored in the register. The second opcode byte provides the remaining 8-bits of data.

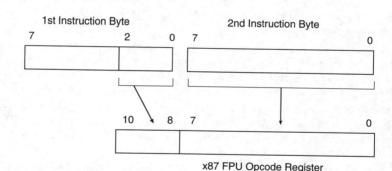

(Courtesy of Intel Corporation)

In previous implementations, the final opcode (or FOP) to be stored in the FOP register is always the FOP of the last non-transparent floating point instruction executed before an FSAVE, FSTENV, or FXSAVE instruction.

However, to improve FPU performance, the Pentium 4 and Xeon processors only store the FOP of the last non-transparent floating point instruction that had an unmasked exception. For backward compatibility, the Pentium 4 and Xeon processors allow programmable control of the FOP register. This is where the **FPU OPCODE Compatible Mode** BIOS feature comes in.

When **enabled**, the processor reverts to the FOP code compatibility mode and stores the last non-transparent floating point instruction in the 11-bit FOP register. Intel recommends that this feature should only be **enabled** if the software was designed to use the fopcode to analyze program performance or to restart the program after an exception has been handled.

When **disabled**, the processor turns off the FOP code compatibility mode and stores only the FOP of the last non-transparent floating point instruction that had an unmasked exception. This allows for better FPU performance.

Therefore, it is recommended that you **disable** this feature. This allows for better FPU performance, although some older programs may require you to **enable** this feature to allow recovery from FPU exceptions.

FSB Spread Spectrum

Common Options: 0.5%, 1.0%, Disabled

When the motherboard's clock generator pulses, the extreme values (spikes) of these signals generated create **EMI** (**Electromagnetic Interference**). This EMI interferes with other electronics in the area. There are also claims that it may allow electronic eavesdropping of the data that is being transmitted.

This BIOS feature allows you to reduce the EMI of the **front side bus** (also known as the **FSB** or processor bus) by modulating the signals it generates so that the spikes are reduced to flatter curves. It achieves this by varying the frequency *slightly* so that the signal does not use any particular frequency for more than a moment. This reduces the amount of EMI generated by the motherboard.

The BIOS usually offers two levels of modulation—**0.5%** or **1.0%**. They denote the amount of modulation or jitter from the baseline signal. The greater the modulation, the greater the reduction of EMI. Therefore, if you need to significantly reduce the front side bus EMI, a modulation of **1.0%** is recommended.

In most conditions, frequency modulation through this feature should not cause any problems. However, system stability may be compromised if you are overclocking the front side bus. Of course, this depends on the amount of modulation, the extent of overclocking, and other factors like temperature, and so forth. As such, the problem may not manifest itself immediately.

Therefore, it is recommended that you **disable** this feature if you are overclocking the front side bus. The risk of crashing your system is not worth the reduction in EMI. Of course, if EMI reduction is important to you, **enable** this feature by all means. However, you should reduce the clock speed a little to provide a margin of safety.

If you are not overclocking, the decision to enable or disable this feature is really up to you. Unless you have EMI problems or sensitive data that must be safeguarded from electronic eavesdropping, it is best to **disable** this feature to remove the possibility of stability issues.

Full Screen Logo

Common Options: Enabled, Disabled

This BIOS feature determines whether the motherboard or system manufacturer's logo appears instead of the usual boot-up screen.

When it is **enabled**, the BIOS displays the full-screen logo during the boot-up sequence.

When it is **disabled**, the BIOS displays the usual boot-up screen instead of the full-screen logo.

Please note that enabling this BIOS feature often adds 2–3 seconds of delay to the booting sequence. This delay ensures that the logo is displayed for a sufficient amount of time.

Therefore, it is recommended that you **disable** this BIOS feature for a faster boot-up time.

G

Gate A20 Option

Common Options: Normal, Fast

This BIOS feature is used to determine the method by which Gate A20 is controlled. The **Normal** option forces the chipset to use the slow keyboard controller to do the switching. The **Fast** option, on the other hand, allows the chipset to use its own 0x92 port for faster switching. No candy for guessing which is the recommended setting!

Please note this feature is only important for operating systems that switch a lot between real mode and protected mode. These operating systems include 16-bit operating systems, such as MS-DOS and 16-bit/32-bit hybrid operating systems like Microsoft Windows 98.

This feature has no effect if the operating system only runs in real mode (no operating system currently in use does that, as far as I know!), or if the operating system operates entirely in protected mode (for example, Microsoft Windows XP). This is because if A20 mode switching is not required, then it does not matter at all if the switching was done by the slow keyboard controller or the faster 0x92 port.

With all that said and done, the recommended setting for this BIOS feature is still **Fast**, even with operating systems that don't do much mode switching. Although using the 0x92 port to control Gate A20 has been known to cause spontaneous reboots in very rare instances, there is really no reason why you should keep using the slow keyboard controller to turn A20 on or off.

Graphic Win Size

Common Options: 4, 8, 16, 32, 64, 128, 256

This BIOS feature does two things. It selects the size of the AGP aperture (hence, the name **Graphic Windows Size**), and it determines the size of the **GART (Graphics Address Relocation Table)**.

The aperture is a portion of the PCI memory address range that is dedicated for use as AGP memory address space, while the GART is a translation table that translates AGP memory addresses into actual memory addresses, which are often fragmented. The GART allows the graphics card to see the memory region available to it as a contiguous piece of memory range.

Host cycles that hit the aperture range are forwarded to the AGP bus without need for translation. The aperture size also determines the maximum amount of system memory that can be allocated to the AGP graphics card for texture storage.

Please note that the AGP aperture is merely address space, *not* actual physical memory in use. Although it is very common to hear people recommending that the AGP aperture size should be *half* the size of system memory, that is *wrong*!

The requirement for AGP memory space *shrinks* as the graphics card's local memory increases in size. This is because the graphics card has more local memory to dedicate to texture storage. So, if you upgrade to a graphics card with more memory, you shouldn't be "deceived" into thinking that you need even more AGP memory! On the contrary, a smaller AGP memory space is required.

It is recommended that you keep the AGP aperture around **64MB** to **128MB** in size, even if your graphics card has a lot of onboard memory. This allows flexibility in the event that you actually need extra memory for texture storage. It also keeps the GART within a reasonable size.

Graphic Window WR Combin

Common Options: Enabled, Disabled

This BIOS feature allows you to control the **USWC** (**Uncached Speculative Write Combining**) write combine buffers. Somehow, they had to give it the badly mangled name of **Graphic Window WR Combin**.

If **enabled**, the write combine buffers will accumulate and combine partial or smaller graphics writes from the processor and write them to the graphics card as burst writes.

If **disabled**, the write combine buffers will be disabled. All graphics writes from the processor will be written to the graphics card directly.

It is highly recommended that you **enable** this feature for improved graphics and processor performance.

However, if you are using an older graphics card, it may not be compatible with this feature. Enabling this feature with such graphics cards will cause a host of problems, such as graphics artifacts, system crashes, and even the inability to boot up properly.

If you face such problems, you should **disable** this BIOS feature immediately.

Graphics Aperture Size

Common Options: 4, 8, 16, 32, 64, 128, 256

This BIOS feature does two things: It selects the size of the AGP aperture, and it determines the size of the **GART** (**Graphics Address Relocation Table**).

The aperture is a portion of the PCI memory address range that is dedicated for use as AGP memory address space, whereas the GART is a translation table that translates AGP memory addresses into actual memory addresses, which are often fragmented. The GART allows the graphics card to see the memory region available to it as a contiguous piece of memory range.

Host cycles that hit the aperture range are forwarded to the AGP bus without need for translation. The aperture size also determines the maximum amount of system memory that can be allocated to the AGP graphics card for texture storage.

Please note that the AGP aperture is merely address space, *not* actual physical memory in use. Although it is very common to hear people recommending that the AGP aperture size should be *half* the size of system memory, that is *wrong*!

The requirement for AGP memory space *shrinks* as the graphics card's local memory increases in size. This is because the graphics card will have more local memory to dedicate to texture storage. So, if you upgrade to a graphics card with more memory, you shouldn't be "deceived" into thinking that you will need even more AGP memory! On the contrary, a smaller AGP memory space will be required.

It is recommended that you keep the AGP aperture around **64MB** to **128MB** in size, even if your graphics card has a lot of onboard memory. This allows flexibility in the event that you actually need extra memory for texture storage. It will also keep the GART (Graphics Address Relocation Table) within a reasonable size.

G

Hardware Reset Protect

Common Options: Enabled, Disabled

This BIOS feature is very useful for file servers and routers that need to be running 24 hours a day, 365 days a year. When it is **enabled**, the hardware reset button is **disabled**. This prevents the possibility of any accidental resets. When **disabled**, the reset button functions as normal.

If you are running a mission-critical server or have kids who just love to press little red buttons, it is highly recommended that you **enable** this feature. Otherwise, it is really up to your preference. Naturally, people using buggy operating systems or applications are advised to keep this feature **disabled** for more convenient reboots.

HDD S.M.A.R.T. Capability

Common Options: Enabled, Disabled

This BIOS feature controls support for the hard disk's **S.M.A.R.T. (Self Monitoring Analysis And Reporting Technology)** capability.

S.M.A.R.T. is supported by all current hard disks and it allows the early prediction and warning of impending hard disk disasters. You should **enable** it if you want to use S.M.A.R.T.-aware utilities to monitor the hard disk's condition. Enabling it also allows the monitoring of the hard disk's condition over a network.

However, there is a possibility that enabling S.M.A.R.T. may cause spontaneous reboots with networked computers. **Johnathan P. Dinan** reported such an issue. Apparently, S.M.A.R.T. continuously sends packets of data through the network even when there is nothing receiving those data packets. This may cause the computer to spontaneously reboot. Therefore, if you experience spontaneous reboots or crashes with a networked computer, try **disabling** this feature.

While S.M.A.R.T. looks like a really great safety feature, it isn't really that useful or even necessary for most users. For S.M.A.R.T. to work, it is not just a matter of enabling it in the BIOS. You must also keep a S.M.A.R.T.-aware hardware monitoring utility running in the background all the time. This means using up some memory and processor time just to monitor S.M.A.R.T. data from the hard disk.

That's quite alright if the hard disk you are using has a spotty reputation and you need advanced warning of any impending failure. However, hard disks these days are mostly reliable enough to make S.M.A.R.T. redundant. Unless you are running mission-critical applications, it is very unlikely that S.M.A.R.T. is of any use at all.

Even then, you must not be misled into thinking that S.M.A.R.T. is a foolproof way to get early warning of impending hard disk failure. S.M.A.R.T. can only detect certain conditions that can lead to hard disk failures. Even with S.M.A.R.T. enabled, a hard disk can still fail without prior warning.

With that said, S.M.A.R.T. is still useful in providing a modicum of data loss prevention by continuously monitoring hard disks for signs of impending failure. If you have critical or irreplaceable data, you should **enable** this BIOS feature and use a S.M.A.R.T.-aware hardware monitoring software. Just don't rely completely on it! Back up your data on a CD or DVD!

Please note that even if you do not use any S.M.A.R.T.-aware utility, enabling S.M.A.R.T. in the BIOS uses up some bandwidth because the hard disk continuously sends out data packets. So, if you do not use S.M.A.R.T.-aware utilities, or if you do not need that level of real-time reporting, **disable** HDD S.M.A.R.T. Capability for better overall performance.

Some of the newer BIOSes now come with S.M.A.R.T. monitoring support built-in. When you enable HDD S.M.A.R.T. Capability, these new BIOSes automatically check the hard disk's S.M.A.R.T. status at boot-up. However, such a feature has very limited utility because it can only tell you the status of the hard disk at boot-up.

It cannot keep track of the hard disk's condition during operation and, therefore, it is far less useful than a proper S.M.A.R.T.-aware monitoring utility. In addition, there have been reports of false alarms raised by such built-in software. Therefore, it is still advisable for you to **disable** HDD S.M.A.R.T. Capability unless you use a proper S.M.A.R.T.-aware monitoring utility.

Host Bus In-Order Queue Depth

Common Options: 1, 4, 8, 12

For greater performance at high clock speeds, motherboard chipsets now feature a pipelined processor bus. The multiple stages in this pipeline can also be used to queue up multiple commands to the processor. This command queuing greatly improves performance because it effectively masks the latency of the processor bus. In optimal situations, the amount of latency between each succeeding command can be reduced to only a single clock cycle!

This BIOS feature controls the use of the processor bus command queue. Normally, there are only two options available. Depending on the motherboard chipset, the options could be (**1** and **4**), (**1** and **8**), or (**1** and **12**). This is because this BIOS feature does not actually allow you to select the number of commands that can be queued.

It merely allows you to disable or enable the command queuing capability of the processor bus pipeline. This is because the number of commands that can be queued depends entirely on the number of stages in the pipeline. As such, you can expect to see this feature associated with options like **Enabled** and **Disabled** in some motherboards.

The first queue depth option is always **1**, which prevents the processor bus pipeline from queuing any outstanding commands. If selected, each command is only issued after the processor has finished with the previous one. Therefore, every command incurs the maximum amount of latency. This varies from **4 clock cycles** for a 4-stage pipeline to **12 clock cycles** for pipelines with 12 stages.

As you can see, this reduces performance as the processor has to wait for each command to filter down the pipeline. The severity of the effect depends greatly on the depth of the pipeline. The deeper the pipeline, the greater the effect.

If the second queue depth option is **4**, this means that the processor bus pipeline has 4 stages in it. Selecting this option allows the queuing of up to 4 commands in the pipeline. Each command can then be processed successively with a latency of only 1 clock cycle.

H

If the second queue depth option is **8**, this means that the processor bus pipeline has 8 stages in it. Selecting this option allows the queuing of up to 8 commands in the pipeline. Each command can then be processed successively with a latency of only 1 clock cycle.

If the second queue depth option is **12**, this means that the processor bus pipeline has 12 stages in it. Selecting this option allows the queuing of up to 12 commands in the pipeline. Each command can then be processed successively with a latency of only 1 clock cycle.

Please note that the latency of only 1 clock cycle is only possible if the pipeline is *completely* filled up. If the pipeline is only partially filled up, then the latency affecting one or more of the commands is more than 1 clock cycle. Still, the average latency for each command is much lower than it would be with command queuing disabled.

In most cases, it is highly recommended that you enable command queuing by selecting the option of **4** / **8** / **12** or, in some cases, **Enabled**. This allows the processor bus pipeline to mask its latency by queuing outstanding commands. You can expect a significant boost in performance with this feature enabled.

Interestingly, this feature also can be used as an aid in overclocking the processor. Although the queuing of commands brings with it a big boost in performance, it may also make the processor unstable at overclocked speeds. To overclock beyond what's normally possible, you can try **disabling** command queuing. This may reduce performance, but it makes the processor more stable and may allow it to be further overclocked.

Please note that the performance deficit associated with deeper pipelines (8 or 12 stages) may not be worth the increase in processor overclockability. This is because the deep processor bus pipelines have very long latencies. If they are not masked by command queuing, the processor may be stalled so badly that you end up with poorer performance even if you are able to further overclock the processor. So, it is recommended that you **enable** command queuing for deep pipelines, even if it means reduced overclockability.

Hyper-Threading Technology

Common Options: Enabled, Disabled

The **Intel Hyper-Threading Technology** is an extension to the IA-32 architecture, which allows a single processor to execute *two or more* separate threads concurrently. When hyper-threading is enabled, multi-threaded software applications can execute their threads in parallel, thereby improving the processor's performance.

The current implementation involves *two* logical processors sharing the processor's execution engine and its bus interface. Each logical processor, however, comes with its own APIC. The other features of the processor are either shared or duplicated in each logical processor.

Here is a list of the features duplicated in each logical processor:

- General registers (EAX, EBX, ECX, EDX, ESI, EDI, ESP, and EBP)
- Segment registers (CS, DS, SS, ES, FS, and GS)
- EFLAGS and EIP registers
- x87 FPU registers (ST0 to ST7, status word, control word, tag word, data operand pointer, and instruction pointer)
- MMX registers (MM0 to MM7)
- XMM registers (XMM0 to XMM7)

- MXCSR register
- Control registers (CR0, CR2, CR3, CR4)
- System table pointer registers (GDTR, LDTR, IDTR, task register)
- Debug registers (DR0, DR1, DR2, DR3, DR6, DR7)
- Debug control MSR (IA32_DEBUGCTL)
- Machine check global status MSR (IA32_MCG_STATUS)
- Machine check capability MSR (IA32_MCG_CAP)
- Thermal clock modulation and ACPI power management control MSRs
- Time stamp counter MSRs
- Most of the other MSR registers including Page Attribute Table (PAT) Local APIC registers

Here are the features shared by the two logical processors:

- A32_MISC_ENABLE MSR
- Memory type range registers (MTRRs)

The following are features that can be duplicated or shared according to requirements:

- Machine check architecture (MCA) MSRs
- Performance monitoring control and counter MSRs

The Intel Hyper–Threading Technology is only supported by the Intel Pentium 4 (officially only those 3.06GHz and faster) and the Intel Xeon processors. Note that for Hyper–Threading to work, you should have the following:

- Intel processor that supports Hyper–Threading
- Motherboard with a chipset and BIOS that support Hyper–Threading
- Operating system that supports Hyper–Threading (Microsoft Windows XP or Linux 2.4.x)

Because it behaves like two separate processors with their own APICs, you should also enable **APIC Function** in the BIOS, which is required for multi-processing.

It is highly recommended that you **enable** Hyper–Threading Technology for improved processor performance.

I

IDE Bus Master Support

Common Options: Enabled, Disabled

This BIOS feature is a misnomer because it doesn't actually control the bus mastering ability of the onboard IDE controller. It is actually a toggle for the built-in driver that allows the onboard IDE controller to perform **DMA (Direct Memory Access)** transfers.

DMA transfer modes allow IDE devices to transfer large amounts of data from the hard disk to the system memory and vice versa with minimal processor intervention. It differs from the older and processor-intensive **PIO (Programmed Input/Output)** transfer modes by offloading the task of data transfer from the processor to the chipset.

Previously, this feature was only available after an operating system supporting DMA transfers (through the appropriate device driver) was loaded. Now, however, many BIOS come with a built-in 16-bit driver that allows DMA transfers. This allows the onboard IDE controller to perform DMA transfers even before the operating system is loaded!

When this BIOS feature is **enabled**, the BIOS loads up the 16-bit busmastering driver for the onboard IDE controller. This allows the IDE controller to transfer data through DMA, resulting in greatly improved transfer rates and lower CPU utilization in real-mode DOS and during the loading of other operating systems.

When this BIOS feature is **disabled**, the BIOS will *not* load up the 16-bit busmastering driver for the onboard IDE controller. The IDE controller then transfers data through PIO.

Therefore, it is recommended that you **enable** IDE Bus Master Support. This greatly improves the IDE transfer rate and reduces CPU utilization during the booting process or when you are using real-mode DOS. Users of DOS-based disk utilities, such as Norton Ghost, can expect to benefit a lot from this feature.

Please note that because current operating systems (for example, Windows XP) load up their own 32-bit busmastering driver, this feature has no effect when such an operating system loads up. Still, it is recommended that you **enable** this feature to improve performance prior to the loading of the operating system's own driver.

IDE HDD Block Mode

Common Options: Enabled, Disabled

This BIOS feature speeds up hard disk access by transferring multiple sectors of data per interrupt instead of using the usual single-sector transfer mode. This mode of transferring data is known as block transfers.

When you enable this feature, the BIOS automatically detects whether your hard disk supports block transfers and sets the proper block transfer settings for it. Depending on the IDE controller, up to **64KB** of data can be transferred per interrupt when block transfers are enabled. Because all current hard disks support block transfers, there is *usually* no reason why IDE HDD Block Mode should be disabled.

However, if you are running on Windows NT 4.0, you might need to disable this BIOS feature because Windows NT 4.0 has a problem with block transfers. According to **Chris Bope**, Windows NT does *not* support IDE HDD Block Mode and enabling this feature can cause data to be corrupted.

According to a Microsoft article (Enhanced IDE operation under Windows NT 4.0), IDE HDD Block Mode and 32-bit Disk Access have been found to cause data corruption in some cases. Therefore, Microsoft recommends that Windows NT 4.0 users **disable** IDE HDD Block Mode.

Microsoft took a serious view of the issue and corrected it in the **Windows NT 4.0 Service Pack 2**. Therefore, it is safe to **enable** IDE HDD Block Mode in a Windows NT 4.0 system, so long as it has been upgraded with Service Pack 2.

Please note that if you **disable** IDE HDD Block Mode, only **512 bytes** of data can transfer per interrupt. Needless to say, this significantly degrades performance.

Therefore, you should **disable** IDE HDD Block Mode *only* if you actually face the possibility of data corruption (with an unpatched version of Windows NT 4.0). Otherwise, it is highly recommended that you **enable** this BIOS feature for significantly better hard disk performance!

Init Display First

Common Options: AGP, PCI

Although the AGP bus was designed exclusively for the graphics subsystem, some users still have to use PCI graphics cards for multi-monitor support. This is because there can be only one AGP port! So, if you want to use multiple monitors, you must either get an AGP card that provides multi-monitor support or use PCI graphics cards.

For those who upgraded from a PCI graphics card to an AGP card, it is certainly enticing to use the old PCI graphics card to support a second monitor. The PCI card does the job just fine because it merely sends display data to the second monitor. You don't need a powerful graphics card to run the second monitor because Microsoft Windows 2000/XP does not support 3D graphics acceleration on the second monitor.

When it comes to a case of an AGP graphics card working in tandem with a PCI graphics card, the BIOS has to determine which graphics card is the primary graphics card. Naturally, the default would be the **AGP** graphics card because, in most cases, it is the faster card.

However, a BIOS switch that allows you to manually select the graphics card with which to boot the system is still required. This is particularly important if you have AGP and PCI graphics cards but only one monitor. This is where the **Init Display First** feature comes in. It allows you to select whether to boot the system using the AGP graphics card or the PCI graphics card.

If you are only using a single graphics card, then the BIOS detects it as such and boots it up, irrespective of what you set the feature to. However, there may be a slight reduction in the time taken to detect and initialize the card if you select the proper setting for this BIOS feature. For example, if you only use an AGP graphics card, then setting Init Display First to **AGP** may speed up your system's booting-up process.

Therefore, if you are only using a single graphics card, it is recommended that you set the Init Display First feature to the proper setting for your system (**AGP** for a single AGP card and **PCI** for a single PCI card).

However, if you are using multiple graphics cards, it is up to you which card you want to use as your primary display card. It is recommended that you select the fastest graphics card as the primary display card.

I

In-Order Queue Depth

Common Options: 1, 4, 8, 12

For greater performance at high clock speeds, motherboard chipsets now feature a pipelined processor bus. The multiple stages in this pipeline can also be used to queue up multiple commands to the processor. This command queuing greatly improves performance because it effectively masks the latency of the processor bus. In optimal situations, the amount of latency between each succeeding command can be reduced to only a single clock cycle!

This BIOS feature controls the use of the processor bus command queue. Normally, there are only two options available. Depending on the motherboard chipset, the options could be (**1** and **4**), (**1** and **8**), or (**1** and **12**). This is because this BIOS feature does not actually allow you to select the number of commands that can be queued.

It merely allows you to disable or enable the command queuing capability of the processor bus pipeline. This is because the number of commands that can be queued depends entirely on the number of stages in the pipeline. As such, you can expect to see this feature associated with options like **Enabled** and **Disabled** in some motherboards.

The first queue depth option is always **1**, which prevents the processor bus pipeline from queuing any outstanding commands. If selected, each command only is issued after the processor has finished with the previous one. Therefore, every command incurs the maximum amount of latency. This varies from **4 clock cycles** for a 4-stage pipeline to **12 clock cycles** for pipelines with 12 stages.

As you can see, this reduces performance as the processor has to wait for each command to filter down the pipeline. The severity of the effect depends greatly on the depth of the pipeline. The deeper the pipeline, the greater the effect.

If the second queue depth option is **4**, this means that the processor bus pipeline has 4 stages in it. Selecting this option allows the queuing of up to 4 commands in the pipeline. Each command then can be processed successively with a latency of only 1 clock cycle.

If the second queue depth option is **8**, this means that the processor bus pipeline has 8 stages in it. Selecting this option allows the queuing of up to 8 commands in the pipeline. Each command then can be processed successively with a latency of only 1 clock cycle.

If the second queue depth option is **12**, this means that the processor bus pipeline has 12 stages in it. Selecting this option allows the queuing of up to 12 commands in the pipeline. Each command then can be processed successively with a latency of only 1 clock cycle.

Please note that the latency of only 1 clock cycle is only possible if the pipeline is *completely* filled up. If the pipeline is only partially filled up, then the latency affecting one or more of the commands is more than 1 clock cycle. Still, the average latency for each command is much lower than it would be with command queuing disabled.

In most cases, it is highly recommended that you enable command queuing by selecting the option of **4 / 8 / 12** or, in some cases, **Enabled**. This allows the processor bus pipeline to mask its latency by queuing outstanding commands. You can expect a significant boost in performance with this feature enabled.

Interestingly, this feature can also be used as an aid in overclocking the processor. Although the queuing of commands brings with it a big boost in performance, it may also make the processor unstable at overclocked speeds. To overclock beyond what's normally possible, you can try **disabling** command queuing. This may reduce performance, but it makes the processor more stable and may allow it to be further overclocked.

However, please note that the performance deficit associated with deeper pipelines (8 or 12 stages) may not be worth the increase in processor overclockability. This is because the deep processor bus pipelines have very long latencies. If they are not masked by command queuing, the processor may be stalled so badly that you may end up with poorer performance even if you are able to further overclock the processor. So, it is recommended that you **enable** command queuing for deep pipelines, even if it means reduced overclockability.

Interrupt Mode

Common Options: PIC, APIC

This BIOS feature is used to enable or disable the motherboard's **APIC** (**Advanced Programmable Interrupt Controller**). The APIC is a new distributed set of devices that make up an interrupt controller. In current implementations, it consists of three parts—a local APIC, an I/O APIC, and an APIC bus.

The local APIC delivers interrupts to a specific processor, so each processor in a system has to have its own local APIC. Therefore, a dual processor system must have two local APICs. Because a local APIC has been integrated into every processor since the debut of the original Intel Pentium P54C processor, there's no need to worry about the number of local APICs.

The I/O APIC is the replacement for the old chained **8259 PIC** (**Programmable Interrupt Controller**) still in use in many motherboards. It collects interrupt signals from I/O devices and sends messages to the local APICs through the APIC bus that connects it to the local APICs.

There can be up to eight I/O APICs in a system, each supporting anywhere from 24 (usually) to 64 interrupt lines. As you can see, this allows a lot more IRQs than is currently possible with the 8259 PIC. Note that without at least one I/O APIC, the local APIC is useless and the system functions as if it's based on the 8259 PIC.

To sum it all up, APIC provides multiprocessor support, more IRQs, and faster interrupt handling, all of which are not possible with the old 8259 PIC. Although they can be used in single-processor boards, you are more likely to find them in multi-processor motherboards. This is because APIC is only supported in Windows NT, 2000, and XP. It is not supported in operating systems that are required to support MS-DOS device drivers, such as Windows 95/98. However, as users transition to Windows XP, you can expect more manufacturers to ship single-processor boards with I/O APICs.

If your single-processor motherboard supports APIC and you are using a Win32 operating system (Windows NT, 2000, and XP), it is recommended that you select **APIC** to allow faster and better IRQ handling. If you are using a multiprocessor motherboard, you must select **APIC** because it is required for IRQ handling in multiprocessor systems.

However, if you are running Windows 95/98 or a DOS-based operating system on a single-processor motherboard, you must select **PIC** instead. This is because MS-DOS drivers assume they can write directly to the 8259 PIC (APIC did not exist yet in those days!) and its associated **IDT (Interrupt Descriptor Table)** entries. Selecting **PIC** forces the APIC to revert to the legacy 8259 PIC mode.

I

IOQD

Common Options: 1, 4, 8, 12

For greater performance at high clock speeds, motherboard chipsets now feature a pipelined processor bus. The multiple stages in this pipeline also can be used to queue up multiple commands to the processor. This command queuing greatly improves performance because it effectively masks the latency of the processor bus. In optimal situations, the amount of latency between each succeeding command can be reduced to only a single clock cycle!

This BIOS feature controls the use of the processor bus command queue. Normally, there are only two options available. Depending on the motherboard chipset, the options could be (**1** and **4**), (**1** and **8**), or (**1** and **12**). This is because this BIOS feature does not actually allow you to select the number of commands that can be queued.

It merely allows you to disable or enable the command queuing capability of the processor bus pipeline. This is because the number of commands that can be queued depends entirely on the number of stages in the pipeline. As such, you can expect to see this feature associated with options like **Enabled** and **Disabled** in some motherboards.

The first queue depth option is always **1**, which prevents the processor bus pipeline from queuing any outstanding commands. If selected, each command only is issued after the processor has finished with the previous one. Therefore, every command incurs the maximum amount of latency. This varies from **4 clock cycles** for a 4-stage pipeline to **12 clock cycles** for pipelines with 12 stages.

As you can see, this reduces performance as the processor has to wait for each command to filter down the pipeline. The severity of the effect depends greatly on the depth of the pipeline. The deeper the pipeline, the greater the effect.

If the second queue depth option is **4**, this means the processor bus pipeline has 4 stages in it. Selecting this option allows the queuing of up to 4 commands in the pipeline. Each command then can be processed successively with a latency of only 1 clock cycle.

If the second queue depth option is **8**, this means that the processor bus pipeline has 8 stages in it. Selecting this option allows the queuing of up to 8 commands in the pipeline. Each command then can be processed successively with a latency of only 1 clock cycle.

If the second queue depth option is **12**, this means that the processor bus pipeline has 12 stages in it. Selecting this option allows the queuing of up to 12 commands in the pipeline. Each command then can be processed successively with a latency of only 1 clock cycle.

Please note that the latency of only 1 clock cycle is only possible if the pipeline is *completely* filled up. If the pipeline is only partially filled up, then the latency affecting one or more of the commands is more than 1 clock cycle. Still, the average latency for each command is much lower than it would be with command queuing disabled.

In most cases, it is highly recommended that you enable command queuing by selecting the option of **4**/**8**/**12** or, in some cases, **Enabled**. This allows the processor bus pipeline to mask its latency by queuing outstanding commands. You can expect a significant boost in performance with this feature enabled.

Interestingly, this feature also can be used as an aid in overclocking the processor. Although the queuing of commands brings with it a big boost in performance, it may also make the processor unstable at overclocked speeds. To overclock beyond what's normally possible, you can try **disabling** command queuing. This may reduce performance but it makes the processor more stable and may allow it to be further overclocked.

However, please note that the performance deficit associated with deeper pipelines (8 or 12 stages) may not be worth the increase in processor overclockability. This is because the deep processor bus pipelines have very long latencies. If they are not masked by command queuing, the processor may be stalled so badly that you may end up with poorer performance even if you are able to further overclock the processor. So, it is recommended that you **enable** command queuing for deep pipelines, even if it means reduced overclockability.

ISA 14.318MHz Clock

Common Options: Enabled, Disabled

The ISA bus (also known as the AT bus) was originally an **8-bit** bus running at just **4.77MHz**. It was then expanded to include a 16-bit bus running initially at 6MHz and later at 8MHz. Eventually, the ISA bus was standardized to run at a maximum speed of **8.33MHz**.

Because each ISA data transfer takes anywhere from two to eight clock cycles to complete, this yields a maximum bandwidth of only **4.77MB/s** for 8-bit cards and **8.33MB/s** for 16-bit cards.

Maximum bandwidth for the 8-bit ISA bus = 8.33MHz × 1 byte (*8-bits*) ÷ 2 clock cycles per transfer = 4.77MB/s

Maximum bandwidth for the 16-bit ISA bus = 8.33MHz × 2 bytes (*16-bits*) ÷ 2 clock cycles per transfer = 8.33MB/s

This BIOS feature allows you to overclock the ISA bus using the reference clock generator speed of **14.318MHz**. This greatly improves the ISA bus speed by running the bus **72%** faster than normal. At this clock speed, 8-bit cards have a bandwidth of **7.16MB/s** while 16-bit cards have a bandwidth of **14.32MB/s**.

In most cases, it is recommended that you **enable** this feature to give the ISA bus a performance boost. Of course, this is only useful if you have ISA devices in your system. Otherwise, this feature is redundant.

Please note that while newer ISA cards are capable of running at this "out-of-spec" speed, older ones may not work properly at this speed. Therefore, if your ISA card fails to function properly, **disable** this feature.

ISA Enable Bit

Common Options: Enabled, Disabled

This is similar to the **AGP ISA Aliasing** BIOS feature.

The origin of this feature can be traced back all the way to the original IBM PC. When the IBM PC was designed, it only had *10* address lines (**10-bits**) for I/O space allocation. Therefore, the I/O space back in those days was only **1KB** or 1024 bytes in size. Out of those 1024 available addresses, the first **256 addresses** were reserved exclusively for the motherboard's use, leaving the last **768 addresses** for use by add-in devices. This would become a critical factor later on.

I

Later, motherboards began to utilize *16* address lines for I/O space allocation. This was supposed to create a contiguous I/O space of 64KB in size. Unfortunately, many ISA devices by then were only capable of doing 10-bit decodes. This was because they were designed for computers based on the original IBM design, which only supported 10 address lines.

To circumvent this problem, they fragmented the 64KB I/O space into **1KB** chunks. Unfortunately, because the first 256 addresses must be reserved exclusively for the motherboard, this means that only the first (or lower) 256 bytes of each 1KB chunk would be decoded in full 16-bits. All 10-bits-decoding ISA devices are, therefore, restricted to the last (or top) 768 bytes of the 1KB chunk of I/O space.

As a result, such ISA devices only have 768 I/O locations to use. Because there were so many ISA devices back then, this limitation created a lot of compatibility problems because the chances of two ISA cards using the same I/O space were high. When that happened, one or both of the cards would not work. Although they tried to reduce the chance of such conflicts by standardizing the I/O locations used by different classes of ISA devices, it still was not good enough.

Eventually, they came up with a workaround. Instead of giving each ISA device all the I/O space it wanted in the 10-bit range, they gave each ISA device a smaller number of I/O locations and made up for the difference by "borrowing" them from the 16-bit I/O space! Here's how they do it.

The ISA device would first take up a small number of I/O locations in the 10-bit range. It then extends its I/O space by using **16-bit aliases** of the few 10-bit I/O locations taken up earlier. Because each I/O location in the 10-bit decode area has **sixty-three** 16-bit aliases, the total number of I/O locations expands from just 768 locations to a maximum of 49,152 locations!

More importantly, each ISA card now requires very few I/O locations in the 10-bit range. This drastically reduced the chances of two ISA cards conflicting each other in the limited 10-bit I/O space. This workaround naturally became known as **ISA Aliasing**.

Now, that's all well and good for ISA devices. Unfortunately, the 10-bit limitation of ISA devices becomes a liability to devices that require 16-bit addressing. AGP and PCI devices come to mind. As noted earlier, only the first 256 addresses of the 1KB chunks support 16-bit addressing. What that really means is all 16-bit addressing devices are thus limited to only 256 bytes of *contiguous* I/O space!

When a 16-bit addressing device requires a larger *contiguous* I/O space, it has to encroach on the 10-bit ISA I/O space. For example, if an AGP card requires 8KB of contiguous I/O space, it takes up *eight* of the 1KB I/O chunks (which are made up of eight 16-bit areas and eight 10-bit areas!). Because ISA devices are using ISA Aliasing to extend their I/O space, there is now a high chance of I/O space conflicts between ISA devices and the AGP card. When that happens, the affected cards will most likely fail to work.

There are two ways out of this mess. Obviously, you can limit the AGP card to a maximum of 256 bytes of contiguous I/O space. Of course, this is not an acceptable solution.

The second, and the preferred method, is to throw away the restriction and provide the AGP card with all the contiguous I/O space it wants.

Here is where the **ISA Enable Bit** BIOS feature comes in. The default setting of **Enabled** forces the system controller to alias ISA addresses using address bits [15:10]—the last 6-bits. Only the first 10-bits (address bits 0 to 9) are used for decoding. This restricts all 16-bit addressing devices to a maximum contiguous I/O space of 256 bytes.

When **disabled**, the system controller does not perform any ISA aliasing and all 16 address lines can be used for I/O address space decoding. This gives 16-bit addressing devices access to the full 64KB I/O space.

It is recommended that you **disable** ISA Enable Bit for optimal AGP (and PCI) performance. It also prevents your AGP or PCI cards from conflicting with your ISA cards. **Enable** it only if you have ISA devices that are conflicting with each other.

I

K7 CLK_CTL Select

Common Options: Default, Optimal

As the name suggests, this is an AMD-specific BIOS feature. It controls the **Clock Control (CLK_CTL) Model Specific Register** (**MSR**), which is part of the AMD Athlon's power management control system.

First of all, we should be aware that the AMD Athlon family of processors has four different power management states:

- Working State (C0)
- Halt State (C1)
- Stop Grant States (C2 and S1)
- Probe State

The Athlon processor can switch to its power-saving mode when it is in the Halt state or one of the Stop Grant states. In those power management states, the processor sends a HLT or STP-CLK# special bus cycle to the north bridge, which disconnects the Athlon system bus. The processor then enters into its power-saving mode.

Now, unlike the Intel Pentium 4 processor, the Athlon processor saves power by actually reducing its *internal* clock speed. The Athlon bus clock speed remains constant, but by using an internal clock divider, the Athlon processor can reduce its internal clock speed to **1/64th** (Palomino cores and older) or **1/8th** (Thoroughbred cores and newer) of its nominal clock speed. That means a 2.0GHz Athlon processor with a Palomino or older core has an internal clock speed of only **31.25MHz** in power-saving mode! However, if the same processor has a Thoroughbred core, the internal clock speed in power-saving mode is **250MHz**.

As you can see, the older Athlon cores run at a much lower internal speed compared to the newer cores. This translates into a much lower power consumption in power-saving modes. For example, Athlon processors with Palomino cores use only **0.86W** of power in power-saving mode. In contrast, the newer Athlon Thoroughbred-B processors in power-saving mode consume about **8.9W** of power. However, the extremely low internal clock speed in the older Athlon cores meant that these cores take a much longer time to ramp up to full clock speed when it "wakes up" from its power-saving mode. This can sometimes cause problems.

The older Athlons have a bug (Errata No. 11) called *PLL Overshoot on Wake-Up from Disconnect Causes Auto-Compensation Circuit to Fail*. What happens is the processor can sometimes overshoot the nominal clock speed when it ramps up after a power-saving session. This causes a reduction in the Athlon bus I/O drive strength levels, which the auto-compensation circuitry attempts to correct. However, because there is not enough time, the proper drive strengths cannot be attained before the processor reconnects to the system bus. This causes the system bus to fail, which results in a system hang.

K

This bug is particularly prominent in the older Athlons that use the 1/64 internal divider because they normally require a longer ramp-up time, which increases the chance for the processor to overshoot the nominal clock speed. Hence, a workaround for this bug was devised whereupon the BIOS manually reprograms the CLK_CTL register to *reduce* the ramp-up time. With a reduced ramp-up time, there is very little chance of the processor overshooting and causing a failure of the system bus.

By default, the BIOS programs the CLK_CTL register with a value of **6003_1223h** during the POST routine. To increase the ramp-up speed, the BIOS has to change the value to **2003_1223h**.

This is where the **K7 CLK_CTL Select** BIOS feature comes in. When set to **Default**, the BIOS programs the CLK_CTL register with a value of **6003_1223h**. Setting to **Optimal** causes the BIOS to program the CLK_CTL register with a value of **2003_1223h**.

If you are using an AMD Athlon processor with a *Palomino or older* core, it is recommended that you set **K7 CLK_CTL Select** to **Optimal**. This prevents Errata No. 11 from manifesting itself and may even provide a speed boost by allowing the processor to disconnect and connect to the system bus faster.

From the **Thoroughbred-A** core (CPUID 680) onward, AMD started using an internal clock divider of only **1/8** with the CLK_CTL value of **6003_1223h**. While this means that the newer cores consume more power during power-saving states, the 1/8 divider allows a much faster ramp-up time. This neatly circumvents the Errata No. 11 problem, although AMD also corrected that bug. With such processors, the CLK_CTL should be set to the **Default** value of **6003_1223h**.

Unfortunately, AMD then did an about-face with the Thoroughbred-B core (CPUID 681) and changed the value associated with the **1/8** divider from **6003_1223h** to **2003_1223h**. Unless the BIOS was updated to recognize this difference, it probably would write the **6003_1223h** value used for the Thoroughbred-A core into the register instead of the correct **2003_1223h** required by the Thoroughbred-B core. When this happens, the processor may become unstable during transitions from sleep mode to active mode.

Therefore, for **Thoroughbred-B** cores and above, you should set the **K7 CLK_CTL Select** BIOS feature to **Optimal** setting to ensure proper setting of the internal clock divider.

KBC Input Clock Select

Common Options: 8MHz, 12MHz, 16MHz

The PS/2 keyboard communicates with the keyboard controller on the motherboard through a serial data link. The speed of the data link depends on the clock signal generated by the keyboard controller. The higher the clock speed, the faster the keyboard interface. This translates into a more responsive keyboard, although not all keyboards can work with higher clock speeds.

This BIOS feature allows you to adjust the keyboard interface clock for a better response or to fix a keyboard problem. It is recommended that you select the **16MHz** option for a better keyboard response. However, if the keyboard performs erratically or fails to initialize, try a lower clock speed.

K

Keyboard Auto-Repeat Delay

Common Options: 1/4 Sec, 1/2 Sec, 3/4 Sec, 1 Sec

This BIOS feature determines how long, in fractions of a second, the keyboard controller waits before it starts repeating the keystroke that you have pressed continuously. The longer the delay, the longer the keyboard controller waits before it starts repeating the keystroke.

Generally, using a short delay is useful for people who type quickly and don't like to wait long for a keystroke to be repeated. On the other hand, a long delay is useful for users who tend to press the keys longer while typing. This prevents the keyboard controller from unnecessarily repeating keystrokes with such users.

Keyboard Auto-Repeat Rate

Common Options: 6/Sec, 8/Sec, 10/Sec, 12/Sec, 20/Sec, 24/Sec, 30/Sec

This BIOS feature determines the rate at which the keyboard repeats a keystroke if you press it continuously.

The available settings are in characters per second. Therefore, a typematic rate of **30/Sec** causes the keyboard to repeat the keystroke at a rate of 30 characters per second if you press a particular key continuously. The higher the typematic rate, the faster the keyboard repeats the keystroke.

The choice of what setting to use is entirely up to your personal preference. Please note that this typematic rate is only applicable in operating systems that communicate with the hardware through the BIOS, like **MS-DOS**. The typematic rate in operating systems like Windows XP is controlled by the keyboard driver's settings.

K

L

L3 Cache

Common Options: Enabled, Disabled

In addition to the Level 1 and Level 2 caches, some processors come with an additional cache called **Level 3 cache** or **L3 cache**.

This Level 3 cache is designed to handle data requests that the Level 1 and Level 2 caches fail to satisfy. Although slower than the Level 2 cache, the Level 3 cache compensates by being much larger in size. While the largest Level 2 cache at this time is only 512KB, Level 3 caches can be as large as 4MB!

Irrespective of the actual numbers, the larger size of the Level 3 cache allows it to store a lot more data than the Level 2 cache. This gives it a high probability of satisfying *cache misses* from the Level 2 cache. With three caches working together, the chance of the processor stalling due to the need to access the much slower RAM is very small.

This is where the **L3 Cache** BIOS feature comes in. It controls the functionality of the processor's Level 3 cache.

Currently, this is an Intel Xeon MP-specific BIOS feature. The Intel Xeon MP processor features an on-die Level 3 cache that can be 512KB, 1MB, or 2MB in size. It is an 8-way set associative sectored cache with 64-byte cache lines.

When **enabled**, the processor's Level 3 cache is allowed to function. This allows the best possible performance from the processor.

When **disabled**, the processor's Level 3 cache is disabled. The processor bypasses the Level 3 cache and relies only on the Level 1 and Level 2 caches. This reduces the performance of the processor.

The recommended setting is obviously **Enabled** because disabling it severely affects the processor's performance. However, the **Disabled** setting is useful as a troubleshooting tool, especially when you are overclocking your processor.

For example, if your processor cannot reach 2GHz, you can try to find out if the cause is the Level 3 cache by **disabling** this BIOS feature. If this allows your processor to run at 2GHz and beyond, then the Level 3 cache is the cause of your processor's failure to run at 2GHz. However, if your processor still cannot run at 2GHz even with the Level 3 cache disabled, then the problem lies elsewhere.

Please note that disabling the Level 3 cache in order to increase the overclockability of the CPU is a *very bad* idea. If the Level 3 cache is disabled, the processor may stall frequently, especially when the system is running memory-intensive applications.

Therefore, except for troubleshooting purposes, this feature should always be left **enabled**.

L

Level 2 Cache Latency

Common Options: Auto, 1 to 15

Whenever the processor's **Level 2 cache** receives a read/write command, a certain period of time passes before the cache can actually process the command. This delay is called latency and the shorter the latency, the faster the Level 2 cache can service data reads/writes.

This BIOS feature enables you to change the latency of the processor's Level 2 cache. By default, this feature is set to **Auto**, which means that the processor's Level 2 cache is left to its default latency setting. This is the safest option.

You can also manually select the latency of the cache. For this purpose, this BIOS feature provides options ranging from **1** clock cycle to **15** clock cycles. Please note that setting the latency too low can cause the Level 2 cache to lose data integrity or fail altogether. This will manifest as a system crash or an inability to boot-up altogether.

Therefore, it is recommended that you start with a high latency and work your way down until you start to encounter stability issues. This allows you to figure out the lowest latency your processor's Level 2 cache can support. Select that latency for optimal performance without stability issues.

Please note that this is a processor-dependent feature. Not all processors support BIOS manipulation of the Level 2 cache latency. If the processor does not allow any manipulation of its Level 2 cache latency, this BIOS feature will not have any effect, irrespective of what was selected.

Master Drive PIO Mode

Common Options: Auto, 0, 1, 2, 3, 4

This BIOS feature is usually found under the **Onboard IDE-1 Controller** or **Onboard IDE-2 Controller** feature. It is linked to one of the IDE channels, so if you disable one, the corresponding Master Drive PIO Mode option for that IDE channel either disappears or becomes grayed out.

This BIOS feature allows you to set the **PIO (Programmed Input/Output)** mode for the Master IDE drive attached to that particular IDE channel. Here is a table of the different PIO transfer rates and their corresponding maximum throughputs.

PIO Data Transfer Mode	Maximum Throughput
PIO Mode 0	3.3 MB/s
PIO Mode 1	5.2 MB/s
PIO Mode 2	8.3 MB/s
PIO Mode 3	11.1 MB/s
PIO Mode 4	16.6 MB/s

Setting this BIOS feature to **Auto** lets the BIOS auto-detect the IDE drive's maximum supported PIO mode at boot-up.

Setting this BIOS feature to **0** forces the BIOS to use **PIO Mode 0** for the IDE drive.

Setting this BIOS feature to **1** forces the BIOS to use **PIO Mode 1** for the IDE drive.

Setting this BIOS feature to **2** forces the BIOS to use **PIO Mode 2** for the IDE drive.

Setting this BIOS feature to **3** forces the BIOS to use **PIO Mode 3** for the IDE drive.

Setting this BIOS feature to **4** forces the BIOS to use **PIO Mode 4** for the IDE drive.

Normally, you should leave it as **Auto** and let the BIOS auto-detect the IDE drive's PIO mode. You should only set it manually for the following reasons:

- If the BIOS cannot detect the correct PIO mode.
- If you want to try forcing the IDE device to use a faster PIO mode than it was designed for.
- If you want to force the IDE device to use a slower PIO mode if it cannot work properly with the current PIO mode (for example, when the PCI bus is overclocked)

Please note that forcing an IDE device to use a PIO transfer rate that is faster than what it is rated for can potentially cause data corruption.

Master Drive UltraDMA

Common Options: Auto, Disabled

This BIOS feature is usually found under the **Onboard IDE-1 Controller** or **Onboard IDE-2 Controller** feature. It is linked to one of the IDE channels, so if you disable one, the corresponding Master Drive UltraDMA function for that IDE channel either disappears or is grayed out.

This BIOS feature allows you to enable or disable **DMA (Direct Memory Access)** support (if available) for the Master IDE device attached to that particular IDE channel. For easy reference, here is a table of the different DMA transfer rates and their corresponding maximum throughputs.

DMA Transfer Mode	Maximum Throughput
DMA Mode 0	4.16 MB/s
DMA Mode 1	13.3 MB/s
DMA Mode 2	16.6 MB/s
UltraDMA 33	33.3 MB/s
UltraDMA 66	66.7 MB/s
UltraDMA100	100.0 MB/s
UltraDMA 133	133.3 MB/s

Setting this BIOS feature to **Auto** lets the BIOS auto-detect the IDE drive's maximum supported DMA mode at boot-up.

Setting this BIOS feature to **Disabled** forces the BIOS to disable DMA transfers for the IDE drive.

Normally, you should leave it as **Auto** and let the BIOS auto-detect the drive's DMA support. If the drive supports DMA transfers, the proper DMA transfer mode is enabled for that drive, allowing it to burst data at anywhere from 33MB/s to 133MB/s (depending on the transfer mode supported).

You should only **disable** it for troubleshooting purposes. For example, certain IDE devices may not run properly using DMA transfers when the PCI bus is overclocked. Disabling DMA support forces the drive to use the slower PIO transfer mode. This may allow the drive to work properly with the higher PCI bus speed.

Please note that setting this to **Auto** does *not* enable DMA transfers for IDE devices that do not support DMA transfers. If your drive does not support DMA transfers, the BIOS automatically sets the drive to do PIO transfers only.

Also note that this BIOS feature merely enables DMA transfers during the booting up process and for operating systems that do not load their own drivers for IDE functions. For operating systems that use their own IDE drivers (for example, Windows 9x/2000/XP), you have to enable DMA support for the drive within the operating system as well.

In Windows 9x, this can be accomplished by ticking the **DMA checkbox** in the properties sheet of the IDE drive in question. In Windows 2000/XP, you have to set the transfer mode of the IDE device to **DMA If Available** in the Advanced Settings tab of the associated IDE channel's properties page.

Master Priority Rotation

Common Options: 1 PCI, 2 PCI, 3 PCI

This BIOS feature controls the priority of the processor's accesses to the PCI bus.

If you choose **1 PCI**, the processor is always granted access right after the **current** PCI bus master completes its transaction, irrespective of how many other PCI bus masters are on the queue. This improves processor-to-PCI performance, at the expense of other PCI transactions.

If you choose **2 PCI**, the processor is always granted access right after the **second** PCI bus master on the queue completes its transaction. This means the processor has to wait for just two PCI bus masters to complete their transactions on the PCI bus before it can gain access to the PCI bus itself. This means slightly poorer processor-to-PCI performance but PCI bus masters enjoy slightly better performance.

If you choose **3 PCI**, the processor is always granted access right after the **third** PCI bus master on the queue completes its transaction. This means the processor has to wait for three PCI bus masters to complete their transactions on the PCI bus before it can gain access to the PCI bus itself. This means poorer processor-to-PCI performance, but PCI bus masters enjoy better performance.

No matter what you choose, the processor is guaranteed access to the PCI bus after a certain number of PCI bus master grants. It doesn't matter if there are numerous PCI bus masters on the queue or when the processor requests access to the PCI bus. The processor is always granted access after one PCI bus master transaction (**1 PCI**), two transactions (**2 PCI**), or three transactions (**3 PCI**).

For better overall performance, it is recommended that you select the **1 PCI** option as this allows the processor to access the PCI bus with minimal delay. However, if you wish to improve the performance of your PCI devices, you can try the **2 PCI** or **3 PCI** options. They ensure that your PCI cards receive greater PCI bus priority.

MD Driving Strength

Common Options: Hi, Lo / High, Low

There is no auto–compensation mechanism for the memory bus. So, it is up to the motherboard designer to determine the amount of driving strength needed to compensate for the motherboard's impedance on the memory bus. The BIOS then loads up the preset driving strength value when it boots up the motherboard.

The default driving strength is usually sufficient for normal DRAM loads. It is kept low in order to reduce **EMI (Electromagnetic Interference)** and power consumption. However, this means that the default driving strength may not be sufficient for heavy DRAM loads (for example, multiple double-sided memory modules).

This is where the **MD Driving Strength** BIOS feature comes in. It offers simplified control of the memory data bus driving strength.

The default value is **Lo** or **Low**. With heavy DRAM loads, you might want to set this feature to **Hi** or **High**.

Due to the nature of this BIOS feature, it is possible to use it as an aid in overclocking the memory bus. Your memory module may not overclock as well as you want it to. By raising the driving strength of the memory bus, it is possible to improve its stability at overclocked speeds.

However, this is not a surefire way of overclocking the memory bus. All you may get at the end of the day is increased EMI and power consumption.

Please note too that increasing the memory bus drive strength does *not* improve the performance of your memory subsystem.

Therefore, it is recommended that you leave the MD Driving Strength at its default **Lo** or **Low** setting. Set it to **Hi** or **High** only if you have a heavy DRAM load or if you are trying to stabilize an overclocked memory module.

Memory Hole At 15M-16M

Common Options: Enabled, Disabled

Certain ISA cards require exclusive access to the 1MB block of memory, from the 15th to the 16th megabyte, to work properly. This BIOS feature allows you to reserve that 1MB block of memory for such cards to use.

If you **enable** this feature, 1MB of memory (the 15th MB) is reserved exclusively for the ISA card's use. This effectively reduces the total amount of memory available to the operating system by 1MB. Therefore, if you have 256MB of memory, the usable amount of memory is reduced to 255MB.

Please note that in certain motherboards, enabling this feature may actually render all memory above the 15th MB unavailable to the operating system! In such cases, you end up with only **14MB** of usable memory, irrespective of how much memory your system actually has.

If you **disable** this feature, the 15th MB of RAM is *not* reserved for the ISA card's use. The full range of memory is therefore available for the operating system to use. However, if your ISA card requires the use of that memory area, it may fail to work.

Because ISA cards are a thing of the past, it is highly recommended that you **disable** this feature. Even if you have an ISA card that you absolutely have to use, you may *not* actually need to enable this feature.

Most ISA cards do *not* need exclusive access to this memory area. Make sure that your ISA card requires this memory area before enabling this feature. You should use this BIOS feature only in a last-ditch attempt to get a stubborn ISA card to work.

MP Capable Bit Identify

Common Options: Enabled, Disabled

There are a few flavors of the AMD Athlon processor, namely the Duron, Athlon XP, Athlon MP, and the mobile Athlon XP (Athlon XP-M). However, they all have the same CPUID. So, processor identification has to be done on the basis of clock speed and L2 cache size variations. This is not a problem for the Duron and Athlon XP-M processors.

Unfortunately, there is nothing to distinguish the Athlon MP from the Athlon XP. Neither clock speed nor L2 cache size can be used to differentiate the two processors.

In addition, AMD don't hardcode the processor name string into the AMD Athlon processors. The BIOS actually detects the processor model during the boot-up process and writes the appropriate name string into the processor. So, the Athlon MP cannot be detected by querying the processor name string.

The only thing that truly distinguishes the Athlon MP processor from the Athlon XP processor is its multi-processing capability.

To solve this problem, AMD used **bit 19** of Athlon's Extended Feature Flags to denote multi-processing capability. It is also known as the **MP Capable** bit, MP for multi-processing.

This bit is set to **0** in the Athlon XP processors and set to **1** in the Athlon MP processors. Below is a table of the MP Capable bit settings for the different AMD Athlon processors.

The MP Capable Bit in Various AMD Processors.

EXHIBIT A: Table 5, Page 31, AMD Processor Recognition Application Note Rev. 3.07.

Processor	CPUID	MP Capable (bit 19 of Extended Feature Flags)	Platform Segment	Recommended Name String[1]
AMD Athlon™ Model 6	660 or 661	Reserved	Multiprocessing	AMD Athlon MP
AMD Athlon Model 6	660 or 661	Reserved	Desktop	AMD Athlon
AMD Athlon Model	660 or 661	Reserved	Mobile	mobile AMD Athlon 4
AMD Athlon Model 6	662	0	Multiprocessing	AMD Athlon XP [xxxxx][2]
AMD Athlon Model 6	662	1	Multiprocessing	AMD Athlon MP [xxxxx][2]
AMD Athlon Model 6	662	N/A	Desktop	AMD Athlon XP [xxxxx][2]
AMD Athlon Model 6	662	N/A	Mobile	mobile AMD Athlon 4

(Continued)

Processor	CPUID	MP Capable (bit 19 of Extended Feature Flags)	Platform Segment	Recommended Name String[1]
AMD Duron™ Model 6	N/A[3]	N/A	Desktop	AMD Duron
AMD Duron Model 6	N/A[3]	N/A	Mobile	mobile AMD Duron
AMD Duron Model 7	N/A[3]	Reserved	Desktop	AMD Duron
AMD Duron Model 7	N/A[3]	Reserved	Mobile	mobile AMD Duron
AMD Athlon Model 8	N/A[3]	0	Multiprocessing	AMD Athlon XP [xxxxx][2]
AMD Athlon Model 8	N/A[3]	1	Multiprocessing	AMD Athlon MP [xxxxx][2]
AMD Athlon Model 8	N/A[3]	0	Desktop	AMD Athlon XP [xxxxx][2]
AMD Athlon Model 8	N/A[3]	1	Desktop	AMD Athlon MP [xxxxx][2]
AMD Athlon Model 8	N/A[3]	N/A	Mobile	mobile AMD Athlon XP [xxxxx][2]
AMD Athlon Model 10	N/A[3]	0	Desktop	AMD Athlon XP [xxxxx][2]
AMD Athlon Model 10	N/A[3]	1	Multiprocessing	AMD Athlon MP [xxxxx][2]
AMD Athlon Model 10	N/A[3]	N/A	OPGA Mobile	mobile AMD Athlon XP-M [xxxxx][2]
AMD Athlon Model 10	N/A[3]	N/A	µPGA Mobile mobile	AMD Athlon XP-M (LV) [xxxxx][2]

1. This name string must be programmed into the processor by the BIOS. See the document, "Displaying and Programming the Processor Name String BIOS Application Note," order# 90056.

2. See Table 7 on page 33 and Table 5 on page 31 of "AMD Processor Recognition Application Note," Publication #20734, February 2004 (Advanced Micro Devices, Inc.), for proper model number to insert into name string.

3. Recommended name strings for the AMD Duron processors models 6 and 7 and the AMD Athlon processors models 8 and 10 do not vary by CPUID stepping value.

© 2004 Advanced Micro Devices, Inc. Reprinted with permission. AMD, the AMD logo, AMD Athlon, AMD Duron, and combinations thereof are trademarks of Advanced Micro Devices, Inc.

Therefore, if the BIOS detects a processor with the MP Capable bit set to **1**, it writes the processor name string of AMD Athlon (tm) MP into the processor.

This BIOS feature determines if the BIOS should query the MP Capable bit to correctly identify an AMD Athlon MP processor.

When set to **Enabled**, the BIOS will query the MP Capable bit at boot-up. If it detects a MP Capable bit setting of **1**, it writes the Athlon MP processor string name into the appropriate registers.

When set to **Disabled**, the BIOS will not query the MP Capable bit at boot-up. The Athlon MP processor will be indistinguishable from the Athlon XP processor, as far as the processor identification is concerned.

If you are using an AMD Athlon MP processor, it is recommended that you enable this BIOS feature to allow proper identification of the processor. If you are using other Athlon processors, you should disable this BIOS feature as the BIOS does not need to query the MP Capable bit to detect the processor correctly.

M

MPS Control Version For OS

Common Options: 1.1, 1.4

This feature is only applicable to multiprocessor motherboards as it specifies the version of the **Multi-Processor Specification** (**MPS**) that the motherboard uses. The MPS is a specification by which PC manufacturers design and build Intel architecture systems with two or more processors.

MPS 1.1 was the original specification. MPS version 1.4 adds extended configuration tables for improved support of multiple PCI bus configurations and greater expandability in the future. In addition, MPS 1.4 introduces support for a secondary PCI bus without requiring a PCI bridge.

Please note that MPS version 1.4 is required for a motherboard to support a secondary PCI bus without the need for a PCI bridge.

If your operating system comes with support for MPS 1.4, you should change the setting from the default of 1.1 to **1.4**. You also need to enable MPS 1.4 support if you need to make use of the secondary PCI bus on a motherboard that doesn't come with a PCI bridge. This is because only MPS 1.4 supports a bridgeless secondary PCI bus.

You should only leave it as **1.1** if you are running an older operating system that only supports MPS 1.1.

As far as Microsoft operating systems are concerned, Windows NT/2000/XP support MPS 1.4.

However, users of the ABIT BP6 motherboard and Windows 2000 should take note of a possible problem with the MPS version set to 1.4. **If** you set the MPS version to 1.4 in the ABIT BP6 motherboard, Windows 2000 does *not* use the second processor. So, if you encounter this problem, set the MPS Version Control For OS to **1.1**.

MPS Revision

Common Options: 1.1, 1.4

This feature is only applicable to multiprocessor motherboards as it specifies the version of the **Multi-Processor Specification** (**MPS**) that the motherboard uses. The MPS is a specification by which PC manufacturers design and build Intel architecture systems with two or more processors.

MPS 1.1 was the original specification. MPS version 1.4 adds extended configuration tables for improved support of multiple PCI bus configurations and greater expandability in the future. In addition, MPS 1.4 introduces support for a secondary PCI bus without requiring a PCI bridge.

Please note that MPS version 1.4 is required for a motherboard to support a secondary PCI bus without the need for a PCI bridge.

If your operating system comes with support for MPS 1.4, you should change the setting from the default of 1.1 to **1.4**. You also need to enable MPS 1.4 support if you need to make use of the secondary PCI bus on a motherboard that doesn't come with a PCI bridge. This is because only MPS 1.4 supports a bridgeless secondary PCI bus.

You should only leave it as **1.1** if you are running an older operating system that only supports MPS 1.1.

As far as Microsoft operating systems are concerned, Windows NT/2000/XP support MPS 1.4.

However, users of the ABIT BP6 motherboard and Windows 2000 should take note of a possible problem with the MPS version set to 1.4. If you set the MPS version to 1.4 in the ABIT BP6 motherboard, Windows 2000 does *not* use the second processor. So, if you encounter this problem, set the MPS Revision to **1.1**.

Multi-Sector Transfers

Common Options: Disabled, 2 Sectors, 4 Sectors, 8 Sectors, 16 Sectors, 32 Sectors, Maximum

This BIOS feature speeds up hard disk access by transferring multiple sectors of data per interrupt instead of using the usual single-sector transfer mode. This mode of transferring data is known as block transfers.

There are a few available options, from **Disabled** to **Maximum** and a few different multiple sectors options.

The **Disabled** option forces your IDE controller to transfer only a single sector (512 bytes) per interrupt. Needless to say, this significantly degrades performance.

The selection of **2 Sectors** to **32 Sectors** allows you to manually select the number of sectors that the IDE controller is allowed to transfer per interrupt.

The **Maximum** option allows your IDE controller to transfer as many sectors per interrupt as the hard disk is able to support.

Because all current hard disks support block transfers, there is *usually* no reason why Multi-Sector Transfers should be disabled.

However, if you are running on Windows NT 4.0, you might need to disable this BIOS feature because Windows NT 4.0 has a problem with block transfers. According to a Microsoft article (*Enhanced IDE Operation under Windows NT 4.0*), IDE HDD Block Mode and 32-bit Disk Access have been found to cause data corruption in some cases. Therefore, Microsoft recommends that Windows NT 4.0 users **disable** IDE HDD Block Mode.

Microsoft took a serious view of the issue and corrected it through the **Windows NT 4.0 Service Pack 2**. Therefore, it is safe to enable Multi-Sector Transfers in a Windows NT 4.0 system, so long as it has been upgraded with Service Pack 2.

Therefore, you should **disable** Multi-Sector Transfers *only* if you actually face the possibility of data corruption (with an unpatched version of Windows NT 4.0). Otherwise, it is highly recommended that you select the **Maximum** option for significantly better hard disk performance!

The manual selection of 2 to 32 sectors is useful if you notice data corruption with the **Maximum** option. It allows you to scale back the multi-sector transfer feature to correct the problem without losing too much performance.

N

N/B Strap CPU As

Common Options: By CPU, PSB400, PSB533, PSB800

This BIOS feature allows you to circumvent the CPU-to-DRAM ratio limitation found in the newer Intel i865/i875-series of chipsets. In those chipsets, Intel has chosen to limit the choices of available CPU-to-DRAM ratios according to the clock speed of the **CPU bus** (also known as **front side bus** or **FSB**).

When a **400MHz FSB** processor is installed, the choice of CPU-to-DRAM ratio is limited to **3:4**.

When a **533MHz FSB** processor is installed, the choices of CPU-to-DRAM ratio are limited to **1:1** or **4:5**.

When a **800MHz FSB** processor is installed, the choices of CPU-to-DRAM ratio are limited to **1:1, 3:2** or **5:4**.

As you can see, this greatly limits the flexibility in selecting the best CPU-to-DRAM ratio for your system. Fortunately, this BIOS feature allows you to circumvent that limitation.

The **N/B Strap CPU As** BIOS feature actually controls the setting of the external hardware reset strap assigned to the **MCH** (**Memory Controller Hub**) of the chipset. By setting it to **PSB400, PSB533,** or **PSB800,** you can trick the chipset into thinking that the **400MHz FSB, 533MHz FSB,** or the **800MHz FSB** is being used.

When this BIOS feature is set to **PSB800,** you are able to access the **800MHz** CPU-to-DRAM ratios of **1:1, 3.2** and **5:4.**

When this BIOS feature is set to **PSB533,** you are able to access the **533MHz** CPU-to-DRAM ratios of **1:1** and **4:5.**

When this BIOS feature is set to **PSB400,** you are able to access the **400MHz** CPU-to-DRAM ratio of **3:4.**

By default, this BIOS feature is set to **By CPU,** whereby the hardware strap is set according to the actual FSB rating of the processor.

Generally, you do not need to manually adjust the hardware strap setting. However, if you require access to the CPU-to-DRAM ratio that normally would not be available to you, then this BIOS feature will be very helpful indeed.

No Mask of SBA FE

Common Options: Enabled, Disabled

This BIOS feature controls the masking of the signal used to calibrate the **SBA** (**Sideband Address**) port. It is used to fix compatibility issues with certain graphics cards.

AGP 3.0-compatible chipsets usually implement dynamic compensation to recalibrate the AGP bus over time. The SBA port of the AGP bus also undergoes recalibration *after* an AGP bus recalibration cycle. The entire process consists of a critical **six clock cycle waiting period** and a subsequent **two cycle recalibration period**.

In certain situations, the recalibration of the SBA port has been known to cause the graphics card to hang. This may be a result of the graphics chip glitching on the SBA strobe lines during the six clock cycle-long waiting period when the strobes must be completely low. Or it could be due to the graphics chip resuming SBA activity before the chipset can finish recalibrating the SBA port.

Whatever the cause, this BIOS feature was implemented to fix the problem by just preventing the SBA port from performing dynamic recalibrations.

When **enabled**, the chipset masks (hides) the SBA calibration signal, so the graphics chip does not initiate the SBA calibration cycle. Since the SBA port is never recalibrated, the issue of the graphics card hanging due to SBA recalibration is avoided.

When **disabled**, the graphics chip is allowed to initiate the SBA calibration cycle right after the AGP bus calibration cycle.

Users of ATI R3xx-based graphics cards (for example, Radeon 9700 Pro, Radeon 9800) are advised to **enable** this BIOS feature if the graphic card hangs or crashes during 3D benchmarking or gaming.

Users of other unaffected graphics cards are advised to **disable** this feature, so the chipset can dynamically calibrate the SBA port.

Onboard FDC Swap A & B

Common Options: No Swap, Swap AB

This BIOS feature is used to logically swap the mapping of drives A: and B:. Therefore, it is only useful if you have two floppy drives.

Normally, the sequence by which you connect the floppy drives to the cable determines which is drive A: and which is drive B:. If you attach the floppy drives the wrong way and obtain a drive mapping that is not to your satisfaction, the usual way of correcting this is to physically swap the floppy cable connectors.

This feature allows you to swap the logical arrangement of the floppy drives without the need to open up the case and physically swap the connectors.

When this BIOS feature is set to **Swap AB**, the floppy drive that originally was mapped to drive A: is remapped to drive B: and vice versa for the drive that was originally set as drive B:.

When this BIOS feature is set to **No Swap**, the floppy drive mapping remains as set by the drive connector arrangement.

Although this appears to be nothing more than a feature of convenience, it can be quite important if you are using two floppy drives of different form factors (3.5" and 5.2"), and you need to boot from the second drive. Because the BIOS can only boot from drive A:, you have to physically swap the drive connections or use this BIOS feature to do it logically.

If your floppy drive mapping is correct or if you only have a single floppy drive, there is no need to set this feature to **Swap AB**. Leave it at the default setting of **No Swap**.

Onboard FDD Controller

Common Options: Enabled, Disabled

This BIOS feature allows you to enable or disable the onboard floppy drive controller.

When **enabled**, the motherboard's onboard floppy drive controller is enabled.

When **disabled**, the motherboard's onboard floppy drive controller is disabled. This frees up the IRQ used by the floppy drive controller.

If you are using a floppy drive connected to the motherboard's built-in floppy drive controller, select the **Enabled** option.

If you are using an add-on floppy drive controller card or if you are not using any floppy drive at all, set it to **Disabled** to save an IRQ that can be used by other devices.

Onboard IDE-1 Controller

Common Options: Enabled, Disabled

This BIOS feature is actually a misnomer because there is only one IDE controller integrated into current chipsets.

This single IDE controller comes with two IDE channels, each of which supports up to two IDE drives. Therefore, the IDE controller supports a total of four IDE devices through two IDE channels. However, it has become common practice to label the two IDE channels as *IDE controllers*.

Therefore, while the name of this BIOS feature suggests that it controls the functionality of the *first* IDE controller, it actually controls only the first IDE channel of the motherboard's single IDE controller.

When **enabled**, the IDE channel is able to provide support for up to two IDE drives.

When **disabled**, the IDE channel is disabled. Any attached IDE drives are not accessible. However, this frees up an IRQ, which can be used by other devices. Disabling this IDE channel also speeds up the booting sequence a little as the BIOS does not need to query this channel for IDE devices when it boots up.

You should leave this **enabled** if you are using this IDE channel. Disabling it prevents any IDE devices attached to this channel from being accessed.

If you are not attaching any IDE devices to this IDE channel (or if you are using a SCSI/add-on IDE card), you can **disable** this IDE channel to free an IRQ and speed up the booting sequence.

Onboard IDE-2 Controller

Common Options: Enabled, Disabled

This BIOS feature is actually a misnomer because there is only one IDE controller integrated into current chipsets.

This single IDE controller comes with two IDE channels, each of which supports up to two IDE drives. Therefore, the IDE controller supports a total of four IDE devices through two IDE channels. However, it has become common practice to label the two IDE channels as *IDE controllers*.

Therefore, while the name of this BIOS feature suggests that it controls the functionality of the *second* IDE controller, it actually controls only the second IDE channel of the motherboard's single IDE controller.

When **enabled**, the IDE channel is able to provide support for up to two IDE drives.

When **disabled**, the IDE channel is disabled. Any attached IDE drives are not accessible. However, this frees up an IRQ, which can be used by other devices. Disabling this IDE channel also speeds up the booting sequence a little as the BIOS does not need to query this channel for IDE devices when it boots up.

You should leave this **enabled** if you are using this IDE channel. Disabling it prevents any IDE devices attached to this channel from being accessed.

If you are not attaching any IDE devices to this IDE channel (or if you are using a SCSI/add-on IDE card), you can **disable** this IDE channel to free an IRQ and speed up the booting sequence.

Onboard IR Function

Common Options: IrDA (HPSIR) mode, ASK IR (Amplitude Shift Keyed IR) mode, Disabled

This BIOS feature is usually found under the **Onboard Serial Port 2** feature because it is slaved to the second serial port. If you disable the second serial port, this BIOS feature either disappears or is greyed out.

There are two different **IR (Infra-Red)** modes—**IrDA** and **ASK IR**.

IrDA, named for the **Infrared Data Association**, provides up to **115.2 kbps** of bandwidth for a distance of about **2 meters**.

ASK IR, on the other hand, is an old IR protocol developed by Sharp for its Wizard organizer and Zaurus PDA. It was also used by Apple for their Newton PDAs. Originally, it provided up to **9.6 kbps** of bandwidth up to **1 meter** but Apple eventually extended the protocol so that it could provide up to **38.4 kbps** of bandwidth. Currently, the maximum speed with this protocol is **57.6 kbps**.

You should select the IR mode that is supported by your external IR device. Choosing the wrong IR mode prevents your computer from communicating with the external IR device.

If there is a choice between IrDA and ASK IR, the natural choice would be **IrDA**, of course! IrDA is faster and has a longer range.

Please note that such IR communications require an IR beam kit to be plugged into the IR header on the motherboard. Without the IR beam kit, this feature won't have any effect.

You should also note that enabling this IR function prevents the second serial port from being used by normal serial devices. Therefore, if you do not need to use the onboard IR function, **disable** this BIOS feature, so the second serial port can be used by normal serial devices.

Onboard Parallel Port

Common Options: 3BCh/IRQ7, 278h/IRQ5, 378h/IRQ7, Disabled

This BIOS feature allows you to select the I/O address and IRQ for the onboard parallel port.

The default I/O address of **378h** and IRQ of **7** should work well in most cases. Unless you have a problem with the parallel port, you should leave it at the default settings.

You should only select an alternative I/O address or IRQ if the default settings are causing a conflict with other devices.

You can also **disable** the onboard parallel port if you do not need to use it. Doing so frees up the I/O port and IRQ used by the parallel port. Those resources can then be reallocated for other devices to use.

Onboard Serial Port 1

Common Options: Auto, 3F8h/IRQ4, 2F8h/IRQ3, 3E8h/IRQ4, 2E8h/IRQ3, Disabled

This BIOS feature allows you to manually select the I/O address and IRQ for the first serial port.

It is recommended that you leave it as **Auto**, so that the BIOS can select the best settings for it. However, if you need a particular I/O port or IRQ that has been taken up by this serial port, you can manually select an alternative I/O port or IRQ for it.

Please note that any I/O port or IRQ can be used for the serial port. There is no advantage or disadvantage in any of the options. As long as you do not select an I/O port or IRQ that has already been allocated to another device, any option will do.

You can also **disable** this serial port if you do not need to use it. Doing so frees up the I/O port and IRQ used by this serial port. Those resources then can be reallocated for other devices to use.

Onboard Serial Port 2

Common Options: Auto, 3F8h/IRQ4, 2F8h/IRQ3, 3E8h/IRQ4, 2E8h/IRQ3, Disabled

This BIOS feature allows you to manually select the I/O address and IRQ for the first serial port.

It is recommended that you leave it as **Auto**, so the BIOS can select the best settings for it. However, if you need a particular I/O port or IRQ that has been taken up by this serial port, you can manually select an alternative I/O port or IRQ for it.

Please note that any I/O port or IRQ can be used for the serial port. There is no advantage or disadvantage in any of the options. As long as you do not select an I/O port or IRQ that has already been allocated to another device, any option will do.

You can also **disable** this serial port if you do not need to use it. Doing so frees up the I/O port and IRQ used by this serial port. Those resources then can be reallocated for other devices to use.

Onboard USB Controller

Common Options: Enabled, Disabled

This BIOS feature is somewhat similar to **Assign IRQ For USB**. It enables or disables the motherboard's onboard USB controller.

However, instead of controlling the assignment of an IRQ to the onboard USB controller, this feature directly controls the USB controller's functionality.

It is recommended that you **enable** this feature, so you can use the onboard USB controller to communicate with your USB devices.

If you **disable** this feature, the USB controller is disabled, and you are not able to use it to communicate with any USB device. This frees up an IRQ for other devices to use. This is useful when you have many devices that cannot share IRQs.

However, it is recommended that you do *not* disable this BIOS feature unless you do not use any USB device, or if you are using a different USB controller for your USB needs.

Disabling this feature is not necessary with **APIC**-capable motherboards because they come with more IRQs.

OS/2 Onboard Memory > 64M

Common Options: Enabled, Disabled

This is similar to the **OS Select For DRAM > 64M** BIOS feature.

When there is more than 64MB of memory in a computer, older versions of IBM's OS/2 operating system differ from other operating systems in the way it manages memory. It is different from the conventional way of memory management. Therefore, a BIOS option was created to provide compatibility for such OS/2 systems.

If you are running an old, unpatched version of OS/2, you must select the **Yes** option. Please note that this is only true for *older* versions of OS/2 that haven't been upgraded using IBM's FixPaks.

Starting with the OS/2 Warp v3.0, IBM changed the memory management system to the more conventional method. IBM also issued FixPaks to address this issue with older versions of OS/2.

Therefore, if you are using OS/2 Warp v3.0 or higher, you should select **No** instead. You should also select **No** if you have upgraded an older version of OS/2 with the FixPaks that IBM has been releasing over the years.

If you select the **Yes** option with a newer or updated version (v3.0 or higher) of OS/2, it causes erroneous memory detection. For example, if you have 64MB of memory, it may only register as 16MB. Or if you have more than 64MB of memory, it may register as only 64MB of memory.

Users of non-OS/2 operating systems (like Microsoft Windows XP) should select the **No** option. Doing otherwise causes memory errors if you have more than 64MB of memory in your system.

In conclusion:

- If you are using an older version of the IBM OS/2 operating system, you should select **Yes**.

- If you are using the IBM OS/2 Warp v3.0 or higher operating system, you should select **No**.

- If you are using an older version of the IBM OS/2 operating system but have already installed all the relevant IBM FixPaks, you should select **No**.

Users of non-OS/2 operating systems (like Microsoft Windows XP) should select the **No** option.

OS Select For DRAM > 64MB

Common Options: OS/2, Non–OS/2

When there is more than 64MB of memory in a computer, older versions of IBM's OS/2 operating system differ from other operating systems in the way it manages memory. It is different from the conventional way of memory management. Therefore, a BIOS option was created to provide compatibility for such OS/2 systems.

If you are running an old, unpatched version of OS/2, you must select the **OS/2** option. Please note that this is only true for *older* versions of OS/2 that haven't been upgraded using IBM's FixPaks.

Starting with the OS/2 Warp v3.0, IBM changed the memory management system to the more conventional method. IBM also issued FixPaks to address this issue with older versions of OS/2.

Therefore, if you are using OS/2 Warp v3.0 or higher, you should select **Non–OS/2** instead. You should also select **Non–OS/2** if you have upgraded an older version of OS/2 with the FixPaks that IBM has been releasing over the years.

If you select the **OS/2** option with a newer or updated version (v3.0 or higher) of OS/2, it causes erroneous memory detection. For example, if you have 64MB of memory, it may only register as 16MB. Or if you have more than 64MB of memory, it may register as only 64MB of memory.

Users of non–OS/2 operating systems (like Microsoft Windows XP) should select the **Non–OS/2** option. Doing otherwise causes memory errors if you have more than 64MB of memory in your system.

In conclusion:

- If you are using an older version of the IBM OS/2 operating system, you should select **OS/2.**
- If you are using the IBM OS/2 Warp v3.0 or higher operating system, you should select **Non–OS/2**.
- If you are using an older version of the IBM OS/2 operating system but have already installed all the relevant IBM FixPaks, you should select **Non–OS/2**.

Users of non–OS/2 operating systems (like Microsoft Windows XP) should select the **Non–OS/2** option.

P

P2C/C2P Concurrency

Common Options: Enabled, Disabled

The BIOS feature allows PCI-to-CPU and CPU-to-PCI traffic to occur concurrently. This means PCI traffic to the CPU and CPU traffic to the PCI bus can occur simultaneously.

This prevents the CPU from being "locked up" during PCI transfers. It also allows PCI traffic to the processor to occur without delay even when the processor is writing to the PCI bus. This may prevent performance issues with certain PCI cards.

Therefore, it is recommended that you **enable** this feature for better performance.

Parallel Port Mode

Common Options: Normal (SPP), ECP, EPP, ECP+EPP

This BIOS feature is usually found under the **Onboard Parallel Port** feature. It is linked to the parallel port, so if you disable the parallel port, this BIOS feature either disappears or is grayed out.

By default, the parallel port is usually set to the **Normal (SPP)** mode. **SPP** stands for **Standard Parallel Port**. It is the original transfer protocol for the parallel port. Therefore, it works with all parallel port devices.

Although the SPP was a unidirectional port originally, it was eventually adapted to work bidirectionally. Such bidirectional SPP ports are also known as PS/2 parallel ports. So, contrary to popular opinion, the SPP mode is capable of bidirectional transfers.

However, it can only receive **4-bits** of data per cycle in this bidirectional mode. Its output, fortunately, remains at **8-bits** per cycle. This gives the parallel port in SPP mode an output rate of **150KB/s** and an input rate of **50KB/s** (due to software reasons).

The **ECP (Extended Capabilities Port)** transfer mode was introduced by Microsoft and Hewlett-Packard to provide fast, bidirectional communication between the computer and high-performance printers and scanners. It uses the DMA protocol to achieve data transfer rates of up to **2MB/s** and provides *symmetric* bidirectional communication.

On the other hand, **EPP (Enhanced Parallel Port)**, now known as **IEEE 1284**, uses existing parallel port signals to provide *asymmetric* bidirectional communication. It was also designed for high-speed communications, offering transfer rates of up to **2MB/s**.

As you can see, SPP is a very slow transfer mode. It should only be selected when faster transfer modes cannot be used (for example, with old printers or scanners). With modern parallel port devices, the ECP and EPP modes are the transfer modes of choice.

Generally, because of its FIFOs and the DMA channel it uses, **ECP** is good at large data transfers. Therefore, it is the transfer mode that works best with scanners and printers. **EPP** is better with devices that switch between reads and writes frequently (like ZIP drives and hard disks).

P

However, you should check your parallel port device's documentation before you set the transfer mode. The manufacturer of your parallel port peripheral may have designated a preferred transfer mode for the device in question. In that case, it is best to follow their recommendation.

If the device documentation did not state any preferred transfer mode and you still do not know what mode to select, you can select the **ECP+EPP** mode. If you select this mode, the BIOS automatically determines the transfer mode to use for your device.

However, this should be considered as a last resort because you may be needlessly tying up a DMA channel for nothing if your device does not use ECP at all. Or the BIOS may not actually select the best parallel port mode for the device. If possible, set the parallel port to the transfer mode that best suits your parallel port device.

Passive Release

Common Options: Enabled, Disabled

If you have already read about the **CPU to PCI Write Buffer** feature, you should know that the chipset has an integrated write buffer to service the processor's PCI writes.

Whenever the processor wants to write to the PCI bus, it no longer needs to arbitrate for the PCI bus and wait for its turn. It can immediately write up to four words of PCI writes to the write buffer. This frees up the processor and allows it to work on other tasks.

This BIOS feature controls the passive release feature of the **CPU to PCI Write Buffer**. Therefore, if the write buffer is disabled, this BIOS feature does not have any effect. However, the reverse is not true. The **CPU to PCI Write Buffer** feature still works even if **Passive Release** is disabled.

When Passive Release is **enabled**, the write buffer independently writes the data to the PCI bus at the first available opportunity. It can do so even when the processor is busy doing something else.

When Passive Release is **disabled**, the write buffer waits until the processor reasserts (retries) the write request. Only then does it write to the PCI bus. This still improves performance because the processor does not need to resend the data. The write buffer is ready to offload the data the moment the PCI bus arbiter releases control of the bus to the processor. However, the write buffer still loses some of its effectiveness because it has to wait for the CPU to retry the transaction.

This can be a particularly big problem when an ISA device engages the ISA bus. Because the ISA bus is very slow, this ties up the PCI bus and prevents the processor from accessing it for a very long time. If the CPU-to-PCI write buffer is enabled, the processor can write to the buffer instead. This allows the processor to engage in other tasks. However, if Passive Release is disabled, the write buffer cannot write its contents to the PCI bus until both the processor is free to retry the write and the PCI bus is free to receive.

Passive Release helps in this situation by allowing the write buffer to "passively write" to the PCI bus without the processor's intervention and even while the ISA device is engaging the PCI bus. This essentially allows the processor to indirectly write to the PCI bus, even when the ISA device has control over it. Without this feature, the PCI bus arbiter only allows other (non-CPU) PCI masters to access the PCI bus.

For best performance, it is highly recommended that you **enable** Passive Release. This dramatically reduces the effect of slow ISA devices hogging the PCI bus. However, some ISA cards may not work well with Passive Release. In such cases, **disable** Passive Release or better yet, throw the card away and get a PCI version instead!

If you don't use any ISA device, this feature should still be **enabled** because it allows the write buffer to offload its data to the PCI bus without waiting for the processor to retry the transaction. This improves the performance of the processor and PCI bus.

Please note again that this BIOS feature has no effect if you disable the **CPU to PCI Write Buffer**.

PCI#2 Access #1 Retry

Common Options: Enabled, Disabled

This BIOS feature is linked to **CPU to PCI Write Buffer**. Therefore, if the write buffer is **disabled**, this BIOS feature does not have any effect. However, the reverse is not true. The **CPU to PCI Write Buffer** feature still works even if **PCI#2 Access #1 Retry** is **disabled**.

When the buffer is **enabled**, the processor writes directly to the buffer instead of the PCI bus. The buffer then attempts to write the data to the PCI bus by **Passive Release**. This allows the processor to perform other tasks without waiting for its data to be written to the PCI bus.

However, the attempted buffer write to the PCI bus may fail because the PCI bus may still be occupied by another device. When that happens, this BIOS feature determines whether the buffer write should be reattempted or sent back for arbitration.

If this BIOS feature is **enabled**, the buffer attempts to write to the PCI bus until it is successful.

If this BIOS feature is **disabled**, the buffer flushes its contents and registers the transaction as failed. The processor now has to write again to the write buffer.

Generally, it is recommended that you **enable** this feature because it improves the processor's performance.

However, if you have many PCI devices and their performance is more important, you may want to **disable** this feature. This prevents excessive generation of retries by the write buffer, which may severely tax the PCI bus. Disabling this feature improves the PCI bus performance, especially with slow PCI devices that hog the bus for long periods of time at a stretch.

Please note again that this BIOS feature has no effect if you disable the **CPU to PCI Write Buffer**.

PCI 2.1 Compliance

Common Options: Enabled, Disabled

This is the same as the **Delayed Transaction** BIOS feature because it refers to the **PCI Delayed Transaction** feature, which is part of the PCI Revision 2.1 specifications.

On the PCI bus, there are many devices that may not meet the PCI target latency rule. Such devices include I/O controllers and bridges (for example, PCI-to-PCI and PCI-to-ISA bridges). To meet PCI 2.1 compliance, the PCI maximum target latency rule must be observed.

According to this rule, a PCI 2.1-compliant device must service a read request within **16** PCI clock cycles (**32** clock cycles for a host bus bridge) for the *initial* read and **8** PCI clock cycles for each *subsequent* read. If it cannot do so, the PCI bus terminates the transaction, so other PCI devices can access the bus. However, instead of rearbitrating for access (and failing to meet the minimum latency requirement again), the PCI 2.1-compliant device can make use of the **PCI Delayed Transaction** feature.

When a master device *reads* from a target device on the PCI bus but fails to meet the latency requirements, the transaction is terminated with a Retry command. The master device then has to rearbitrate for bus access. However, if **PCI Delayed Transaction** had been enabled, the target device can independently continue the read transaction. So, when the master device successfully gains control of the bus and reissues the read command, the target device has the data ready for immediate delivery. This ensures that the retried read transaction can be completed within the stipulated latency period.

If the delayed transaction is a *write*, the target device latches on the data and terminates the transaction if it cannot be completed within the target latency period. The master device then rearbitrates for bus access while the target device completes writing the data. When the master device regains control of the bus, it reissues the same write request. This time, instead of returning data (in the case of a read transaction), the target device sends the completion status to the master device to complete the transaction.

One advantage of using **PCI Delayed Transaction** is that it allows other PCI masters to use the bus while the transaction is being carried out on the target device. Otherwise, the bus is left idling while the target device completes the transaction.

PCI Delayed Transaction also allows write-posted data to remain in the buffer, while the PCI bus initiates a non-postable transaction, and yet still adhere to the PCI ordering rules. The write-posted data is written to memory while the target device is working on the non-postable transaction and flushed before the transaction is completed on the master device. Without **PCI Delayed Transaction**, all write-posted data has to be flushed before another PCI transaction can occur.

As you can see, the **PCI Delayed Transaction** feature uses the PCI bus more efficiently, resulting in better PCI performance by allowing write-posting to occur concurrently with non-postable transactions. In this BIOS, the **PCI 2.1 Compliance** option allows you to enable or disable the **PCI Delayed Transaction** feature.

It is highly recommended that you **enable** PCI 2.1 Compliance for better PCI performance and to meet PCI 2.1 specifications. **Disable** it only if your PCI cards cannot work properly with this feature enabled or if you are using PCI cards that are *not* PCI 2.1-compliant.

Please note that while many manuals and even earlier versions of the BIOS Optimization Guide have stated that this is an ISA bus-specific BIOS feature that enables a 32-bit write-posted buffer for faster PCI-to-ISA writes, they are *incorrect!* This BIOS feature is *not* ISA bus-specific and it does *not* control any write-posted buffers. It merely allows write-posting to continue while a non-postable PCI transaction is underway.

PCI Chaining

Common Options: Enabled, Disabled

This BIOS feature is designed to speed up writes from the processor to the PCI bus by allowing write combining to occur at the PCI interface.

When PCI chaining is **enabled**, up to four quadwords of processor writes to *contiguous* PCI addresses are chained together and written to the PCI bus as a single PCI burst write.

When PCI chaining is **disabled**, each processor write to the PCI bus is handled as separate non-burstable writes.

Needless to say, writing four quadwords of data in a single PCI write is much faster than doing so in four separate non-burstable writes. A single PCI burst write also reduces the amount of time the processor has to wait while writing to the PCI bus.

Therefore, it is recommended that you **enable** this feature for better CPU to PCI write performance.

PCI Clock / CPU FSB Clock

Common Options: 1/2, 1/3, 1/4, 1/5, 1/6

The PCI bus was designed to run at a maximum clock speed of 33MHz. The processor bus, on the other hand, always has a much higher clock speed than the PCI bus. Even the slowest processors these days run on a 100MHz processor bus. Newer processors utilize processor buses that run from 133MHz to 200MHz.

Knowledge about the clock speed of your processor bus is important because the PCI bus speed is actually derived from the processor's bus speed. It does this with the use of clock speed dividers.

For example, if you have a 100MHz processor bus, a 1/3 PCI bus divider is used to allow the PCI bus to run at the specified clock speed of 33MHz. Systems that use a 133MHz processor bus utilize a 1/4 divider to maintain the PCI bus at the standard 33MHz clock speed.

Please note that motherboards claiming to have 200MHz to 800MHz processor bus speeds are actually only running from 100MHz to 200MHz. For example, current AMD-based motherboards sport bus speeds of 200MHz and 266MHz, although the processor bus is only running at 100MHz and 133MHz, respectively. This is achieved by transferring data on both edges of the clock signal, thereby doubling the bandwidth of the processor bus.

The same goes for Intel-based motherboards that tout 400MHz, 533MHz, and 800MHz processor buses. These actually run at 100MHz, 133MHz, and 200MHz, respectively. The 400MHz, 533MHz, and 800MHz Intel processor buses are actually quad-pumped. While they actually run at only 100MHz, 133MHz, and 200MHz, they can transfer four times as much data per clock cycle.

So, when you want to calculate the suitable PCI bus divider for your system, please take the information above into account. As far as this BIOS feature is concerned, such motherboards are only running at 100MHz to 133MHz. If you do not calculate properly, you force the PCI bus to run beyond its rated speed of 33MHz. This may result in an unstable system and corruption of data on your hard disk.

This BIOS feature allows you to manually select the PCI bus clock divider. Because this divider determines the speed at which the PCI bus runs, manipulation of this feature allows you some control over the PCI bus speed.

It was meant to keep the PCI bus running within specifications when you overclock the processor bus, but you can also use it to overclock the PCI bus. With that said, you should keep in mind that the recommended safe limit for an overclocked PCI bus is **37.5MHz**. This is the speed at which practically all new PCI cards can run without breaking a sweat.

Of course, running at a higher speed is definitely possible. However, the risk of data corruption is particularly worrisome because the IDE controller runs off the PCI bus. If you intend to overclock beyond 37.5MHz, test your system thoroughly and make sure that your IDE devices are running fine before you do any serious work!

Selecting the clock divider of **1/2** makes the PCI bus run at half the processor bus speed. If your processor bus is set to 100MHz, the PCI bus speed is 50MHz. As such, this clock divider is useful for processor bus speeds of **66MHz to 75MHz**. Within that range, the PCI bus runs from 33MHz to 37.5MHz.

Selecting the clock divider of **1/3** makes the PCI bus run at a third of the processor bus speed. As such, this clock divider is useful for processor bus speeds of **100MHz to 112.5MHz**. Within that range, the PCI bus runs from 33MHz to 37.5MHz.

Selecting the clock divider of **1/4** makes the PCI bus run at a quarter of the processor bus speed. As such, this clock divider is useful for processor bus speeds of **133MHz to 150MHz**. Within that range, the PCI bus runs from 33MHz to 37.5MHz.

Selecting the clock divider of **1/5** makes the PCI bus run at a fifth of the processor bus speed. As such, this clock divider is useful for processor bus speeds of **166MHz to 187.5MHz**. Within that range, the PCI bus runs from 33MHz to 37.5MHz.

Selecting the clock divider of **1/6** makes the PCI bus run at a sixth of the processor bus speed. As such, this clock divider is useful for processor bus speeds of **200MHz to 225MHz**. Within that range, the PCI bus runs from 33MHz to 37.5MHz.

You are probably wondering about the gaps in the processor bus speeds listed above. For your convenience, only processor bus speeds that produce PCI clock speeds within the range of optimal PCI clock speeds (33MHz to 37.5MHz) are displayed above. The other processor bus speeds either produce a slow PCI bus or an excessively overclocked one.

Therefore, for optimal PCI bus performance, try to shoot for one of the processor bus speed-divider combinations shown above.

PCI Delay Transaction

Common Options: Enabled, Disabled

On the PCI bus, there are many devices that may not meet the PCI target latency rule. Such devices include I/O controllers and bridges (for example, PCI-to-PCI and PCI-to-ISA bridges). To meet PCI 2.1 compliance, the PCI maximum target latency rule must be observed.

According to this rule, a PCI 2.1-compliant device must service a read request within **16** PCI clock cycles (**32** clock cycles for a host bus bridge) for the *initial* read and **8** PCI clock cycles for each *subsequent* read. If it cannot do so, the PCI bus terminates the transaction, so other PCI devices can access the bus. However, instead of rearbitrating for access (and failing to meet the minimum latency requirement again), the PCI 2.1-compliant device can make use of the **PCI Delayed Transaction** feature.

When a master device *reads* from a target device on the PCI bus but fails to meet the latency requirements, the transaction is terminated with a Retry command. The master device then has to rearbitrate for bus access. However, if **PCI Delayed Transaction** had been enabled, the target device can independently continue the read transaction. So, when the master device successfully gains control of the bus and reissues the read command, the target device has the data ready for immediate delivery. This ensures that the retried read transaction can be completed within the stipulated latency period.

If the delayed transaction is a *write*, the target device latches on the data and terminates the transaction if it cannot be completed within the target latency period. The master device then rearbitrates for bus access while the target device completes writing the data. When the master device regains control of the bus, it reissues the same write request. This time, instead of returning data (in the case of a read transaction), the target device sends the completion status to the master device to complete the transaction.

One advantage of using **PCI Delayed Transaction** is that it allows other PCI masters to use the bus while the transaction is being carried out on the target device. Otherwise, the bus is left idling while the target device completes the transaction.

PCI Delayed Transaction also allows write-posted data to remain in the buffer, while the PCI bus initiates a non-postable transaction, and yet still adhere to the PCI ordering rules. The write-posted data is written to memory while the target device is working on the non-postable transaction and flushed before the transaction is completed on the master device. Without **PCI Delayed Transaction**, all write-posted data has to be flushed before another PCI transaction can occur.

As you can see, the **PCI Delayed Transaction** feature uses the PCI bus more efficiently as well as increases PCI performance by allowing write-posting to occur concurrently with non-postable transactions. In this BIOS, the **PCI Delay Transaction** option allows you to enable or disable the **PCI Delayed Transaction** feature.

It is highly recommended that you **enable** PCI Delay Transaction for better PCI performance and to meet PCI 2.1 specifications. **Disable** it only if your PCI cards cannot work properly with this feature enabled or if you are using PCI cards that are not PCI 2.1-compliant.

Please note that while many manuals and even earlier versions of the BIOS Optimization Guide have stated that this is an ISA bus-specific BIOS feature that enables a 32-bit write-posted buffer for faster PCI-to-ISA writes, they are *incorrect*! This BIOS feature is *not* ISA bus-specific, and it does *not* control any write-posted buffers. It merely allows write-posting to continue while a non-postable PCI transaction is underway.

PCI Dynamic Bursting

Common Options: Enabled, Disabled

This BIOS feature is similar to the **Byte Merge** feature.

If you have already read about the **CPU to PCI Write Buffer** feature, you should know that the chipset has an integrated PCI write buffer that allows the CPU to immediately write up to **four words** (or 64-bits) of PCI writes to it. This frees up the CPU to work on other tasks while the PCI write buffer writes them to the PCI bus.

Now, the CPU doesn't always write 32-bit data to the PCI bus. 8-bit and 16-bit writes can also take place. However, while the CPU may only write 8-bits of data to the PCI bus, it is still considered a single PCI transaction. This makes it equivalent to a 16-bit or 32-bit write in terms of PCI bandwidth! This reduces the effective PCI bandwidth, especially if there are many 8-bit or 16-bit CPU-to-PCI writes.

To solve this problem, the write buffer can be programmed to accumulate and merge 8-bit and 16-bit writes into 32-bit writes. The buffer then writes the merged data to the PCI bus. As you can see, merging the smaller 8-bit or 16-bit writes into a few large 32-bit writes reduces the number of PCI transactions required. This increases the efficiency of the PCI bus and improves its bandwidth.

This is where the **PCI Dynamic Bursting** BIOS feature comes in. It controls the byte merging capability of the PCI write buffer.

If it is **enabled**, every write transaction goes straight to the write buffer. They are accumulated until there is enough to be written to the PCI bus in a single burst. This improves the PCI bus performance.

If you **disable** byte merging, all writes still go to the PCI write buffer (if the **CPU to PCI Write Buffer** feature has been enabled). However, the buffer does not accumulate and merge the data. The data is written to the PCI bus as soon as the bus becomes free. This reduces PCI bus efficiency, particularly when 8-bit or 16-bit data is written to the PCI bus.

Therefore, it is recommended that you **enable** PCI Dynamic Bursting for better performance.

Please note that, like **Byte Merge**, this feature may not be compatible with certain PCI network interface cards. For example, 3Com's 3C905-series of NICs won't work properly with Byte Merge enabled.

So, if your NIC (Network Interface Card) won't work properly, try **disabling** Byte Merge. Otherwise, you should **enable** Byte Merge for better performance.

PCI IDE Busmaster

Common Options: Enabled, Disabled

This BIOS feature is a misnomer because it doesn't actually control the bus mastering ability of the onboard IDE controller. It is actually a toggle for the built-in driver that allows the onboard IDE controller to perform **DMA (Direct Memory Access)** transfers.

DMA transfer modes allow IDE devices to transfer large amounts of data from the hard disk to the system memory and vice versa with minimal processor intervention. It differs from the older and processor-intensive **PIO (Programmed Input/Output)** transfer modes by offloading the task of data transfer from the processor to the chipset.

Previously, this feature is only available after an operating system that supports DMA transfers (through the appropriate device driver) is loaded up. Now, many BIOS come with a built-in 16-bit driver that allows DMA transfers. This allows the onboard IDE controller to perform DMA transfers even before the operating system is loaded up!

When this BIOS feature is **enabled**, the BIOS loads up the 16-bit busmastering driver for the onboard IDE controller. This allows the IDE controller to transfer data through DMA, resulting in greatly improved transfer rates and lower CPU utilization in real-mode DOS and during the loading of other operating systems.

When this BIOS feature is **disabled**, the BIOS does *not* load up the 16-bit busmastering driver for the onboard IDE controller. The IDE controller then transfers data through PIO.

Therefore, it is recommended that you **enable** PCI IDE Busmaster. This greatly improves the IDE transfer rate and reduces the CPU utilization during the booting process or when you are using real-mode DOS. Users of DOS-based disk utilities like Norton Ghost can expect to benefit a lot from this feature.

Please note that because current operating systems (for example, Windows XP) load up their own 32-bit busmastering driver, this feature has no effect once such an operating system loads up. Still, it is recommended that you **enable** this feature to improve performance prior to the loading of the operating system's own driver.

PCI IRQ Activated By

Common Options: Edge, Level

This BIOS feature allows you to set the method by which the IRQs for your PCI devices are activated or triggered.

ISA and old PCI devices are **edge-triggered** (using a single voltage level) while newer PCI and AGP devices are **level-triggered** (using multiple voltage levels). This is important mainly because PCI devices must be level-triggered to share IRQs.

The multiple voltage levels supported by level-triggered cards are used to activate the proper device among multiple devices sharing the same IRQ. Edge-triggered devices only support a single voltage level, which can only be used to activate or deactivate their IRQs. Therefore, IRQs allocated to edge-triggered devices cannot be shared with other devices.

When PCI devices were initially introduced, they were almost always *edge-triggered* and, therefore, did not support IRQ sharing. That is why the default and recommended setting for such devices was invariably **Edge**. Unfortunately, that misled people into thinking that it would be the same for newer PCI devices.

Current PCI devices are all *level-triggered* and so support IRQ sharing. This is critical in allowing the use of the numerous PCI devices in current computers. Without IRQ sharing, IRQ conflicts make PCI configuration a real hassle.

Of course, the introduction of the **Advanced Programmable Interrupt Controller** or **APIC** solves this problem completely by providing anywhere from 24 to 512 IRQ lines! However, until all motherboards ship with APIC, IRQ sharing will continue to play an important role in allowing multiple PCI devices to work in harmony.

Because all PCI devices currently in the market are level-triggered, it is recommended that you set this BIOS feature to **Level**, so your PCI devices can share IRQs.

However, if you are still using old edge-triggered devices, select **Edge** to force the chipset to allow only edge-triggering of PCI devices. This may cause configuration problems if there are IRQ conflicts, but it prevents system lockups that can occur if the chipset erroneously attempts to level-trigger an edge-triggered PCI device.

PCI Latency Timer

Common Options: 0–255

This BIOS feature controls how long a PCI device can hold the PCI bus before another takes over. The longer the latency, the longer the PCI device can retain control of the bus before handing it over to another PCI device.

As each access to the bus comes with an initial delay before any transaction can be made, a short PCI latency time reduces the effective PCI bandwidth because the PCI device only has a short time to perform transactions on the PCI bus. Longer latencies actually improve the effective PCI bandwidth by allowing the PCI device to perform more transactions with the same amount of delay.

On the other hand, the response time of PCI devices suffers with longer PCI latencies. A long PCI latency allows the active PCI device to use the bus longer but at the expense of other PCI devices queuing up to use the bus. All PCI devices therefore have to wait longer before gaining access to the bus.

Normally, the PCI Latency Timer is set to **32 cycles**. This means the active PCI device has to complete its transactions within 32 clock cycles or hand it over to the next PCI device.

For better PCI performance, a longer latency should be used. Try increasing it to **64 cycles** or even **128 cycles**. The optimal value for every system is different. You should benchmark your PCI cards' performance after each change to determine the optimal PCI latency time for your system.

Please note that a longer PCI latency isn't necessarily better. A long latency can also reduce performance because the other PCI devices queuing up may be stalled for too long. This is especially true with systems with many PCI devices or PCI devices that continuously write short bursts of data to the PCI bus. Such systems work better with shorter PCI latencies because they allow rapid access to the PCI bus.

In addition, some time-critical PCI devices may not agree with a long latency. Such devices require priority access to the PCI bus, which may not be possible if the PCI bus is held up by another device for a long period. In such cases, it is recommended that you keep to the default PCI latency of **32 cycles**.

PCI Master 0 WS Read

Common Options: Enabled, Disabled

This BIOS feature determines whether the chipset inserts a delay before any reads from the PCI bus.

If **PCI Master 0 WS Read** is **enabled**, read requests to the PCI bus are executed immediately (with zero wait states), if the PCI bus is ready to send data.

If PCI Master 0 WS Read is **disabled**, every read request to the PCI bus is delayed by one wait state.

It is recommended that you **enable** this feature for better PCI read performance.

However, **disabling** it may be useful if you are attempting to stabilize an overclocked PCI bus. The delay generally improves the overclockability and stability of the PCI bus.

PCI Master 0 WS Write

Common Options: Enabled, Disabled

This BIOS feature determines whether the chipset inserts a delay before any writes from the PCI bus.

If **PCI Master 0 WS Write** is **enabled**, write requests to the PCI bus are executed immediately (with zero wait states), if the PCI bus is ready to send data.

If PCI Master 0 WS Write is **disabled**, every write request to the PCI bus is delayed by one wait state.

It is recommended that you **enable** this feature for better PCI write performance.

However, **disabling** it may be useful if you are attempting to stabilize an overclocked PCI bus. The delay generally improves the overclockability and stability of the PCI bus.

PCI Master Read Caching

Common Options: Enabled, Disabled

This is an AMD-specific BIOS feature. It determines whether the processor's L2 cache is used to cache PCI bus master reads. However, like **Video RAM Cacheable**, this BIOS feature may actually reduce performance.

If this feature is enabled, the processor's L2 cache is used to cache PCI bus master reads. This boosts the performance of PCI bus masters. On the other hand, it reduces the processor's performance because it uses up some of the precious L2 cache.

This is why motherboard manufacturers like ASUS recommend that only systems using AMD Athlon processors should **enable** this feature. Duron users should **disable** this feature because its small L2 cache is not able to cache the PCI reads without causing a massive hit to memory bandwidth.

However, it is questionable that even AMD Athlon systems benefit from this feature. For one thing, the Athlon is not so well-endowed in L2 cache that using some of it to boost the performance of PCI bus masters won't detrimentally affect its performance.

In addition, such a caching scheme requires the two-way use of the Athlon processor bus. This reduces its efficiency and bandwidth as well as the processor's performance.

So, does the boost in PCI bus master performance justify the loss in processor and memory performance? Although the final word is still in the air, I recommend **disabling** this feature. The use of precious L2 cache to cache PCI bus masters is not worth the potential benefit in PCI bus performance.

PCI Pipelining

Common Options: Enabled, Disabled

This BIOS feature determines whether PCI transactions to the memory subsystem are pipelined.

The pipelining of PCI transactions allows their latencies to be masked (hidden). This greatly improves the efficiency of the PCI bus. However, this is only true for multiple transactions in the same direction. Pipelining doesn't help with PCI devices that switch between reads and writes often.

This feature is different from a burst transfer where multiple data transactions are executed consecutively with a single command. In PCI pipelining, different transactions are progressively processed in the pipeline without waiting for the current transaction to finish. Normally, outstanding transactions have to wait for the current one to complete before they are initiated.

If the PCI pipeline feature is **enabled**, the memory controller allows PCI transactions to be pipelined. This masks the latency of each PCI transaction and improves the efficiency of the PCI bus.

Please note that once the transactions are pipelined, they are flagged as performed, even though they have not actually been completed. As such, data coherency problems *may* occur when other devices write to the same memory block. This may cause valid data to be overwritten by outdated or expired data, causing problems like data corruption or system lock-ups.

If the PCI pipeline feature is **disabled**, the memory controller is forced to check for outstanding transactions from other devices to the same block address that each PCI transaction is targeting.

If there is a match, the PCI transaction is stalled until the outstanding transaction to the same memory block is complete. This essentially forces the memory controller to hold the PCI bus until the PCI transaction is cleared to proceed. It also prevents other PCI transactions from being pipelined. Both factors greatly reduce performance.

For better PCI performance, the PCI pipeline should be **enabled**. This allows the latency of the bus to be masked for consecutive transactions.

However, if your system constantly locks up for no apparent reason, try **disabling** this feature. Disabling PCI Pipelining reduces performance but ensures that data coherency is strictly maintained for maximum reliability.

PCI Prefetch

Common Options: Enabled, Disabled

This feature controls the system controller's **PCI Prefetch** capability. When **enabled**, the system controller prefetches eight quadwords (one cache line) of data whenever a PCI device reads from the system memory. Here's how it works.

Whenever the system controller reads PCI-requested data from the system memory, it also reads the subsequent cache line of data. This is done on the assumption that the PCI device requests the subsequent cache line. When the PCI device actually initiates a read command for that cache line, the system controller can immediately send it to the PCI device.

This speeds up PCI reads because the PCI device doesn't need to wait for the system controller to read from the system memory. As such, PCI Prefetch allows contiguous memory reads by the PCI device to proceed with minimal delay.

Therefore, it is recommended that you **enable** this feature for better PCI read performance. Please note that PCI writes to the system memory do not benefit from this feature.

PCI Target Latency

Common Options: Enabled, Disabled

This BIOS feature determines whether the system controller should conform to the PCI maximum target latency rule.

According to the PCI maximum target latency rule, the PCI device must service a read request within **16** PCI clock cycles (**32** PCI clock cycles if it is a host bus bridge) for the *initial* read and **8** PCI clock cycles for each *subsequent* read. Please note that this only applies to the PCI bus. It does not apply to the AGP bus.

When this feature is **enabled**, the system controller disconnects the PCI bus master when it cannot service a read request within 32 PCI clock cycles for the initial read and 8 PCI clock cycles for subsequent reads. The PCI bus master then rearbitrates for access to the PCI bus.

When this feature is **disabled**, the PCI bus master is *not* disconnected when it cannot service a read request within the stipulated 32 PCI clock cycles for the initial read and 8 PCI clock cycles for subsequent reads. The PCI bus master is allowed to complete with its transactions.

Compliance to the PCI maximum target latency rule is important because it ensures that fair access for all PCI devices to the PCI bus. In addition, if a PCI device hogs the PCI bus beyond the target latency, it may cause the system to lock-up when there is PCI to AGP traffic.

It is recommended that you **enable** this feature to enforce the PCI maximum target latency rule and prevent potential deadlocks.

PCI to DRAM Prefetch

Common Options: Enabled, Disabled

This feature controls the system controller's PCI prefetch capability. When **enabled**, the system controller prefetches eight quadwords (one cache line) of data whenever a PCI device reads from the system memory. Here's how it works.

Whenever the system controller reads PCI-requested data from the system memory, it also reads the subsequent cache line of data. This is done on the assumption that the PCI device requests the subsequent cache line. When the PCI device actually initiates a read command for that cache line, the system controller can immediately send it to the PCI device.

This speeds up PCI reads because the PCI device doesn't need to wait for the system controller to read from the system memory. As such, PCI to DRAM Prefetch allows contiguous memory reads by the PCI device to proceed with minimal delay.

Therefore, it is recommended that you **enable** this feature for better PCI read performance. Please note that PCI writes to the system memory do not benefit from this feature.

PCI/VGA Palette Snoop

Common Options: Enabled, Disabled

This BIOS feature determines whether your graphics card should allow VGA palette snooping by a fixed function display card. It is only useful if you use a fixed-function display card that requires a VGA-compatible graphics card to be present (for example, MPEG decoder card).

Such fixed-function display cards generally do not have their own VGA palette. So, they have to "snoop" VGA palette data from the graphics card to generate the proper colors. Normally, the graphics card's **Feature Connector** is used for this purpose.

When this feature is **enabled**, the graphics card does not respond to framebuffer writes. It forwards them to the fixed-function display card through its Feature Connector. The fixed-function display card then snoops the palette data and generates the proper colors.

This ensures accurate color reproduction. It also prevents the monitor from displaying a blank screen after the fixed-function card's capabilities are not required (for example, when you stop playing MPEG video using the MPEG decoder card).

When this feature is **disabled**, the graphics card displays all framebuffer writes.

It is recommended that you **disable** this feature if you do not use any fixed-function display card like a MPEG decoder card.

However, if you are using a fixed-function display card that requires palette snooping, enable this feature. Otherwise, the colors displayed may not be accurate and the monitor will blank out once you stop using the fixed-function display card.

PIO Mode

Common Options: Auto, 0, 1, 2, 3, 4

This BIOS feature allows you to set the **PIO (Programmed Input/Output)** mode for the IDE drive. Here is a table of the different PIO transfer rates and their corresponding maximum throughputs.

PIO Data Transfer Mode	Maximum Throughput
PIO Mode 0	3.3 MB/s
PIO Mode 1	5.2 MB/s
PIO Mode 2	8.3 MB/s
PIO Mode 3	11.1 MB/s
PIO Mode 4	16.6 MB/s

Setting this BIOS feature to **Auto** lets the BIOS auto-detect the IDE drive's maximum supported PIO mode at boot-up.

Setting this BIOS feature to **0** forces the BIOS to use **PIO Mode 0** for the IDE drive.

Setting this BIOS feature to **1** forces the BIOS to use **PIO Mode 1** for the IDE drive.

Setting this BIOS feature to **2** forces the BIOS to use **PIO Mode 2** for the IDE drive.

Setting this BIOS feature to **3** forces the BIOS to use **PIO Mode 3** for the IDE drive.

Setting this BIOS feature to **4** forces the BIOS to use **PIO Mode 4** for the IDE drive.

Normally, you should leave it as **Auto** and let the BIOS auto-detect the IDE drive's PIO mode. You should only set it manually for the following reasons:

- If the BIOS cannot detect the correct PIO mode.
- If you want to try forcing the IDE device to use a faster PIO mode than it was designed for.
- If you want to force the IDE device to use a slower PIO mode if it cannot work properly with the current PIO mode (for example, when the PCI bus is overclocked).

Please note that forcing an IDE device to use a PIO transfer rate that is faster than what it is rated for can potentially cause data corruption.

PIRQ x Use IRQ No.

Common Options: Auto, 3, 4, 5, 7, 9, 10, 11, 12, 14, 15

This BIOS feature allows you to manually set the IRQ for a particular device installed on the AGP and PCI buses.

It is especially useful when you are transferring a hard disk from one computer to another and you don't want to reinstall your operating system to redetect the IRQ settings. By setting the IRQs to fit the original settings, you can circumvent a lot of configuration problems after installing the hard disk in a new system. However, this is only true for non–ACPI systems.

Here are some important notes from the reference motherboard (may vary between motherboards):

- If you specify a particular IRQ here, you can't specify the same IRQ for the ISA bus. If you do, you will cause a hardware conflict.
- Each PCI slot is capable of activating up to 4 interrupts[md]INT A, INT B, INT C, and INT D.
- The AGP slot is capable of activating up to 2 interrupts[md]INT A and INT B.

Normally, each slot is allocated INT A. The other interrupts are reserves and used only when the PCI/AGP device requires more than one IRQ or if the IRQ requested has been used up.

The AGP slot and PCI slot #1 share the same IRQ.

PCI slot #4 and #5 share the same IRQs.

USB uses PIRQ_4.

The following is a table showing the relationship between PIRQ (Programmable Interrupt Request) signals and INT in the reference motherboard:

Signals	AGP Slot/	PCI Slot 2 / PCI Slot 1	PCI Slot 3	PCI Slot 4/ PCI Slot 5
PIRQ_0	**INT A**	INT D	INT C	INT B
PIRQ_1	INT B	**INT A**	INT D	INT C
PIRQ_2	INT C	INT B	**INT A**	INT D
PIRQ_3	INT D	INT C	INT B	**INT A**

Notice that the interrupts are staggered, so conflicts do not happen easily. The INT A entries are in **bold** to highlight the staggered arrangement.

Even then, you should try not to use up paired slots that share the same set of IRQs. In this reference motherboard, such paired slots are **AGP slot and PCI slot 1** or **PCI slots 4 and 5**. In such cases, it is recommended that you use only one of the two slots.

In most cases, you should just leave the setting as **Auto**. This allows the motherboard to assign the IRQs automatically. However, if you need to assign a particular IRQ to a device on the AGP or PCI bus, here is how you can make use of this BIOS feature.

1. Determine the slot in which the device is located.
2. Check your motherboard's **PIRQ table** (in the manual) to determine the slot's primary PIRQ. For example, if you have a PCI network card in PCI slot 3, the table above shows that the slot's primary PIRQ is PIRQ_2. Remember, all slots are first allocated INT A if it is available.
3. You then select the IRQ you want by assigning the IRQ to the appropriate PIRQ. In our network card example, if the card requires IRQ 7, set PIRQ_2 to use IRQ 7. The BIOS then allocates IRQ 7 to PCI slot 3. It is that easy!:

Just remember that the BIOS always tries to allocate the PIRQ linked to INT A for each slot. So, in our reference motherboard, the primary PIRQ for the AGP slot and PCI slot 1 is PIRQ_0, while the primary PIRQ for PCI slot 2 is PIRQ_1, and so on. It is just a matter of linking the IRQ you want to the correct PIRQ for that slot.

Please note the table, notes, and INT details are only examples provided by the reference motherboard. They may vary between motherboards. For example, Intel i8xx chipsets have 8 interrupt lines (INT A to INT H). In i8xx motherboards, the AGP slot always has its own IRQ.

PNP OS Installed

Common Options: Yes, No

This BIOS feature is quite misleading because its name suggests that you should set it to **Yes** if you have an operating system that supports **Plug and Play** (**PnP**). Unfortunately, it isn't quite so simple.

What this BIOS feature actually does is determine what devices are configured by the BIOS when the computer boots up and what are left to the operating system. This is rather different from what the name implies, right?

Before you can determine the appropriate setting for this feature, you should first determine the kind of BIOS that came with your motherboard. For the purpose of this discussion, the BIOS can be divided into two types—**ACPI BIOS** and **Non-ACPI BIOS**.

You also need to find out if your operating system supports *and* is currently running in ACPI mode. Please note that while an operating system may tout ACPI support, it is possible to force the operating system to use the older PnP mode. So, find out if your operating system is actually running in ACPI mode. Of course, this is only possible if your motherboard comes with an ACPI BIOS. With a Non-ACPI BIOS, all ACPI-compliant operating systems automatically revert to PnP mode.

Non-ACPI BIOSes are found in older motherboards that do not support the new **ACPI** (**Advanced Configuration and Power Interface**) initiative. This can be either the ancient non-PnP BIOS (or Legacy BIOS) or the newer PnP BIOS. With such a BIOS, setting the PNP OS Installed feature to **No** allows the BIOS to configure all devices under the assumption that the operating system cannot do so. Therefore, all hardware settings are fixed by the BIOS at boot up and are not changed by the operating system.

On the other hand, if you set the feature to **Yes**, the BIOS only configures critical devices required to boot up the system, for example, the graphics card and the hard disk. The other devices are then configured by the operating system. This allows the operating system some flexibility in shuffling system resources, like IRQs and IO ports, to avoid conflicts. It also gives you some degree of freedom when you want to manually assign system resources.

While all this flexibility in hardware configuration sounds like a good idea, shuffling resources can sometimes cause problems, especially with a buggy BIOS. Therefore, it is recommended that you set this feature to **No** to allow the BIOS to configure all devices. You should only set this feature to **Yes** if the Non-ACPI BIOS cannot configure the devices properly or if you want to manually reallocate hardware resources in the operating system.

Of course, all current motherboards now ship with the new **ACPI BIOS**. If you are using an ACPI-compliant operating system (such as Windows 98 and above) with an ACPI BIOS, then this PNP OS Installed feature is no longer relevant. It actually does not matter what setting you select. This is because the operating system uses the ACPI BIOS interface to configure all devices as well as retrieve system information. There is no longer a need to specifically split the job up between the BIOS and the operating system.

However, if your operating system does not support ACPI, then the BIOS falls back to PNP mode. In this situation, consider the BIOS as you would a **Non-ACPI BIOS**. If there is no need to configure any hardware manually, it is again recommended that you set this feature to **No**.

Please note that bugs in some ACPI BIOS can cause even an ACPI-compliant operating system to disable ACPI. This reverts the BIOS to PnP mode. However, there is an additional catch to it. Certain operating systems (for example, Windows 98 and above) only access the buggy BIOS in *read-only* mode. This means the operating system relies entirely on the BIOS to configure all devices and provide it with the hardware configuration. As such, you must set the feature to **No** if you have a buggy ACPI BIOS.

Linux is not really PnP-compatible, but most distributions use a software called ISAP-NPTOOLS to set up ISA cards. If PnP OS is set to **No**, the BIOS will attempt to configure the ISA cards, but that won't work with Linux. Worse, if ISAPNPTOOLS is used to configure the ISA cards as well, it may lead to conflicts between the two.

Therefore, it is recommended that you set PnP OS to **Yes** in Linux and allow ISAPNPTOOLS to handle the task instead.

As far as OS/2 is concerned, PnP OS should be set to **No**, especially in a multi-boot system. In addition, if you add or change hardware, you should enable full hardware detection during the initial boot sequence of OS/2. This allows OS/2 to properly register the hardware changes. You can do so by pressing Alt-F1 at the boot screen, and then pressing the F5 key.

Robert Kirk of IBM has this to say about PnP OS :

> *"Actually, the setting 'PnP OS' is really misnamed. A better thing would be to say 'do you want the system to attempt to resolve resource conflicts, or do you want the OS to resolve system conflict?' Setting the system to PnP OS says that even if the machine determines some kind of resource problem, it should not attempt to handle it . . . . Rather, it should pass it on to the OS to resolve the issue. Unfortunately, the OS can't resolve some issues . . . . which sometimes results in a lock or other problems.*
>
> *For stability reasons, it is better to set EVERY motherboard's PnP OS option to **No**, regardless of manufacturer, but still allow the BIOS to autoconfigure PnP devices. Just leave the PnP OS to **No**. It won't hurt a thing, you lose nothing, your machine will still autoconfigure PnP devices, and it will make your system more stable."*

To sum it all up, except for certain cases, it is highly recommended that you to set this BIOS feature to **No**, irrespective of the operating system you actually use. Exceptions to this would be the inability of the BIOS to configure the devices properly in PnP mode and a specific need to manually configure one or more of the devices.

Post Write Combine

Common Options: Enabled, Disabled

This is similar to the **USWC Write Posting** BIOS feature.

Current processors are heavily optimized for burst operations, which allows for very high memory bandwidth. Unfortunately, graphics writes from the processor are mostly pixel writes that are 8 to 32-bits in nature. Because they do not fill up an entire cache line, such writes are not burstable. This results in poor graphics write performance.

To correct this deficiency, processors now come with one or more internal write combine buffers. These buffers are designed to accumulate graphics writes from the processor. These partial or smaller writes are then combined and written to the graphics card as burst writes.

The use of these internal write combine buffers provides many benefits:

1. Partial or smaller graphics writes from the processor are now combined into burstable writes. This greatly increases the performance of the processor and AGP (or PCI) buses.

2. Graphics writes require fewer transactions on the processor and AGP (or PCI) bus. This improves the bandwidth of those buses.

3. The processor only needs to write to its internal write combine buffers instead of to the processor bus. This improves its performance by allowing it to work on other tasks while the write combine buffers handle the actual write transaction.

Because the write combine buffers allow speculative reads, this feature is known as the **USWC (Uncached Speculative Write Combining)** feature. The older method of writing all processor writes directly to the graphics card is known as **UC (UnCached)**.

This BIOS feature allows you to control the **USWC (Uncached Speculative Write Combining)** write combine buffers.

If **enabled**, the write combine buffers accumulate and combine partial or smaller graphics writes from the processor and write them to the graphics card as burst writes.

If **disabled**, the write combine buffers are disabled. All graphics writes from the processor are written to the graphics card directly.

It is highly recommended that you **enable** this feature for improved graphics and processor performance.

Please note that this feature also must be supported by the graphics card, the operating system, and the graphics driver for it to work properly.

All Microsoft operating systems from Windows NT 4.0 onward support USWC, so you do not need to worry if you are using a Windows NT 4.0 or newer operating system from Microsoft. Because this feature has been around for some time, drivers of USWC-compatible graphics cards fully support this feature.

However, if you are using an older graphics card, it may not be compatible with this feature. Older graphics cards make use of a **FIFO (First In, First Out)** I/O model, which can only support the **UnCached (UC)** type of transaction. Enabling this feature with such graphics cards causes a host of problems such as graphics artifacts, system crashes, and even the inability to boot up properly.

If you face such problems, you should **disable** this BIOS feature immediately.

Power On Function

Common Options: Button Only, Keyboard 98, Hot Key, Mouse Left, Mouse Right

This BIOS feature allows you to select the method with which to turn on your computer.

By default, this feature is set to **Button Only**. This allows your computer to be started up only through the use of the power button or switch. Other available options:

- A Keyboard 98-compatible keyboard (that comes with a wake-up button)
- A keyboard hot key (for non-Keyboard 98 keyboards)
- A mouse button (either the right or left button)

If you select the **Mouse Left** option, the left button of the mouse is used to start up the system. The **Mouse Right** option selects the right mouse button as the power on button instead.

Please note that only PS/2 mice support the **Mouse Left** or **Mouse Right** options. Mice using serial or USB connections do not support this power on function.

The **Keyboard 98** option only works if you are using Windows 98 or better and have the appropriate keyboard. Then you can use the keyboard's wake-up or power-on button to start up the computer.

Older keyboards that do not conform to the *Keyboard 98* standard, and therefore do not have the special wake-up button, can use the **Hot Key** option instead. There are 12 hot keys available: **Ctrl-F1** through **Ctrl-F12**. Select the hot key you want and you will be able to start up the computer using that hot key.

There is no performance advantage in choosing any of the options above. So, choose the option that you are most comfortable with.

Primary Graphics Adapter

Common Options: AGP, PCI

Although the AGP bus was designed exclusively for the graphics subsystem, some users still have to use PCI graphics cards for multi-monitor support. This is because there can be only one AGP port! So, if you want to use multiple monitors, you must either get an AGP card that provides multi-monitor support or use PCI graphics cards.

For those who upgraded from a PCI graphics card to an AGP card, it is certainly enticing to use the old PCI graphics card to support a second monitor. The PCI card can do the job just fine because it merely sends display data to the second monitor. You don't need a powerful graphics card to run the second monitor because Microsoft Windows 2000/XP does not support 3D graphics acceleration on the second monitor.

When it comes to a case of an AGP graphics card working in tandem with a PCI graphics card, the BIOS has to determine which graphics card is the primary graphics card. Naturally, the default would be the **AGP** graphics card because, in most cases, it would be the faster card.

However, a BIOS switch that allows you to manually select the graphics card to boot the system with is still required. This is particularly important if you have AGP and PCI graphics cards but only one monitor. This is where the **Primary Graphics Adapter** feature comes in. It allows you to select whether to boot the system using the AGP graphics card or the PCI graphics card.

If you are only using a single graphics card, then the BIOS detects it as such and boots it up, irrespective of what you set the feature to. However, there may be a slight reduction in the time taken to detect and initialize the card if you select the proper setting for this BIOS feature. For example, if you only use an AGP graphics card, then setting Primary Graphics Adapter to **AGP** may speed up your system's booting-up process.

Therefore, if you are only using a single graphics card, it is recommended that you set the Primary Graphics Adapter feature to the proper setting for your system (**AGP** for a single AGP card and **PCI** for a single PCI card).

However, if you are using multiple graphics cards, it is up to you which card you want to use as your primary display card. It is recommended that you select the fastest graphics card as the primary display card.

Primary VGA BIOS

Common Options: AGP VGA Card, PCI VGA Card

Although the AGP bus was designed exclusively for the graphics subsystem, some users still have to use PCI graphics cards for multi-monitor support. This is because there can be only one AGP port! So, if you want to use multiple monitors, you must either get an AGP card that provides multi-monitor support or use PCI graphics cards.

For those who upgraded from a PCI graphics card to an AGP card, it is certainly enticing to use the old PCI graphics card to support a second monitor. The PCI card can do the job just fine because it merely sends display data to the second monitor. You don't need a powerful graphics card to run the second monitor because Microsoft Windows 2000/XP does not support 3D graphics acceleration on the second monitor.

When it comes to a case of an AGP graphics card working in tandem with a PCI graphics card, the BIOS has to determine which graphics card is the primary graphics card. Naturally, the default would be the **AGP** graphics card because, in most cases, it would be the faster card.

However, a BIOS switch that allows you to manually select the graphics card to boot the system with is still required. This is particularly important if you have AGP and PCI graphics cards but only one monitor. This is where the **Primary VGA BIOS** feature comes in. It allows you to select whether to boot the system using the AGP graphics card or the PCI graphics card.

If you are only using a single graphics card, then the BIOS detects it as such and boots it up, irrespective of what you set the feature to. However, there may be a slight reduction in the time taken to detect and initialize the card if you select the proper setting for this BIOS feature. For example, if you only use an AGP graphics card, then setting Primary VGA BIOS to **AGP VGA Card** may speed up your system's booting-up process.

Therefore, if you are only using a single graphics card, it is recommended that you set the Primary VGA BIOS feature to the proper setting for your system (**AGP VGA Card** for a single AGP card and **PCI VGA Card** for a single PCI card).

However, if you are using multiple graphics cards, it is up to you which card you want to use as your primary display card. It is recommended that you select the fastest graphics card as the primary display card.

Processor Number Feature

Common Options: Enabled, Disabled

This BIOS feature allows you to control the use of the processor's embedded **unique identification number**. Therefore, it is only valid if you are using a processor that features such a feature.

This infamous "feature" debuted in the Intel Pentium III processor and is mainly found only in that processor. The Transmeta Crusoe processor also supports this feature. However, most manufacturers have refrained from integrating such a feature in their processors. Even Intel has declined to add this feature to the Intel Pentium 4 processors.

If **enabled**, the processor's identification number can be read by external programs. It used to be required for certain secure transactions. However, this is no longer true because the initiative has long been abandoned.

If **disabled**, the processor's identification number cannot be read by external programs.

It is highly advisable that you **disable** this feature because it no longer has a use. Even worse, it can actually be misused to track your online activities. Disabling this feature safeguards your privacy by preventing the identification of your computer by the processor's identification number.

PS/2 Mouse Function Control

Common Options: Enabled, Auto

IRQ12 is the interrupt usually reserved for the PS/2 mouse's use. This BIOS feature determines whether the BIOS should reserve IRQ12 for the PS/2 mouse or allow other devices to make use of this IRQ.

Setting this BIOS feature to **Auto** allows the BIOS to allocate IRQ12 to the PS/2 mouse if the mouse is detected at startup. Otherwise, IRQ12 is released for use by other devices in the system.

Setting this BIOS feature to **Enabled** forces the BIOS to reserve IRQ12 even if a PS/2 mouse was not detected at startup.

It is recommended that you leave this BIOS feature at its default setting of **Auto**. This allows your BIOS to release IRQ12 for other devices to use if it doesn't detect the presence of a PS/2 mouse during startup.

Q

Quick Boot

Common Options: Enabled, Disabled

This BIOS feature allows you to decrease the time it takes to boot up the computer by shortening or skipping certain standard booting procedures.

However, it is not the same as the **Quick Power On Self Test** feature, which just shortens or skips certain system tests. Quick Boot further shortens the booting process by using a few additional tricks. Therefore, the Quick Power On Self Test should be considered a subset of the Quick Boot feature.

If **enabled**, the BIOS shortens the booting process by skipping some tests and shortening others. In addition, it also performs the following tricks to further speed up the booting process:

- Spin up the hard disks as soon as power is supplied (or as soon as possible)
- Initialize only critical parts of the chipset
- Read memory size from the **SPD** (**Serial Presence Detect**) chip on the memory modules
- Eliminate logo delays (inserted by many manufacturers)

If **disabled**, the BIOS runs the whole gamut of boot-up tests.

It is recommended that you **disable** this feature when you boot up a new computer for the first time or whenever you install a new piece of hardware. This allows the BIOS to run full diagnostic tests to detect any problems that may slip past Quick Boot's abbreviated testing scheme.

After a few error-free test runs, you should **enable** this feature for much faster booting.

Quick Power On Self Test

Common Options: Enabled, Disabled

This BIOS feature allows you to decrease the time it takes to boot up the computer by shortening or skipping certain standard booting procedures.

If **enabled**, the BIOS shortens the booting process by skipping some tests and shortening others.

If **disabled**, the BIOS runs the whole gamut of boot-up tests.

It is recommended that you **disable** this feature when you boot up a new computer for the first time or whenever you install a new piece of hardware. This allows the BIOS to run full diagnostic tests to detect any problems that may slip past the abbreviated testing scheme.

After a few error-free test runs, you should **enable** this feature for much faster booting.

R

Rank Interleave

Common Options: Enabled, Disabled

Rank is a new term used to differentiate physical banks on a particular memory module from internal banks within the memory chip. Single-sided memory modules have a single rank while double-sided memory modules have two ranks.

This BIOS feature is similar to **SDRAM Bank Interleave**. Interleaving allows banks of SDRAM to alternate their refresh and access cycles. One bank undergoes its refresh cycle while another is being accessed. This improves memory performance by masking the refresh cycles of each memory bank. The only difference is that **Rank Interleave** works between different physical banks or, as they are called now, **ranks**.

Because a minimum of two ranks are required for interleaving to be supported, double-sided memory modules are a must if you wish to enable Rank Interleave. Enabling Rank Interleave with single-sided memory modules does not result in any performance boost.

Please note that Rank Interleave currently works only if you are using double-sided memory modules. Rank Interleave does not work with two or more single-sided memory modules. The interleaving ranks must be on the same memory module.

It is highly recommended that you **enable** Rank Interleave for better memory performance. You can also **enable** Rank Interleave if you are using a mixture of single- and double-sided memory modules. However, if you are using only single-sided memory modules, it's advisable to **disable** Rank Interleave.

R

Read-Around-Write

Common Options: Enabled, Disabled

This BIOS feature allows the processor to execute read commands out of order as if they are independent from the write commands. It does this by using a Read-Around-Write buffer.

If this BIOS feature is **enabled**, all processor writes to memory are first accumulated in that buffer. This allows the processor to execute read commands without waiting for the write commands to be completed.

The buffer then combines the writes and writes them to memory as burst transfers. This reduces the number of writes to memory and boosts the processor's write performance.

Incidentally, until its contents have been written to memory, the Read-Around-Write buffer also serves as a cache of the data that it is storing. These tend to be the most up-to-date data because the processor has just written them to the buffer.

Therefore, if the processor sends out a read command whose memory address shows that the latest copy is still in the Read-Around-Write buffer, the processor can read directly from the buffer instead. This greatly improves read performance because the processor does not need to wait for the memory controller to access the data. The buffer is much closer logically, so reading from it is much faster than reading from memory.

If this BIOS feature is **disabled**, the processor writes directly to the memory controller. All writes have to be completed before the processor can execute a read command. It also prevents the buffer from being used as a temporary cache of processor writes. This reduces the processor's read performance.

Therefore, it is highly recommended that you **enable** this feature for better processor read and write performance.

Read Wait State

Common Options: 0 Cycle, 1 Cycle

This BIOS feature determines how long the memory controller should wait before sending read data to the data requester (for example, processor, graphics card, and so forth).

If this feature is set to **1 Cycle**, the memory controller imposes a delay of **one clock cycle** before the data is sent to the requester. This reduces memory read performance because the memory controller delays the transfer of each piece of requested data by one clock cycle.

In addition, read and write requests can overlap each other when the Read Wait State is set to **1 Cycle**. To prevent this, when this BIOS feature is set to **1 Cycle**, the memory controller automatically inserts an additional delay cycle between every read cycle that is followed immediately by a write cycle.

This is similar to **disabling** the **Fast R-W Turn Around** feature. This results in reduced memory write performance.

If this feature is set to **0 Cycle**, the memory controller transfers read data to the data requester without any delay. This improves memory read performance. It also improves memory write performance because there is no longer a need to insert an additional delay cycle to prevent read and write requests from overlapping each other.

Therefore, it is recommended that you set the Read Wait State to **0 Cycle** for better memory read and write performance.

Please note that this may cause system instabilities in certain configurations. When that happens, just reset the value to **1 Cycle**.

Refresh Interval

Common Options: 7.8 μsec, 15.6 μsec, 31.2 μsec, 64 μsec, 128 μsec, Auto

Memory cells normally need to be refreshed every 64 msec. However, simultaneously refreshing all the rows in a typical memory chip causes a big surge in power requirements. In addition, a simultaneous refresh causes all data requests to stall, which greatly impacts performance.

To avoid both problems, refreshes are normally staggered according to the number of rows. Because a typical memory chip contains 4096 rows, the memory controller usually refreshes a different row every **15.6 μsec** (64,000 μsec / 4096 rows = 15.6 μsec). This reduces the amount of current used during each refresh, and it allows data to be accessed from rows that are not being refreshed.

Usually, memory modules that use **128Mbit** or smaller memory chips have **4096 rows** while memory chips with higher capacity (256Mbit and above) have **8192 rows**. For memory chips that come with 8192 rows, the refresh interval needs to be halved to **7.8 μsec** because there are now twice as many rows to serviced within the stipulated 64 msec for the entire chip.

Therefore, the typical refresh interval for 128Mbit (not MB!) or smaller memory chips is **15.6 μsec**, while those for 256Mbit or larger memory chips are **7.8 μsec**. Please note that if you are using a mix of 128Mbit and 256Mbit memory modules, the fail-safe Refresh Interval is 7.8 μsec, *not* 15.6 μsec.

Although JEDEC standards call for a **64 msec** refresh cycle, memory chips these days can actually hold data for longer than that. So, using a longer refresh cycle is quite possible. With a longer refresh cycle, the memory chips are refreshed less often, reducing both the amount of bandwidth wasted on refreshes and the amount of power consumed (which is great for laptops and other portable devices).

This BIOS feature allows you to set the refresh interval of the memory chips. There are three different settings as well as an **Auto** option. If the **Auto** option is selected, the BIOS queries the memory modules' SPD chips and uses the lowest setting found for maximum compatibility.

For better performance, you should consider increasing the **Refresh Interval** from the default values (15.6 μsec for 128Mbit or smaller memory chips and 7.8 μsec for 256Mbit or larger memory chips) up to **128 μsec**. Please note that if you increase the **Refresh Interval** too much, the memory cells may lose their contents.

Therefore, you should start with small increases in the **Refresh Interval** and test your system after each hike before increasing it further. If you face stability problems upon increasing the refresh interval, reduce the refresh interval step by step until the system is stable.

Refresh Mode Select

R

Common Options: 7.8 μsec, 15.6 μsec, 31.2 μsec, 64 μsec, 128 μsec, Auto

Memory cells normally need to be refreshed every 64 msec. However, simultaneously refreshing all the rows in a typical memory chip causes a big surge in power requirements. In addition, a simultaneous refresh causes all data requests to stall, which greatly impacts performance.

To avoid both problems, refreshes are normally staggered according to the number of rows. Because a typical memory chip contains 4096 rows, the memory controller usually refreshes a different row every **15.6 μsec** (64,000 μsec / 4096 rows = 15.6 μsec). This reduces the amount of current used during each refresh, and it allows data to be accessed from rows that are not being refreshed.

Usually, memory modules that use **128Mbit** or smaller memory chips have **4096 rows**, while memory chips with higher capacity (256Mbit and above) have **8192 rows**. For memory chips that come with 8192 rows, the refresh interval needs to be halved to **7.8 μsec** because there are now twice as many rows to serviced within the stipulated 64 msec for the entire chip.

Therefore, the typical refresh interval for 128Mbit (not MB!) or smaller memory chips is **15.6 μsec**, while those for 256Mbit or larger memory chips is **7.8 μsec**. Please note that if you are using a mix of 128Mbit and 256Mbit memory modules, the fail-safe Refresh Mode Select is **7.8 μsec**, *not* 15.6 μsec.

Although JEDEC standards call for a **64 msec** refresh cycle, memory chips these days can actually hold data for longer than that. So, using a longer refresh cycle is quite possible. With a longer refresh cycle, the memory chips are refreshed less often, reducing both the amount of bandwidth wasted on refreshes and the amount of power consumed (which is great for laptops and other portable devices).

This BIOS feature allows you to set the refresh interval of the memory chips. There are three different settings as well as an **Auto** option. If the **Auto** option is selected, the BIOS queries the memory modules' SPD chips and uses the lowest setting found for maximum compatibility.

For better performance, you should consider increasing the **Refresh Mode Select** from the default values (15.6 μsec for 128Mbit or smaller memory chips and 7.8 μsec for 256Mbit or larger memory chips) up to **128 μsec**. Please note that if you increase the **Refresh Mode Select** too much, the memory cells may lose their contents.

Therefore, you should start with small increases in the **Refresh Mode Select** and test your system after each hike before increasing it further. If you face stability problems upon increasing the refresh interval, reduce the refresh interval step by step until the system is stable.

Report No FDD For Win95

Common Options: Enabled, Disabled

This BIOS feature allows you to set whether the BIOS should report the absence of a floppy disk drive to Windows 95.

For some reason, the Microsoft Windows 95 operating system requires a floppy disk drive to be present. However, in an age of USB flash media and CD/DVD writers, not all computers come with a floppy disk drive. Such computers fail to boot up Windows 95 without a floppy disk drive.

Therefore, to meet Microsoft Windows 95's logo certification, and yet allow computers sans floppy disk drives to boot Windows 95 normally, motherboards provide this BIOS feature.

If this feature is **enabled**, the BIOS assigns IRQ 6 (which is designated for the floppy disk drive's use) to another device, presumably to trick Windows 95 into thinking that a floppy disk drive exists. This allows computers with no floppy disk drives to boot into Windows 95 normally.

If this feature is **disabled**, Windows 95 detects the absence of the floppy disk drive and halts the system with an error message.

If you are using Windows 95 *without* a floppy disk drive, you have to **enable** this feature to allow Windows 95 to boot up normally.

If you are using Windows 95 *with* a floppy disk drive, you can **enable** or **disable** this feature. Windows 95 boots up normally either way.

Please note that this BIOS feature has no relevance in other operating systems. Only Windows 95 is affected. It does not matter what you set this BIOS option to if you are using other operating systems.

Reset Configuration Data

Common Options: Enabled, Disabled

The **ESCD (Extended System Configuration Data)** is a feature of the Plug and Play BIOS that allows the BIOS to re-use system configuration data.

Whenever the BIOS boots up, it needs to configure the ISA, PCI and AGP devices in the system (Plug and Play-capable or otherwise). However, because the installed devices are unlikely to change from one booting to another, the system configuration data actually remains the same. Therefore, if it can be stored and re-used, the BIOS can skip configuring the same devices every time you boot up the system.

This is where the ESCD feature comes in. It stores the IRQ, DMA, I/O and memory configurations of your system's devices in a special area of the BIOS Flash ROM. The BIOS snoops and re-uses the stored configuration data when it boots up the system. As long as there are no hardware changes, the BIOS does not need to reconfigure the ESCD.

If you install a new piece of hardware or modify your computer's hardware configuration, the BIOS automatically detects the changes and reconfigures the ESCD. Therefore, there is usually no need to manually force the BIOS to reconfigure the ESCD.

However, the occasion may arise where the BIOS may not be able to detect the hardware changes. A serious resource conflict may occur and the operating system may not even boot as a result. This is where the **Reset Configuration Data** BIOS feature comes in.

This BIOS feature allows you to manually force the BIOS to clear the previously saved ESCD data and reconfigure the settings. All you need to do is **enable** this BIOS feature and then reboot your computer. The new ESCD should resolve the conflict and allow the operating system to load normally.

Please note that the BIOS automatically resets it to the default setting of **Disabled** after reconfiguring the new ESCD. So, there is no need for you to manually **disable** this feature after rebooting.

Resource Controlled By

Common Options: Auto, Manual

This BIOS feature determines whether the BIOS should automatically configure IRQ and DMA resources.

If this feature is set to **Auto**, the BIOS automatically assigns IRQs and DMA channels for all your devices. All IRQ and DMA assignment fields below this BIOS feature disappear or become grayed out.

If this feature is set to **Manual**, the BIOS allows you to manually configure the IRQs and DMA channels for your devices.

The BIOS is generally capable of automatically configuring IRQ and DMA resources for the devices in your computer. Therefore, it is advisable that you set this feature to **Auto**.

However, if the BIOS has problems assigning the resources properly, you can select the **Manual** option to reveal the IRQ and DMA assignment fields. You can then assign each IRQ or DMA channel to either **Legacy ISA** or **PCI/ISA PnP** devices.

Legacy ISA devices are compliant with the original PC AT bus specification and require a specific interrupt and/or DMA channel to function properly. **PCI/ISA PnP** devices, on the other hand, adhere to the Plug and Play standard and can use any interrupt or DMA channel.

RxD, TxD Active

Common Options: Hi, Hi or Lo, Lo or Hi, Lo or Lo, Hi

This BIOS feature allows you to set the infra-red reception (**RxD**) and transmission (**TxD**) polarity.

It is usually found under the **Onboard Serial Port 2** BIOS feature and is linked to the second serial port. So, if you disable that port, this feature disappears from the screen or appears grayed out.

There are four options available, based on combinations of Hi and Lo. You'll need to consult your IR peripheral's documentation to determine the correct polarity. Choosing the wrong polarity prevents a proper IR connection from being established with the IR peripheral.

S

S2K Bus Driving Strength

Common Options: Auto, Manual

The S2K bus is another name for the AMD Athlon processor bus. Therefore, this BIOS feature determines whether the motherboard chipset should automatically adjust the drive strength of the Athlon processor bus or allow manual configuration.

If you set this feature to **Auto**, the chipset is allowed to dynamically adjust the S2K bus strength or use values pre-set by the manufacturer.

If you set this feature to **Manual**, the chipset's dynamic compensation circuitry for the S2K bus is turned off. You can then manually set the S2K bus strength.

Generally, it is recommended that you set this feature to **Auto**, so the S2K bus strength can be dynamically adjusted by the chipset. However, there may be occasions when manual configuration of the S2K bus driving strength may be desirable.

It is possible to make use of this feature for overclocking purposes. Increasing the drive strength increases the stability of the S2K bus by reducing the impedance from the motherboard and boosting the signal strength. However, please be very circumspect when you increase the S2K bus drive strength with an overclocked processor because you may irreversibly damage the processor!

If you want to manually configure the S2K bus driving strength, you must set the S2K Bus Driving Strength to **Manual**. This allows you to manually set the S2K bus driving strength value through the **S2K Strobe P Control** and **S2K Strobe N Control** BIOS features.

S2K Strobe N Control

Common Options: 0 to F (Hex numbers), 0h to Fh

This BIOS feature determines the N transistor drive strength of the S2K bus. It is used in conjunction with **S2K Bus Driving Strength** and **S2K Strobe P Control** to bypass the motherboard chipset's dynamic compensation for the S2K bus.

It is slaved to the **Manual** option of the **S2K Bus Driving Strength** feature. Therefore, if you set S2K Bus Driving Strength to **Auto**, then the value you choose for this function has no effect. For this function to have any effect, you must set S2K Bus Driving Strength to **Manual**.

The N transistor drive strength is represented by Hex values from **0** to **F** (**0** to **15** in decimal). The default N transistor drive strength differs between motherboards. However, the higher the drive strength, the greater the compensation for the motherboard's impedance on the S2K bus.

Due to the nature of this BIOS feature, it is possible to use it as an aid in overclocking the S2K bus. A higher N (and P) transistor drive strength may be just what you need to overclock the S2K bus higher than is normally possible. By raising the drive strength of the S2K bus, you can improve its stability at overclocked speeds.

Please be very circumspect when you increase the S2K drive strength with an overclocked processor because you may irreversibly damage the processor!

Also, contrary to popular opinion, increasing the S2K drive strength does *not* improve the performance of your AMD processor. It is not a performance-enhancing feature, so you should not increase the N transistor drive strength unnecessarily.

S2K Strobe P Control

Common Options: 0 to F (Hex numbers), 0h to Fh

This BIOS feature determines the P transistor drive strength of the S2K bus. It is used in conjunction with **S2K Bus Driving Strength** and **S2K Strobe P Control** to bypass the motherboard chipset's dynamic compensation for the S2K bus.

It is slaved to the **Manual** option of the **S2K Bus Driving Strength** feature. Therefore, if you set S2K Bus Driving Strength to **Auto**, then the value you choose for this function has no effect. For this function to have any effect, you must set S2K Bus Driving Strength to **Manual**.

The P transistor drive strength is represented by Hex values from **0** to **F** (**0** to **15** in decimal). The default P transistor drive strength differs between motherboards. However, the higher the drive strength, the greater the compensation for the motherboard's impedance on the S2K bus.

Due to the nature of this BIOS feature, it is possible to use it as an aid in overclocking the S2K bus. A higher P (and N) transistor drive strength may be just what you need to overclock the S2K bus higher than is normally possible. By raising the drive strength of the S2K bus, you can improve its stability at overclocked speeds.

Please be very circumspect when you increase the S2K drive strength with an overclocked processor because you may irreversibly damage the processor!

Also, contrary to popular opinion, increasing the S2K drive strength does *not* improve the performance of your AMD processor. It is not a performance-enhancing feature, so you should not increase the P transistor drive strength unnecessarily.

SDRAM 1T Command

Common Options: Enabled, Disabled, Auto

Whenever there is a memory read request from the operating system, the memory controller does not actually receive the physical memory addresses where the data is located. It is only given a virtual address space, which it has to translate into physical memory addresses. Only then can it issue the proper read commands. This produces a slight delay at the start of every new memory transaction.

Instead of immediately issuing the read commands, the memory controller asserts the Chip Select signal to the physical bank that contains the requested data. What this Chip Select signal does is activate the bank, so it is ready to accept the commands. In the meantime, the memory controller is busy translating the memory addresses. After the memory controller has the physical memory addresses, it starts issuing read commands to the activated memory bank.

As you can see, the command delay is not caused by any latency inherent in the memory module. Rather, it is determined by the time taken by the memory controller to translate the virtual address space into physical memory addresses.

Naturally, because the delay is due to translation of addresses, the memory controller requires more time to translate addresses in high-density memory modules due to the higher number of addresses. The memory controller also takes a longer time if there is a large number of physical banks.

This BIOS feature allows you to select the delay between the assertion of the Chip Select signal until the time the memory controller starts sending commands to the memory bank. The lower the value, the sooner the memory controller can send commands out to the activated memory bank.

When this feature is **enabled**, the memory controller only inserts a command delay of **one clock cycle** or **1T**.

When this feature is **disabled**, the memory controller inserts a command delay of **two clock cycles** or **2T**.

The **Auto** option allows the memory controller to use the memory module's SPD value for command delay.

If the SDRAM command delay is too long, it can reduce performance by unnecessarily preventing the memory controller from issuing the commands sooner.

However, if the SDRAM command delay is too short, the memory controller may not be able to translate the addresses in time and the "bad commands" that result cause data loss and corruption.

Fortunately, all unbuffered SDRAM modules are capable of a 1T command delay up to four memory banks per channel. After that, a 2T command delay may be required. However, support for 1T command delay varies between chipsets and even between motherboard models. You should consult your motherboard manufacturer to see whether your motherboard supports a command delay of 1T.

It is recommended that you **enable** SDRAM 1T Command for better memory performance. However, if you face stability issues, **disable** this BIOS feature.

SDRAM 1T Command Control

Common Options: Enabled, Disabled, Auto

Whenever there is a memory read request from the operating system, the memory controller does not actually receive the physical memory addresses where the data is located. It is only given a virtual address space, which it has to translate into physical memory addresses. Only then can it issue the proper read commands. This produces a slight delay at the start of every new memory transaction.

Instead of immediately issuing the read commands, the memory controller asserts the Chip Select signal to the physical bank that contains the requested data. What this Chip Select signal does is activate the bank, so it is ready to accept the commands. In the meantime, the memory controller is busy translating the memory addresses. After the memory controller has the physical memory addresses, it starts issuing read commands to the activated memory bank.

As you can see, the command delay is not caused by any latency inherent in the memory module. Rather, it is determined by the time taken by the memory controller to translate the virtual address space into physical memory addresses.

Naturally, because the delay is due to translation of addresses, the memory controller requires more time to translate addresses in high-density memory modules due to the higher number of addresses. The memory controller also takes a longer time if there is a large number of physical banks.

This BIOS feature allows you to select the delay between the assertion of the Chip Select signal until the time the memory controller starts sending commands to the memory bank. The lower the value, the sooner the memory controller can send commands out to the activated memory bank.

When this feature is **enabled**, the memory controller only inserts a command delay of **one clock cycle** or **1T**.

When this feature is **disabled**, the memory controller inserts a command delay of **two clock cycles** or **2T**.

The **Auto** option allows the memory controller to use the memory module's SPD value for command delay.

If the SDRAM command delay is too long, it can reduce performance by unnecessarily preventing the memory controller from issuing the commands sooner.

However, if the SDRAM command delay is too short, the memory controller may not be able to translate the addresses in time and the "bad commands" that result cause data loss and corruption.

Fortunately, all unbuffered SDRAM modules are capable of a 1T command delay up to four memory banks per channel. After that, a 2T command delay may be required. However, support for 1T command delay varies between chipsets and even between motherboard models. You should consult your motherboard manufacturer to see whether your motherboard supports a command delay of 1T.

It is recommended that you **enable** SDRAM 1T Command Control for better memory performance. However, if you face stability issues, **disable** this BIOS feature.

SDRAM Active to Precharge Delay

Common Options: 4, 5, 6, 7, 8, 9

Whenever a read command is issued, a memory row is activated using the **RAS (Row Address Strobe)**. Then, to read data from the target memory cell, the appropriate column is activated using the **CAS (Column Address Strobe)**. Multiple cells can be read from the same active row by applying the appropriate CAS signals.

However, when data has to be read from a different row, the active row has to be deactivated. However, the row cannot be deactivated until the **Minimum Row Active Time** or **tRAS** has elapsed.

The appropriate delay for your memory module is reflected in its rated timings. In JEDEC specifications, it is the *fourth* number in the four-number sequence. For example, if your memory module has the rated timings of 2-3-4-**7**, its rated tRAS delay would be 7 clock cycles.

Like **DRAM Act to PreChrg CMD**, this BIOS feature controls the memory bank's **tRAS**. This constitutes the time when a row is activated until the time the same row can be deactivated. It is also the length of time the row will remain open for data transfers.

If the tRAS period is too long, it can reduce performance by unnecessarily delaying the deactivation of active rows. Reducing the tRAS period allows the active row to be deactivated earlier.

However, if the tRAS period is too short, there may not be enough time to complete a burst transfer. This reduces performance and data may be lost or corrupted.

For optimal performance, use the lowest value you can. Usually, this should be **CAS latency + tRCD + 2 clock cycles**. For example, if you set the CAS latency to 2 clock cycles and the tRCD to 3 clock cycles, the optimum tRAS value would be 7 clock cycles.

However, if you start getting memory errors or system crashes, increase the tRAS value one clock cycle at a time until your system becomes stable.

SDRAM Bank Interleave

Common Options: 2–Bank, 4–Bank, Disabled

This BIOS feature enables you to set the interleave mode of the SDRAM interface.

Interleaving allows banks of SDRAM to alternate their refresh and access cycles. One bank undergoes its refresh cycle while another is being accessed. This improves memory performance by masking the refresh cycles of each memory bank. A close examination reveals that because the refresh cycles of all the memory banks are staggered, this produces a kind of pipelining effect.

If there are four banks in the system, the processor can ideally send one data request to each memory bank in just four clock cycles. In the first clock cycle, the processor sends an address to Bank 0 and then sends the next address to Bank 1 in the second clock cycle before sending the third and fourth addresses to Banks 2 and 3 in the third and fourth clock cycles, respectively. The sequence looks something like this:

1. Processor sends address #0 to **Bank 0**
2. Processor sends address #1 to **Bank 1** and receives data #0 from **Bank 0**
3. Processor sends address #2 to **Bank 2** and receives data #1 from **Bank 1**
4. Processor sends address #3 to **Bank 3** and receives data #2 from **Bank 2**
5. Processor receives data #3 from **Bank 3**

As you can see, the data from all four requests arrives consecutively from the memory banks without any delay in between. However, if interleaving was *not* enabled, the same 4-address transaction may appear like this (worst–case scenario):

1. SDRAM refreshes
2. Processor sends address #0 to SDRAM
3. Processor receives data #0 from SDRAM
4. SDRAM refreshes
5. Processor sends address #1 to SDRAM
6. Processor receives data #1 from SDRAM
7. SDRAM refreshes
8. Processor sends address #2 to SDRAM
9. Processor receives data #2 from SDRAM

10. SDRAM refreshes

11. Processor sends address **#3** to SDRAM

12. Processor receives data **#3** from SDRAM

With interleaving enabled, the first bank can start transferring data to the processor in the same cycle that the second bank receives an address. However, if interleaving is disabled, the processor has to send the address to the memory bank, receive the requested data, and then wait for the memory bank to refresh before initiating the second data transaction. This wastes a lot of clock cycles and results in reduced bandwidth.

Interleaving allows you to mask the refresh cycles. This essentially produces a pipelining effect that greatly increases throughput.

However, bank interleaving only works if the addresses requested consecutively are not in the same bank. If they are in the same memory bank, then the data transactions behave as if the banks were not interleaved. The processor has to wait until the first data transaction clears and that memory bank refreshes before it can send another address to that bank.

Each SDRAM module is internally divided into either **two** or **four** banks of memory. Double-banked SDRAM modules generally use **16Mbit** SDRAM chips and are usually **32MB** or smaller in size. Quad-banked SDRAM modules, on the other hand, usually use higher density (**64Mbit-256Mbit**) SDRAM chips. All SDRAM modules of at least **64MB** in size are quad-banked in nature.

If you are using a *single* double-banked SDRAM module, set this feature to **2-Bank**. This is the only option available for the single double-banked SDRAM module.

If you are using at least *two* double-banked SDRAM modules, you can use the **4-Bank** option as well as the **2-Bank** option. Of course, it is recommended that you select **4-Bank** for better interleaving performance.

If you are using quad-banked SDRAM modules, you can use either interleave options. Of course, it is recommended that you select **4-Bank** for better interleaving performance.

Because a 4-bank interleave always allows for better interleaving performance, it is highly recommended that you select the **4-Bank** option if your system supports it. Use the **2-Bank** option only if you are using a single double-banked SDRAM module.

Please note that **Award** (now part of **Phoenix Technologies**) recommends that SDRAM bank interleaving be **disabled** if **16Mbit** SDRAM modules are used. This is because early 16Mbit SDRAM modules have stability problems with bank interleaving. The good news is all current SDRAM modules support bank interleaving.

SDRAM Bank-to-Bank Delay

Common Options: 2 cycles, 3 cycles

The **Bank-to-Bank Delay** or **tRRD** is a DDR timing parameter that specifies the minimum amount of time between successive ACTIVATE commands to the *same* DDR device, even to **different** internal banks. The shorter the delay, the faster the next bank can be activated for read or write operations. However, because row activation requires a lot of current, using a short delay may cause excessive current surges.

Because this timing parameter is DDR device-specific, it may differ from one DDR device to another. DDR DRAM manufacturers typically specify the tRRD parameter based on the row ACTIVATE activity to limit current surges within the device. If you let the BIOS automatically configure your DRAM parameters, it retrieves the manufacturer-set tRRD value from the **SPD (Serial Presence Detect)** chip. However, you may want to manually set the tRRD parameter to suit your requirements.

For desktop PCs, a delay of **2 cycles** is recommended because current surges aren't really important. This is because the desktop PC essentially has an unlimited power supply and even the most basic desktop cooling solution is sufficient to dispel any extra thermal load that the current surges may impose. The performance benefit of using the shorter 2 cycles delay is of far greater interest. The shorter delay means every back-to-back bank activation takes one clock cycle less to perform. This improves the DDR device's read and write performance.

Note that the shorter delay of **2 cycles** works with most DDR DIMMs, even at 133MHz (266MHz DDR). However, DDR DIMMs running beyond 133MHz (266MHz DDR) may need to introduce a delay of 3 cycles between each successive bank activation. Select **2 cycles** whenever possible for optimal DDR DRAM performance. Switch to **3 cycles** only when there are stability problems with the 2 cycles setting.

In mobile devices like laptops however, it is advisable to use the longer delay of **3 cycles**. Doing so limits the current surges that accompany row activations. This reduces the DDR device's power consumption and thermal output, both of which should be of great interest to the road warrior.

SDRAM Burst Len

Common Options: 4, 8

This is the same as the **SDRAM Burst Length** BIOS feature, only with a weirdly truncated name. Surprisingly, many manufacturers are using it. Why? Only they know.:

Burst transactions improve SDRAM performance by allowing the reading or writing of whole blocks of contiguous data with only one column address.

In a burst sequence, only the *first* read or write transfer incurs the initial latency of activating the column. The subsequent reads or writes in that burst sequence then can follow behind without any further delay. This allows blocks of data to be read or written with far less delay than non-burst transactions.

For example, a burst transaction of four writes can incur the following latencies: **4-1-1-1**. In this example, the total time it takes to transact the four writes is merely **7** clock cycles.

In contrast, if the four writes are not written by burst transaction, they incur the following latencies: **4-4-4-4**. The time it takes to transact the four writes becomes **16** clock cycles, which is 9 clock cycles longer or more than twice as slow as a burst transaction.

This is where the **SDRAM Burst Len** BIOS feature comes in. It is a BIOS feature that allows you to control the length of a burst transaction.

When this feature is set to **4**, a burst transaction can only be comprised of up to **four** reads or **four** writes.

When this feature is set to **8**, a burst transaction can only be comprised of up to **eight** reads or **eight** writes.

S

As the initial CAS latency is fixed for each burst transaction, a longer burst transaction allows more data to be read or written for less delay than a shorter burst transaction. Therefore, a burst length of 8 is faster than a burst length of 4.

For example, if the memory controller wants to write a block of contiguous data 8 units long to memory, it can do it as a *single* burst transaction 8 units long or *two* burst transactions, each 4 units in length. The hypothetical latencies incurred by the single 8-unit long transaction would be **4-1-1-1-1-1-1-1** with a total time of **11** clock cycles for the entire transaction.

However, if the eight writes are written to memory as two burst transactions of 4 units in length, the hypothetical latencies incurred would be **4-1-1-1-4-1-1-1**. The time taken for the two transactions to complete would be **14** clock cycles. As you can see, this is slower than a single transaction 8 units long.

Therefore, it is recommended that you select the longer burst length of **8** for better performance.

SDRAM Burst Length

Common Options: 4, 8

Burst transactions improve SDRAM performance by allowing the reading or writing of whole blocks of contiguous data with only one column address.

In a burst sequence, only the *first* read or write transfer incurs the initial latency of activating the column. The subsequent reads or writes in that burst sequence then can follow behind without any further delay. This allows blocks of data to be read or written with far less delay than non-burst transactions.

For example, a burst transaction of four writes can incur the following latencies: **4-1-1-1**. In this example, the total time it takes to transact the four writes is merely **7** clock cycles.

In contrast, if the four writes are not written by burst transaction, they incur the following latencies: **4-4-4-4**. The time it takes to transact the four writes becomes **16** clock cycles, which is 9 clock cycles longer or more than twice as slow as a burst transaction.

This is where the **SDRAM Burst Length** BIOS feature comes in. It is a BIOS feature that allows you to control the length of a burst transaction.

When this feature is set to **4**, a burst transaction can only be comprised of up to **four** reads or **four** writes.

When this feature is set to **8**, a burst transaction can only be comprised of up to **eight** reads or **eight** writes.

As the initial CAS latency is fixed for each burst transaction, a longer burst transaction allows more data to be read or written for less delay than a shorter burst transaction. Therefore, a burst length of 8 is faster than a burst length of 4.

For example, if the memory controller wants to write a block of contiguous data 8 units long to memory, it can do it as a *single* burst transaction 8 units long or *two* burst transactions, each 4 units in length. The hypothetical latencies incurred by the single 8-unit long transaction would be **4-1-1-1-1-1-1-1** with a total time of **11** clock cycles for the entire transaction.

However, if the eight writes are written to memory as two burst transactions of 4 units in length, the hypothetical latencies incurred would be **4-1-1-1-4-1-1-1**. The time taken for the two transactions to complete would be **14** clock cycles. As you can see, this is slower than a single transaction 8 units long.

Therefore, it is recommended that you select the longer burst length of **8** for better performance.

SDRAM CAS Latency Time

Common Options: 2, 3 (SDR memory) or 1.5, 2, 2.5, 3 (DDR memory)

Whenever a read command is issued, a memory row is activated using the **RAS**. Then, to read data from the target memory cell, the appropriate column is activated using the **CAS**.

Multiple cells can be read from the same active row by applying the appropriate CAS signals. However, there is a short delay after each assertion of the CAS signal before data can be read from the target memory cell. This delay is known as the **CAS latency**.

The appropriate delay for your memory module is reflected in its rated timings. In JEDEC specifications, it is the *first* number in the three or four number sequence. For example, if your memory module has the rated timings of **2-3-4-7**, its rated CAS latency would be 2 clock cycles.

This BIOS feature controls the delay (in clock cycles) between the assertion of the CAS signal and the availability of the data from the target memory cell. It also determines the number of clock cycles required for the completion of the first part of a burst transfer. In other words, the lower the CAS latency, the faster memory reads or writes can occur.

Because column activation occurs every time a new memory cell is read from, the effect of CAS latency on memory performance is significant, especially with SDR SDRAM. Its effect is less obvious in DDR SDRAM.

Please note that some memory modules may not be able to handle the lower latency and may lose data. Therefore, while it is recommended that you reduce the **SDRAM CAS Latency Time** to **2** or **2.5** clock cycles for better memory performance, you should increase it if your system becomes unstable.

Interestingly, increasing the CAS latency time often allows the memory module to run at a higher clock speed. So, if you hit a snag while overclocking your SDRAM modules, try increasing the CAS latency time.

This is particularly true for DDR SDRAM memory because CAS latency has much less effect on performance with such memory, compared to the older SDR memory. The improvement in overclockability with higher CAS latencies cannot be underestimated. If you are interested in overclocking your DDR SDRAM modules, you might want to consider increasing the CAS latency. The huge increase in overclockability far outweighs the minor loss in performance.

SDRAM Command Leadoff Time

Common Options: 3, 4

To meet different timing requirements, the memory controller drives signals onto the address and command lines one clock cycle before they are actually needed. This gives the memory controller some additional time to meet the timing requirements of the motherboard.

Although you may think that the early assertion of the address and command lines helps improve performance, that is not true. Even if the memory controller drives the address and command signals one clock cycle earlier, those signals are only latched onto the memory module when none of the memory banks are active.

Once the signals are latched onto the memory module, the target bank is activated and the memory controller starts reading from the active bank. Now, because of the pre-driving of the address and command lines, the activation of the target memory bank is controlled by the **command leadoff time**.

By definition, the **command leadoff time** is the period between the assertion of the address/command lines and the activation of the target memory bank. This BIOS feature allows you to adjust the command leadoff time to meet timing variances of the motherboard as well as the memory module.

The shorter the leadoff time, the earlier the target bank can be activated. This allows faster access to the data in the memory module. Therefore, it is recommended that you set the SDRAM Command Leadoff Time to **3** clock cycles for better memory performance.

However, your motherboard and memory combination may not be able to support the tighter command leadoff time of **3** clock cycles. If your system becomes unstable with a command leadoff time of **3** clock cycles, revert to the slower command leadoff time of **4** clock cycles.

SDRAM Command Rate

Common Options: 1T, 2T

Whenever there is a memory read request from the operating system, the memory controller does not actually receive the physical memory addresses where the data is located. It is only given a virtual address space that it has to translate into physical memory addresses. Only then can it issue the proper read commands. This produces a slight delay at the start of every new memory transaction.

Instead of immediately issuing the read commands, the memory controller asserts the Chip Select signal to the physical bank that contains the requested data. What this Chip Select signal does is activate the bank, so it is ready to accept the commands. In the meantime, the memory controller is busy translating the memory addresses. Once the memory controller has the physical memory addresses, it starts issuing read commands to the activated memory bank.

As you can see, the command delay is not caused by any latency inherent in the memory module. Rather, it is determined by the time taken by the memory controller to translate the virtual address space into physical memory addresses.

Naturally, because the delay is due to translation of addresses, the memory controller requires more time to translate addresses in high-density memory modules due to the higher number of addresses. The memory controller also takes a longer time if there is a large number of physical banks.

This BIOS feature allows you to select the delay between the assertion of the Chip Select signal until the time the memory controller starts sending commands to the memory bank. The lower the value, the sooner the memory controller can send commands out to the activated memory bank.

If the SDRAM command delay is too long, it can reduce performance by unnecessarily preventing the memory controller from issuing the commands sooner.

However, if the SDRAM command delay is too short, the memory controller may not be able to translate the addresses in time and the "bad commands" that result cause data loss and corruption.

Fortunately, all unbuffered SDRAM modules are capable of a 1T command delay up to four memory banks per channel. After that, a 2T command delay may be required. However, support for 1T command delay varies between chipsets and even between motherboard models. You should consult your motherboard manufacturer to see if your motherboard supports a command delay of 1T.

It is recommended that you try the **1T** command delay for better memory performance. However, if you face stability issues, increase the command delay to **2T**.

SDRAM Cycle Length

Common Options: 2, 3 (SDR memory) or 1.5, 2, 2.5, 3 (DDR memory)

Whenever a read command is issued, a memory row is activated using the **RAS**. Then, to read data from the target memory cell, the appropriate column is activated using the **CAS**.

Multiple cells can be read from the same active row by applying the appropriate CAS signals. However, there is a short delay after each assertion of the CAS signal before data can be read from the target memory cell. This delay is known as the **CAS latency**.

The appropriate delay for your memory module is reflected in its rated timings. In JEDEC specifications, it is the *first* number in the three or four number sequence. For example, if your memory module has the rated timings of 2–3–4–7, its rated CAS latency would be 2 clock cycles.

This BIOS feature is same as the **SDRAM CAS Latency Time** BIOS feature. It controls the delay (in clock cycles) between the assertion of the CAS signal and the availability of the data from the target memory cell. It also determines the number of clock cycles required for the completion of the first part of a burst transfer. In other words, the lower the CAS latency, the faster memory reads or writes can occur.

Because column activation occurs every time a new memory cell is read from, the effect of CAS latency on memory performance is significant, especially with SDR SDRAM. Its effect is less obvious in DDR SDRAM.

Please note that some memory modules may not be able to handle the lower latency and may lose data. Therefore, while it is recommended that you reduce the **SDRAM CAS Latency Time** to **2** or **2.5** clock cycles for better memory performance, you should increase it if your system becomes unstable.

Interestingly, increasing the CAS latency time often allows the memory module to run at a higher clock speed. So, if you hit a snag while overclocking your SDRAM modules, try increasing the CAS latency time.

This is particularly true for DDR SDRAM memory because CAS latency has much less effect on performance with such memory compared to the older SDR memory. The improvement in overclockability with higher CAS latencies cannot be underestimated. If you are interested in overclocking your DDR SDRAM modules, you might want to consider increasing the CAS latency. The huge increase in overclockability far outweighs the minor loss in performance.

S

SDRAM Cycle Time Tras/Trc

Common Options: 5/6, 6/8

This BIOS feature determines the **tRAS** and the **tRC** parameters of the SDRAM memory module.

tRAS refers to the SDRAM **Row Active Time**, which is the length of time the row remains open for data transfers.

tRC, on the other hand, refers to the SDRAM **Row Cycle Time**, which determines the minimum number of clock cycles a memory row takes to complete a full cycle, from row activation up to the precharging of the active row.

The default setting is **6/8**, which is more stable and slower than **5/6**. The **5/6** setting cycles faster, however, it may not leave the row open long enough for burst transactions to complete. When this happens, data may be lost and the contents of the memory cells may be corrupted. This is especially true at clock speeds above 100MHz.

For better memory performance, you should try the **5/6** setting. However, increase it to **6/8** if your system becomes unstable. You can also use the slower **6/8** setting if you are trying to overclock your memory modules because increasing the timings may allow them to run at a higher clock speed.

SDRAM ECC Setting

Common Options: Disabled, Check Only, Correct Errors, Correct+Scrub

This BIOS feature is the extended version of the **DRAM Data Integrity Mode** BIOS feature. It is found in newer chipsets that support more than just simple **ECC** (**Error Checking and Correction**).

This BIOS feature controls the enhanced error correcting capabilities of the memory controller, which includes memory scrubbing. There are actually five ECC modes, although only four are of practical use and available through this BIOS feature:

- Disabled
- Check Only
- Correct Errors
- Correct+Scrub

The first mode is **Disabled**, which disables the memory controller's ECC capabilities. If you are *not* using ECC memory modules, you must select this option. If you are using ECC memory modules, this mode provides the best memory performance, although it doesn't improve data integrity at all.

The **Check Only** mode forces the memory controller to only check for errors. The memory controller detects and reports single- and double-bit errors, however, it does *not* correct them. This mode offers minimal performance degradation, but it doesn't improve data integrity at all.

If you select the **Correct Errors** mode, the memory controller not only checks for and detects single- and double-bit errors, it also corrects single-bit errors. The correction of single-bit errors takes up one extra clock cycle, so this mode has a higher overhead. The plus side is it improves data integrity by seamlessly correcting single-bit errors. Double-bit errors are not corrected, however.

The final ECC mode is **Correct+Scrub**, which is the most reliable ECC mode. It combines ECC with memory scrubbing. With this mode enabled, the memory controller not only detects multiple-bit errors and corrects single-bit errors, it also writes the corrected single-bit value back into memory! This offers the highest level of data integrity of all four modes. However, the scrubbing operation results in even more overhead.

Generally speaking, the **Check Only** mode isn't particularly useful because it only offers error checking and reporting. Users of ECC memory modules should focus mainly on the **Correct Errors** and **Correct+Scrub** modes because they actually improve data integrity by correcting single-bit errors. Of course, if you are using normal, non-ECC memory modules, you must select the **Disabled** mode!

For more information on how ECC works, please refer to the **DRAM Data Integrity Mode** BIOS feature.

SDRAM Idle Limit

Common Options: Disabled, 0 Cycle, 8 Cycles, 12 Cycles, 16 Cycles, 24 Cycles, 32 Cycles, 48 Cycles

The memory controller allows a number of memory pages to remain open. If a processor cycle to the SDRAM falls within those open pages, it can be satisfied without delay. This naturally improves performance.

However, these pages can only remain open for so long. They eventually have to be closed and precharged. If the page closes when the memory controller attempts to read from it, then the read operation is stalled until the page is activated again. Such a page miss is expensive in terms of clock cycles.

This is where the **SDRAM Idle Limit** BIOS feature comes in. This feature sets the number of idle cycles that is allowed before the memory controller forces such open pages to close and precharge.

The premise behind this BIOS feature is the concept of **temporal locality**. According to this concept, the longer the open page is left idle, the less likely it is accessed again before it needs to be precharged. Therefore, it would be better to prematurely close and precharge the page, so it can be opened quickly when a data request comes along.

It can be set to a variety of clock cycles from **0 Cycle** to **48 Cycles**. This sets the number of clock cycles the open pages are allowed to idle before they are closed and precharged. **Disabled** is also an option.

If you select **0 Cycle**, then the memory controller immediately precharges the open pages as soon as there's an idle cycle.

If you select **Disabled**, the memory controller never precharges the open pages prematurely. The open pages are left activated until they have to be precharged.

The default value is **8 cycles**, which allows the memory controller to precharge the open pages after 8 idle cycles have passed.

Increasing the SDRAM Idle Limit to more than the default of **8 cycles** allows the SDRAM bank to delay recharging longer during times of no activity, so if a read or write command comes along, it can be instantly satisfied.

However, this is limited by the refresh cycle already set by the BIOS. That means the open page refreshes when it needs to be recharged whether or not the number of idle cycles have reached the SDRAM Idle Limit. So, the SDRAM Idle Limit setting only can be used to force the refreshing of the SDRAM bank *before* the set refresh cycle but not to actually delay the refresh cycle.

Reducing the number of cycles from the default of 8 cycles to **0 cycles** forces the memory controller to close all open pages after no valid requests are sent to the memory controller. In short, the open pages are refreshed as soon as data requests stop coming. Theoretically, this *may* increase the efficiency of the memory subsystem because the effects of refreshing the open pages are masked by precharging during idle cycles. However, any data requests that comes along after the page is closed have to wait until it is refreshed and activated before they can be satisfied.

Because refreshes do not occur that often (usually only about once every 64 msec), the impact of refreshes on memory performance is really quite minimal. The apparent benefits of masking the refreshes during idle cycles is not noticeable, especially because memory systems these days already use bank interleaving to mask refreshes.

With a **0 cycle** setting, data requests are also likely to get stalled because even a single idle cycle causes the memory controller to close *all* open pages! In desktop applications, most memory reads favor the **spatial locality** concept whereby if one data bit is read, chances are high that the next data bit is also read. That's why closing open pages prematurely using SDRAM Idle Limit most likely causes reduced performance in desktop applications.

On the other hand, using a 0 or 8 idle cycles limit ensures that all memory contents are refreshed more often, thereby preventing the loss of data due to insufficiently refreshed memory cells. Forcing the memory controller to precharge open pages more often also ensures that in the event of a very long read, the pages can be opened long enough to fulfill the data request.

For general desktop use, it is recommended that you **disable** this feature, so precharging can be delayed for as long as possible. This reduces the number of refreshes and increases the effective memory bandwidth.

For applications (for example, servers) that perform a lot of random accesses, it is advisable that you select **0 Cycle** because subsequent data requests are most likely fulfilled by other pages. Closing open pages to precharge prepares those pages for the next data request that hits them. There's also the added benefit of increased data integrity due to more frequent refreshes.

Alternatively, you can greatly increase the value of the **Refresh Interval** or **Refresh Mode Select** feature to boost bandwidth and use this BIOS feature to maintain the data integrity of the memory cells. As ultra-long refresh intervals (for example, 64 or 128 µsec) can cause memory cells to lose their contents, setting a low SDRAM Idle Limit, like **0 Cycle** or **8 Cycles**, allows the memory cells to be refreshed more often with a high chance of those refreshes being done during idle cycles. This appears to combine the best of both worlds—a long bank active period when the memory controller is being stressed and more refreshes when the memory controller is idle.

In reality, however, this is not a reliable way of ensuring sufficient refresh cycles because it depends on the vagaries of memory usage to provide sufficient idle cycles to trigger the refreshes. If your memory subsystem is under extended load, there may not be any idle cycle to trigger an early refresh. This may cause the memory cells to lose their contents.

Therefore, it is recommended that you maintain a proper refresh interval and **disable** this feature (for desktops). This allows you to boost memory bandwidth, by delaying refreshes for as long as possible, and still maintain the data integrity of the memory cells through regular and reliable refresh cycles.

For servers, it is recommended that you maintain a proper refresh interval and use the **0 Cycle** setting. This precharges all open pages whenever there's an idle cycle.

SDRAM Leadoff Command

Common Options: 3, 4

This BIOS feature is actually a misnomer. It actually should be called the **SDRAM Command Leadoff Time**.

To meet different timing requirements, the memory controller will drive signals onto the address and command lines one clock cycle before they are actually needed. This gives the memory controller some additional time to meet the timing requirements of the motherboard.

Although you may think that the early assertion of the address and command lines will help improve performance, that is not true. Even if the memory controller drives the address and command signals one clock cycle earlier, those signals are only latched onto the memory module when none of the memory banks are active.

Once the signals are latched onto the memory module, the target bank is activated and the memory controller starts reading from the active bank. Now, because of the pre-driving of the address and command lines, the activation of the target memory bank is controlled by the **command leadoff time**.

By definition, the **command leadoff time** is the period between the assertion of the address/command lines and the activation of the target memory bank. This BIOS feature allows you to adjust the command leadoff time to meet timing variances of the motherboard as well as the memory module.

The shorter the leadoff time, the earlier the target bank can be activated. This allows faster access to the data in the memory module. Therefore, it is recommended that you set the SDRAM Leadoff Command to **3** clock cycles for better memory performance.

However, your motherboard and memory combination may not be able to support the tighter command leadoff time of **3** clock cycles. If your system becomes unstable with a command leadoff time of **3** clock cycles, revert to the slower command leadoff time of **4** clock cycles.

SDRAM Page Closing Policy

Common Options: One Bank, All Banks

This BIOS feature is similar to **SDRAM Precharge Control**.

The memory controller allows up to four pages to be opened at any one time. These pages have to be in separate memory banks and only one page may be open in each memory bank. If a read request to the SDRAM falls within those open pages, it can be satisfied without delay. This naturally improves performance.

However, if a read request cannot be satisfied by any of the four open pages, there are two possibilities. Either one page is closed and the correct page opened or all open pages are closed and new pages opened up. Either way, the read request suffers the full latency penalty.

This BIOS feature determines if the chipset should try to leave the pages open (by closing just one open page) or keep them closed (by closing all open pages) whenever there is a page miss.

The **One Bank** setting forces the memory controller to close only one page whenever a page miss occurs. This allows the other open pages to be accessed at the cost of only one clock cycle.

However, when a page miss occurs, there is a chance that subsequent data requests result in page misses as well. In long memory reads that cannot be satisfied by any of the open pages, this may cause up to *four* full latency reads to occur. Naturally, this greatly impacts memory performance.

Fortunately, after the four full latency reads, the memory controller can often predict what pages are needed next. It then can open them for minimum latency reads. This somewhat reduces the negative effect of consecutive page misses.

The **All Banks** setting, on the other hand, forces the memory controller to send an **All Banks Precharge Command** to the SDRAM interface whenever there is a page miss. This causes all the open pages to close (precharge). Therefore, subsequent reads only need to activate the necessary memory bank.

This is useful in cases where subsequent data requests also result in page misses. This is because the memory banks already are precharged and ready to be activated. There is no need to wait for the memory banks to precharge before they can be activated. However, it also means that you won't be able to benefit from data accesses that could have been satisfied by the previously opened pages.

As you can see, both settings have their advantages and disadvantages. However, you should see better performance with the **One Bank** setting because the open pages allow very fast accesses. The **All Banks** setting, however, has the advantage of keeping the memory contents refreshed more often. This improves data integrity, although it is only useful if you have chosen a SDRAM **refresh interval** that is longer than the standard 64 msec.

Therefore, it is recommended that you select the **One Bank** setting for better memory performance. The **All Banks** setting can improve data integrity but if you are keeping the SDRAM refresh interval within specification, then it is of little use.

SDRAM Page Hit Limit

Common Options: 1 Cycle, 4 Cycles, 8 Cycles, 16 Cycles, 32 Cycles

The memory controller allows up to four pages to be opened at any one time. These pages have to be in separate memory banks and only one page may be open in each memory bank. If a read request to the SDRAM falls within those open pages, it can be satisfied without delay. This is known as a page hit.

Normally, consecutive page hits offer the best memory performance for the requesting device. However, a flood of consecutive page hit requests can cause non-page hit requests to be delayed for an extended period of time. This does not allow fair system memory access to all devices and may cause problems for devices that generate non-page hit requests.

This BIOS feature is designed to reduce the data starvation that occurs when pending non-page hit requests are unduly delayed. It does so by limiting the number of consecutive **page hit** requests that are processed by the memory controller before attending to a **non-page hit** request.

Please note that whatever you set for this BIOS feature determines the maximum number of consecutive page hits, irrespective of whether the page hits are from the same memory bank or different memory banks. The default value is often **8** consecutive page hit accesses (described erroneously as cycles).

Generally, the default value of **8 Cycles** should provide a balance between performance and fair memory access to all devices. However, you can try using a higher value (**16 Cycles**) for better memory performance by giving priority to a larger number of consecutive page hit requests. A lower value is not advisable because this normally results in a higher number of page interruptions.

SDRAM PH Limit

Common Options: 1 Cycle, 4 Cycles, 8 Cycles, 16 Cycles, 32 Cycles

The memory controller allows up to four pages to be opened at any one time. These pages have to be in separate memory banks and only one page may be open in each memory bank. If a read request to the SDRAM falls within those open pages, it can be satisfied without delay. This is known as a **page hit** (**PH**).

Normally, consecutive page hits offer the best memory performance for the requesting device. However, a flood of consecutive page hit requests can cause non-page hit requests to be delayed for an extended period of time. This does not allow fair system memory access to all devices and may cause problems for devices that generate non-page hit requests.

This BIOS feature is designed to reduce the data starvation that occurs when pending non-page hit requests are unduly delayed. It does so by limiting the number of consecutive **page hit** requests that are processed by the memory controller before attending to a **non-page hit** request.

Please note that whatever you set for this BIOS feature determines the maximum number of consecutive page hits, irrespective of whether the page hits are from the same memory bank or different memory banks. The default value is often **8** consecutive page hit accesses (described erroneously as cycles).

Generally, the default value of **8 Cycles** should provide a balance between performance and fair memory access to all devices. However, you can try using a higher value (**16 Cycles**) for better memory performance by giving priority to a larger number of consecutive page hit requests. A lower value is not advisable because this normally results in a higher number of page interruptions.

S

SDRAM Precharge Control

Common Options: Enabled, Disabled

This BIOS feature is similar to **SDRAM Page Closing Policy**.

The memory controller allows up to four pages to be opened at any one time. These pages have to be in separate memory banks and only one page may be open in each memory bank. If a read request to the SDRAM falls within those open pages, it can be satisfied without delay. This naturally improves performance.

However, if a read request cannot be satisfied by any of the four open pages, there are two possibilities. Either one page is closed and the correct page opened or all open pages are closed and new pages opened up. Either way, the read request suffers the full latency penalty.

This BIOS feature determines whether the chipset should try to leave the pages open (by closing just one open page) or keep them closed (by closing all open pages) whenever there is a page miss.

When **enabled**, the memory controller only closes one page whenever a page miss occurs. This allows the other open pages to be accessed at the cost of only one clock cycle.

However, when a page miss occurs, there is a chance that subsequent data requests result in page misses as well. In long memory reads that cannot be satisfied by any of the open pages, this may cause up to *four* full latency reads to occur. Naturally, this greatly impacts memory performance.

Fortunately, after the four full latency reads, the memory controller can often predict what pages are needed next. It can then open them for minimum latency reads. This somewhat reduces the negative effect of consecutive page misses.

When **disabled**, the memory controller sends an **All Banks Precharge Command** to the SDRAM interface whenever there is a page miss. This causes all the open pages to close (precharge). Therefore, subsequent reads only need to activate the necessary memory bank.

This is useful in cases where subsequent data requests also result in page misses. This is because the memory banks already are precharged and ready to be activated. There is no need to wait for the memory banks to precharge before they can be activated. However, it also means that you won't be able to benefit from data accesses that could have been satisfied by the previously opened pages.

As you can see, both settings have their advantages and disadvantages. However, you should see better performance with this feature **enabled** because the open pages allow very fast accesses. **Disabling** this feature, however, has the advantage of keeping the memory contents refreshed more often. This improves data integrity, although it is only useful if you have chosen a SDRAM **refresh interval** that is longer than the standard 64 msec.

Therefore, it is recommended that you **enable** this feature for better memory performance. **Disabling** this feature can improve data integrity, however, if you are keeping the SDRAM refresh interval within specification, then it is of little use.

SDRAM RAS Precharge Delay

Common Options: 2, 3, 4, 5

Whenever a read command is issued, a memory row is activated using the **RAS**. Then, to read data from the target memory cell, the appropriate column is activated using the **CAS**. Multiple cells can be read from the same active row by applying the appropriate CAS signals.

However, when data has to be read from a different row, the active row has to be deactivated. This introduces a short delay before another row can be activated. This delay is known as the **RAS Precharge Time** or **tRP**.

The appropriate delay for your memory module is reflected in its rated timings. In JEDEC specifications, it is the *third* number in the three or four number sequence. For example, if your memory module has the rated timings of 2-3-4-7, its rated RAS Precharge delay would be 4 clock cycles.

This BIOS feature sets the number of cycles required for the RAS to accumulate its charge before another row can be activated. If the RAS Precharge Time is too long, it will reduce performance by delaying all row activations. Reducing the precharge time to **2** improves performance by allowing a new row to be activated earlier.

However, the short precharge time of 2 may be insufficient for some memory modules. In such cases, the active row may lose its contents before they can be returned to the memory bank and the row deactivated. This may cause data loss or corruption when the memory controller attempts to read from the active row or write to it.

Therefore, it is recommended that you reduce the SDRAM RAS Precharge Delay to **2** for better performance but increase it to **3** or **4** if you experience system stability issues after reducing the precharge time.

SDRAM RAS Precharge Time

Common Options: 2, 3, 4

Whenever a read command is issued, a memory row is activated using the **RAS**. Then, to read data from the target memory cell, the appropriate column is activated using the **CAS**. Multiple cells can be read from the same active row by applying the appropriate CAS signals.

However, when data has to be read from a different row, the active row has to be deactivated. This introduces a short delay before the another row can be activated. This delay is known as the **RAS Precharge Time** or **tRP**.

The appropriate delay for your memory module is reflected in its rated timings. In JEDEC specifications, it is the *third* number in the three- or four-number sequence. For example, if your memory module has the rated timings of 2-3-4-7, its rated RAS Precharge delay is 4 clock cycles.

This BIOS feature sets the number of cycles required for the RAS to accumulate its charge before another row can be activated. If the RAS Precharge Time is too long, it reduces performance by delaying all row activations. Reducing the precharge time to **2** improves performance by allowing a new row to be activated earlier.

However, the short precharge time of 2 may be insufficient for some memory modules. In such cases, the active row may lose its contents before they can be returned to the memory bank and the row deactivated. This may cause data loss or corruption when the memory controller attempts to read from the active row or write to it.

Therefore, it is recommended that you reduce the SDRAM RAS Precharge Time to **2** for better performance but increase it to **3** or **4** if you experience system stability issues after reducing the precharge time.

SDRAM RAS Pulse Width

Common Options: 4, 5, 6, 7, 8, 9

Whenever a read command is issued, a memory row is activated using the **RAS**. Then, to read data from the target memory cell, the appropriate column is activated using the **CAS**. Multiple cells can be read from the same active row by applying the appropriate CAS signals.

However, when data has to be read from a different row, the active row has to be deactivated. However, the row cannot be deactivated until the **Minimum RAS Pulse Width** or **tRAS** has elapsed.

The appropriate delay for your memory module is reflected in its rated timings. In JEDEC specifications, it is the *fourth* number in the four number sequence. For example, if your memory module has the rated timings of 2-3-4-**7**, its rated tRAS delay is 7 clock cycles.

Like **DRAM Act to PreChrg CMD**, this BIOS feature controls the memory bank's minimum row active time (**tRAS**). This constitutes the time when a row is activated until the time the same row can be deactivated.

If the tRAS period is too long, it can reduce performance by unnecessarily delaying the deactivation of active rows. Reducing the tRAS period allows the active row to be deactivated earlier.

However, if the tRAS period is too short, there may not be enough time to complete a burst transfer. This reduces performance and data may be lost or corrupted.

For optimal performance, use the lowest value you can. Usually, this should be **CAS latency + tRCD + 2 clock cycles**. For example, if you set the CAS latency to 2 clock cycles and the tRCD to 3 clock cycles, the optimum tRAS value is 7 clock cycles.

However, if you start getting memory errors or system crashes, increase the tRCD value one clock cycle at a time until your system becomes stable.

SDRAM RAS-to-CAS Delay

Common Options: 2, 3, 4

Whenever a read command is issued, a memory row is activated using the **RAS**. Then, to read data from the target memory cell, the appropriate column is activated using the **CAS**.

However, there is a short delay before the CAS signal can be applied. Because this delay occurs between the Row Address Strobe and the Column Address Strobe, it is known as the **RAS-to-CAS Delay** or **tRCD**. After this delay, multiple columns on the same row can be activated subsequently without incurring the same RAS-to-CAS delay, unless a new row is activated or the row is refreshed.

The appropriate delay for your memory module is reflected in its rated timings. In JEDEC specifications, it is the *second* number in the three or four number sequence. For example, if your memory module has the rated timings of 2-**3**-4-7, its rated RAS-to-CAS delay is 3 clock cycles.

This BIOS feature allows you to set the delay between the RAS and CAS signals. Because this delay occurs whenever the row is refreshed or a new row is activated, reducing the delay improves performance.

Therefore, it is recommended that you **reduce** the delay to **3** or **2** for better memory performance. However, the improvement in performance when you reduce the RAS-to-CAS delay isn't as significant as when you reduce the CAS latency.

Please note that if you use a value that is too low for your memory module, the memory controller may generate the CAS signal before the active row is ready. This can cause the system to be unstable. If your system becomes unstable after you reduce the RAS-to-CAS delay, you should increase the delay or reset it to the rated delay.

Interestingly, increasing the RAS-to-CAS delay may allow the memory module to run at a higher clock speed. So, if you hit a snag while overclocking your SDRAM modules, you can try **increasing** the RAS-to-CAS delay.

SDRAM Row Active Time

Common Options: 4, 5, 6, 7, 8, 9

Whenever a read command is issued, a memory row is activated using the **RAS**. Then, to read data from the target memory cell, the appropriate column is activated using the **CAS**. Multiple cells can be read from the same active row by applying the appropriate CAS signals.

However, when data has to be read from a different row, the active row has to be deactivated. However, the row cannot be deactivated until the **Minimum Row Active Time** or **tRAS** has elapsed.

The appropriate delay for your memory module is reflected in its rated timings. In JEDEC specifications, it is the *fourth* number in the four-number sequence. For example, if your memory module has the rated timings of 2-3-4-**7**, its rated tRAS delay is 7 clock cycles.

Like **DRAM Act to PreChrg CMD**, this BIOS feature controls the memory bank's minimum row active time (**tRAS**). This constitutes the time when a row is activated until the time the same row can be deactivated. It is also the length of time the row remains open for data transfers.

If the tRAS period is too long, it can reduce performance by unnecessarily delaying the deactivation of active rows. Reducing the tRAS period allows the active row to be deactivated earlier.

However, if the tRAS period is too short, there may not be enough time to complete a burst transfer. This reduces performance and data may be lost or corrupted.

For optimal performance, use the lowest value you can. Usually, this should be **CAS latency + tRCD + 2 clock cycles**. For example, if you set the CAS latency to 2 clock cycles and the tRCD to 3 clock cycles, the optimum tRAS value is 7 clock cycles.

However, if you start getting memory errors or system crashes, increase the tRAS value one clock cycle at a time until your system becomes stable.

SDRAM Row Cycle Time

Common Options: 7, 8, 9, 10, 11, 12, 13

This BIOS feature controls the memory module's **Row Cycle Time** or **tRC**. The row cycle time determines the minimum number of clock cycles a memory row takes to complete a full cycle, from row activation up to the precharging of the active row.

Formula-wise, the row cycle time (**tRC**) = minimum row active time (**tRAS**) + row precharge time (**tRP**). Therefore, it is important to find out what the tRAS and tRP parameters are before setting the row cycle time.

The appropriate delay for the **tRAS** delay is reflected in your memory module's rated timings. In JEDEC specifications, it is the *fourth* number in the four number sequence. For example, if your memory module has the rated timings of 2-3-4-**7**, its rated tRAS delay is 7 clock cycles.

S

The appropriate delay for the **tRP** delay is reflected in your memory module's rated timings. In JEDEC specifications, it is the *third* number in the three or four number sequence. For example, if your memory module has the rated timings of 2-3-**4**-7, its rated tRP delay is 4 clock cycles.

If the row cycle time is too long, it can reduce performance by unnecessarily delaying the activation of a new row after a completed cycle. Reducing the row cycle time allows a new cycle to begin earlier.

However, if the row cycle time is too short, a new cycle may be initiated before the active row is sufficiently precharged. When this happens, there may be data loss or corruption.

For optimal performance, use the lowest value you can, according to the **tRC = tRAS + tRP** formula. For example, if your memory module's tRAS is 7 clock cycles and its tRP is 4 clock cycles, then the row cycle time or tRC should be 11 clock cycles.

SDRAM Tras Timing Value

Common Options: 4, 5, 6, 7, 8, 9

Whenever a read command is issued, a memory row is activated using the **RAS**. Then, to read data from the target memory cell, the appropriate column is activated using the **CAS**. Multiple cells can be read from the same active row by applying the appropriate CAS signals.

However, when data has to be read from a different row, the active row has to be deactivated. However, the row cannot be deactivated until the **Minimum Row Active Time** or **tRAS** has elapsed.

The appropriate delay for your memory module is reflected in its rated timings. In JEDEC specifications, it is the *fourth* number in the four number sequence. For example, if your memory module has the rated timings of 2-3-4-**7**, its rated tRAS delay is 7 clock cycles.

Like **DRAM Act to PreChrg CMD**, this BIOS feature controls the memory bank's minimum row active time (**tRAS**). This constitutes the time when a row is activated until the time the same row can be deactivated. It is also the length of time the row remains open for data transfers.

If the tRAS period is too long, it can reduce performance by unnecessarily delaying the deactivation of active rows. Reducing the tRAS period allows the active row to be deactivated earlier.

However, if the tRAS period is too short, there may not be enough time to complete a burst transfer. This reduces performance and data may be lost or corrupted.

For optimal performance, use the lowest value you can. Usually, this should be **CAS latency + tRCD + 2 clock cycles**. For example, if you set the CAS latency to 2 clock cycles and the tRCD to 3 clock cycles, the optimum tRAS value is 7 clock cycles.

However, if you start getting memory errors or system crashes, increase the tRAS value one clock cycle at a time until your system becomes stable.

SDRAM Trc Timing Value

Common Options: 7, 8, 9, 10, 11, 12, 13

This BIOS feature controls the memory module's **Row Cycle Time** or **tRC**. The row cycle time determines the minimum number of clock cycles a memory row takes to complete a full cycle, from row activation up to the precharging of the active row.

Formula-wise, the row cycle time (**tRC**) = minimum row active time (**tRAS**) + row precharge time (**tRP**). Therefore, it is important to find out what the tRAS and tRP parameters are before setting the row cycle time.

The appropriate delay for the **tRAS** delay is reflected in your memory module's rated timings. In JEDEC specifications, it is the *fourth* number in the four-number sequence. For example, if your memory module has the rated timings of 2-3-4-**7**, its rated tRAS delay is 7 clock cycles.

The appropriate delay for the **tRP** delay is reflected in your memory module's rated timings. In JEDEC specifications, it is the *third* number in the three or four number sequence. For example, if your memory module has the rated timings of 2-3-**4**-7, its rated tRP delay is 4 clock cycles.

If the row cycle time is too long, it can reduce performance by unnecessarily delaying the activation of a new row after a completed cycle. Reducing the row cycle time allows a new cycle to begin earlier.

However, if the row cycle time is too short, a new cycle may be initiated before the active row is sufficiently precharged. When this happens, there may be data loss or corruption.

For optimal performance, use the lowest value you can, according to the **tRC = tRAS + tRP** formula. For example, if your memory module's tRAS is 7 clock cycles and its tRP is 4 clock cycles, then the row cycle time or tRC should be 11 clock cycles.

SDRAM Trcd Timing Value

Common Options: 2, 3, 4

Whenever a read command is issued, a memory row is activated using the **RAS**. Then, to read data from the target memory cell, the appropriate column is activated using the **CAS**.

However, there is a short delay before the CAS signal can be applied. Because this delay occurs between the Row Address Strobe and the Column Address Strobe, it is known as the **tRCD timing value** or **tRCD**. After this delay, multiple columns on the same row can be activated subsequently without incurring the same tRCD delay, unless a new row is activated or the row is refreshed.

The appropriate delay for your memory module is reflected in its rated timings. In JEDEC specifications, it is the *second* number in the three or four number sequence. For example, if your memory module has the rated timings of 2-**3**-4-7, its rated tRCD timing value is 3 clock cycles.

This BIOS feature allows you to set the delay between the RAS and CAS signals. Because this delay occurs whenever the row is refreshed or a new row is activated, reducing the delay improves performance.

Therefore, it is recommended that you **reduce** the delay to **3** or **2** for better memory performance. However, the improvement in performance when you reduce the tRCD timing value won't be as significant as when you reduce the CAS latency.

Please note that if you use a value that is too low for your memory module, the memory controller may generate the CAS signal before the active row is ready. This can cause the system to be unstable. If your system becomes unstable after you reduce the tRCD timing value, you should increase the delay or reset it to the rated delay.

Interestingly, increasing the tRCD timing value may allow the memory module to run at a higher clock speed. So, if you hit a snag while overclocking your SDRAM modules, you can try **increasing** the tRCD timing value.

S

SDRAM Trp Timing Value

Common Options: 2, 3, 4

Whenever a read command is issued, a memory row is activated using the **RAS**. Then, to read data from the target memory cell, the appropriate column is activated using the **CAS**. Multiple cells can be read from the same active row by applying the appropriate CAS signals.

However, when data is read from a different row, the active row must be deactivated. This introduces a short delay before the another row can be activated. This delay is known as the **RAS Precharge Time** or **tRP**.

The appropriate delay for your memory module is reflected in its rated timings. In JEDEC specifications, it is the *third* number in the three or four number sequence. For example, if your memory module has the rated timings of 2-3-4-7, its rated tRP delay is 4 clock cycles.

This BIOS feature sets the number of cycles required for the RAS to accumulate its charge before another row can be activated. If the tRP timing value is too long, it reduces performance by delaying all row activations. Reducing the precharge time to **2** improves performance by allowing a new row to be activated earlier.

However, the short precharge time of 2 may be insufficient for some memory modules. In such cases, the active row may lose its contents before they can be returned to the memory bank and the row deactivated. This may cause data loss or corruption when the memory controller attempts to read from the active row or write to it.

Therefore, it is recommended that you reduce the SDRAM tRP timing value to **2** for better performance but increase it to **3** or **4** if you experience system stability issues after reducing the precharge time.

SDRAM Trrd Timing Value

Common Options: 2 cycles, 3 cycles

The **Bank-to-Bank Delay** or **tRRD** is a DDR timing parameter which specifies the minimum amount of time between successive ACTIVATE commands to the **same** DDR device, even to **different** internal banks. The shorter the delay, the faster the next bank can be activated for read or write operations. However, because row activation requires a lot of current, using a short delay may cause excessive current surges.

Because this timing parameter is DDR device-specific, it may differ from one DDR device to another. DDR DRAM manufacturers typically specify the tRRD parameter based on the row ACTIVATE activity to limit current surges within the device. If you let the BIOS automatically configure your DRAM parameters, it retrieves the manufacturer-set tRRD value from the **SPD** (**Serial Presence Detect**) chip. However, you may want to manually set the tRRD parameter to suit your requirements.

For desktop PCs, a delay of **2 cycles** is recommended because current surges aren't really important. This is because the desktop PC essentially has an unlimited power supply and even the most basic desktop cooling solution is sufficient to dispel any extra thermal load that the current surges may impose. The performance benefit of using the shorter 2 cycles delay is of far greater interest. The shorter delay means every back-to-back bank activation takes one clock cycle less to perform. This improves the DDR device's read and write performance.

Note that the shorter delay of **2 cycles** works with most DDR DIMMs, even at 133MHz (266MHz DDR). However, DDR DIMMs running beyond 133MHz (266MHz DDR) may need to introduce a delay of 3 cycles between each successive bank activation. Select **2 cycles** whenever possible for optimal DDR DRAM performance. Switch to **3 cycles** only when there are stability problems with the 2 cycles setting.

In mobile devices like laptops however, it is advisable to use the longer delay of **3 cycles**. Doing so limits the current surges that accompany row activations. This reduces the DDR device's power consumption and thermal output, both of which should be of great interest to the road warrior.

SDRAM Write Recovery Time

Common Options: 1 Cycle, 2 Cycles, 3 Cycles

This BIOS feature controls the **Write Recovery Time (tWR)** of the memory modules.

It specifies the amount of delay (in clock cycles) that must elapse after the completion of a valid write operation before an active bank can be precharged. This delay is required to guarantee that data in the write buffers can be written to the memory cells before precharge occurs.

If the delay is too short, the bank may be precharged before the active bank has enough time to store the write data in the memory cells. This causes data to be lost or corrupted.

Please note that this BIOS feature does *not* determine the time it takes for the bank to precharge. It only controls how soon the bank can *start* precharging right after a write operation to the same bank.

The shorter the delay, the earlier the bank can be precharged for another read/write operation. This improves performance but runs the risk of corrupting data written to the memory cells.

The default value is **2 Cycles**, which meets JEDEC specifications in DDR200 and DDR266 memory modules. DDR333 and DDR400 memory modules require a Write Recovery Time of **3 Cycles**.

It is recommended that you select **2 Cycles** if you are using DDR200 or DDR266 memory modules and **3 Cycles** if you are using DDR333 or DDR 400 memory modules. You can try using a shorter delay for better memory performance, however, if you face stability issues, revert to the specified delay to correct the problem.

S

SDRAM Write to Read Command Delay

Common Options: 1 Cycle, 2 Cycles

This BIOS feature controls the **Write Data In to Read Command Delay (tWTR)** memory timing. This constitutes the minimum number of clock cycles that must occur between the last valid write operation and the next *read* command to the **same** internal bank of the DDR device.

Please note that this is only applicable for read commands that follow a write operation. Consecutive read operations or writes that follow reads are not affected.

If a **1 Cycle** delay is selected, every read command that follows a write operation is delayed **one clock cycle** before it is issued.

If a **2 Cycles** delay is selected, every read command that follows a write operation is delayed **two clock cycles** before it is issued.

The **1 Cycle** option naturally offers faster switching from writes to reads and, consequently, better read performance.

The **2 Cycles** option reduces read performance, however, it improves stability, especially at higher clock speeds. It may also allow the memory chips to run at a higher speed. In other words, increasing this delay may allow you to overclock the memory module higher than is normally possible.

By default, this BIOS feature is set to **2 Cycles**. This meets JEDEC's specification of 2 clock cycles for write-to-read command delay in DDR400 memory modules. DDR266 and DDR333 memory modules require a write-to-read command delay of only 1 clock cycle.

It is recommended that you select the **1 Cycle** option for better memory read performance if you are using DDR266 or DDR333 memory modules. You can also try using the **1 Cycle** option with DDR400 memory modules. However, if you face stability issues, revert to the default setting of **2 Cycles**.

Second Boot Device

Common Options: Floppy, LS/ZIP, HDD-0, SCSI, CDROM, HDD-1, HDD-2, HDD-3, LAN, Disabled

This BIOS feature allows you to select the **second** device from which the BIOS attempts to load an operating system. If the BIOS finds and loads an operating system from the device selected through this feature, it doesn't load another operating system, even if you have one on a different device.

For example, if you set **Floppy** as the first boot device and **HDD-0** as the second boot device, the BIOS boots straight into the Windows 98 installation on your hard disk and ignores the Windows XP installation CD in your CD-ROM drive *if* there is no bootable disk in the floppy drive. In short, this feature allows you to choose the second device from which to boot.

By default, **HDD-0** is the second boot device in practically all motherboards. However, unless you boot often from the floppy drive (which is often the first boot device), it is better to set your hard disk (**HDD-0**) as the first boot device. This shortens the boot process because the BIOS no longer needs to check the floppy drive for a bootable operating system.

More importantly, doing so prevents the BIOS from loading the wrong operating system in case you forgot to remove the boot disk from the floppy drive! This also indirectly prevents the loading of any virus-infected floppy disk that was left in the drive during booting.

Security Setup

Common Options: System, Setup

This BIOS feature controls the application of the BIOS' password protection. It only works after you have created a password through the **Password Setting** option in the main BIOS screen.

Selecting the **System** option forces the BIOS to ask for the password every time the system boots up.

If you choose **Setup**, then the password is only required for access to the BIOS. This option is useful for system administrators or computer resellers who need to keep novice users from messing around with the BIOS.:

Shadowing Address Ranges

Common Options: C8000–CBFFF, CC000–CFFFF, D0000–D3FF, D4000–D7FFF, D8000–DBFFF, DC000–DFFFF, Disabled

This BIOS feature allows you to cordon off specific memory blocks (xxxx–xxxx) to shadow the BIOS of certain add-on cards. This improves the performance of cards that are accessed and controlled through their BIOS, as opposed to drivers. Currently, this is mostly limited to bootable network cards.

For most users, there is absolutely no need for this feature as modern operating systems directly access hardware through drivers. Shadowing your device's BIOS just wastes memory. Therefore, it is recommended that you **disable** this feature.

According to the Microsoft article *Shadowing BIOS Under WinNT 4.0*, shadowing the BIOS (irrespective of what BIOS it is) does not bring about any performance enhancements because it is not used by Windows NT. It only wastes memory. Although the article did not say anything about other versions of Microsoft Windows, this is true for all versions of Microsoft Windows, from Windows 95 onward.

In addition, if you are using an add-on card that uses the CXXXX–EFFFF area for I/O, shadowing that memory block may prevent the card from working because read or write requests might not be passed on to the ISA bus.

Share Memory Size

Common Options: 1MB, 4MB, 8MB, 16MB, 32MB, 64MB

Some motherboard chipsets come with an integrated **GPU (Graphics Processing Unit)**. This GPU usually makes use of the **UMA (Unified Memory Architecture)** for its memory requirements. This means the graphics processor will take a portion of the system memory to use as its own memory buffer.

Using a portion of system memory for the graphics processor's use allows the motherboard manufacturer to offer a low-cost graphics solution. It also allows the user to change the size of the graphics memory buffer to suit different applications.

However, this technology has the following disadvantages:

- Allocating system memory to the GPU reduces the amount of system memory available for the operating system and programs to use.
- Sharing system memory with the GPU saturates the memory bus and reduces the amount of memory bandwidth for both the processor and the graphics processor.

Therefore, integrated GPUs are usually unsuitable for high-demand 3D applications and games. They are best used for basic 2D graphics and video functions.

This BIOS feature controls the amount of system memory that is allocated to the integrated GPU.

The selection of memory sizes allows you to select how much system memory you want to allocate to the integrated GPU. The amount you allocate to the GPU is deducted from the amount of system memory available to your operating system and programs.

Please note that unlike the **AGP Aperture Size**, once the system memory ia allocated to the GPU, it cannot be used by anything else. Even if the GPU does not make use of it, it is not available to the operating system.

Therefore, it is recommended that you select the absolute minimum amount of system memory that the GPU requires for your monitor. You can calculate it by multiplying the resolution and color depth that you are using.

For example, if you use a resolution of 1600×1200 and a color depth of 32-bit, the amount of memory your GPU requires will be $1600 \times 1200 \times 32\text{-bits} = 61,440,000$ bits or 7.68MB. You should set this BIOS feature to **8MB** in this example.

Slave Drive PIO Mode

Common Options: Auto, 0, 1, 2, 3, 4

This BIOS feature is usually found under the **Onboard IDE-1 Controller** or **Onboard IDE-2 Controller** feature. It is linked to one of the IDE channels, so if you disable one, the corresponding Slave Drive PIO Mode option for that IDE channel either disappears or becomes grayed out.

This BIOS feature allows you to set the **PIO (Programmed Input/Output)** mode for the Slave IDE drive attached to that particular IDE channel. Here is a table of the different PIO transfer rates and their corresponding maximum throughputs.

PIO Data Transfer Mode	Maximum Throughput
PIO Mode 0	3.3 MB/s
PIO Mode 1	5.2 MB/s
PIO Mode 2	8.3 MB/s
PIO Mode 3	11.1 MB/s
PIO Mode 4	16.6 MB/s

Setting this BIOS feature to **Auto** lets the BIOS auto-detect the IDE drive's maximum supported PIO mode at boot-up.

Setting this BIOS feature to **0** forces the BIOS to use **PIO Mode 0** for the IDE drive.

Setting this BIOS feature to **1** forces the BIOS to use **PIO Mode 1** for the IDE drive.

Setting this BIOS feature to **2** forces the BIOS to use **PIO Mode 2** for the IDE drive.

Setting this BIOS feature to **3** forces the BIOS to use **PIO Mode 3** for the IDE drive.

Setting this BIOS feature to **4** forces the BIOS to use **PIO Mode 4** for the IDE drive.

Normally, you should leave it as **Auto** and let the BIOS autodetect the IDE drive's PIO mode. You should only set it manually for the following reasons:

- If the BIOS cannot detect the correct PIO mode.
- If you want to try forcing the IDE device to use a faster PIO mode than it was designed for.
- If you want to force the IDE device to use a slower PIO mode if it cannot work properly with the current PIO mode (for example, when the PCI bus is overclocked).

Please note that forcing an IDE device to use a PIO transfer rate that is faster than what it is rated for can potentially cause data corruption.

Slave Drive UltraDMA

Common Options: Auto, Disabled

This BIOS feature is usually found under the **Onboard IDE-1 Controller** or **Onboard IDE-2 Controller** feature. It is linked to one of the IDE channels, so if you disable one, the corresponding Slave Drive UltraDMA function for that IDE channel either disappears or is grayed out.

This BIOS feature allows you to enable or disable **DMA** (**Direct Memory Access**) support (if available) for the Slave IDE device attached to that particular IDE channel. For easy reference, here is a table of the different DMA transfer rates and their corresponding maximum throughputs.

DMA Transfer Mode	Maximum Throughput
DMA Mode 0	4.16 MB/s
DMA Mode 1	13.3 MB/s
DMA Mode 2	16.6 MB/s
UltraDMA 33	33.3 MB/s
UltraDMA 66	66.7 MB/s
UltraDMA 100	100.0 MB/s
UltraDMA 133	133.3 MB/s

Setting this BIOS feature to **Auto** lets the BIOS autodetect the IDE drive's maximum supported DMA mode at boot-up.

Setting this BIOS feature to **Disabled** forces the BIOS to disable DMA transfers for the IDE drive.

Normally, you should leave it as **Auto** and let the BIOS autodetect the drive's DMA support. If the drive supports DMA transfers, the proper DMA transfer mode is enabled for that drive, allowing it to burst data at anywhere from 33MB/s to 133MB/s (depending on the transfer mode supported).

You should only **disable** it for troubleshooting purposes. For example, certain IDE devices may not run properly using DMA transfers when the PCI bus is overclocked. Disabling DMA support forces the drive to use the slower PIO transfer mode. This may allow the drive to work properly with the higher PCI bus speed.

Please note that setting this to **Auto** does *not* enable DMA transfers for IDE devices that do not support DMA transfers. If your drive does not support DMA transfers, the BIOS automatically sets the drive to do PIO transfers only.

Also note that this BIOS feature merely enables DMA transfers during the booting up process and for operating systems that do not load their own drivers for IDE functions. For operating systems that use their own IDE drivers (for example, Windows 9x/2000/XP), you have to enable DMA support for the drive within the operating system as well.

In Windows 9x, this can be accomplished by ticking the **DMA checkbox** in the properties sheet of the IDE drive in question. In Windows 2000/XP, you have to set the transfer mode of the IDE device to **DMA If Available** in the Advanced Settings tab of the associated IDE channel's properties page.

Speed Error Hold

Common Options: Enabled, Disabled

This BIOS feature prevents accidental overclocking by preventing the system from booting up if the processor clock speed was not properly set.

It is very useful for novice users who want nothing to do with overclocking. Yet, they may inadvertently set the wrong processor speed in the BIOS and either prevent the system from booting up at all or cause the system to crash or hang.

When **enabled**, the BIOS checks the processor clock speed at boot up and halts the boot process if the clock speed is different from that imprinted in the processor ID. It also displays an error message to warn you that the processor is running at the wrong speed.

To correct the situation, you have to access the BIOS and correct the processor speed. Most BIOSes, however, automatically reset the processor to the correct speed. All you have to do then is access the BIOS, verify the clock speed, and save the changes made in the BIOS.

If you are thinking of overclocking the processor, you must **disable** this feature because it prevents the motherboard from booting up with an overclocked processor. When **disabled**, the BIOS does *not* check the processor clock speed at boot up. It allows the system to boot with the clock speed set in the BIOS, even if it does not match the processor's rated clock speed (as imprinted in the processor ID).

Although this may seem really obvious, I have seen countless overclocking initiates puzzling over the error message whenever they try to overclock their processors. So, before you start pulling your hair out and screaming hysterically that Intel or AMD has finally implemented a clock speed lock on their processors, try **disabling** this feature.

Split Lock Operations

Common Options: Enabled, Disabled

This is a debug feature specific to the Intel Pentium 4 and the Intel Pentium 4 Xeon processors. It allows you to prevent the processor from issuing split lock cycles to the processor bus if such operations cause problems.

Split lock cycles can potentially cause problems in certain situations—for example, the **Split Lock Cycles** bug in the Intel 82860 MCH. This bug causes the system to hang when two split-locked cycles are issued to a write-only **PAM (Programmable Attribute Map)** region, followed by two more writes to the same region.

Usually, it is recommended that you leave Split Lock Operation at its default setting of **Enabled**. This allows the processor to issue split lock cycles to the processor bus.

However, if you are using a motherboard based on the Intel 82860 chipset, you should **disable** this feature. This forces the processor to issue Alignment Check (#AC) exceptions to the processor bus instead of split lock cycles.

There may be other situations where split lock cycles can cause problems. If your system hangs or crashes for no apparent reason, you can try disabling this feature and see if it solves the problem. Otherwise, leave it **Enabled**.

Spread Spectrum

Common Options: 0.25%, 0.5%, Smart Clock, Disabled

When the motherboard's clock generator pulses, the extreme values (spikes) of these signals generated create **EMI (Electromagnetic Interference)**. This EMI interferes with other electronics in the area. There are also claims that it may allow electronic eavesdropping of the data that is being transmitted.

This BIOS feature allows you to reduce the EMI of your motherboard by modulating the signals it generates, so the spikes are reduced to flatter curves. It achieves this by varying the frequency *slightly*, so the signal does not use any particular frequency for more than a moment. This reduces the amount of EMI generated by the motherboard.

The BIOS usually offers two levels of modulation—**0.25%** or **0.5%**. They denote the amount of modulation or jitter from the baseline signal. The greater the modulation, the greater the reduction of EMI. Therefore, if you need to significantly reduce your motherboard's EMI, a modulation of **0.5%** is recommended.

In most conditions, frequency modulation through this feature should not cause any problems. However, system stability may be slightly compromised in certain situations. For example, this BIOS feature may cause improper functioning of timing-critical devices, such as clock-sensitive SCSI devices.

Spread Spectrum can also cause problems with overclocked systems, especially those that have been taken to extremes. Even a slight modulation of frequency may cause the processor or any other overclocked components of the system to fail, leading to very predictable consequences. Of course, this depends on the amount of modulation, the extent of overclocking and other factors like temperature, and so forth. As such, the problem may not manifest itself immediately.

Therefore, it is recommended that you **disable** this feature if you are overclocking your system. The risk of crashing your system is not worth the reduction in EMI. Of course, if EMI reduction is important to you, **enable** this feature by all means. However, you should reduce the clock speed a little to provide a margin of safety.

If you are not overclocking, the decision to enable or disable this feature is really up to you. However, unless you have EMI problems or sensitive data that must be safeguarded from electronic eavesdropping, it is best to **disable** this feature to remove the possibility of stability issues.

S

Some BIOSes also offer a **Smart Clock** option. This works differently from Spread Spectrum, although it is usually offered as a Spread Spectrum option.

Instead of modulating the frequency of signals over time, Smart Clock turns off the AGP, PCI, and SDRAM clock signals that are not in use. Therefore, EMI can be reduced *without* compromising system stability. As a bonus, using Smart Clock also helps reduce power consumption. The degree of EMI and power reduction depends on the number of empty AGP, PCI, and SDRAM slots. However, generally, Smart Clock is unable to reduce EMI as effectively as simple frequency modulation.

With that said, it is recommended that you **enable Smart Clock** instead of using the **0.25%** or **5%** option, if the option is available to you. It allows you to reduce some EMI without any risk of compromising your computer's stability.

Super Bypass Mode

Common Options: Enabled, Disabled

This BIOS feature basically allows the **memory request organizer** (**MRO**) of the memory controller to skip certain pipeline stages while transferring data to and from the memory subsystem.

This improves memory performance by allowing lower latency accesses to the memory subsystem. However, this feature only can be safely enabled if the following conditions are true:

1. The system only has a *single processor* present. Systems using dual-processor motherboards can enable this feature if only *one* processor is present.

2. The processor clock speed multiplier must be *4 or greater*. This means the processor must be running at least four times faster than its bus speed.

For better memory performance, it is recommended that you **enable** this feature. However, you must make sure that you are only using a single processor that is running at least four times faster than the processor bus. You should **disable** this feature if your system does not meet the two requirements stated above.

Super Bypass Wait State

Common Options: 0 Cycle, 1 Cycle

This BIOS feature is used to fine-tune the **Super Bypass** feature to correct for internal timing variations.

When set to **0 Cycle**, the memory controller initiates all super bypass requests without delay.

When set to **1 Cycle**, the memory controller forces a wait state delay for all super bypass requests.

Official documents recommend that a wait state be added for a 133MHz (266MHz DDR) memory bus. Systems using a 100MHz (200MHz DDR) memory bus do not need this delay. Of course, those are just safe, official recommendations for this feature.

Forcing a wait state on all super bypass requests reduces the effectiveness of the **Super Bypass** feature. Therefore, it is recommended that you try using the **0 Cycle** setting for maximum performance. It should work even with memory clock speeds that are greater than 133MHz (266MHz DDR).

However, if you experience system stability issues after using this **0 Cycle** setting, set this feature to **1 Cycle**. This slows down super bypass transactions but allows your system to use the **Super Bypass** feature at higher clock speeds.

SuperStability Mode

Common Options: Enabled, Disabled

This is a **NVIDIA nForce** chipset-specific BIOS feature. It controls the hitherto hidden "feature" of the nForce chipset, which *locks* the memory clock at **200MHz** instead of the rated **266MHz** when it detects a memory module that is not compatible with the motherboard. This allows the use of substandard or incompatible memory modules, albeit at reduced performance.

At boot-up, the nForce chipset reads the SPD values from each memory module to detect its rated speed, timings, and size. This is where the **SuperStability** feature kicks in.

The chipset only allows the memory clock to be set at 266MHz when it is satisfied that each and every memory module installed has met its standard. If even a single module fails to meet the standard, the chipset locks the memory clock at 200MHz, irrespective of the clock speed at which it was set to run. Even if you attempt to run it at a higher speed, the memory clock remains locked at 200MHz.

Although NVIDIA claims that this feature allows nForce motherboards to work with substandard or incompatible memory modules that would otherwise be unusable, there have been reports that even compatible memory modules are being locked down to 200MHz. Apparently, loading the second slot (Slot B) of the second memory controller with a **double-sided** DIMM also causes SuperStability to kick in.

As you know, the NVIDIA nForce is the first chipset to offer a dual-channel DDR interface, albeit with only three DIMM slots. NVIDIA arranged it so the first DIMM slot has a memory controller all to itself, while the second and third DIMM slots have to share the second memory controller. It is the second slot of this second memory controller that is not compatible with double-sided memory modules.

However, it is not clear if this is due to a bug in the chipset or because the slot was not designed or rated for double-sided modules. What is clear is that if a double-sided module is inserted into the second slot (Slot B) of the second memory controller, it causes the SuperStability feature of the nForce chipset to lock the memory clock at 200MHz.

Please note that Slot B of the second memory controller is not necessarily the third DIMM slot. It can vary between motherboard models. The only way to identify Slot B of the second memory controller is to test it yourself.

After this feature was discovered by Chris Connolly of GamePC, the BIOS was revised to include this **SuperStability Mode** feature. This allows you to switch the SuperStability feature on or off.

When left at the default setting of **Enabled**, the nForce chipset lock the memory clock at 200MHz if it detects an incompatible memory module or if Slot B of the second memory controller is filled with a double-sided memory module.

S

When **disabled**, the nForce chipset does not check the memory modules for incompatibility or Slot B of the second memory controller for a double-sided memory module. The memory modules are allowed to run at the clock speed you set.

It is highly recommended that you **disable** SuperStability Mode for better SDRAM performance, especially if you use all three DIMM slots. There is really no need to enable it because you can lower the memory clock speed yourself or increase their timings in order to use incompatible memory modules.

Swap Floppy Drive

Common Options: Enabled, Disabled

This BIOS feature is used to logically swap the mapping of drives A: and B:. Therefore, it is only useful if you have two floppy drives.

Normally, the sequence by which you connect the floppy drives to the cable determines which is drive A: and which is drive B:. If you attach the floppy drives the wrong way and obtain a drive mapping that is not to your satisfaction, the usual way of correcting this is to physically swap the floppy cable connectors.

This feature allows you to swap the logical arrangement of the floppy drives without the need to open up the case and physically swap the connectors.

When this BIOS feature is **enabled**, the floppy drive that originally was mapped to drive A: is remapped to drive B: and vice versa for the drive that was originally set as drive B:.

When this BIOS feature is **disabled**, the floppy drive mapping remains as that set by the drive connector arrangement.

Although this appears to be nothing more than a feature of convenience, it can be quite important if you are using two floppy drives of different form factors (3.5" and 5.25") and you need to boot from the second drive. Because the BIOS can only boot from drive A:, you have to physically swap the drive connections or use this feature to do it logically.

If your floppy drive mapping is correct or if you only have a single floppy drive, there is no need to enable this feature. Leave it at the default setting of **disabled**.

Synchronous Mode Select

Common Options: Synchronous, Asynchronous

This BIOS feature controls the signal synchronization of the DRAM-CPU interface.

When set to **Synchronous**, the chipset synchronizes the signals from the DRAM controller with signals from the CPU bus (or front side bus). Please note that for the signals to be synchronous, the DRAM controller and the CPU bus must run at the same clock speed.

When set to **Asynchronous**, the chipset decouples the DRAM controller from the CPU bus. This allows the DRAM controller and the CPU bus to run at different clock speeds.

Generally, it is advisable to use the **Synchronous** setting because a synchronized interface allows data transfers to occur without delay. This results in a much higher throughput between the CPU bus and the DRAM controller.

However, the **Asynchronous** mode does have its uses. Users of multiplier-locked processors and slow memory modules may find that using the Asynchronous mode allows them to over-clock the processor much higher without the need to buy faster memory modules.

The **Asynchronous** mode is also useful for those who have very fast memory modules and multiplier-locked processors with low bus speeds. Running the fast memory modules synchro-nously with the low CPU bus speed forces the memory modules to run at the same slow speed. Running asynchronously, therefore, allows the memory modules to run at a much higher speed than the CPU bus.

However, please note that the performance gains of running synchronously cannot be underesti-mated. Synchronous operations are generally much faster than asynchronous operations running at a higher clock speed. It is advisable that you compare benchmark scores of your computer running asynchronously (at a higher clock speed) and synchronously to determine the best option for your system.

System BIOS Cacheable

Common Options: Enabled, Disabled

This BIOS feature is only valid if the motherboard BIOS is shadowed. However, because moth-erboard BIOS shadowing is hardwired into most motherboards, this is really a moot point.

Enabling this feature allows the caching of the motherboard BIOS ROM from **F0000h** to **FFFFFh** by the processor's **Level 2 cache**. This greatly speeds up accesses to the BIOS.

However, this does not translate into better system performance because modern operating sys-tems like Microsoft Windows XP do not need to communicate with the hardware through the BIOS. Current operating systems make use of drivers to access the hardware directly.

Therefore, it would be a waste of the Level 2 cache's bandwidth if the motherboard BIOS was cached instead of data that are more critical to the system's performance. The motherboard BIOS is loaded only when the computer boots up and rarely thereafter. It is very unlikely to be requested again, so it is really quite pointless to cache it.

In addition, if any errant program writes into this memory area, it results in a system crash. Therefore, it is highly recommended that you **disable** this feature for better system performance.

You should only consider **enabling** this BIOS feature if you are using an operating system that still communicates with hardware through the BIOS like **MS-DOS**. If so, caching the mother-board BIOS boosts performance.

S

T

Third Boot Device

Common Options: Floppy, LS/ZIP, HDD-0, SCSI, CDROM, HDD-1, HDD-2, HDD-3, LAN, Disabled

This BIOS feature allows you to select the **third** device from which the BIOS attempt to load an operating system. If the BIOS finds and loads an operating system from the device selected through this feature, it won't load another operating system, even if you have one on a different device.

For example, if you set **Floppy** as the first boot device, **HDD-0** as the second boot device, and **SCSI** as the third boot device, the BIOS boots straight into the Windows 98 installation on your SCSI hard disk and ignores the Windows XP installation CD in your CD-ROM drive *if* there is no bootable IDE hard disk or bootable floppy disk. In short, this feature allows you to choose the third device from which to boot.

By default, **LS/ZIP** is the third boot device in practically all motherboards. Because the third boot device is only tried after no bootable operating system can be found in the first two boot devices, it is of little consequence what you set here. Therefore, the choice of boot device for this BIOS feature is entirely up to your personal preference.

TX, RX Inverting Enable

Common Options: No-No, No-Yes, Yes-No, Yes-Yes

This BIOS feature allows you to set the infra-red reception (**RxD**) and transmission (**TxD**) polarity.

It is usually found under the **Onboard Serial Port 2** BIOS feature and is linked to the second serial port. So, if you disable that port, this feature disappears from the screen or appears grayed out.

There are four options available, based on combinations of **Yes** (read as **High**) and **No** (read as **Low**). You'll need to consult your IR peripheral's documentation to determine the correct polarity. Choosing the wrong polarity prevents a proper IR connection from being established with the IR peripheral.

Typematic Rate

Common Options: 6, 8, 10, 12, 15, 20, 24, 30

This BIOS feature only works if the **Typematic Rate Setting** feature has been **enabled**.

This feature determines the rate at which the keyboard repeats a keystroke if you press it continuously.

The available settings are in characters per second. Therefore, a typematic rate of **30** causes the keyboard to repeat the keystroke at a rate of 30 characters per second if you press a particular key continuously. The higher the typematic rate, the faster the keyboard repeats the keystroke.

The choice of what setting to use is entirely up to your personal preference. However, note that this typematic rate is only applicable in operating systems that communicate with the hardware through the BIOS, like **MS-DOS**. The typematic rate in operating systems like Windows XP are controlled by the keyboard driver's settings.

Typematic Rate Delay

Common Options: 250, 500, 750, 1000

This BIOS setting only works if the **Typematic Rate Setting** feature has been enabled.

This feature determines how long, in **milliseconds** (thousandths of a second), the keyboard controller waits before it starts repeating the keystroke that you have pressed continuously. The longer the delay, the longer the keyboard controller waits before it starts repeating the keystroke.

Generally, using a short delay is useful for people who type quickly and don't like to wait long for a keystroke to be repeated. On the other hand, a long delay is useful for users who tend to press the keys longer while typing. This prevents the keyboard controller from unnecessarily repeating keystrokes with such users.

Typematic Rate Setting

Common Options: Enabled, Disabled

This BIOS feature allows you to gain manual control of the keystroke repeat feature.

When **enabled**, you are given access to these two typematic controls:

- Typematic Rate
- Typematic Rate Delay

They allow you to manually adjust the **Typematic Rate** and the **Typematic Rate Delay**.

If you **disable** this feature, the two typematic controls are disabled and grayed out. The keyboard controller thereby uses the default typematic rate and typematic rate delay.

T

Ultra DMA Mode

Common Options: Disabled, 0, 1, 2, 3, 4, 5, 6, Auto

This BIOS feature allows you to enable or disable **DMA (Direct Memory Access)** support (if available) for the IDE device. For easy reference, here is a table of the different DMA transfer rates and their corresponding maximum throughputs.

DMA Transfer Mode	Maximum Throughput
DMA Mode 0	4.16 MB/s
DMA Mode 1	13.3 MB/s
DMA Mode 2	16.6 MB/s
UltraDMA 33	33.3 MB/s
UltraDMA 66	66.7 MB/s
UltraDMA 100	100.0 MB/s
UltraDMA 133	133.3 MB/s

Setting this BIOS feature to **Disabled** forces the BIOS to disable DMA transfers for the IDE drive.

Setting this BIOS feature to **0** forces the BIOS to use **DMA Mode 0** for DMA transfers.

Setting this BIOS feature to **1** forces the BIOS to use **DMA Mode 1** for DMA transfers.

Setting this BIOS feature to **2** forces the BIOS to use **DMA Mode 2** for DMA transfers.

Setting this BIOS feature to **3** forces the BIOS to use **UltraDMA 33** for DMA transfers.

Setting this BIOS feature to **4** forces the BIOS to use **UltraDMA 66** for DMA transfers.

Setting this BIOS feature to **5** forces the BIOS to use **UltraDMA 100** for DMA transfers.

Setting this BIOS feature to **6** forces the BIOS to use **UltraDMA 133** for DMA transfers.

Setting this BIOS feature to **Auto** lets the BIOS auto-detect the IDE drive's maximum supported DMA mode at boot-up.

Normally, you should leave it as **Auto** and let the BIOS auto-detect the drive's DMA support. If the drive supports DMA transfers, the proper DMA transfer mode is enabled for that drive, allowing it to burst data from anywhere between 33MB/s to 133MB/s (depending on the transfer mode supported).

You should only **disable** it for troubleshooting purposes. For example, certain IDE devices may not run properly using DMA transfers when the PCI bus is overclocked. Disabling DMA support forces the drive to use the slower PIO transfer mode. This may allow the drive to work properly with the higher PCI bus speed.

Please note that setting this to **Auto** or any of the DMA options does *not* enable DMA transfers for IDE devices that do not support DMA transfers. If your drive does not support DMA transfers, the BIOS automatically sets the drive to do PIO transfers only.

Also note that this BIOS feature merely enables DMA transfers during the booting up process and only for operating systems that do not load their own drivers for IDE functions. For operating systems that use their own IDE drivers (for example, Windows 9x/2000/XP), you have to enable DMA support for the drive within the operating system as well.

In Windows 9x, this can be accomplished by ticking the **DMA checkbox** in the properties sheet of the IDE drive in question. In Windows 2000/XP, you have to set the transfer mode of the IDE device to **DMA If Available** in the Advanced Settings tab of the associated IDE channel's properties page.

UltraDMA-100 IDE Controller

Common Options: Enabled, Disabled

This BIOS feature is only found in certain motherboards that come with an additional built-in IDE controller. It allows you to enable or disable the function of that IDE controller.

Please note that the IDE controller covered by this BIOS feature is different from the chipset's own IDE controller. This extra UltraDMA/100 IDE controller is often added to provide UltraDMA/100 support in motherboards with chipsets that do not support UltraDMA/100.

Even if the motherboard's chipset has an IDE controller that supports UltraDMA/100, it is not controlled by this BIOS feature. This BIOS feature is only used to control the additional IDE controller built into the motherboard.

To avoid confusion, I shall henceforth refer to the chipset's IDE controller as the **internal** IDE controller while the additional IDE controller will be known as the **external** IDE controller.

If you want to attach one or more IDE devices to the external UltraDMA/100 controller, you should **enable** this feature. You should only **disable** this BIOS feature for the following reasons:

- If you do not have any IDE device attached to the external UltraDMA/100 controller
- For troubleshooting purposes

Disabling the external IDE controller frees up two IRQs, which can be used by other devices in the system. It also speeds up the boot-up sequence because the external IDE controller's BIOS no longer needs to be loaded. Your system is also able to skip the external controller's long boot-up check and initialization sequence.

Therefore, if you do not use the external IDE controller, it is recommended that you **disable** it for a much faster booting process.

UltraDMA-133 IDE Controller

Common Options: Enabled, Disabled

This BIOS feature is only found in certain motherboards that come with an additional built-in IDE controller. It allows you to enable or disable the function of that IDE controller.

Please note that the IDE controller covered by this BIOS feature is different from the chipset's own IDE controller. This extra UltraDMA/133 IDE controller is often added to provide UltraDMA/133 support in motherboards with chipsets that do not support UltraDMA/133.

Even if the motherboard's chipset has an IDE controller that supports UltraDMA/133, it is not controlled by this BIOS feature. This BIOS feature is only used to control the additional IDE controller built into the motherboard.

To avoid confusion, I shall henceforth refer to the chipset's IDE controller as the **internal** IDE controller while the additional IDE controller will be known as the **external** IDE controller.

If you want to attach one or more IDE devices to the external UltraDMA/133 controller, you should **enable** this feature. You should only **disable** this BIOS feature for the following reasons:

- If you do not have any IDE device attached to the external UltraDMA/133 controller
- For troubleshooting purposes

Disabling the external IDE controller frees up two IRQs, which can be used by other devices in the system. It also speeds up the boot-up sequence because the external IDE controller's BIOS no longer needs to be loaded. Your system is also able to skip the external controller's long boot-up check and initialization sequence.

Therefore, if you do not use the external IDE controller, it is recommended that you **disable** it for a much faster booting process.

UltraDMA-66 IDE Controller

Common Options: Enabled, Disabled

This BIOS feature is only found in certain motherboards that come with an additional built-in IDE controller. It allows you to enable or disable the function of that IDE controller.

Please note that the IDE controller covered by this BIOS feature is different from the chipset's own IDE controller. This extra UltraDMA/66 IDE controller is often added to provide UltraDMA/66 support in motherboards with chipsets that do not support UltraDMA/66.

Even if the motherboard's chipset has an IDE controller that supports UltraDMA/66, it is not controlled by this BIOS feature. This BIOS feature is only used to control the additional IDE controller built into the motherboard.

To avoid confusion, I shall henceforth refer to the chipset's IDE controller as the **internal** IDE controller while the additional IDE controller will be known as the **external** IDE controller.

If you want to attach one or more IDE devices to the external UltraDMA/66 controller, you should **enable** this feature. You should only **disable** this BIOS feature for the following reasons:

- If you do not have any IDE device attached to the external UltraDMA/66 controller
- For troubleshooting purposes

Disabling the external IDE controller frees up two IRQs, which can be used by other devices in the system. It also speeds up the boot-up sequence because the external IDE controller's BIOS no longer needs to be loaded. Your system is also able to skip the external controller's long boot-up check and initialization sequence.

Therefore, if you do not use the external IDE controller, it is recommended that you **disable** it for a much faster booting process.

USB Controller

Common Options: Enabled, Disabled

This BIOS feature is somewhat similar to **Assign IRQ For USB**. It enables or disables the motherboard's onboard USB controller.

However, instead of controlling the assignment of an IRQ to the onboard USB controller, this feature directly controls the USB controller's functionality.

It is recommend that you **enable** this feature, so you can use the onboard USB controller to communicate with your USB devices.

If you **disable** this feature, the USB controller is disabled and you are unable to use it to communicate with any USB device. This frees up an IRQ for other devices to use. This is useful when you have many devices that cannot share IRQs.

However, it is recommended that you do *not* disable this BIOS feature unless you do not use any USB device or if you are using a different USB controller for your USB needs.

Disabling this feature is unnecessary with **APIC**-capable motherboards because they come with more IRQs.

USB Keyboard Support

Common Options: OS, BIOS

This BIOS feature determines whether support for the USB keyboard should be provided by the operating system or the BIOS. Therefore, it only affects those who are using USB keyboards.

If your operating system offers native support for USB keyboards, you should select the **OS** option. This provides much greater functionality. However, if you are using DOS or operating systems that do not offer support for USB keyboards, then using the OS optionessentially disables the keyboard because these operating systems cannot detect or work with USB keyboards.

This is where the **BIOS** option comes in. When selected, the BIOS provides support for the USB keyboard. You are able to use the keyboard with both operating systems that do not support USB keyboards and those that do.

However, the BIOS option offers only rudimentary support for the USB keyboard, so using it strips the keyboard of all except basic functions. Therefore, you should *not* select this option if you are using an operating system that supports USB keyboards. It is recommended that you select the **OS** option if you are using a current operating system like Windows XP.

However, don't forget to switch from the **OS** option to the **BIOS** option whenever you want to boot up using a DOS boot disk. Even if the boot disk was created by a USB-aware operating system like Windows XP, it will *not* support the USB keyboard.

USB Mouse Support

Common Options: OS, BIOS

This BIOS feature determines whether support for the USB mouse should be provided by the operating system or the BIOS. Therefore, it only affects those who are using USB mice.

If your operating system offers native support for USB mice, you should select the **OS** option. This provides much greater functionality. However, if you are using DOS or operating systems that do not offer support for USB mice, then using the OS option essentially disables the mouse because these operating systems cannot detect or work with USB mice.

This is where the **BIOS** option comes in. When selected, the BIOS provides support for the USB mouse. You are able to use the mouse with both operating systems that do not support USB mice and those that do.

However, the BIOS option offers only rudimentary support for the USB mouse, so using it strips the mouse of all except basic functions. Therefore, you should *not_select* this option if you are using an operating system that supports USB mice. It is recommended that you select the **OS** option if you are using a current operating system like Windows XP.

However, don't forget to switch from the **OS** option to the **BIOS** option whenever you want to boot up using a DOS boot disk. Even if the boot disk was created by a USB-aware operating system like Windows XP, it does *not* support the USB mouse.

USWC Write Posting

Common Options: Enabled, Disabled

Current processors are heavily optimized for burst operations, which allows for very high memory bandwidth. Unfortunately, graphics writes from the processor are mostly pixel writes, which are 8- to 32-bits in nature. Because they do not fill up an entire cache line, such writes are not burstable. This results in poor graphics write performance.

To correct this deficiency, processors now come with one or more internal write combine buffers. These buffers are designed to accumulate graphics writes from the processor. These partial or smaller writes are then combined and written to the graphics card as burst writes.

The use of these internal write combine buffers provides many benefits:

1. Partial or smaller graphics writes from the processor are now combined into burstable writes. This greatly increases the performance of the processor and AGP (or PCI) buses.

2. Graphics writes require fewer transactions on the processor and AGP (or PCI) bus. This improves the bandwidth of those buses.

3. The processor only needs to write to its internal write combine buffers instead of the processor bus. This improves its performance by allowing it to work on other tasks while the write combine buffers handle the actual write transaction.

Because the write combine buffers allow speculative reads, this feature is known as the **USWC (Uncached Speculative Write Combining)** feature. The older method of writing all processor writes directly to the graphics card is known as **UC (UnCached)**.

This BIOS feature allows you to control the **USWC (Uncached Speculative Write Combining)** write combine buffers.

If **enabled**, the write combine buffers accumulate and combine partial or smaller graphics writes from the processor and write them to the graphics card as burst writes.

If **disabled**, the write combine buffers are disabled. All graphics writes from the processor are written to the graphics card directly.

It is highly recommended that you **enable** this feature for improved graphics and processor performance.

Please note that this feature must also be supported by the graphics card, the operating system, and the graphics driver for it to work properly.

All Microsoft operating systems from Windows NT 4.0 onward support USWC, so you do not need to worry if you are using a Windows NT 4.0 or newer operating system from Microsoft. Because this feature has been around for some time, drivers of USWC-compatible graphics cards fully support this feature.

However, if you are using an older graphics card, it may not be compatible with this feature. Older graphics cards make use of a **FIFO** (**First In, First Out**) I/O model, which can only support the **UnCached** (**UC**) type of transaction. Enabling this feature with such graphics cards causes a host of problems, such as graphics artifacts, system crashes, and even the inability to boot up properly.

If you face such problems, you should **disable** this BIOS feature immediately.

V

Video BIOS Cacheable

Common Options: Enabled, Disabled

This BIOS feature aims to further boost the performance of a shadowed video BIOS by caching it using the processor's Level 2 cache. It works in conjunction with **Video BIOS Shadowing** and is only valid when the **Video BIOS Shadowing** feature is enabled.

If this BIOS feature is **enabled**, a 32KB block of the video BIOS from **C0000h-C7FFFh** is cached by the processor's Level 2 cache. This greatly speeds up *subsequent consecutive* accesses to the video BIOS.

If this BIOS feature is **disabled**, the video BIOS is not cached. The video BIOS is read from the system memory (if it has been shadowed) or directly from the BIOS chip.

However, caching the video BIOS does not necessarily translate into better system performance. First of all, modern operating systems like Microsoft Windows XP do not need to use the video BIOS. They bypass the BIOS completely and use the graphics card's driver instead. This provides the operating systems with direct access to the graphics card and allows them to make full use of the card's capabilities. With such a driver, these operating systems do not need to make any BIOS calls. Therefore, absolutely no benefit can be realized by caching the BIOS.

And unlike system memory, which can be a gigabyte or more, the processor's L2 cache is a limited resource. Most processors come with L2 caches of only 128KB to 512KB in size. Diverting such a large portion of the L2 cache for the purpose of caching the video BIOS deprives the processor of L2 cache for its own data. Consequently, there is a significant deterioration in processor performance whenever the video BIOS is cached.

There are some who reason that because the video BIOS is only cached when needed, the processor does not actually lose 32KB of L2 cache. The video BIOS is flushed out of the L2 cache when it is not needed. That's true. However, whenever the video BIOS is cached, it still takes up 32KB of L2 cache and the processor's performance suffers at that point.

As with the **Video BIOS Shadowing** feature, Flash ROM upgrades should not be attempted if the video BIOS is cached. If the video BIOS is cached, any attempt at flashing the video BIOS will likely result in a system crash. This is because the location pointer for the video BIOS now points to a location in the processor's L2 cache, not the Flash ROM!

Worst of all, because only 32KB of the video BIOS is cached, part of the new video BIOS overwrites that cached portion, while the rest would overwrite the contents of the Flash ROM. Because the video BIOS in the Flash ROM was only partially overwritten, the end result is usually a corrupted video BIOS.

Of course, caching the video BIOS theoretically provides a significant boost in real-mode DOS games or certain operating systems in fail-safe mode. However, the loss of the processor's L2 cache negates any performance advantage gained by caching the video BIOS.

Therefore, it is recommended that you **disable** Video BIOS Caching, even if you play a lot of real-mode DOS games or work with operating systems running in fail-safe mode. It is better just to rely on video BIOS shadowing to provide a boost in the video BIOS' performance.

V

Video BIOS Shadowing

Common Options: Enabled, Disabled

This BIOS feature allows faster access to the video BIOS by *shadowing* or making a copy of it in the system memory. Shadowing the video BIOS improves its performance because the BIOS now can be read by the CPU through the **64-bit** memory bus as opposed to the slow **8-bit** XT bus (used in older motherboards) or the newer LPC bus (used in current motherboards).

This appears quite an attractive feature because it results in at least a thousand-fold improvement in video BIOS performance, and the only price you pay is losing the small amount of system memory used to mirror the video BIOS. Unfortunately, the truth is not so simple.

Modern operating systems do not even use the video BIOS. They bypass the BIOS completely and use the graphics card's driver instead. This provides the operating system with direct access to the graphics card and allows it to make full use of the card's capabilities. With such a driver, these operating systems do not need to make any BIOS calls. Therefore, absolutely no benefit can be realized by shadowing the BIOS.

According to a Microsoft article about *Shadowing BIOS under WinNT 4.0*, shadowing the BIOS (irrespective of what BIOS it is) does not bring about any performance enhancements because it is not used by Windows NT. It just wastes memory. Although the article did not say anything about other versions of Microsoft Windows, this is true for all versions of Microsoft Windows from Windows 95 onward.

In addition, shadowing the video BIOS can sometimes cause conflicts to occur. There is always a risk of certain software writing to the RAM region used to shadow the video BIOS. When this happens, a conflict occurs and the system crashes. Fortunately, this is no longer an issue in current motherboards because the shadowed RAM region now has been moved far from the reach of programs.

What could be a bigger issue is the shadowing of just a portion of the video BIOS. Newer video BIOSes are generally much larger than 32KB in size. However, most motherboards shadow only a 32KB block from **C0000** to **C7FFF**. If only this region of the video BIOS is shadowed and the rest is left unshadowed, applications may have trouble accessing the video BIOS properly. Therefore, if you intend to shadow the video BIOS, you must ensure that the *entire* video BIOS is shadowed. To do this, you need to:

- Enable video BIOS shadowing (for the C0000–C7FFF region)
- Enable the shadowing of the remaining portions, for example C8000–CBFFF, until the entire video BIOS is shadowed.

Finally, all graphics cards now use Flash ROM, which is much faster than the ROM or EEPROM chips used in older graphics cards. Flash ROM also allows easy upgrading of the firmware by a simple BIOS flash. However, if the video BIOS is shadowed, any attempt at flashing the video BIOS will likely result in a system crash. This is because the location pointer for the video BIOS now points to a location in the system memory, not the Flash ROM!

It could be even worse if only a *portion* of the video BIOS had been shadowed when the video BIOS upgrade was attempted. Part of the new video BIOS overwrites the portion of the video BIOS that was shadowed in the system memory while the rest overwrites the contents of the Flash ROM. Because the video BIOS in the Flash ROM was only partially overwritten, the end result is usually a corrupted video BIOS.

Therefore, video BIOS shadowing must be **disabled** if you want to flash the Flash ROM of the graphics card.

Some of you probably wonder why we should continue to update the video BIOS even though it appears to be useless in most cases. The answer is simple—the video BIOS does not contain only standard VGA functions. The video BIOSes of current graphics cards also contain code for 2D, 3D, and video acceleration. Therefore, using the latest video BIOS is likely to boost performance as well as correct bugs in the previous BIOS versions. There may also be occasions when the latest drivers may not work with older versions of the video BIOS. Therefore, it is advisable to keep updating the video BIOS whether or not you use real-mode DOS.

With all that said, there may still be a use or two for this BIOS feature. For one thing, most real-mode DOS games use the video BIOS's VGA functions because they cannot directly access the graphics processor. Such games benefit from the shadowing of the video BIOS. If you still play old real-mode DOS games, you can try enabling **Video BIOS Shadowing** for better performance.

Shadowing of the video BIOS also provides performance benefits when it comes to the fail-safe mode of certain operating systems (for example, Safe Mode in Microsoft Windows XP). These operating systems fall back on the video BIOS because all video BIOSes contain the same, standardized VGA functions. In such cases, shadowing the video BIOS can provide a substantial boost to graphics performance. Of course, no one uses Safe Mode in Windows all the time!

If this BIOS feature is **enabled**, the video BIOS is shadowed in system memory. This improves graphics rendering performance if the VGA functions of the video BIOS are used.

If this BIOS feature is **disabled**, the video BIOS is *not* shadowed in system memory. Any access to the video BIOS has to go through the XT or LPC bus.

Because drivers have replaced the video BIOS as the interface between the graphics hardware and the operating system, it is recommended that you **disable** Video BIOS Shadowing. The risk of crashes and BIOS corruptions due to this BIOS feature is not worth the benefits it provides in certain circumstances.

However, if you do play a lot of old real-mode DOS games or work a lot in safe-mode Windows, then you should shadow the video BIOS for improved performance.

Video Memory Cache Mode

Common Options: USWC, UC

This is yet another BIOS feature with a misleading name. It does not cache the video memory or even graphics data (such data is uncacheable anyway). It is actually similar to the **USWC Write Posting** BIOS feature.

Current processors are heavily optimized for burst operations, which allows for very high memory bandwidth. Unfortunately, graphics writes from the processor are mostly pixel writes that are 8- to 32-bits in nature. Because they do not fill up an entire cache line, such writes are not burstable. This results in poor graphics write performance.

To correct this deficiency, processors now come with one or more internal write combine buffers. These buffers are designed to accumulate graphics writes from the processor. These partial or smaller writes are then combined and written to the graphics card as burst writes.

The use of these internal write combine buffers provides many benefits:

1. Partial or smaller graphics writes from the processor are now combined into burstable writes. This greatly increases the performance of the processor and AGP (or PCI) buses.
2. Graphics writes require fewer transactions on the processor and AGP (or PCI) bus. This improves the bandwidth of those buses.
3. The processor only needs to write to its internal write combine buffers instead of the processor bus. This improves its performance by allowing it to work on other tasks while the write combine buffers handle the actual write transaction.

Because the write combine buffers allow speculative reads, this feature is known as the **USWC (Uncached Speculative Write Combining)** feature. The older method of writing all processor writes directly to the graphics card is known as **UC (UnCached)**.

This BIOS feature allows you to control the **USWC (Uncached Speculative Write Combining)** write combine buffers.

If **enabled**, the write combine buffers accumulates and combines partial or smaller graphics writes from the processor and writes them to the graphics card as burst writes.

If **disabled**, the write combine buffers are disabled. All graphics writes from the processor are written to the graphics card directly.

It is highly recommended that you **enable** this feature for improved graphics and processor performance.

Please note that this feature must also be supported by the graphics card, the operating system, and the graphics driver for it to work properly.

All Microsoft operating systems from Windows NT 4.0 onward support USWC, so you do not need to worry if you are using a Windows NT 4.0 or newer operating system from Microsoft. Because this feature has been around for some time, drivers of USWC-compatible graphics cards fully support this feature.

However, if you are using an older graphics card, it may not be compatible with this feature. Older graphics cards make use of a **FIFO (First In, First Out)** I/O model, which can only support the **UnCached (UC)** type of transaction. Enabling this feature with such graphics cards causes a host of problems, such as graphics artifacts, system crashes, and even the inability to boot up properly.

If you face such problems, you should **disable** this BIOS feature immediately.

Video RAM Cacheable

Common Options: Enabled, Disabled

The **Upper Memory Area (UMA)** is a 384KB block of memory at the top of the first megabyte of memory that is reserved for the system's use in DOS. A portion of this Upper Memory Area is reserved as video RAM memory.

The video RAM memory area is a 128KB block from A0000h to BFFFFh. Of this 128KB, the first half (A0000h–AFFFFh) is reserved for use in VGA graphics mode. The other half is used for monochrome text mode (B0000h–B7FFFh) and color text mode (B8000h–BFFFFh). This video RAM memory area is the only portion of the graphics card's memory that the processor has direct access to in VGA mode.

The graphics card and the processor use this memory area to write pixel data when the computer is operating in VGA mode. This is why all VGA graphics modes take up less than 64KB of memory. The most common VGA mode is mode 0x13, which has a resolution of 320 x 200 in 256 colors. This mode uses up exactly 64,000 bytes of memory and fits nicely into the 64KB block from A0000h to AFFFFh.

This BIOS feature aims to boost VGA graphics performance by using the processor's Level 2 cache to cache the 64KB VGA graphics memory area from **A0000h** to **AFFFFh**.

If this BIOS feature is **enabled**, the VGA graphics memory area is cached by the processor's **Level 2 cache**. This speeds up accesses to the VGA graphics memory area.

If this BIOS feature is **disabled**, the VGA graphics memory area is *not* cached by the processor's **Level 2 cache**.

From what we have discussed so far, it sounds like caching the VGA graphics memory area is logically the way to go. Caching the VGA graphics memory area definitely speeds up VGA graphics performance by caching accesses to the graphics memory area. This is great for those old DOS games, although it won't do anything for VGA text modes.

However, reality is far less ideal. For one thing, VGA modes are hardly used at all these days. For compatibility reasons, VGA is still used in Windows XP's **Safe Mode**. It is also used in real mode DOS, if you still use that. Other than that, there is no more use for VGA modes. If VGA graphics modes are not used, no benefit can possibly be realized by enabling this BIOS feature.

Even if you use DOS modes a lot, is there even a point in caching the VGA graphics memory area for better performance? Even the slowest computer today is more than capable of handling VGA graphics with ease. In short, caching the VGA graphics memory area not bring any noticeable advantage.

On the other hand, caching this memory area will cost you some processor performance. Because some of the processor's Level 2 cache is being diverted to cache the VGA graphics memory area, there is less to keep the processor supplied with data. Consequently, the processor's performance suffers.

If the use of the processor's Level 2 cache can bring about significant improvement in the performance of the graphics subsystem, it would have been worth it. Unfortunately, the VGA graphics modes are rarely used at all. Even when used, there is little or no real benefit in caching the memory area. This BIOS feature essentially wastes the processor's Level 2 cache on something that cannot possibly improve the system's graphics performance.

Therefore, it is highly recommended that you **disable** this BIOS feature. There is no reason to enable it even if you use real mode DOS a lot or work a lot in Windows Safe Mode.

Virus Warning

Common Options: Enabled, Disabled

This BIOS feature provides rudimentary anti-virus protection by monitoring writes to the boot sector and partition table.

If this feature is **enabled**, the BIOS halts the system and flashes a warning message whenever it detects an attempt to write to the boot sector or the partition table. Please note that this only protects the boot sector and the partition table, not the entire hard disk.

If this feature is **disabled**, the BIOS does not monitor writes to the boot sector and partition table.

This feature can cause problems with software that need to access the boot sector. One good example is the installation routine of all versions of Microsoft Windows from Windows 95 onward. When **enabled**, this feature causes the installation routine to fail. Also, many disk diagnostic utilities that access the boot sector can also trigger the system halt and error message as well. Therefore, you should **disable** this feature before running such software.

Note that this feature is useless for hard disks that run on external controllers with their own BIOS. Boot sector viruses bypass the system BIOS with its anti-virus protection features and write directly to the hard disks. Such controllers include additional IDE or SCSI controllers that are either built into the motherboard or available through add-on cards.

VLink 8X Support

Common Options: Enabled, Disabled

V-Link is the name of the proprietary interchip bus used in new VIA chipsets. Previously, VIA used the PCI bus to connect the North Bridge and the South Bridge of their chipsets. However, with high-speed PCI devices already saturating the PCI bus, there was little bandwidth left for interchip communications.

So, following Intel's lead with the **Intel Hub Architecture**, they designed a fast dedicated bus to link the North Bridge with the South Bridge chips in their chipsets. They christened this new interchip bus as the V-Link bus.

The initial version used a quad-pumped 8-bit bus running at 66MHz to provide **266MB/s** of interchip bandwidth. This gave them a dedicated bus with twice the bandwidth of the PCI bus (which also has to be shared with other PCI devices). The V-Link debuted in the VIA Apollo KT266 chipset.

VIA recently enhanced their V-Link bus to provide even more bandwidth for interchip communications. Starting with the Apollo KT400 and P4X400 chipsets, the clock speed of the V-Link bus has been doubled to 133MHz. This doubles the bandwidth of the V-Link bus to **533MB/s**. Although the new bus is only four times faster than the PCI bus, VIA chose to call the new bus **8X V-Link**.

The **VLink 8X Support** BIOS feature is used to toggle the V-Link bus mode between the original V-Link and the newer and faster 8X V-Link.

If this feature is **enabled**, the quad-pumped 8-bit V-Link bus switches to the new 8X V-Link mode, which runs at 133MHz and delivers a bandwidth of 533MB/s.

If this feature is **disabled**, the V-Link bus uses a clock speed of 66MHz, essentially reverting to the original V-Link standard. It then delivers a bandwidth of 266MB/s.

This BIOS feature was most likely included for troubleshooting purposes. It is highly recommended that you **enable** this BIOS feature for better performance.

V

Watchdog Timer

Common Options: Enabled, Disabled

The **Watchdog Timer (WDT)** is an independent monitoring circuit built into the chipset to detect when a computer malfunctions due to a software or hardware error. It does this by employing a countdown timer that limits the amount of time a particular task is allowed to take.

Every time the operating system performs a task, the countdown timer keeps track of the amount of time taken. If the task cannot be completed within a predetermined time, the Watchdog Timer assumes that the computer has locked up and initiates a number of actions. These may be attempts at correcting the problem, like generating a non-maskable interrupt; or the Watchdog Timer may just reboot or shut down the computer.

The WDT timer ticks approximately once every 0.6 seconds, but there is a one-tick uncertainty. This means that the very first timer tick may occur immediately when the timer is started or up to 0.6 seconds later.

By default, the WDT timer is set to **04h**, which allows a timeout period of 1.8 to 2.4 seconds. The timer can be set up to a maximum value of **3Fh**, which gives a timeout period of approximately 37.5 seconds.

This BIOS feature controls the operation of the chipset's Watchdog Timer.

When **enabled**, the Watchdog Timer will monitor the time taken for each task performed by the operating system. Any timeout will cause it to initiate corrective actions like generate a non-maskable interrupt or reboot the computer.

When **disabled**, the Watchdog Timer will not monitor the time taken for each task performed by the operating system. Even if the system locks up, the Watchdog Timer will not initiate any corrective action.

It is recommended that you **enable** the Watchdog Timer to automatically detect hardware and software errors that lock up the computer. While it may do nothing more than automatically reboot or shut down the computer when an irresolvable error occurs, there is a chance it may allow the correction of the problem and allow the computer to function normally.

Write Data In to Read Delay

Common Options: 1 Cycle, 2 Cycles

This BIOS feature controls the **Write Data In to Read Command Delay (tWTR)** memory timing. This constitutes the minimum number of clock cycles that must occur between the last valid *write* operation and the next *read* command to the *same* internal bank of the DDR device.

Please note that this is only applicable for read commands that follow a write operation. Consecutive read operations or writes that follow reads are not affected.

If a **1 Cycle** delay is selected, every read command that follows a write operation is delayed **one clock cycle** before it is issued.

If a **2 Cycles** delay is selected, every read command that follows a write operation is delayed **two clock cycles** before it is issued.

The **1 Cycle** option naturally offers faster switching from writes to reads and, consequently, better read performance.

The **2 Cycles** option reduces read performance but it improves stability, especially at higher clock speeds. It may also allow the memory chips to run at a higher speed. In other words, increasing this delay may allow you to overclock the memory module higher than is normally possible.

By default, this BIOS feature is set to **2 Cycles**. This meets JEDEC's specification of 2 clock cycles for write-to-read command delay in DDR400 memory modules. DDR266 and DDR333 memory modules require a write-to-read command delay of only 1 clock cycle.

It is recommended that you select the **1 Cycle** option for better memory read performance if you are using DDR266 or DDR333 memory modules. You can also try using the **1 Cycle** option with DDR400 memory modules. However, if you face stability issues, revert to the default setting of **2 Cycles**.

Write Recovery Time

Common Options: 1 Cycle, 2 Cycles, 3 Cycles

This BIOS feature controls the **Write Recovery Time (tWR)** of the memory modules.

It specifies the amount of delay (in clock cycles) that must elapse after the completion of a valid write operation before an active bank can be precharged. This delay is required to guarantee that data in the write buffers can be written to the memory cells before precharge occurs.

If the delay is too short, the bank may be precharged before the active bank has enough time to store the write data in the memory cells. This causes data to be lost or corrupted.

Please note that this BIOS feature does *not* determine the time it takes for the bank to precharge. It only controls how soon the bank can *start* precharging right after a write operation to the same bank.

The shorter the delay, the earlier the bank can be precharged for another read/write operation. This improves performance but runs the risk of corrupting data written to the memory cells.

The default value is **2 Cycles**, which meets JEDEC specifications in DDR200 and DDR266 memory modules. DDR333 and DDR400 memory modules require a Write Recovery Time of **3 Cycles**.

It is recommended that you select **2 Cycles** if you are using DDR200 or DDR266 memory modules and **3 Cycles** if you are using DDR333 or DDR 400 memory modules. You can try using a shorter delay for better memory performance, but if you face stability issues, revert to the specified delay to correct the problem.

Acronym List

Acronym	Definition
#	
#AC	Alignment Check Interrupt
μsec	Microsecond
2D	Two Dimensional
3D	Three Dimensional
A	
ACPI	Advanced Configuration and Power Interface
AGP	Accelerated Graphics Port
ALU	Arithmetic Logic Unit
AMD	Advanced Micro Devices, Inc.
API	Application Program Interface
APIC	Advanced Programmable Interrupt Controller
AT	Advanced Technology
ATA	Advanced Technology Attachment
ATI	Allied Telesyn International
B	
BIOS	Basic Input Output System
C	
CAS	Column Address Strobe
CD	Compact Disc
CD-ROM	Compact Disc – Read Only Memory
CLK	Clock
CLK_CTL	Clock Control
CMD	Command
CMOS	Complementary Metal-Oxide Semiconductor
CPU	Central Processing Unit
CTRL	Control

D	
DBI	Dynamic Bus Inversion
DDR	Double Data Rate
DIMM	Dual Inline Memory Module
DIP	Dual Inline Package
DMA	Direct Memory Access
DMI	Desktop Management Interface
DOS	Disk Operating System
DRAM	Dynamic Random Access Memory
DVD	Digital Versatile Disc / Digital Video Disc
E	
EA	(USN Rating) Engineering Aide
ECC	Error Checking and Correction
ECP	Extended Capabilities Port
EMI	Electromagnetic Interference
EPP	Enhanced Parallel Port
EPROM	Electrically Programmable Read Only Memory
ESCD	Extended System Configuration Data
EXT	Extension
F	
FAQ	Frequently Asked Questions
FDC	Floppy Disk Controller
FDD	Floppy Disk Drive
FIFO	First In, First Out
FOP	Final Opcode
FPU	Floating-Point Unit
FSB	Front-Side Bus
G	
GART	Graphics Address Relocation Table
GB	Gigabyte
GB/s	Gigabytes per Second

GHz	Gigahertz
GPU	Graphics Processing Unit
GUI	Graphical User Interface

H	
HDD	Hard Disk Drive
Hex	Hexadecimal
HPSIR	Hewlett-Packard Serial Infra-Red

I	
IBM	International Business Machines Corporation
IDE	Integrated Drive Electronics
IDT	Interrupt Descriptor Table
IEEE	Institute of Electrical & Electronics Engineers
INT	Interrupt
I/O	Input/Output
IR	Infra-Red
IrDA	Infrared Data Association
IRQ	Interrupt Request
ISA	Industry Standard Architecture

J	
JEDEC	Joint Electron Device Engineering Council

K	
KB	Kilobyte

L	
LAN	Local Area Network
Lat	Latency
LPC	Low Pin Count

M	
MB	Megabyte
Mbit	Megabit
MB/s	Megabytes per Second
MCA	Micro Channel Architecture

MCH	Memory Controller Hub
MHz	Megahertz
MMX	Multi-Media Extensions
MPEG	Moving Picture Experts Group
MPS	Multi-Processor Specification
MRO	Memory Request Organizer
MS-DOS	Microsoft Disk Operating System
msec	Millisecond
MSR	Model Specific Register
MTRR	Memory Type Range Register
N	
NA	Not Applicable
NIC	Network Interface Card
ns	Nanosecond
NT	New Technology
O	
OEM	Original Equipment Manufacturer
OS	Operating System
OS/2	Operating System 2 (IBM)
P	
PAM	Programmable Attribute Map
PC	Personal Computer
PCI	Peripheral Component Interconnect
PDA	Personal Digital Assistant
PH	Page Hit
PIC	Programmable Interrupt Controller
PIO	Programmed Input/Output
PIRQ	Programmable Interrupt Request
PLCC	Plastic Leaded Chip Carrier
PnP	Plug and Play
POST	Power-On Diagnostic Test

PROCHOT#	Processor Hot Interrupt
PS/2	Personal System 2 (IBM)

Q

QDR	Quad Data Rate
QW	Quadword

R

RAID	Redundant Array of Inexpensive Disks
RAM	Random-Access Memory
RAS	Row Address Strobe
ROM	Read-Only Memory
R/W	Read/Write
RxD	Data Reception

S

SBA	Sideband Address
SCSI	Small Computer System Interface
SDRAM	Synchronous Dynamic Random Access Memory
Sec	Second(s)
SIMD	Single Instruction-Stream, Multiple Data-Stream
S.M.A.R.T.	Self Monitoring Analysis And Reporting Technology
SMI	System Management Interrupt
SPD	Serial Presence Detect
SPP	Standard Parallel Port
SRAM	Static RAM
SSE	Streaming SIMD Extensions
STR	Suspend To RAM

T

TCC	Thermal Control Circuit
tRAS	Minimum Row Active Time
tRC	Row Cycle Time
tRCD	Row Address to Column Address Delay
tRP	RAS Precharge Time

tRRD	Bank-to-Bank Delay
tWR	Write Recovery Time
tWTR	Write Data In to Read Command Delay
TxD	Data Transmission

U

UC	Uncached
UMA	Upper Memory Area or Unified Memory Architecture
USB	Universal Serial Bus
USWC	Uncacheable, Speculative Write Combine

V

VGA	Video Graphics Adapter

W

WDT	Watchdog Timer

X

XMM	Extended Memory Manager
XP	Experience (Microsoft Windows XP)
XT	Extended Technology

Index

About the Author

Adrian Wong has been part of the online hardware community since 1996 when he first set up Adrian's Rojak Pot. Since then, the author has written many authoritative articles and guides on computers.

Here's a short list of some of his previous works:

The Motherboard BIOS Flashing Guide

The Video BIOS Flashing Guide

The Hot Flashing Guide

Hard Disk Myths Debunked!

The Definitive Swapfile Optimization Guide

The Definitive Battery Extender Guide

The Compression Comparison Guide

The Definitive Maxtor Silent Store Guide

The Windows 2000 Hints & Tips Guide

The Definitive Disk Cache Optimization Guide

The Definitive Chunksize Optimization Guide

The Definitive IDE Block Mode Guide

The Definitive Video RAM Caching Guide

Adrian's articles and guides are considered reference material by the computer hardware community. In fact, the author regularly receives accolades from both peers and members of the industry.

Adrian currently divides his time between medical school and Adrian's Rojak Pot in Melaka, Malaysia.

About Adrian's Rojak Pot

Adrian initially started **Adrian's Rojak Pot** (http://www.rojakpot.com/) as nothing more than a personal homepage on Tripod in 1996. Considering that he had absolutely no knowledge of HTML, it's amazing that Adrian's Rojak Pot was even born!

Thanks to Microsoft's FrontPage 98, Adrian found that it wasn't as hard as it appeared. Of course, he never had to write a single line of HTML code! Nevertheless, it galvanized him to work on his homepage, so that on the remote chance some lost soul happened upon the page, he wouldn't think Adrian was a dull boy.

Eventually, Adrian started writing some short articles and guides on how to optimize the computer. Although he had no intention of creating a computer hardware site, people started visiting his site, and he soon developed a reputation among fellow enthusiasts for his reviews and guides.

One thing led to another and Adrian's Rojak Pot is now Malaysia's top hardware site! The metamorphosis from Adrian's personal homepage to the current hardware site was long and painful due to Adrian's commitment to his medical studies.

However, Adrian's Rojak Pot is now a sleek hardware site with its own server and a dedicated team to run it. In addition, it is host to a flourishing community in its discussion forums.

If you are interested in finding out more about Adrian's Rojak Pot and Team ARP, head over to http://www.rojakpot.com/about_us.aspx

If you want to visit the ARP forums and hang out with the regulars (who label themselves Rojakpotters), head over to http://forums.rojakpot.com

What's Rojak?

Well, rojak is a distinctly Malaysian fare. It is a dish of fruits, vegetables, crackers, fried soybean curd, and practically anything else the connoisseur wants, mixed well with a spicy, sweet, and sticky paste made of prawns, chili, and belacan. A generous amount of shredded peanuts are then sprinkled on the dish.

Yum, yum! Yes, it's delicious, and it suits different palates because it can be anything and everything you want it to be. Colloquially, rojak also means "mixed up" because the dish is really a mix of many different ingredients. The pot that is used to mix the assorted ingredients is, of course, called the rojak pot, hence, the origin of the website's name, Adrian's Rojak Pot. Why? Read on to find out!

Why Adrian's Rojak Pot?

Well, first of all, you have to understand a tiny part of the Malaysian culture—Malaysians love to eat. Malaysia is one of the few places on Earth where you can find food stalls and even restaurants open 24 hours a day, 7 days a week. No, no, we're not talking about 7–Eleven; we're talking about bona fide *mamak* and hawker stalls. All of this just to cater to the Malaysian's desire to eat at any time of the day or night.

With such a national food obsession, Adrian believes his website should at least give a nod in that direction, and what better way to do that than to name it after one of Malaysia's favorite dishes?

In addition, the name conjures up an image of a site that publishes a variety of articles, as varied and delectable as the ingredients of rojak. It also points to the diversity of visitors the site aims to attract. While Adrian's website is Malaysian in origin, it does not restrict itself to Malaysia. The Internet is borderless and welcomes diversity!

Finally, Adrian feels that Adrian's Rojak Pot is a unique name for a unique site. What better name could there be?

About the BIOS Optimization Guide

Of all the articles and guides Adrian has written, none has been more highly praised or talked about than his online *BIOS Optimization Guide*. Adrian started writing it in July of 1999 after noticing that far too many people had misconceptions about optimizing the BIOS.

Instead of just telling people what to do, Adrian decided to write down everything he knew about each BIOS option. Then he wrote his recommendations and the reasons for them. Adrian believes this is the best way to teach people about BIOS optimization.

Did he succeed? Apparently so!

The online *BIOS Optimization Guide* (or, as it is affectionately known, BOG) is now the Internet's ultimate reference on BIOS optimization. It is frequently quoted in online arguments about BIOS settings. In fact, Adrian's peers now refer their visitors to his online *BIOS Optimization Guide* whenever they ask about BIOS settings.

Although unfortunate, the best indicator of the online *BIOS Optimization Guide's* popularity is the numerous times it has been plagiarized. As they say, imitation is the highest form of flattery; and so, plagiarism has always been the bane of the guide's existence.

The online *BIOS Optimization Guide* has the dubious honor of being the only *free* online guide that has been plagiarized countless times by individuals and websites from all over the world!

Currently, the online version of *The BIOS Optimization Guide* is in its eighth revision, and it covers more than 230 different BIOS options. More are being added every month. If you want to see the online version of *The BIOS Optimization Guide*, head over to http://www.rojakpot.com/bog.aspx

Breaking Through the BIOS Barrier: The BIOS Optimization Guide will not only break the BIOS barrier, it will also break the barrier between printed media and online media. This book comes with a FREE subscription to the online BIOS Optimization Guide for a period of three months (valued at more than $10). This gives you the best of both worlds—a book you can carry and consult whenever and wherever you want; and the latest updates to the guide! To register for your FREE subscription, log on to http://www.phptr.com/biosguide.

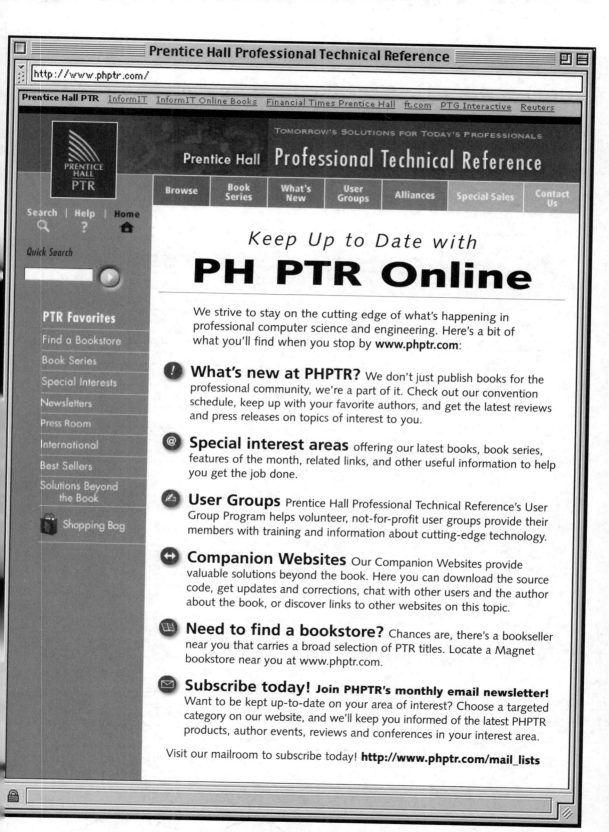

BIOS Option	Quick Review	Detailed Description	BIOS Option	Quick Review	Detailed Description
Memory Subsystem (Continued)					
SDRAM Write to Read Command Delay	129	301	SuperStability Mode	134	309
Shadowing Address Ranges	130	303	Write Data in to Read Delay	147	326
Super Bypass Mode	134	308	Write Recovery Time	148	327
Super Bypass Wait State	134	308			
Miscellaneous					
Anti-Virus Protection	40	178	Parallel Port Mode	95	249
Duplex Select	62	204	Power On Function	107	267
Flash BIOS Protection	65	208	PS/2 Mouse Function Control	108	269
Floppy 3 Mode Support	65	209	RxD, TxD Active	114	276
Full Screen Logo	68	212	Security Setup	130	302
Hardware Reset Protect	72	216	Spread Spectrum	133	307
KBC Input Clock Select	80	229	TX, RX Inverting Enable	137	312
Keyboard Auto-Repeat Delay	80	230	Typematic Rate	137	312
Keyboard Auto-Repeat Rate	80	230	Typematic Rate Delay	138	313
Onboard IR Function	92	245	Typematic Rate Setting	141	313
Onboard Parallel Port	92	245	USB Controller	141	317
Onboard Serial Port 1	92	246	USB Keyboard Support	141	317
Onboard Serial Port 2	93	246	USB Mouse Support	141	318
Onboard USB Controller	93	246	Virus Warning	145	324
Processor					
Athlon 4 SSED Instruction	42	174	CPU Drive Strength	48	181
Auto Turn Off PCI Clock Pin	43	175	CPU Fast String	48	182
Clock Throttle	47	180	CPU Hyper-Threading	49	182
Compatible FPU OPCODE	47	181	CPU L2 Cache ECC Checking	49	184